Distance and Campus Universities: Tensions and Interactions

A Comparative Study of Five Countries

ISSUES IN HIGHER EDUCATION
Series Editor: GUY NEAVE, International Association of Universities, Paris, France

Editorial Advisory Board:
JOSE JOAQUIM BRUNNER, Director FLACSO (Latin American Faculty for Social Sciences), Santiago, Chile
BURTON R CLARK, Graduate School of Education, University of California, Los Angeles, USA
DAN LEVY, Professor of Educational Administration and Policy Studies, State University of New York, Albany, USA
LYNN MEEK, Department of Public Administration and Studies in Higher Education, University of New England Armidale, New South Wales, Australia
HASSAN MEKOUAR, University Mohammed V, Morocco
KETO MSHIGENI, The Graduate School, University of Dar-es-Salaam, Tanzania
GUY NEAVE, International Association of Universities, Paris, France
JAN SADLAK, Higher Education Division, UNESCO, Paris
AGILAKPA SAWYERR, African Association of Universities, Accra, Ghana
ULRICH TEICHLER, Director of the Research Centre for Higher Education and the Labour Market, University of Kassel, Germany
MORIKAZU USHIOGI, Department of Higher Education, Nagoya University, Japan
FRANS VAN VUGHT, Rector Magnificus, University of Twente, Enschede, The Netherlands
FANG MIN WEI, Institute of Higher Education at Beijing University, The People's Republic of China

Other titles in the series include

GOEDEGEBUURE *et al.*
Higher Education Policy: An International Comparative Perspective

NEAVE & VAN VUGHT
Government and Higher Education Relationships Across Three Continents: The Winds of Change

SALMI & VERSPOOR
Revitalizing Higher Education

YEE
East Asian Higher Education: Traditions and Transformations

DILL & SPORN
Emerging Patterns of Social Demand and University Reform: Through a Glass Darkly

MEEK *et al.*
The Mockers and Mocked: Comparative Perspectives on Differentiation, Convergence and Diversity in Higher Education

BENNICH-BJORKMAN
Organizing Innovative Research: The Inner Life of University Departments

HUISMAN & MAASSEN
Higher Education and the Nation State

CLARK
Creating Entrepreneurial Universities: Organizational Pathways of Transformation

Distance and Campus Universities: Tensions and Interactions

A Comparative Study of Five Countries

Sarah Guri-Rosenblit

IAU

Published for the IAU Press
PERGAMON

UK   Elsevier Science Ltd, The Boulevard, Langford Lane, Kidlington, Oxford OX5 1GB, UK

USA   Elsevier Science Inc., 655 Avenue of the Americas, New York, NY 10010, USA

JAPAN Elsevier Science Japan, Higashi Azabu 1-chome Building 4F, 1-9-15, Higashi Azabu, Minato-ku, Tokyo 106, Japan

---

First edition 1999

Library of Congress Cataloging in Publication Data
A catalog record for this book is available from the US Library of Congress

British Library Cataloguing in Publication Data
A catalogue record for this book is available from the British Library.

ISBN 0 08 043066 X

The opinions expressed by the author do not engage the responsibility of the IAU nor of its Administrative Board.

The IAU

The International Association of Universities (IAU), founded in 1950, is a worldwide organisation with member institutions in over 120 countries, which cooperates with a vast network of international, regional and national bodies. Its permanent Secretariat, the International Universities Bureau, is located at UNESCO, Paris, and provides a wide variety of services to Member Institutions and to the international higher education community at large.

Activities and Services

* IAU–UNESCO Information Centre on Higher Education

* International Information Networks

* Meetings and seminars

* Research and studies

* Promotion of academic mobility and cooperation

* Credential evaluation

* Consultancy

* Exchange of publications and materials

Publications

* International Handbook of Universities

* World List of Universities

* Issues in Higher Education (monographs)

* Papers and Reports

* Higher Education Policy (quarterly)

* IAU Bulletin (bimonthly)

To Buma and Gideon

Introduction to Issues in Higher Education

For the past quarter century, higher education has been high on the agenda of governments and central to the fortune of nations. Similarly, this same period has seen quite massive changes in direction, in the complexity of systems, in the underlying rationale which has accompanied such changes and in the sheer size of the enterprise in terms of students, staff and budgets, not to mention social and economic purpose. It is not surprising then that the study of higher education itself has broadened and now encompasses some 20 different disciplines, ranging from Anthropology through to Women's Studies, each with its own particular paradigms, methodologies and perspectives.

Against this background, the comparative analysis of higher education policy which has always occupied a crucial place in understanding the contextual setting of reform in individual countries, has acquired a new significance as the pace of "internationalisation" itself quickens. There are many reasons why this should be so: the creation of new economic blocs and, in the case of Europe, the gradual emergence of a trans-national policy for higher education across the EC countries; the triumph of one industrial ethnic and the collapse of another, the rise of new economies in Asia, etc. The breakdown of a seemingly established order has ushered in a renewed interest in other models of higher education and in how other nations are going about tackling often similar issues though in different ways. This series has the purpose of examining issues and testing theories in the field of higher education policy which are of current and practical concern to its main constituencies—national and institutional leadership, administrators, teachers, those researching in this domain and students. As a series, it will focus on both advanced industrial and also on developing systems of higher education.

Issues in Higher Education will be resolutely comparative in its approach and will actively encourage original studies which are firmly based around an international perspective. Individual volumes will be based on a minimum of two different countries so as to bring out the variations occurring in a given problématique. Every encouragement will be given to the drawing of clear and explicit comparisons between the higher education systems covered.

As the editor, I wish to thank the members of the Educational Advisory Board for their part in developing this series. They are:

Jose Joaquim Brunner, *FLACSO (Latin American Faculty for Social Sciences), Santiago, Chile*
Burton R. Clark, *Emeritus Professor, Graduate School of Education, University of California, Los Angeles*
Dan Levy, *Professor of Educational Administration and Policy Studies, State University of New York, Albany, USA*
Lynn Meek, *Department of Public Administration and Studies in Higher Education, University of New England Armidale, New South Wales, Australia*
Hassan Mekouar, *University Mohammed V, Morocco*
Keto Mshigeni, *The Graduate School, University of Dar-es-Salaam, Tanzania*
Jan Sadlak, *Higher Education Division, UNESCO, Paris*
Agilakpa Sawyerr, *African Association of Universities, Accra, Ghana*
Ulrich Teichler, *Director of the Research Centre for Higher Education and the Labour Market, University of Kassel, Germany*
Morikazu Ushiogi, *Department of Higher Education, Nagoya University, Japan*
Frans van Vught, *Rector Magnificus, University of Twente, Enschede, The Netherlands*
Fang Min Wei, *Institute of Higher Education at Beijing University, The People's Republic of China*

GUY NEAVE
International Association of Universities
Paris, France

Foreword
On Prospects, Distant and not so Distant

One of the more spectacular developments in higher education over the past quarter century or so must surely be the speed at which innovation translates into established routine. And whilst this axiom is held to apply generally to progress in the area of high technology, it also, despite all that the more unobservant and tendentious would have us believe, applies to the supposed Ivory Tower of the University. What was yesterday's "alternative form"—alternative of course, to that other bugaboo, the "classical" university—has been assimilated very rapidly into what may, for lack of a better term, stand as "main line provision". Similarly, breakthroughs pioneered by the bold and hardy, once such efforts are seen to work, suddenly acquire a quite astounding attraction for those who earlier shook their grey locks and judged such ventures to be mere folly. Change by imitation may not be daring. It may indeed be very fashionable. But it is, for all that, a powerful and, in times when speed is its own merit, a most desirable force.

There is no better illustration of this general trend than the rise of distance teaching universities. Over the past three decades, they have migrated from what was once cast as one particular form of peripheral provision in higher education. Today, they have come to occupy a strategic position at the very centre of current thinking. In this extraordinary saga of progress, they have acquired a weight and an influence which is both pervasive and difficult to underestimate. It is not exaggerating to say that, with the rise of the "Knowledge Society" or the "Learning Society"—themselves the encapsulation of this speeding up of education's adaptation to a changing world—what was once heralded as the daring experiment in distance teaching universities has now become the template: the referential vision against which even well-established universities now seek, in varying degrees of accommodation, to align themselves.

In itself, as Sarah Guri-Rosenblit points out, distance education has a surprisingly long history. It can be traced back across the millennia. But, to continue the Biblical analogy, it was very much like John the Baptist "a thin, small voice crying in the wilderness". The forces which impelled distance teaching universities towards the centre of the higher education stage are, of course, precisely those which tore higher learning from the possession of the few to become the rightful expectation of the many—namely, the rise of mass higher education and the striving between nations to secure themselves a place in the knowledge-based economy.

Yet, if launched on the wave of mass demand and often as a belated recognition that in its "classic" form, higher education provision was in truth, unable wholly to meet such unleashed hopes, distance teaching universities owe no small part of their subsequent fortunes to the early and rapid marriage with communications technology. Today, there is to all intents and purposes, no establishment of higher learning which is not directly affected—or, more to the point, holds itself to be so—by the communications revolution. Though we are only beginning to appreciate the repercussions the communications revolution has already had upon the social, political and economic fabric and by natural extension, upon all aspects of learning, of one thing we may be certain—namely, that it will continue to reconvert established practice into a series of reopened "problematiques". To give one example of this modern-day edition of the world turned upside down: take the issue of the so-called "unprepared student". This figure, horrendous in symbol if never in person, stood as one of the more recurrent nightmares of the "classic" university. By contrast, it was precisely how the interests of such students ought to be—and could be—handled which constituted the main concern of distance teaching universities. As a result, the issue is becoming defined in new terms and often, most vociferously. Can one indeed speak of "unprepared students"? Is it not more appropriate in times of mass higher education, to talk about "unprepared universities"?

This is only one particular illustration of the Umwertung aller Werte which distance teaching universities, in combination with the harnessing to learning of advanced communications techniques, pose for higher education in general. There are others and not least amongst them, the possible repercussions upon the academic profession, its structure, its standing and those who are deemed its members. That which affects learning must by the same logic, also bear down upon the ways in which those who teach are organised, quite apart from the range of responsibilities they are called upon to assume.

How far those techniques, whether pedagogic, of materials development, course design or of "delivery" systems pioneered by distance teaching universities will be "the shape of things to come" brooks no easy answer. Either way, however, there is much that higher education institutions which still subscribe to the three historical unities—unity of place, of time involved in studying and unity of age [though the latter in many industrial countries is rapidly fraying at the edges]—may learn from the rise of the distance teaching universities and may do so with advantage.

Sarah Guri-Rosenblit, as Dean of the Education and Psychology Department at the Open University of Israel, brings an immense knowledge and first-hand experience to this rapidly evolving domain. Systematic and comparative studies of distance teaching universities and systems are of especial importance, not simply for themselves but also because they may render particular service to other sectors of higher education and most of all at a time when increasingly governments and inter-governmental bodies are turning towards the fundamental issue of how to adapt mass higher education to life-long learning. Amongst recent examples of this gathering momentum are the 1995 White Paper of the European Union, Teaching and Learning: Towards the Learning Society and the 1997 British Report, Higher Education in the Learning Society, otherwise known as the Dearing Report, after its chairman, Ron Dearing.

The "distance teaching university" is, of course, a generic term and as such covers many variations and differences in purpose, practice and paths of development. Professor Guri-Rosenblit explores these variations in depth and systematically across five different institutions ranging from the pioneer of them all, the British Open University through the Spanish National Distance Teaching University, the FernUniversität at Hagen in Germany, her own establishment in Israel, through to Athabasca University in Canada. Hers is a fascinating and an exciting account of an institutional form which has been— and continues still to serve as—a catalytic agent not only within its respective home system, but also abroad.

Comparative studies of distance teaching universities are not unknown. They tend, however, usually to focus on bilateral comparison. Few, if any, set out to analyse and to compare the workings of distance teaching universities within the context of the systems of higher education in which these pioneers are located. In effect, most studies on distance teaching universities group them generically together, rather than examining the similarities and differences between them. Yet, differences there are and it is important to look closely at them, especially at a time when this particular mode of learning is gathering increasing attention around it.

Innovative institutions deserve equally innovative treatment. And this Professor Guri-Rosenblit does in full measure. By increasing the number of models analysed, not only does she open up further vistas of enquiry. She brings out clearly those features and characteristics which cannot fail to be crucial to those who wish to develop such provision for themselves. It is, as she points out in Chapter 8, essential for new patterns of distance teaching systems to be planned not simply with reference to the needs of "learners". It is no less essential that their planning take account of those norms already present in established systems of higher education, of the various academic cultures which flourish there and, above all, to be sensitive to the degree of openness— or, for that matter, its absence—that system already displays. In addition, she reminds us that in an age which claims to be the first example of a "global economy", there are also corresponding "global" forms of higher education.

It is for these reasons that distance teaching universities deserve our closest scrutiny and attention as a very substantial Issue in Higher Education.

GUY NEAVE
Paris/Enschede
November 1998

Contents

Acknowledgements

The idea of conducting a comparative study on the interrelations between distance and campus universities started to dwell in my mind many years ago. But, the actual work began in 1992 on my first summer sabbatical at the Centre for Studies in Higher Education in the University of California at Berkeley. I was greeted by the tremendously warm hospitality of Sheldon Rothblatt, the Director of the Centre and my host, who opened for me doors and windows to a highly exciting world of comparative research on higher education. He and Barbara, his wife, became close and dear friends. Sheldon's exquisite personality, breathtaking scope of knowledge and wit had turned the centre into a unique place, which enhanced international scholarship of a very high standard. I would like to express my heartiest thanks to Sheldon for his overall guidance and support, and for exposing me to the intricate meanings attached to the 'idea of a university'.

The centre at Berkeley has provided fertile grounds for the exchange of ideas between scholars from all over the world. On my two sabbaticals in the centre, in 1992 and 1994, I had the privilege of getting to know wonderful people and first class scholars. Through the international network of the centre I met, among others, Martin Trow, the former Director of the centre in Berkeley; Guy Neave, Director of Research of the International Association of Universities; Ulrich Teichler, Director of the *Wissenschaftliches Zentrum für Berufs und Hochschulforschung* of the University of Kassel; Frans van Vught, the Director of the Centre for Higher Education Policy Studies of Twente University; and Michael Gibbons, Secretary-General of the Association of Commonwealth Universities. Their personal works introduced me to the overt and subtle underpinnings of academic cultures of the countries that I chose to compare. Their expertise and advice provided me with invaluable insights, which were pertinent to the theme of my study. I salute them and extend my gratitude to all of them.

I am particularly indebted to Guy Neave for generously inviting me to publish my study in this series under his editorship, for his insightful critique of my first chapters, for kindly agreeing to write a foreword to this book, and for serving in the capacity of a 'walking encyclopaedia' on numerous occasions. Guy seems to know literally everything on anything in higher education—a real erudite. All of my questions and queries always got in-depth answers, encompassing a wealth of knowledge. It is my pleasure to express my hearty thanks for his help.

I would like to acknowledge the contribution of many colleagues who greatly assisted me in getting updated and detailed data on those universities that are examined in my study. They include: Ellison Platt, Keith Harry, Alan Tait, Steve Sykes and Mike Flude from the British Open University; Jose-Luis García-Garrido and Manuel Moreno from *Universidad Nacional de Educación a Distancia*; Rudolf Schuemer from the *Zentrales Institut für Fernstudien-forschung* of the FernUniversität; Chris Nash, David Rawlence and Pam Patten from Athabasca University. My special thanks to Harold Silver from Oxford Brookes University and the Open University Validation Services for the detailed explanation on the external examiners system and validation and accreditation procedures in the UK.

My university helped me in many ways by enabling me to find 'extra' time to write the book while directing the Department of Education and Psychology, and providing me with all the necessary technological and technical infra-structure. Conversations with Abraham Ginzburg, who served as the president of the Open University of Israel from 1975 to 1987, helped to illuminate important issues in the formative years of the University. I thank him whole-heartedly for his insights and contribution. I would like to recognise the assistance of Tirza Posner and Bat-Sheva Engelberg in the last stage of editing and preparing the final manuscript.

Finally, I would like to express my eternal gratitude and affection to Buma and Gideon—my husband and son—for their unlimited patience, love and encouragement throughout the five-year odyssey of conducting this study. They crossed the Atlantic Ocean twice with me on our way to Berkeley, and accompanied me on my voyages to many more places to which this study took me, both real and virtual. I dedicate the book to them.

Preface

I started working at the Open University of Israel in 1976 when it was in its infancy and had just opened the gates to its first students. Since then, I have followed closely its development, both in the context of the Israeli higher education system and in comparison with other distance teaching universities, also born in the early 1970s, and based on the model of the British Open University. The development of the large, autonomous distance teaching universities caught my curiosity and academic interest. The enthusiasm of their initiators, academics and administrators was striking. Their plans, activities and future policies were coloured by a strong social mission, a spirit of adventure and novelty, a deep dedication and a pioneering zeal—all of which combined to produce a unique *esprit de corps*. The overriding feeling among distance educators and a handful of outsiders was one of taking part in a revolutionary change, a breakthrough in higher education.

In order to follow the impact of the distance teaching universities on their national higher education systems and to comprehend fully their functional roles, it seemed natural to examine the evolving relations and interrelations between them and the conventional, campus universities. Throughout the last two decades I have read dozens of books and articles on distance education, attended and participated in numerous conferences and become acquainted with many colleagues working at sister distance teaching universities. To some of the questions which were of great interest to me I have found no satisfactory answers in the existing distance education literature, such as:

- Have the distance teaching universities been a major innovation in their higher education systems in the 1970s or have they been merely one amongst several reforms aimed at solving emerging problems, such as widening access to higher education, cutting costs per student, diversifying the higher education system?

- What was the broad historical, socio-political background of founding the distance teaching universities in different countries?
- To what extent do the distance teaching universities differ from traditional universities in each national setting and to what extent do they resemble each other?
- What kind of relations have been established between the distance teaching universities and their conventional counterparts since their birth in the early 1970s to this date?
- How can the distance teaching universities' academic status in each country be defined?

The evolving distance education literature in the last twenty years has related to distance teaching universities as a generic phenomenon and highlighted their common features in an effort to emphasise their novelty as compared with both classical universities and former providers of distance education, and to establish distance education as a separate field of study. General contextual background as to other developments that took place concurrently with the emergence of the distance teaching universities in each national setting and the relative innovative characteristics of each distance teaching university as compared with its national, traditional counterparts were, by and large, lacking. In order to get information on these missing links in the distance education literature, I have turned to the general comparative literature on higher education. There I found answers to most of the above questions, but at the same time was greatly amazed and struck by the wide discrepancies as to the portrayal of distance teaching universities in these two sets of reference.

Whereas in the distance education literature, distance teaching universities were characterised by many as the most important evolution in higher education since the middle ages, as the new temples of learning, as a radical challenge to the concept of university, in the general higher education literature quite often the very existence of the distance teaching universities was not mentioned at all, or they were referred to either as marginal developments or, at best, as unique establishments with special tasks outside the realm of regular universities.

My initial astonishment grew over the years to a strong conviction that, only by analysing the operation of the distance teaching universities in the broad context of their higher education systems, is it possible to fully grasp their mission, and get a reflective exposition of their functions within diverse national milieux and on the international scene. This conviction led me into a long and exciting journey in which I have tried to synthesise between the general higher education literature and the distance education literature in order to get a balanced representation of the distance teaching universities' academic status and their particular roles in each national setting. The results and conclusions of this journey are set out in this book.

I chose to focus the comparative analysis only on single-mode distance teaching universities, which were born in the early 1970s and which have introduced into higher education a new-brand university. The newness of the distance teaching universities' underlying ideas, in relation both to the former generation of correspondence institutions and to mainstream universities, has singled them out as a unique group. Thus, neither the dual-mode or consortia-type universities, nor distance teaching universities established since the late 1970s were included in the study. I found it most challenging to follow the evolutionary path of distance teaching universities that were founded in the same period and yet proceeded in different directions.

The five distance teaching universities that are examined in this study are: the British Open University, the Spanish Universidad de Educación a Distancia, the Open University of Israel, the German FernUniversität, and the Canadian Athabasca University, all of which started operating in the early 1970s. These universities have similar roots and resemble each other in many respects. But they also have sufficiently great differences to make comparisons interesting and illuminating: some are national distance teaching universities, others are provincial; some are mega-universities whereas others are relatively small-scale distance teaching universities; they operate within large to very small countries; some teach the full range of degrees from bachelor to doctoral levels, while others mainly confine themselves to undergraduate studies; they teach in four different languages; and each of them has been influenced deeply by differential academic cultures in each national setting.

The major thrust of the book is to examine the subtle and intricate relations and tensions between the distance teaching universities and conventional universities and to analyse the impact they have had on each other. In the process of conducting the study, I became convinced that not only could distance educators benefit from a comparative analysis of distance teaching universities, but policy makers, administrators and academics in conventional universities might also gain important insights into emerging issues that had been first taken care of by distance teaching universities and which subsequently gradually moved to the centre stage of higher education. Distance teaching universities can be viewed in many respects as forerunners in facing and dealing early on with challenges confronting higher education systems today, such as: providing lifelong study opportunities to working adults; defining flexible access policies for second-chance students; teaching unprepared students; designing flexible curricula for a rich spectrum of clienteles; experimenting with innovative learning/teaching modes; employing quality assurance measures for academic teaching; harnessing advanced technologies to the use of higher education; reducing costs per student and providing economies of scale; creating virtual classrooms/settings; managing huge mega-universities; operating intensive support systems; enhancing greater interface with labour markets and business; and promoting globalisation and international cooperation. Many of these themes have been initially treated by distance teaching universities, and within a decade or two, started to feature conspicuously in the agendas of traditional, campus universities. Distance teaching universities can scarcely be viewed as marginal, unique phenomena, but rather as harbingers of future trends whose evolutionary path may have important implications for the planning and development of mainstream universities.

An additional purpose of this study is to identify significant divergences between distance teaching universities operating in various national contexts. Most of the existing distance education literature emphasises the commonalties between distance teaching universities. They are classified in many distance education taxonomies as a generic group contrasted with other establishments and forms of distance education, such as dual-mode universities (which teach both on-campus and off-campus students), extension departments, extramural studies, private correspondence institutions, and consortia-type universities. It is quite natural for entrepreneurs of new academic institutions to mobilise all of their energies to emphasise the common features of these institutions compared with long-standing establishments. After almost thirty years of operation, the time is ripe to observe unique variable national impacts on shaping the nature and the innovative profile of each distance teaching university. As a matter of fact, a natural path of many new-born theories now reaching a stage of maturity, is to observe differences between individual group members, as Burton Clark described: "Any theory of convergence that highlights common drift into complexity, will need in time to shade into a theory of divergence that observes individual national evolutions" (Clark, 1993, 263). The depiction of special functions of each distance teaching university in its national milieu has the potential both to deepen our comprehension of its degree of novelty in its natural context of operation, and to highlight its relevance to future developments in other parts of the world.

Methodologically, it is quite an ambitious task to compare all of the five higher education settings single-handedly. With the exception of Israel, the outsider position assisted me in unveiling and unfolding many features and principles inherent in each system by asking naive questions which were not self-evident and clear to external eyes. Naturally, I have engaged in ongoing dialogues and electronic correspondence with colleagues closely acquainted with each distance teaching university to deepen my understanding and to reveal further layers beneath the existing literature and primary resources. It was a most illuminating and rewarding effort, thanks to which I have acquired a wealth of knowledge, which has shed new light on old and familiar phenomena. For instance, the mechanism and rationale of the external examiner system and the BA honours degrees, so basic in the British university world and so totally alien to the academic cultures of Germany, Israel and Spain, became clear to me only after several personal discussions and correspondence with expert colleagues; it was most fascinating to discover the connections between the relatively high status of UNED in the Spanish higher education, its attractiveness to reputable academics, its location in Madrid and the fact that Spanish academics are civil servants; and it was revealing to learn that the German FernUniversität was just one out of twelve Gesamthochschulen established in the early 1970s in West Germany. Obviously, the amount of documentation on each distance teaching university varies greatly. Thus, some of the descriptions and analyses are thicker and more colourful while others are slimmer in scope and perspective.

The book is composed of eight chapters. Each chapter examines the following major questions:

- **Chapter 1**: To what extent have the new distance teaching universities, born in the early 1970s, departed from the underlying premises of the first-generation correspondence institutions? To what extent have they presented a challenge to the existing ethos and long-standing practices of well-established campus-centred universities? What was the broad socio-political background of establishing each of the distance teaching universities under scrutiny? What were the social and academic missions the distance teaching universities were expected to fulfil and promote?

- **Chapter 2:** In which aspects do the distance teaching universities differ from each other? To what degree is each distance teaching university innovative in its national milieu? How does the innovative cluster of each Distance Teaching University affect its relations with its national counterparts?

- **Chapter 3:** To what extent do the profiles and roles of students and academic faculty in each distance teaching university differ from those of students and faculty in campus universities? What are the implications of the distribution of the teaching responsibilities between many actors on the nature of the learning/teaching processes? How do the absence of a campus atmosphere and the lack of peer group interaction affect the quality of students' academic experiences? What are the reasons for the relatively high drop-out rates at distance teaching universities? How can the dangers of potential indoctrination in teaching large numbers of students by distance teaching media be tackled? Which kind of support systems exist in distance teaching settings and what are their major functions?

- **Chapter 4:** What fields of study has each distance teaching university chosen to concentrate on? To what extent do the distance teaching universities' academic curricula differ from one another and from regular, classical universities? Which kind of degrees and diplomas do the distance teaching universities offer? Are distance teaching universities more market-oriented and geared towards professional training? Are there special subjects that lend themselves more easily to being taught via distance education methods? Which kind of openness and closure dimensions characterises the academic programs of various distance teaching universities?

- **Chapter 5:** What are the unique features of the varying technologies employed by distance education providers for producing and delivering study materials? Which kinds of technology are used for interactive communication purposes? How will advanced computer technologies, such as electronic publishing, affect the design and development of academic curricula at the distance teaching universities, and shape the content and didactics of self-study materials? To what extent will the third generation interactive information and communication media shape the learning/ teaching processes both in distance and in conventional education settings? In which ways will the new advanced technologies affect the interrelations between distance teaching universities and campus universities? What are the main criteria for choosing a balanced mix of media?

- **Chapter 6:** In which aspects do the governance organs and executive officers of distance teaching universities resemble or differ from those of campus universities? How is the financial base of distance teaching universities organised, and in which aspects does their funding differ from that of conventional universities? To what extent do distance teaching universities provide economies of scale? What kind of relations exists between the headquarters and the regional and local study centres in each distance teaching university?

- **Chapter 7:** Which kind of path has each distance teaching university followed in interacting with the regular universities in each national setting? What were the main reasons for the waves of criticism and hostility toward most distance teaching universities in the 1970s? In which areas do the distance teaching universities and their conventional counterparts cooperate? What are the effects of the blurring of boundaries between distance and campus universities and the growing competition between them on their future relations?

- **Chapter 8:** What are the implications that administrators, academics and policy makers in higher education might deduce from the distance teaching universities' experience with regard to the policy planning and actual operation of mainstream establishments? In which areas can the distance teaching universities be regarded as trend-setters in current and future higher education? What are the future prospective scenarios for distance higher education, and distance teaching universities, in particular? To what extent will globalisation and international networking trends have an impact on the developments of distance higher education and mass higher education, in general? What are the main guidelines to be considered for setting up new distance teaching universities in the future, based on the past experiences of veteran distance teaching universities?

1

The Idea of a Distance Teaching University

By eliminating the lecture hall, seminar room and university library and placing the student at home, the distance teaching universities have presented the most radical challenge yet to the traditional concept of a university.

Keegan and Rumble (1982, 24)

The rise of the open universities has surely been one of the most important events— perhaps the most important—since the birth of the ancient universities in the Middle Ages. It has carried out a change in the concept of university.

García-Garrido (1988, 200)

Introduction

The idea of a *distance teaching university* can be fully grasped only by contrasting it with the idea of a traditional, campus-based university. A distance teaching university is not an independent concept, but rather a derivative, a unique interpretation, a modern evolution of the generic notion of what a university is and how it should operate. The *idea of a university*, as expressing its essence and mission, has long preoccupied academics and policy-makers (Kerr, 1963; Ross, 1976; Clark, 1983; Rothblatt, 1989, 1997; Barnett, 1992; Clark & Neave, 1992; Wilson, 1992; Rothblatt & Wittrock, 1993a,b). The university is amongst the oldest and most prestigious institutions in Western society. Since its inception in the eleventh century it has evolved in diverse directions in different places and at different times. On a more general level, the common denominator of all universities through the centuries is their ability to combine certain definite intrinsic and extrinsic qualities (van Vught, 1994). The intrinsic qualities are related to the ideals of the search for truth, and the conservation and transmission of knowledge, while the extrinsic qualities are expressed in the services the universities provide to society. With each passing decade, universities are expected to do more for society, and to react to changing trends and needs in their contextual settings. Certain university traditions have proven very persistent and remarkably resilient to change, while some other elements were more transient. Scott (1995) stressed that the university as an institution has survived so long, because it has changed so much. Clark (1983) argued that the peculiar characteristics and structure of the universities have enabled them to bend and adapt to a whole variety of circumstances and changes in their environments, thus producing diversity among universities, but at the same time: "to maintain an appearance of similarity that allows us to recognise them in all the guises they take" (*ibid.*, 187).

Clearly, there are several university models. Cardinal Newman's notion of a collegiate university as providing a special environment in which both the pursuit of knowledge and the nurturing of gentlemen take place, differs meaningfully from the *Humboldtian* idea of a research-oriented university (Rothblatt, 1989, 1997; Wittrock, 1993). The nature of the modern *multiversity* as portrayed by Clark Kerr (1963) is drastically opposed to the academic ethos of the small elitist colleges, following the Oxbridge tradition. But all of these manifestations of the idea, or more precisely the ideas, of a university entail the notion of a geographical location, drawing students and teachers from distant places to come together for the purpose of learning and pursuing knowledge in various fields of study, be it a spacious green campus or an urban institution interspersed amongst city buildings. *The idea of a distance teaching university* adopts the opposite course. Instead of assembling students from dispersed destinations in one place, it reaches out to students wherever they live or wish to study. Nowadays, many classical universities offer distance education and reach out to students gathered in virtual classrooms or distant locations via advanced information technologies. In retrospect, the distance teaching universities might be viewed as pioneers experimenting on a large scale with designing virtual university settings.

Apart from abolishing the physical campus and the educational and social atmosphere it entails, the distance teaching universities have challenged some other long-standing sets of beliefs and ongoing practices of their older and respectable counterparts, the most important of which will be elaborated further on.

Distance education by correspondence is not a recent, modern phenomenon. Examples of an intensive exchange of letters for educational purposes have been known since ancient times. Such is the correspondence between Plato and Cicero with their students. The Apostle Paul sent letters to early Christian communities to discuss questions of dogma and the interpretation of Christ's message (Peters, 1994a, 61; Daniel, 1995a, 5–6). In Judaism, the

Questions and Answers (known academically as Responsa) constituted a most important vehicle of communication between the Jewish leadership and diverse diasporas, both for imparting knowledge and elaborating on dilemmas of everyday life. It can be traced back to as early as the eighth century. The invention of printing, the advent of a publishing industry and the development of the modern postal services boosted the utilisation of correspondence for educational purposes. Glatter and Wedell (1971) in an extensive survey on correspondence studies provided data on hundreds of thousands of students in Europe, as well as in other parts of the world, who were studying by correspondence towards external academic degrees, and mainly for advanced professional qualifications, ever since the nineteenth century.

Evidently, distance education as a form of higher and continuing education offered by universities has existed since the early half of the nineteenth century (Rumble & Harry, 1982; Holmberg, 1986, 1995; Bell & Tight, 1993). The University of London, which got its Royal Charter as a distance examining body in 1836, enabled students studying in private correspondence colleges in any part of the British Empire to take its examinations. From 1858 it opened all of its non-medical examinations, from matriculation level upwards, to candidates anywhere in the world, regardless of their method of preparation. The University was not concerned whether the students had pursued a course of study at a recognised institution, had studied with a recognised tutor or had gained knowledge purely by self-study. This all-encompassing policy lasted till 1950, when external students in several subjects, for instance engineering and pharmacy, were required to study in institutions authorised for that purpose by the University. But in many subjects the external degree of the London University is offered to this day (Bell & Tight, 1993).

St. Andrews University, which is the oldest Scottish university, offered between 1877 and 1931 an external, higher education degree designed specifically for women (the Licentiate in Arts) scattered in over one hundred centres world-wide and in places as diverse as China, Palestine and Kenya (Smart, 1968; Bell & Tight, 1993).

The foundation of a correspondence programme at Illinois State University in 1874 can be taken as the start of distance education at university level in the USA (Keegan & Rumble, 1982). In 1883 the State of New York authorised the Chautauqua Institute to award degrees through its method. Chautauqua was a summer training programme for Sunday school teachers who continued to receive instruction by mail after they returned to their homes (Watkin & Wright, 1991; Mood, 1995; Moore & Kearsley, 1996). The University of Chicago under William Harper offered the first university sponsored correspondence course in 1891; and the University of Wisconsin offered an extension course in 1892 (Verduin & Clark, 1991; Moore, 1987). In the USA, distance education courses at university level have been provided by independent study divisions within the extension colleges or continuing education departments of conventional universities.

Distance education at university level was initiated in Canada at Queens University in Kingston, Ontario in 1889 (Keegan & Rumble, 1982). Many of the Canadian universities operate correspondence and distance education programmes.

University-level distance teaching in the former Soviet Union has a history that goes back to 1926 (Keegan & Rumble, 1982; Glatter & Wedell, 1971). When Otto Peters undertook a comparative study of all distance teaching universities in the eastern and western world in the early 1960s, his analysis of the universities then teaching at a distance led him to the conclusion that the Republic of South Africa and the USSR were the only countries with distance teaching universities (Peters, 1965). In the Soviet Union he identified eleven distance teaching universities and over a hundred departments of conventional universities which offered courses through correspondence in a wide array of subjects. Similar institutions were established after the Second World War in other socialist regimes of Eastern Europe including East Germany, Poland, Hungary and Czechoslovakia (Glatter & Wedell, 1971). Since the Eastern European model emphasised formal class meetings organised periodically during the year as an essential part of the correspondence education, this model was termed as the *consultation model* (Keegan & Rumble, 1982).

The model of the University of London as a federal examining body was adopted as a basis for universities not only in England, but also in Ireland, Wales, Canada, Australia, New Zealand, India and South Africa (Houle, 1974; Rothblatt, 1987). The University of South Africa (UNISA) is held to be the first full-fledged autonomous distance teaching university (Boucher, 1973; Rumble & Harry, 1982; Peters, 1965; Holmberg, 1986, 1995). Established in 1873 as the University of the Cape of Good Hope, it was based on the model of the University of London as an external examining board. It started teaching at a distance in 1946, after all of its eleven constituent colleges had gradually developed into autonomous degree-granting institutions. It was reconstituted in 1951 to provide degree courses for external students only. In 1962 it was officially established as a distance teaching university through a governmental decree (Boucher, 1973; Holmberg, 1995).

In the 1970s a new brand of institution, foreshadowed by UNISA, emerged —the autonomous stand-alone *distance teaching universities*. They are independent universities, responsible for establishing their curricula, developing self-study courses, providing support and counselling services, conducting the tutoring and assessment of student performances and awarding academic degrees and qualifications.

The establishment of the British Open University in 1969 marked a new era in distance higher education. It constituted a landmark occasion, one that gave distance education a new legitimacy and opened up new prospects. Lord Ashby commented that the foundation of the British Open University was the most striking event in the history of higher education since the establishment of the land-grant universities in the USA in the 1860s (Perry, 1977). Many others have heralded the new distance teaching universities as the most conspicuous development in higher education systems in recent decades, as "a new academic tradition" (Shaw & Taylor, 1984), as "a radical challenge to the concept of a university" (Keegan & Rumble, 1982; García-Garrido, 1988; Peters, 1992a), as "the most developed stage yet in the evolution of the concept of a university" (Keegan, 1993a), as "the new temples of learning" (Reddy, 1988a,b), and as "a new species of university" (Perry, 1996).

Rather than viewing the new distance teaching universities as revolutionary developments, some argue that they are a natural evolution from the first generation of distance education institutions, called by a plethora of terms in different parts of the world: "external studies", "extra-mural studies", "off-campus", "correspondence education", "home-study", "independent study", "non-traditional learning", "open learning", "outreach programs". Bell and Tight (1993) claimed vehemently that all of the new open universities might be regarded in their proper historical context "as a part of a continuing and developing pattern rather than as major innovations, as they have raised much the same concerns and faced much the same problems as their predecessors" (*ibid.*, 1).

In an attempt to examine to what extent the distance teaching universities, born in the 1970s, presented a challenge to the idea of a conventional, campus-based university, and to what extent they departed from the conceptual framework and the operating practices of the first generation of correspondence and extension institutions, their underlying premises and goals are examined below. The analysis is divided into two parts. The first part describes the socio-political context in which each of the five distance teaching universities, which are investigated in this book, has been conceived. The second part discusses their major distinctive features.

Top-Down Planning by Governments

One conspicuous factor that distinguishes the new distance teaching universities from most of their early predecessors is their being a product of governmental planning as large-scale higher education institutions set to fulfil national missions. Until the 1970s, distance education was roundly criticised for the malpractice of some private practitioners (Keegan, 1993b, 2). In many Western European countries correspondence education was used mainly by commercially motivated individuals who set up schools and colleges to enable people who work during the day to study for qualifications offered by a variety of academic, vocational and professional institutions. Many of these private providers sent materials of poor quality and offered little or no support during the learning/teaching process, aiming mainly to maximise their profits (Perry, 1992). Most correspondence schools were perceived as second-class education (Glatter & Wedell, 1971). It is important to note however that private correspondence schools operated mainly in Western Europe. Correspondence education was fully established as a tool of government policy in the former Soviet Union and other Eastern European countries, as has been pointed out (Peters, 1965; Tait, 1994a).

Not all correspondence institutions operating prior to the 1970s deserved a bad reputation. Some, such as the National Extension College in Cambridge, Wolsey Hall in Oxford and Hermods in Sweden, attempted to offer their students a real chance of successfully completing their studies (Glatter & Wedell, 1971; Holmberg, 1986, 1995; Perry, 1992). But the drastic shift from private to public-sponsored distance education on a wide-scale took place in Europe, as well as in some other parts of the world, in the early 1970s. The new generation of the autonomous, fully fledged distance teaching universities moved distance higher education from the margins to the mainstream (Tait, 1994a). A new phase, and a new generation of distance education came into existence.

The distance teaching universities of the 1970s are a clear example of institutions initiated and planned by national governments. They were born in a period characterised by an almost unlimited trust in the potential and power of education in society and its continuing expanding resources (Cerych & Sabatier, 1986), by a huge expansion of higher education systems world-wide following the Second World War, and by an increasingly weighty intervention of governments in higher education planning.

Before the Second World War the main preoccupation with equity in education was focused on entry to secondary schools. Over the past three decades, with secondary schooling becoming universal, attention has perforce shifted onto entry to higher education (Halsey, 1993). After the War, in most Western industrialised countries governments assumed an increasingly pro-active role in higher education (Neave & van Vught, 1991). How to transform the small elite university systems of the nineteenth century and the first half of the twentieth century into mass higher education constituted a major problem from the early 1950s till the mid 1970s in most Western countries (Trow, 1974, 1996a).

Governments funnelled public funds into higher education for the building of new institutions, the expanding of the existing ones, and the support of students who attended them. In the 1960s and the 1970s the higher education systems in Western Europe and in North America "in overall enrolment, government expenditure, the number of institutions, and staff size... [had] at least doubled and often tripled or quadrupled within a period of less than a decade and a half" (Wittrock, 1993, 334).

The distance teaching universities were only a partial, though an important, solution to the increased demand for higher education and the growing political concern for greater equality of opportunity of access to higher education. All of the distance teaching universities were initiated by high ranking politicians and sponsored as large-scale institutions by national governments. A brief description of the political climate in which each of the five distance teaching universities analysed in this book was initiated is undertaken below.

British Open University

The British higher education system was considered in the 1960s as the most elitist in Europe, "enrolling the smallest proportion of the age grade... of any modern industrial society" (Trow, 1993, 280). Several important committees were set up by the government in the 1960s to review and recommend measures to be taken to extend the boundaries of higher education. Two important reports contributed to the policy of the higher education expansion. The Anderson Committee's Report recommended financial support to all students who gained a full-time place at a university (Anderson, 1960). This was implemented, and so the ability to pay was no longer a major obstacle to entering a university for competent high-school graduates (Blackburn & Jarman, 1993). The Robbins Report on Higher Education emphasised the principle that university education should be available to all those with the ability and qualifications to benefit from it (Prime Minister's Committee on Higher Education, 1963). The Report stated that the universities should expand to meet the increased demand of qualified school graduates, and that there was a large, untapped pool of adults in the UK who could benefit from university education but who "had missed out earlier in their lives" (Harry, 1982, 170). The Robbins Report suggested expanding significantly access to existing universities, establishing new universities and upgrading existing post-secondary and professional institutions. Martin Trow highlighted the main developments of the mainstream British higher education in the two decades following the Second World War, before and immediately after the Robbins Report's recommendations: "Post-war expansion in Britain took the form of the establishment of colleges of advanced technology and their incorporation in the 1960s into the university system; the creation of new *plate glass* universities in the cathedral towns, small by American standards and only marginally different from the *red brick* universities; and the establishment of the polytechnics in the 1960s as a *public sector* side by side with the universities, though maintaining (at least in principle) the same standards of admission and the same high level of first degree" (Trow, 1993, 298).

It was the elitism and the preservation of meritocracy implicit in the British university system, even in its newly established higher education institutions, and particularly the disregard and indifference towards the adult, part-time students, that led Harold Wilson, then the leader of the Opposition, to propose in a speech in Glasgow in 1963 the creation of the *University of the Air*, a consortium of existing universities using broadcasting and tuition by correspondence to bring their teaching to adult students wherever they live or wish to study. Wilson was greatly impressed by the extensive use of correspondence education in the Soviet higher education and the education television employed in the USA (Perry, 1976, 1997; Tait, 1994a). At that time his idea of a University of the Air attracted little interest. It was regarded as another hopelessly impractical socialist election promise (Cerych & Sabatier, 1986). The editorial in the *Times Educational Supplement* written immediately after the proposal of the new university was published in 1966, when Wilson was already Prime Minister, declared that: "Mr. Wilson's pipe dream of a University of the Air, now adumbrated in a White Paper... as vague as it is insubstantial, is just the sort of cosy scheme that shows the socialists at their most endearing and impractical worst" (in Perry, 1996, 63).

In a foreword written in 1976 to a book by Lord Walter Perry, the first Vice Chancellor of the British Open University, Wilson himself asserted that: "The decision to create the Open University, then known as The University of the Air, was a political act" (Perry, 1976, XI). Lord Perry, looking back after nearly thirty years, admitted that: "There was only one factor which actually led to the establishment of the Open University, namely political determination. Its creation was a political act. It would never have been started by the academic world" (Perry, 1997, 8).

After the 1964 election Harold Wilson became Prime Minister, and in 1965 he appointed Jennie Lee as Secretary of State within the Department of Education and Science (DES), with special responsibility for the Arts and the University of the Air. Under Jennie Lee's leadership, the concept of the newly planned university changed its essence. It was to be a fully independent university, offering access to applicants without any specific entry requirements and equal in its quality and standards to any other British university. Perry admitted that: "Mr. Wilson's plan for the University of the Air may bear little relation to the Open University as it exists today, but it was to be the key that opened the door. It was the first expression of interest, by a powerful political figure in the provision of opportunities for higher education to adults, studying part-time while in full employment" (Perry, 1976, 9).

Jennie Lee fought long and hard to win the finance, cooperation and academic recognition that was crucially needed to establish the British Open University. "She succeeded to *outsnob the snobs* as she put it herself" (Smith, 1992, 3). On 18 September 1967 a Planning Committee was set up. The Planning Committee's Report was published on 28 January 1969, providing a blueprint for the University (Open University Planning Committee, 1969). Walter Perry was appointed as Vice Chancellor in May 1968. A Royal Charter, granted in June 1969, established the Open University as an independent and autonomous university authorised to confer its own degrees.

The fact that the British Open University received a Royal Charter, without even a probation period, was most significant to its academic status within the British higher education system. The authority to award degrees in the UK is jealously guarded and associated with the granting of a royal charter, but only to institutions which can demonstrate that they can teach and examine to high and common academic standards (Trow, 1988, 1993). Other higher education institutions established concurrently with the British Open University in the late 1960s and early 1970s did not obtain the autonomous status of a university. After the Robbins Report (though against its advice) the Labour Government grouped some of the English and Welsh colleges of technology, art and commerce (plus one in Northern Ireland) into thirty polytechnics, run by local governments, and intended to be more vocationally-oriented than the universities, thus creating what is known as the binary system which lasted until 1992 (Watson, 1989; Eustace, 1992; Parry, 1995, 1997). The polytechnics were not authorised to grant their own degrees, but had rather to teach toward the Council of National Academic Awards (CNAA) degrees. The CNAA, set up in 1964 by a Royal Charter, was an accrediting body, not a teaching institution, responsible for validating and conferring degrees of studies pursued at colleges and polytechnics other than the universities. Its function was comparable with the external examining system of the University of London, described earlier. The CNAA had the power of accreditation not only of institutions but also of each course within these institutions. Following the 1992 Education Act, the CNAA was abolished and the polytechnics were upgraded to university status. Hence the fact that the British Open University was granted a Royal Charter to confer its own degrees, while the polytechnics at the same time were put under the auspices of the CNAA, is most significant and crucially important to its initial status within the British higher education system.

The Conservative victory in 1970 threatened the very existence of the British Open University. Lord Perry declared that the British Open University's birth "was nearly a still-birth, because the Labour Party which had founded it, lost power before the first students began their studies" (Perry, 1992, 227). The idea of the British Open University was opposed not only by the Conservatives but also by many in academia, the media and the civil service (Perry, 1976, 1996, 1997; Harry, 1986). It survived, and the first students were admitted in 1971. Over 40,000 people applied, and 19,581 were admitted (Open University, 1993a; EADTU, 1994, 125).

In spite of the fact that there are many documents demonstrating the open hostility of the Conservative Party to the idea of the British Open University, Cerych and Sabatier (1986) claimed that the British Open University's goals had obvious political advantages of potential appeal to both left and right in the UK. To the supporters of Labour its open admission policy allowing for increased access to higher education among historically disadvantaged groups was most attractive. To the Conservatives the notion of providing opportunity of quality university education to those willing to work hard to obtain a degree appealed to the Conservatives' ideology of self-help. In addition, the reduced capital expenditure in distance higher education compared to the traditional research universities, an important aspect that will be discussed further on, was attractive to both left and right. It is claimed that Margaret Thatcher rescued the British Open University when some of her political colleagues had advised closing it, because she was particularly interested in its potential for reducing the costs of higher education. She perceived the British Open University as a possible way of avoiding the expense of having to establish quite so many new conventional universities as suggested by the Robbins Report (Daniel, 1995b; Perry, 1997).

Lord Perry stated that already in 1976 the British Open University "has gained its proper position as an institution outside politics and is no longer a pawn in the party political game" (Perry, 1976, 30). But from the point of view of the Labour Party it is still conceived as a great Labour creation. Andrew Smith, M.P., Labour's Higher and Continuing Education Spokesperson, declared in a position paper published in 1992 that the British Open University is "one of Labour's proudest achievements... When Harold Wilson resigned in 1976 and was asked what he considered his proudest achievement in his four terms as Prime Minister, he had no hesitation in singling out the Open University" (Smith, 1992, 2, 4).

Universidad Nacional de Educación a Distancia

The establishment of the Universidad Nacional de Educación a Distancia (UNED), the Spanish distance teaching university, was part of an overall, macro-organisational reform of the Spanish educational system from pre-school education upwards (James, 1982; García-Garrido, 1988). The Spanish Cortes had approved on 4 August 1970 the General Law of Education. This Law laid down the structure and sequence of the Spanish education system, which was divided into four stages: (1) pre-school education from four years of age to six, defined as optional; (2) primary and lower secondary education from six to fourteen (General Basic Education) declared mandatory; (3) higher secondary education (*Bachillerato*) or vocational training was to be optional only to General Basic Education graduates; (4) university education—special arrangements were defined for transfer from academic to vocational training, and vice versa (García-Garrido, 1976; García-Garrido, 1988).

The 1970 General Law of Education specified the need to provide educational opportunities to those who, for a variety of reasons, had no access to education, either because they lived in remote areas or belonged to marginalised segments of the society. The Law dictated that: "In order to offer possibilities of continuing their studies to those who could not attend regularly the official Centres or follow the common timetables, the Ministry of Education and Science, in collaboration with institutions involved, would regulate the different types of correspondence education, education by radio and TV" (in Popa-Lisseanu, 1986, 115). This law laid the basis for establishing distance education frameworks at all educational levels. Two distance education institutions for primary and secondary education were created as a result of this

Law. One was the National Centre for Basic Education at a Distance (CENEBAD), and the other the National Institute for Secondary Education at a Distance (INBAD). The initiation of UNED was a natural consequence that followed the overall restructuring of the education system.

A formal planning committee for the new university was established by the government on 6 May 1971 (García-Garrido, 1976; James, 1982). Members of the Committee were sent on exploratory study visits to compare various models of distance higher education. They visited the very young British Open University, the American Consortium for Distance Education and the University of the Air in Japan, which was at the planning stage. They were most impressed by the British Open University and recommended modelling the UNED as much as possible on this template (García-Garrido, 1976; García-Garrido, 1988).

UNED was formally constituted on 18 August 1972. On 15 September 1972, the first Rector of UNED, Manuel Jésus García-Garrido was appointed. The first group of 12,452 students began their studies on 6 February 1973 (Popa-Lisseanu, 1986, 115).

The University Reform Act of 1984 conferred on UNED an autonomous status identical to that of all other universities. This Act defined clearly the financial and legal authorities by which each university was to shape its own and distinct character. Apart from its distance education method, UNED was designed from the outset to be equal in every way to conventional Spanish universities. Its degrees were to be of equal status, and its students able to transfer credits between UNED and other Spanish universities (UNED, 1996). In addition, since UNED, through it special statutes, is defined as a national university, it should pay special attention to the national requirements and needs, and establish relations with a variety of regional educational authorities. UNED is the only national university in Spain, directly dependent on the Central Ministry of Education and Science. Spanish universities depend functionally on the educational committees of their autonomous regions (Popa-Lisseanu, 1986; UNED, 1996).

The Open University of Israel

The establishment of the Open University of Israel was the outcome of successful collaboration between a government initiative and an influential private philanthropic foundation. Until 1987, the Open University of Israel was called *Everyman's University* in English, though in Hebrew it was called from its first days *Hauniversita HaPetucha*, which means *The Open University*.

Yigal Allon, who became Minister of Education and Culture and Deputy Prime Minister in 1969, was determined "to make advances in higher education the hallmark of his tenure in office" (Halperin, 1984, 28). Just as some of his predecessors as Ministers of Education had pioneered large reforms in elementary and secondary education in Israel during the 1950s and the 1960s, Allon put his imprint on Israeli higher education by greatly expanding the power of the existing Council for Higher Education to plan and budget the universities and by supporting what soon became the powerful Planning and Budgeting Committee. The Council for Higher Education is the only authority empowered, subject to final Government approval, to grant academic recognition to new institutions and accredit them to award appropriate academic degrees. It is also responsible for approving new departments or new academic programmes in existing universities and academic colleges. The Planning and Budgeting Committee was modelled to a great extent on the British University Grants Committee (UGC).

Allon was impressed not only by the British UGC, but also by the new British Open University. When a graduate student in Britain during the early 1960s, Allon met his friend and colleague Harold Wilson and was greatly intrigued by the emerging idea of establishing a University of the Air (Halperin, 1984). By the time Allon had become Israel's Minister of Education and Culture in 1969, Wilson had become Britain's Prime Minister and the British Open University was about to be launched. Allon encouraged Elad Peled, then the Director-General of the Ministry of Education and Culture, and Samuel Bendor, the head of its Foreign Relations Department, to visit Jennie Lee, the principal champion of the British Open University, and study the newly established university at Walton Hall.

In the early 1970s the Israeli higher education system was composed of seven universities. No other higher education institutions existed outside the university sector. The total student population amounted to 35,374 (Council for Higher Education, 1995, 1). From the very start a strong focus on research characterised the Israeli universities. Germany provided the Humboldtian model of unity of research and teaching for the first two foundations, the Hebrew University, established in 1925, and the Technion at Haifa, established in 1924 (Ben-David, 1986). The remaining five universities, founded between 1949 and 1965, imitated the two older institutions in style. In reviewing the dilemmas of growth, diversification and administration of the Israeli universities Ben-David remarked that the Humboldtian idea of a strong emphasis on research had been adopted more vigorously by the Israeli universities than by any university elsewhere, Germany included (*ibid.*, 112). In Israel all undergraduate teaching was carried out until the mid-1970s in relatively high-cost research universities (Guri-Rosenblit, 1993a, 1996a).

Faced with some radical reforms in secondary schooling during the 1960s, it became more and more apparent that the universities were both unable and unwilling to respond to some urgent needs of the Israeli society at the post-secondary level. No first degree curricula were offered, neither for those wishing to study for general education purposes without a particular interest in a specific discipline, nor for those who sought to upgrade their professional education. The need to upgrade the professional education of teachers was

particularly urgent. Most teachers did not possess the minimum entry qualifications to be admitted to universities.

In addition, there has been a tremendous disparity between the representation of students of Ashkenazi (European-Western) origin and Sephardic
(Oriental, from North-African and Middle-Eastern countries) origin both
amongst high-school graduates and university students. In Israel, admission to
universities depends on the completion of a matriculation examination, *Bagrut*,
which resembles the German *Abitur* and French *Baccalauréat* (Guri-Rosenblit,
1996a). In the 1960s only 6% of Sephardic origin students of the relevant age
cohort passed the *Bagrut*, compared with 30% of the students of Ashkenazi
background (Gottlieb & Chen, 1995, 159), despite the fact that in the total
population, each of the two groups fluctuated around 50%. In 1969 students of
Sephardic origin constituted only 13.5% of the total student body in the
universities (*ibid.*). Several reforms were implemented in the 1960s at
secondary-level to close this social gap. The search for alternative paths of
continuing and higher education outside the university sector, to accommodate the needs of large segments of the Israeli population, unprovided for by
the universities, was a natural follow-on to the reforms in secondary education.

On 5 May 1970, the Council for Higher Education and the Ministry of Education appointed an ad hoc Committee on Post-Secondary Education, chaired
by Professor Shneuer Lifson of the Weizmann Institute, to carry out a broad
review of that field and to suggest how to solve the tapped problems. The
report of this Committee was submitted in December 1971 and recommended,
among other things, the establishment of an Open University based on the
British model, run in cooperation with a network of regional colleges. The
Committee proposed that the new Open University should utilise the latest
learning technologies to offer solid academic education leading to a bachelor's
degree.

Concurrently with the work of the Lifson Committee, Allon sought for
private philanthropic resources to launch the new-style university, "realising
that his Government colleagues would better warm to the idea of a new
university if it entailed no immediate budgetary outlays and if the initiative for
such a venture came from a body as prestigious and above reproach as *Hanadiv*
(The Benefactor)—The Rothschild Foundation which had, for almost 100
years, done so much to develop the land and institutions of the Jewish community in Palestine" (Halperin, 1984, 29). Allon began a series of negotiations
with the Rothschild family in London, and with Max Rowe, the Secretary-
General of the Foundation operating out of Geneva, and frequently from
Tel-Aviv. On 7 September 1971, the Rothschild Foundation had appointed an
Enquiry Commission "to assess the feasibility, practicability, and economics of
an Everyman's University for Israel" (Schramm et al., 1972, 16). This Commission was chaired by Prof. Wilbur Schramm, then the Director of the
Institute for Research of Communication at Stanford University. Its two other
members were Prof. David Hawkridge, Director of the Institute of Edu-

cational Technology at the British Open University, and Harold Howe II, the Vice President of the Ford Foundation for Education and Research. On 15 September 1972, the Schramm Commission issued its final report, calling for the creation of Everyman's University, an institution similar, but not identical to the British Open University. The Commission recommended that the new university offer a real alternative, rather than duplicating the existing universities. It should serve a wide spectrum of needs beyond the secondary school; offer students learning opportunities without limitations of place, age and traditional entry qualifications; and work with innovative methods of education and technology.

Hanadiv Foundation approved the recommendations of the Schramm Commission and expressed its readiness to finance the new venture during its early years. On 25 April 1973, the Rothschild Foundation formally committed itself to the funding of the new University for a seven-year period, as a pilot project, with the understanding that the Government would gradually assume financial responsibility for the University. On 19 August 1972, the Israeli Cabinet, then headed by Prime Minister Golda Meir, unanimously approved the establishment of Everyman's University. On 2 October 1973, the Council for Higher Education also unanimously approved Everyman's University as a pilot project along the lines proposed by Hanadiv Foundation. In a letter addressed to Mrs. Dorothy de Rothschild, Allon described the Cabinet meeting, in which Everyman's University was approved, as "one of the most stimulating and rewarding events which I have yet experienced in this forum. The ministers displayed great interest in the functions and goals of the university and were unanimous in recognising the benefits which Everyman's University would confer upon Israeli society" (Allon, 1973). Max Rowe was nominated as its first president. The Open University of Israel was officially established on 14 April 1974. The first 2,267 students were admitted in October 1976 (Halperin, 1984, 40).

Unlike the British Open University and UNED, which were established as totally autonomous full-fledged universities empowered to award degrees at the outset including master and doctoral degrees, the Open University of Israel was established as a pilot project. It had yet to prove its credibility as a university. The rules of academic recognition in Israel require a new academic institution to undergo a probation period, and only after several years of operation may it be recognised as an autonomous university or college. 1974, the year which saw the Open University of Israel beginning to operate, also witnessed the establishment of the Planning and Budgeting Committee, as a powerful organ of the Council for Higher Education to budget and plan the higher education system, with powers to decide whether a need for a new institution or a new department or a new programme were justified, and what were the financial implications of new ventures in the higher education system. The Open University of Israel was born in a period of growing control and intervention of the Israeli government in the planning and development of the universities and other higher education institutions. In June 1980, the Council for Higher Education recognised the Open University of Israel as an institution of higher education and authorised it to award bachelor degrees.

The Open University of Israel was the last university founded in Israel. The non-university sector started to develop in the same year in which the Open University of Israel was founded. The first authorisation to award professional bachelor's degrees was granted in 1974 to the Rubin Academy of Music. Since then the non-university sector has grown enormously (Guri-Rosenblit, 1993a, 1996a). In 1995, 28 colleges authorised to award first degrees operated in Israel (Israel Central Bureau of Statistics, 1995). Like the British Open University, it was important for the academic status of the Open University of Israel that it was established as a university. By contrast all the other new higher education institutes founded then and since were confined to college-level education only.

FernUniversität in Germany

The FernUniversität is not a national distance teaching university like the British Open University, UNED and the Open University of Israel. It was founded by the Land of North Rhine-Westphalia, one of the eleven Länder (states) which then composed the Federal Republic of Germany, and the most populous and industrialised state (Bartels & Peters, 1986). The FernUniversität was created as part of a broad attempt to restructure the German higher education system in the late 1960 and the early 1970s.

In the late 1960s general policy favoured expansion and diversification of the German higher education system as a response to the growing age cohorts entitled to take up university education (Teichler, 1986; Peisert & Framheim, 1990). Upgrading the less prestigious sectors of post-secondary education and establishing a new type of higher education institutions was the major thrust. The first step towards a diversified higher education system involved an agreement between the eleven German Länder in 1968 to upgrade former engineering schools and higher vocational schools to Fachhochschulen (vocational colleges) in the year 1971 (ibid.). Merging institutions of higher education with universities, whenever feasible, enjoyed considerable popularity in the early 1970s.

In 1970, the Minister of Education and Science of the Federal Republic of Germany presented a set of "fourteen theses" as a preliminary to a framework law covering all higher education institutions (Cerych & Sabatier, 1986). According to this law, German higher education, including its universities, Fachhochschulen, teacher training colleges, colleges of fine arts and other post-secondary establishments, were to be reorganised into Gesamthochschulen type institutions, and every new university would develop as a Gesamthochschule. The frequently used English translation for Gesamthochschulen is "comprehensive university". The framework law proposing Gesamthochschulen was passed in 1976.

The reform of the German higher education system flopped. Its impact was limited. Mainly due to the resistance of the universities, the model of the *Gesamthochschulen* lost its earlier appeal. At the end of the 1970s, only eleven *Gesamthochschulen* existed out of a total of 266 higher education institutions in Germany (Cerych & Sabatier, 1986, 200). Out of the eleven Länder only three had created *Gesamthochschulen*—North Rhine-Westphalia, Hesse and Bavaria. None of the *Gesamthochschulen* incorporated an established university (Teichler, 1986). Several new universities were founded in the 1970s (e.g., Oldenburg, Bayreuth, Passau), but none adopted the Gesamthochschulen nature. Paradoxically, after 1976, when the framework law governing the *Gesamthochschulen* was passed officially, none of the higher education institutions became a *Gesamthochschule*. Currently, there are only seven *Gesamthochschulen*, six in North Rhine-Westphalia (Duisburg, Essen, Paderborn, Siegen, Wuppertal and the FernUniversität in Hagen), and one in Hesse (Kassel).

The planning of a federal distance teaching university in Germany had been discussed by many higher education policy-makers since the late 1960s. But, as Otto Peters, the first Rector of the FernUniversität, noted: "The combined efforts of the universities, the governments of the Länder, of the Federal Government as well as of the broadcasting corporations to establish a university for distance education, had lasted for years and had come to a complete impasse" (Peters, 1994b, 179). When it became obvious that the different groups planning the federal scheme of a national distance teaching university would never agree, mainly for financial reasons, the Minister of Higher Education and Research of North Rhine-Westphalia, Johannes Rau, decided to establish a distance teaching university in his Land. In Peters' judgement: "He did so with a sense of proportion, a nose for political timing, an instinct for the successful approach, and with extraordinary personal involvement" (*ibid.*).

Looking back over twenty years, Peters attributed the establishment and success of the FernUniversität to Johannes Rau, a tribute which highlighted the crucial role of determined and powerful politicians in initiating and seeing innovations through complex systems: "His contribution cannot be overrated. Describing his role reveals the irony of development. Whereas the joint effort of Länder, universities and broadcasting corporations depended on the work of many commissions and sub-commissions, in which countless professors, administrators and experts from all over Germany met regularly at changing places for many years, the new project was conceived, planned, initiated and conducted only by him and a small planning group in one place and in an unbelievably short time. He initiated all necessary activities: the setting up of a planning commission in the ministry which studied the possibilities of distance education and described the project, the adoption of the project by the cabinet, the passing of the FernUniversität (Establishment) Act in parliament, the appointment of the Planning Committee, the selection of the first professors and the quick employment of a core of competent administrative experts" (Peters, 1997, 59). Johannes Rau was a leading exponent for expanding higher education in his Land. Six out of seven *Gesamthochschulen* currently existing in Germany are in North Rhine-Westphalia.

Johannes Rau had used as a clinching argument—the success of the British Open University which had shown distance education to be both feasible and efficient (Reddy, 1988c; Peters, 1994c, 1997). The Cabinet of North Rhine-Westphalia agreed on the establishment of the FernUniversität on 9 October 1973. The impetus for founding it was the unexpected and unusually high increase in the numbers entitled to enrol at a university. Early plans envisaged distant students who had just graduated from secondary school. It was also to become a Comprehensive University, similar to the other five new universities in North Rhine-Westphalia, which included professional and vocational training in addition to traditional university subjects.

However, the Planning Committee decided to impose a quota of 50% for working adults. It also ruled that continuing education was to be another important priority of the newly founded university (Keegan, 1982; Peters, 1994c, 1997). A decision was also taken that anyone should be able to enrol for single courses. The radical change of the FernUniversität's potential clientele, from high-school graduates to adults, was a significant alteration of the original FernUniversität vision. Peters claimed that it persuaded most of those pressing for continuing education at all universities to support the establishment of the FernUniversität: "The suspicion of the other universities grew a little less as the FernUniversität was no longer expected to become a rival institution to them" (Peters, 1994c, 174).

On 26 November 1974, the FernUniversität Act was passed by the Parliament of North Rhine-Westphalia. Otto Peters was appointed as its Rector. Peter Glotz, then the Secretary of State, told the audience at the opening ceremony: "The foundation of the FernUniversität was one of the greatest achievements in education policy we have seen in the recent years" (Peters, 1997, 63). The first 1,331 students were enrolled in September 1975 (*ibid.*, 69). The FernUniversität, like other German universities, is open to German students from other Länder, as well as to foreign applicants.

Athabasca University

Athabasca University, like the FernUniversität, is not a national distance teaching university. It was established in Alberta, one of the ten provinces and two territories that comprise Canada. It was born in a period of an unparalleled upsurge in university enrolment across the country during the 1960s (Hughes, 1980; Byrne, 1989). In response to the increased demand for university education, many provincial governments enlarged the existing universities and built new ones. From 48 universities and colleges in Canada in 1960, higher education rose to 67 universities and colleges in 1970. Enrolment grew from 116,466 in 1960 to 303,510 in 1970 (Ross, 1976, 56; Andrews et al., 1997).

Athabasca University was planned in 1970 largely as a response to enrolment pressures on the University of Alberta, which had reached the upper limits of growth. It was established by an Order in Council of the Government of Alberta, to be an undergraduate, campus-based university, and the fourth university in Alberta (in addition to the University of Alberta, Calgary University and Lethbridge University). From the outset, its mandate was "to explore and institute, if deemed desirable, new procedures in curriculum, organisation and instruction" (Shale, 1982, 34).

As in the case of the British Open University, the change of political power in 1970 threatened to close the University in its early stage of planning. The ruling Social Credit Party lost the provincial election in August 1971, after 36 years in power in Alberta. Not only was Athabasca University's future clouded in terms of its political affiliation. "Its necessity as a relief valve for student enrolments pressures came into serious question at the same time" (Hughes, 1980, 42). Far from increasing by 12% and 13%, as had been the pattern during the 1960s, a drop of one percent in full-time enrolment struck in the fall of 1971. It raised doubts about the wisdom of setting up a fourth university in the province (*ibid.*). Within two months of returning to power, the Conservative government, led by Peter Lougheed, halted the physical planning of Athabasca University. However, a small ad-hoc committee, including Dr. Tym Byrne and Dr. Sam Smith, later to become the first two presidents of the University, was asked to continue the academic planning of the university, though the government provided no guarantee about its eventual establishment.

The success of the British Open University was a source of inspiration to Byrn. He approached the Lougheed government and persuaded them to start an experiment in Alberta, namely to establish the first open university in Canada, following the British model (Morrison & Saraswati, 1988). "By the end of October 1971, what stood between a tenuous life for Athabasca University and total collapse was Tim Byrne. A lesser president, someone more career oriented, would simply cut and run... Tim hung tough because he deeply believed in the Athbasca University's academic concept and in the model which had been structured upon this concept" (Hughes, 1980, 44).

Athabasca University was re-established on 20 December 1972 by an Order in Council as an experimental project, due to end in 1975. This order authorised the University Interim Governing Council "to undertake a pilot project for the production, testing and application of learning systems to provide study programmes in the arts and sciences leading to undergraduate degrees, and for the application of learning systems and new procedures to improve educational opportunities for adults generally" (Shale, 1982, 35). Thus, Athabasca University was given the mandate and challenge to prove whether a fully fledged distance teaching university was feasible in Alberta. Like the Open

University of Israel, it had rapidly to prove its worth as an experimental project, in order to become permanent.

The three years of the pilot project from 1972 to 1975 were characterised by "much frenetic activity by a tiny staff of about 35" (Morrison & Saraswati, 1988, 21). Athabasca University enrolled its first students in October 1973. By the time the pilot project ended in November 1975, the University's leaders had convinced the Government that distance higher education could be made to work in Alberta. Another Order in Council gave Athabasca University permanent status in 1975. The legislative commitment, however, was not made until April 1978, when Athabasca University was established as the fourth permanent university of the Alberta province under the authority of the Universities Act. In 1975, Athabasca University enrolled 726 students, and by 1978 1,824 (Shale, 1982, 49). Enrolment at the Athabasca University is open to all Canadian students, and to a limited extent also to foreigners. In 1980, it was decided to relocate Athabasca University in Athabasca, 145 kilometres north of Edmonton. The new University's facilities were officially opened in 1985 (Andrews et al., 1997, 64)

The Impact of the British Open University Model

The emergence of these distance teaching universities described above demonstrates their political importance as a tool for governments to expand and open up higher education systems within national or provincial boundaries. Conspicuously striking, however, is the impact the British Open University had on the other four distance teaching universities (as well as on many others), even in its earliest days of operation. Policy makers and academics in Spain, Israel, Germany and Canada referred to the British Open University as a convincing model that a distance teaching university is a viable and efficient alternative to campus-based universities, for serving a wide clientele, particularly part-time adult students. The British Open University was the first of its kind, and unlike other distance teaching universities, it had thus no example to follow. Mugridge stressed that: "The achievement of establishing the British Open University without a model is extraordinary and the influence of the British Open University on the development of modern distance education has been and continues to be enormous" (Mugridge, 1997b, 169).

The persuasive influence of the British Open University is best summarised by Lord Perry, its first Vice Chancellor: "There was enormous interest in the experiment of the Open University, emanating from almost every country in the world. It was marked by an enthusiasm and an absence of the criticism so common in this country, and did much to offset the depressing effect of the continuous flow of adverse comments at home. We were indeed in the position of the prophet without honour in his own land" (Perry, 1976, 33). In the opinion of Bell and Tight: "In any estimation the Open University idea must rank as one of the major British intellectual exports of the last two decades" (1993, 128).

Lord Ashby, a weighty commentator on university affairs, remarked on the outstanding pace of British Open University's development and success. The founding of the British Open University was comparable to the establishment of the land-grant universities in the United States in the 1860s. Each form of higher education provided serious and sustained learning opportunities for large numbers of people for whom higher education had never previously been available, he thought. To achieve this: "It was necessary in both cases to develop new methods, materials, instructional designs, and forms of admini-stration" (Perry, 1977, IX). But the major difference between the American land-grant universities and the British Open University was that: "The first institution took at least seventy five years to achieve a fully established place in American society, while the second had to be brought into full-scale operation in less than three years" (*ibid.*).

Peters endorsed the noteworthy impact the British Open University had on the FernUniversität: "When the FernUniversität was founded, the British Open University was already a shining example of a modern distance teaching university. Its main contribution to the founding of the FernUniversität was that it had improved the image of distance education enormously. We could point to it in order to demonstrate in Germany that higher education at a distance was possible and that it should and could be organised by the state as teaching at a distance was no longer a dubious and questionable activity. This made it easier to convince sceptical politicians and educationalists" (Peters, 1997, 67).

The impact of the British Open University on the development of distance teaching universities worldwide has been extraordinary. While struggling for respect at home, it served as a model of imitation and guidance abroad. In a growing international and inter-connected planet successful innovations are most influential. As Clark and Neave suggested in the preface to the Encyclo-paedia of Higher Education: "Regardless of motive, systems are now clearly interacting. What is perceived as the success of one quickly becomes the model for others to emulate. Whether the graft will take root in foreign soil is a matter of faith, hope and money" (Clark & Neave, 1992, XXVII).

Distinctive Features of Distance Teaching Universities

The distance teaching universities born in the 1970s display salient features and specific goals which distinguish them as special universities. Their distinctive features are analysed below in terms of seven issues: broadening access to higher education; large-scale operation; changes in student-faculty interaction; high quality university-level textbooks; multi-media; reduced capi-tal expenditure; non-campus university.

Broadening Access to Higher Education

All distance teaching universities reflect a concern with widening access to higher education. Distance teaching universities have opened the gates of academia to varied and diverse clienteles, which remained outside the conventional university. They equalised opportunity of access to higher education by opening up admission requirements to hitherto underprivileged groups (Perraton, 1981; Rumble & Harry, 1982; Cerych & Sabatier, 1986). All the distance teaching universities founded in the 1970s offered a *second chance* of part-time study to adults, regardless of work, geography, family commitments and constraints. From the outset, some set their sights at younger segments of society as well. The underlying philosophy of each of the distance teaching universities in respect of access is examined below, whilst further light on students' characteristics is shed in Chapter 3.

The British Open University was clearly committed to part-time adult students. Leslie Wagner (1984) contended that the opening of access to degree level higher education for adults was undoubtedly the *raison d'être* of the British Open University. By the end of the 1970s, it provided more opportunities for adults to study at undergraduate level than the rest of the higher education system put together (universities, polytechnics and colleges). In 1971, the British Open University admitted 19,581 students, five times more than the total of part-time undergraduates then in universities, and nearly three-quarters of all part-time undergraduates in the UK (Smith, 1992, 4). Between 1971 and 1991, over one and a half million adults had taken a British Open University course of one kind or another (*ibid.*). In 1995, it counted 151,331 students in degree programmes, and 65,473 individuals learning through a variety of non-credit-bearing study-packs (Open University, 1995, Daniel, 1996a, 31).

The British Open University was keen to have it known that it was conceived for a very different clientele compared with traditional universities. Although committed to an open admission policy, it restricted access to applicants of at least 21 years of age (Perry, 1976, 1996). A pilot project was undertaken in 1974 at the request of the Conservative Government into the possibility of admitting the 18–21 age group. But the small number of applicants and the relatively poor results led to the conclusion that it was not a priority area for the university (Woodley & McIntosh, 1980). The age limit of 21 was, however, removed in 1986 (Harry, 1986, 91; Schutze, 1986, 21). The decision to recruit only adult part-timers was influenced by the policy not to compete with mainline universities, but rather to play up the differences in its student body, and its special mission in British higher education.

From the outset, the Spanish UNED aimed at both adult part-timers and at young high-school graduates. Its formal objectives were: "To provide higher education at home... to all those who missed their first educational opportunity or were unable to attend existing institutions of learning without disrupting their normal occupations or because of distance, sickness, inflexible schedules, etc.; to substitute the *free learning* offered to those who for some reason or other, could not attend a class, and hence, had to study independently as best as they could...; to become an efficient instrument to the implementation of equal opportunities in higher education in Spain; to increase the enrolment capacity of Spanish universities" (García-Garrido, 1988, 202–203).

In February 1973, UNED admitted 12,452 students (Popa-Lisseanu, 1986, 115), and by 1979 it already totalled 45,146 students (James, 1982, 155). In that same year 24% of its students were under 25 years of age (Rumble & Keegan, 1982, 211). In 1984 its student population reached 87,300 (García-Garrido, 1988, 208), and in 1995 it had attained 136,480 (UNED, 1996). Currently, UNED is the second largest university in Spain.

Although its target population was diverse from the start, the average age of students is higher than in traditional Spanish universities; most students work full-time and are employed by public administration or by the private sector (García-Garrido, 1988, 207). UNED has not taken up the open admission policy of the British Open University. It has, however, put on a special access course for those 25 years and older who do not possess sufficient entry qualifications—usually those without the *Bachillerato* certificate. Those completing this Admission Course successfully are admitted to degree level studies at UNED or other Spanish universities; 17,645 students were enrolled in this course in 1995 (UNED, 1996).

The Israeli Open University was created mainly to provide *second chance* higher education for adults, and in this is similar to the British Open University. It too has an open admission policy. Its goals were set out as: "To make academic degrees accessible to large segments of the public; to provide persons who have interrupted their studies with suitable study frameworks to broaden their education and improve their vocational skills; to assist in raising the educational levels of teachers" (Everyman's University of Israel, 1982, 2).

In 1976 the Open University of Israel enrolled 2,267 students. In 1984 it had 12,871 (Halperin, 1984, 40); and in 1995 its students numbered 28,771 (President's Report, 1997, 119). Halperin conducted a study on the Open University of Israel's performance after ten years of activity and concluded that it "does more to serve the disadvantaged, to train teachers and to offer second chances to persons unable to benefit from regular study programmes than any of its conventional academic counterparts" (Halperin, 1984, 38).

Young students, many of whom are conscripted soldiers, are a special segment at the Open University of Israel. In 1984, they amounted to 16% of students (*ibid.*, 42), and in 1994, 14% (President's Report, 1995, 115). Many of them enrol full time at one of the conventional universities on completing their military service. Another special group at the Open University of Israel is high-school students of at least 16 years of age. Unlike the British Open University, the Open University of Israel has no limitations on admitting young students. The percentage of students of 20 or under grew from 1.2% in 1976 (Halperin, 1984, 41) to 6% in 1995 (President's Report, 1997, 119).

The three prime goals of the German FernUniversität were: "To create additional capacity for academic study and thus contribute to the increase in capacity of the German university system; to develop a system of academic continuing education; to be engaged in the reform of university teaching" (Keegan, 1982, 92).

As mentioned before, the FernUniversität was originally intended to cater for high-school graduates, however, definition of the target groups changed already at the planning stage. The FernUniversität's Planning Committee recommended a quota of 50% for adults in employment, another 25% for students taking single courses, and thus leaving only 25% of places for high-school graduates (Peters, 1994c, 1997). The shift in focus to adults was echoed in a speech delivered by Johannes Rau, then Minister of Higher Education and Research in North Rhine-Westphalia, on 13 June 1977, to the first meeting of the FernUniversität's Advisory Board: "He surprised many participants when he presented the three main goals of the FernUniversität in a new sequence. According to this, the FernUniversität was firstly to contribute to university reform, secondly to develop higher continuing education, and thirdly to increase the capacity of the universities. The original first goal, which, as described, had caused the planning of the FernUniversität, was now relegated to third place" (*ibid.*, 177).

By 1993, the FernUniversität was describing itself as "particularly designed to meet the needs of learners who are not able to study with traditional universities. But of course it equally suits the purposes of full-time study" (Schmidtchen, 1993, 3–4).

Unlike the British Open University and the Open University of Israel, but similar to UNED, the FernUniversität did not adopt an open admission policy. In 1975, it enrolled 1,331 students (Peters, 1997, 63), in 1981 46,669, of whom 26.2% were under 25 years of age (Keegan, 1982, 91; Rumble & Keegan, 1982, 211). In 1995, the FernUniversität had some 54,630 students (Schuemer, 1997).

The Canadian Athabasca University operates an open access policy like the British Open University and the Open University of Israel. Its main mission was set out as: "The removal of barriers that traditionally restrict access to and success in university-level studies and the increase of equality of educational opportunity for all adult Canadians regardless of their geographical location and prior academic credentials" (Athabasca University, 1992a, 1).

In 1975, Athabasca University had 776 students (Shale, 1982, 49). From 1980 to 1991, student numbers more than tripled from 3,466 in 1980 to 11,229 (Athabasca University, 1992a, 2). Since the early 1990s, student enrolments remained constant. In 1995, for instance, 10,974 students were enrolled at Athabasca University (Patten, 1997). Athabasca University's students were very similar to part-time students at conventional universities in Alberta. They were, on average, older than full-time undergraduates (Shale, 1982). In 1977, 25% of students were under 24 years old. The corresponding statistic fifteen years later in 1995 was almost 20% (Athabasca University, 1992b).

This brief outline of the admission policies and student numbers at each of the five distance teaching universities reveals their substantial contribution to widening access to university level education, to democratisation and opening up of higher education systems. Most distance teaching universities attract large numbers. In some instances, they are impressive and by any yardstick towering (Reddy, 1988b; Daniel, 1996a). Able to handle large student numbers, at relatively low cost, distance teaching universities have "done their bit" in the move from elite to mass higher education. Their special commitment to part-time adults sets them apart from conventional campus-based universities, which in the 1970s were geared mainly, and in some cases even exclusively, to high-school graduates. By encouraging working adults to pursue higher education, distance teaching universities developed a more extensive interface with employment. Individuals work while studying. They suffer no loss of income, and maybe their country suffers no loss of productivity.

Large-scale Operation

In surveying the theory and practice of distance education, Holmberg (1986, 1995) distinguished between *large-scale* and *small-scale* systems of distance education. Holmberg believed that the *large-scale* institutions, like autonomous distance teaching universities, could be regarded as innovations outside traditional higher education, in so far as they apply what Peters (1983, 1994d) called "industrial working methods". *Small-scale* organisations— private correspondence schools or extension departments—find it more rewarding to remain within the mainstream of education.

Peters suggested that the salient feature of distance education was its high degree of industrialisation (Peters, 1983, 1994d). He claimed that this encompassed its structural uniqueness, separated it sharply from all conventional forms of face-to-face instruction, thus presenting a new and radical form of university education, and very different from traditional didactics. As in industrial production, the process of developing materials for learning and teaching at a distance were moulded by the principles of rationalisation, the most important of which were the division and sub-division of labour, specialisation, objectification and automation. Peters defined distance teaching as follows: "Distance study is a rationalised method—involving the division of labour—of providing knowledge which, as a result of applying the principles of industrial organisation as well as the extensive use of technology, thus facilitating the reproduction of objective teaching activity in any numbers, allows a large number of students to participate in university study simultaneously regardless of their place of residence and occupation" (Peters, 1994d, 125). An illuminating example indeed, which clarified the underlying premises of the distance teaching university and the need to plan it as a large-scale operation was provided by Peters: if a Minister of Education accepts the idea of an open university, but suggests it should begin with a small unit later to grow in subsequent years, that Minister is labouring under a deep misconception as to what a distance teaching university is: "As it is an industrialised process based on division of labour, a high degree of mechanisation and the economy of scale, it is absurd to plan a small beginning" (Peters, 1994e, 11).

Perry, addressing an American audience, quipped that: "Everything about distance learning systems must, like everything in Texas, be big" (Perry, 1991, 10). Instructional materials of quality are expensive to produce, and large numbers of students must use them before the cost per head becomes reasonable. Distance teaching universities, *sui generis*, have to be established and to operate as large-scale organisations, otherwise their *raison d'être* may be compromised.

Daniel (1990) views the interpretation of distance education as an industrial form of education as simplistic. It is more reasonable to see distance teaching universities as forerunners of information-based organisations of the 21st century. Running the printing process and arranging the course material warehouse may well be done by traditional industrial methods, activities such as designing and developing a distance teaching course by teamwork require the most modern methods of project management.

Whether based on an industrial model or on a project management techniques, distance teaching universities demand massive organisational efforts to lay down a specialised infrastructure for producing and dispatching study materials, for monitoring and evaluating teaching and learning. Neither conventional universities, nor first-generation correspondence institutions possessed or possess such a complete infrastructure.

Changing the Student–Faculty Interaction

Distance education implies the physical separation of students from academic faculty in most stages of their study. To compensate for this, self-study materials are built around a *guided didactic conversation* (Holmberg, 1986, 1995), which enables students to study by themselves whenever they wish to do so, but without the presence of a teacher or a tutor. In distance teaching, it is learning materials, developed by the institution, which take over the responsibility of instruction. Therefore the *venia legendi* (the right to teach) is vested in the study materials rather than in the individual lecturer, as is the case in classical universities. The involvement of senior faculty in teaching, the nature of the student support services, the roles of junior academic staff (course coordinators, teaching assistants, tutors) are subject to considerable variation from one distance teaching university to another. These aspects are discussed in detail in Chapter 3.

The last decade has seen student support services grow rapidly in most distance teaching universities. If the 1970s were taken up with the quest for effective models of course design, interest in the 1980s shifted to student learning environments. It became evident that completion rates in distance teaching systems depended greatly upon effective support mechanisms (Guri-Rosenblit, 1989, 1990a, 1993a; EADTU, 1993b). This was especially true for students from disadvantaged backgrounds.

Over the past decade, some distance teaching universities have provided campus-like conditions for students who prefer frequent face-to-face tutorials. In addition, new information technologies linking satellite and computer networks, have introduced a new dimension of student–faculty interaction. For most of the distance teaching universities analysed here, this is an important development. Chapter 5 looks at this aspect in greater detail.

High Quality University-level Textbooks

One of the more enterprising ventures which accompanied the rise to fortune of many distance teaching universities was the production of high-quality learning materials, designed to stimulate and improve self-study. Special attention is paid to the quality of teaching rather than to research. The preparation of materials stands at the centre of learning and teaching in all distance teaching universities and takes up the largest proportion of the academic staff's time. It is the emphasis on teaching which distinguishes distance teaching universities from both campus-based universities—primarily oriented towards research—and correspondence institutions that act mainly as examining agencies and do not generally spend great efforts to develop special learning materials for their students. The course materials produced by distance teaching universities are—like any textbook—open to scrutiny and to criticism. Thus, by virtue of its public nature, there is control over the quality of instruction (Perry, 1976, 1996; Reddy, 1988b; Guri-Rosenblit, 1993a).

Designing and developing self-study materials by a course team are very expensive. In the British Open University the cost of producing courses (which equal one-sixth of a degree) ranges from £500,000 to £1,000,000 (Perry, 1997). In the Israeli Open University, the development of a course (which is approximately 1,000 pages long) takes three to five years and costs over $250,000 (Guri-Rosenblit, 1997a). Hence, distance teaching universities cannot afford to develop courses in highly peripheral areas that attract only small numbers of students. Sometimes, they arrange for such courses to be diffused via satellites, computer networks or face-to-face seminar settings.

However, students at distance teaching universities are not the only beneficiaries. Faculty and students at many main line universities frequently use the materials developed by distance teaching universities as set books, because of their clarity, their integrated structure and overall presentation (Guri, 1987; Guri-Rosenblit, 1990). Some distance teaching universities have become the biggest academic publishing houses in their countries. All of the distance teaching universities analysed here have contributed very substantially to the production of high-level university textbooks, at undergraduate level.

Multi-media

At the heart of distance education universities lie the employment of a multi-media approach and the utilisation of advanced communication technology (Reddy, 1988a; Daniel, 1995a, 1996a). In setting up the British Open University, Prime Minister Wilson wanted the technology of mass communication to be harnessed to the service of higher education. The Canadian Athabasca University was a pilot project for the application of technology and new procedures to improve educational opportunities for adults. UNED, the Open University of Israel and the FernUniversität have been urged to utilise new technologies to improve university teaching. And all new distance teaching universities have been heralded as universities of the air. By emphasising communication technology they have thrown off the image of the correspondence college which clung to many of the private and mixed correspondence institutions which earlier supplied teaching at a distance (Rumble & Harry, 1982; Glatter & Wedell, 1971).

Looking back on distance teaching universities of the 1970s, they enjoyed an overriding public association with the use of multi-media techniques. They played down, however, the practice of correspondence teaching based mainly on print technology. During the 1970s and 1980s, the implementation of multi-media was far less successful than expected (Paul, 1990). Most distance teaching universities still rely mainly on the written text. None of those in this study depends on electronic or advanced technology for primary instruction.

Unquestionably, new technologies, developed mainly since the 1990s, bear an enormous potential for improving and refining the delivery systems in distance teaching universities, and they are also being tested by conventional universities (Bates, 1989a, 1990a,b, 1995, 1997; Daniel, 1995a, 1996a; Perry, 1996). Distance education, even so, is well placed to utilise different technologies, not only to improve dissemination and delivery, but also to improve the quality of learning and teaching. New technologies allow a far greater interaction between learner and instructor and open new avenues of communication. An impressive list of technologies is utilised in distance teaching settings, including radio, television, audio and video cassettes, interactive videodiscs, telephone, audio and video conferencing, computer-based programmes and computer-mediated communication.

Reduced Capital Expenditure

The search for less expensive ways of providing higher education to growing numbers of students was one of the main considerations behind the establishment of distance teaching universities in the 1970s. However, comparison on the basis of cost between distance and mainstream systems is by no means easy. Their cost structures are very different (Perraton, 1993).

The total costs of each institution are made up of both fixed and variable costs. In the area of fixed costs, distance teaching universities do not support a campus or residential facilities, so they are significantly cheaper compared with campus-based universities. On the other hand, they require heavy investment to set up the infrastructure for the production of the study materials even before a single student is enrolled. The capital costs of distance teaching universities are also altered by the choice of media (TV productions are amazingly expensive, for example), the number of subject areas covered, and the number of courses provided (Rumble, 1993).

Course materials are produced centrally by a relatively small academic staff. As the number of students increases, the cost per student decreases. In traditional universities, the variable costs increase almost directly with the volume of activity, i.e., more students require more staff. For distance teaching universities, the more students, the lower the variable cost per student (Granger, 1990; Smith, 1992; Perraton, 1993; Rumble, 1993; Holmberg, 1995). In short, while the start-up costs of distance teaching universities are high, the marginal cost per student decreases the more students enrol.

A small distance teaching university might face difficulties in achieving economies of scale. In the case of the Canadian Athabasca University, when some 4,400 students were on the books in 1981, the costs per course enrolment were comparable with those of other universities in Alberta (Rumble, 1993, 105). For a large distance teaching university it is easier to achieve economies of scale. Leslie Wagner calculated that in the first three years of the British Open University, it cost less than a third to teach an undergraduate compared with other British universities (Wagner, 1980, 21). Sir John Daniel, its Vice Chancellor, remarked in 1995: "Now that all English universities are funded on a common basis comparisons can readily be made. These show that the cost to the public purse of a full-time-equivalent student at the Open University in each discipline is just over half the average for other universities" (Daniel, 1995b, 402–403). García-Aretio's studies conducted in UNED, found that "in UNED the costs of studying a specific subject in an official branch of learning is only 41 percent of the cost of studying in a conventional university" (García-Aretio, 1995, 94).

In an examination of a series of cost studies at different distance teaching universities, Rumble concluded: "Given the differences in the structure of costs between distance and traditional education systems, the former can be cheaper per student, per credit hour or graduate than the latter" (Rumble, 1993, 106). More details on the cost structures of the distance teaching universities are given in Chapter 6.

Furthermore, since most distance teaching university students are part-timers, they continue to work while studying, and this is no less an important economic factor, though omitted from the classical calculation of per student costs. Since most distance teaching universities contribute to raising the quality of academic textbooks, as we have mentioned earlier, this too is a significant element and it too remains excluded from the usual formulae of fixed and variable costs of a university.

Non-campus University

Disbanding the campus and reaching out to students wherever they prefer and whenever they may wish to study, is the feature which distinguishes distance teaching universities from the mainline, residential universities. A *campus* incarnates not only the distinctive physical qualities of a university, but also its educational and social ideals. The term *campus* was first used to describe the grounds of Princeton University around 1770 (Turner, 1984, 47). Campus in its Latin meaning of a field, is an allusion perhaps to the Campus Martius of ancient Rome, and by imaginative licence enshrined the green expansiveness distinctive to certain American universities. The term gradually assumed a broader significance, until at most universities it encompassed the entire property, including buildings. One could even allude to an "urban campus" which was nothing remotely resembling a field. In 1925, the German city planner Werner Hegemann, writing on America, defined *campus* for his countrymen as a "piece of land that is covered with buildings of an American university" (*ibid.*, 4). The purely physical meaning aside, it has taken on other connotations, the pervasive spirit of a university, its *genius loci* embodied in architecture and grounds. By the 1870s the term had become so evocative that an observer of one of the American colleges wrote: "There is no spell more powerful to recall the memories of college life than the word Campus" (*ibid.*). Campus superseded yard and grounds. By the 1820s, it had been borrowed by most American universities, imported to Europe, though more sparingly.

Campus universities include not only lecture halls, seminar rooms, laboratories and libraries, but also residential arrangements and recreational facilities—tennis courts, football fields, theatres, subsidised dining rooms, cafeterias and so on. A campus entails the grounds both for faculty–student dialogue interaction as well as for student–student meeting points. Perhaps too great an emphasis has been laid in the distance education literature on physical separateness between faculty and students, and by the same token too little is said about the lack of exchange between students.

It was not coincidental that the British Open University insisted on defining its students as part-time adults. Be that as it may, until very recently, most British universities were predominantly residential. That students and teachers live together in small, tightly regulated colleges represents the ideal of a collegiate university as a self-contained community. Historically the metropolitan University of London was a challenge to the collegiate model. The British Open University went even further down this road by eliminating the campus. It catered for part-time adults for whom campus life was either of lesser attraction or impossible. In the minds of its planners a distance teaching university like the British Open University is not an alternative form of under-graduate education for young school graduates, for whom work, play and sports, which a campus-based university makes available, are of great importance.

Continental European universities are focused more on academic studies, and pay little, if any, attention to their students' extracurricular life. Distance teaching universities in Spain and in Germany were a far less radical challenge to the notion of a campus-based university. It explains partially why they could cater for full-time young students together with part-time working adults. This pattern applies also to the Israeli and Canadian distance teaching universities, which took their place in systems where comprehensive, multiversities operate, and where many of their students live at home and combine study with work. The broader implications that arise from disbanding the campus and the effects on distance teaching university students and on learning and teaching are analysed in Chapter 3.

2

Distance Teaching Universities in Their National Settings

Any theory of convergence that highlights common drift into complexity, and similar forms of accommodation, will need in time shade into a theory of divergence that observes individual national evolutions.

Clark (1993, 263)

While the main features of most open universities are similar they are different from each other in several respects. Each has been established taking into account the peculiar conditions of its country. In other words, each open university has its own national characteristics.

Reddy (1988b, 7)

Introduction

In Chapter 1, the major characteristics of the autonomous distance teaching universities were analysed as a means of highlighting the essential differences between them and campus-based universities, as well as between them and the first generation of correspondence institutions. All of the large distance teaching universities have abolished the physical campus, opened up the university gates to heterogeneous populations and contributed most significantly to the democratisation of their higher education systems. They pay pre-eminent attention to the quality of instruction and to the quality of the study textbooks. They employ multi-media in teaching and learning. They utilise industrial and advanced technological methods for course development, production and dispatch. They are cost-effective. They contribute to closer ties with work and the business sector.

All five distance teaching universities chosen for this comparative study possess and portray these characteristics. Moreover, all of them were established overtly and explicitly on the model of the British Open University. Although they resemble each other in many respects, they also differ from each other. Their great resemblance makes it even more interesting to analyse both the explicit and subtle differences between them, as a reflection of the diverse academic cultures in each of their national settings. Clearly, each national higher education system has it own peculiar features and qualities. As Clark put it: "National systems of higher education vary in their organisation and structure... Different national structures then produce different responses to common trends or demands. The structure of a national system is generally the primary determinant of the direction and intensity of change within it, and the degree of success in deliberate reforms" (Clark, 1986, 259).

It is natural for the initiators of an emerging academic model and a new field of study to mobilise at the outset all their energies to portray the unique features of the innovative phenomenon in contrast to longstanding practices. Most of the relevant literature on distance education in the last two decades has done exactly this; it has emphasised the special characteristics of distance teaching universities and other distance education institutions as set against traditional, conventional educational establishments. It has highlighted the resemblance between different distance teaching universities (Rumble & Harry, 1982; Sewart et al., 1983; Keegan, 1986; Holmberg, 1986, 1995; van Enckevort et al., 1986; Smith & Kelly, 1987; Paul, 1990; Verduin & Clark, 1991; Harry et al., 1993; Keegan, 1993b; Moore & Kearsley, 1996; Mugridge, 1997a).

In a recent account of the history of nine distance teaching universities, from the perspective of their founding presidents, Mugridge (1997a) recalled, while attending in 1982 an international panel on distance education represented by five different institutions, that: "My prevailing impression as the five presentations drew to a close was that, allowing for differences of location, stages of institutional development and style of presentation, there would have been little comment if we had delivered one another's scripts... I have sometimes had a very similar feeling as I read the ten contributions to this collection. The experiences of founding distance teaching universities recorded here are spread over almost a thirty year period and cover institutions in nine countries, on three continents. Yet the stories that the contributors have to tell are uniformly illustrative of the problems facing those attempting to establish distance teaching programmes in any part of the world with which I am familiar" (Mugridge, 1997b, 166).

I would depart from the sweeping tendency to relate to all distance teaching universities as a generic group. Most meaningful and important differences do exist between various distance teaching universities and it is most illuminating to observe their divergences if one is to grasp each distance teaching university's functional roles and academic status within its national setting. Nowadays, the distance education field seems mature enough to engage in what Clark defined as a "theory of divergence that observes individual national evolutions" (Clark, 1993, 263). To observe the differential functions of each distance teaching university in its national academic milieu enriches our understanding of its contribution to the higher education system at large and deepens our comprehension of the scope involved in the novelty and innovation within each national context (Guri-Rosenblit, 1996b, 1997b). A given feature, such as open access, might constitute a great revolutionary idea in an elitist higher education system, but a relatively minor change in a higher education system which rests on the premises of mass or universal access.

Already in the brief description of the major and leading goals of each of the five distance teaching universities presented in Chapter 1, it is possible to observe certain obvious differences between the five universities, and divide them into sub-groups according to certain parameters. For example, three of the distance teaching universities are national universities (British Open University, UNED, Open University of Israel), while two are provincial (Fern-Universität, Athabasca University). This alone is an important variation. National universities are geared to accommodate national priorities on a large scale. Smaller provincial universities tend to operate on a different scale and on a different philosophy. Three of the distance teaching universities were initially given full authority to operate as fully fledged universities and to grant academic degrees from Bachelor up to PhD (British Open University, UNED, FernUniversität). By contrast, the other two were established as experimental projects, and at the beginning were authorised to award only bachelor degrees (Open University of Israel, Athabasca University). Three distance teaching universities adopted an open admission policy (British Open University, Open University of Israel, Athabasca University), while two require the same entry requirements as the conventional universities (UNED, FernUniversität). Even these brief comparisons reveal the impossibility of grouping various distance teaching universities into definite categories. Each comparison divided the five distance teaching universities into different sub-groups. The division into sub-groups depends on the parameters of comparison. In one case, the British Open University was grouped with UNED and the Open University of Israel; in the second, with UNED and the FernUniversität; and in the third with the Open University of Israel and Athabasca University.

In this chapter, we will examine the degree of novelty and innovation, which each of the distance teaching universities has introduced into its national higher education system, on the basis of the following eight parameters: distance teaching at university level; access–exit requirements; part-time adults; ethos of academic freedom; size of a distance teaching university; modular credit accumulation; academic year calendar; use of mass communication.

Some of the distance teaching universities are also called *open universities*, and the terms *open learning* and *distance education* are often used interchangeably in the literature. Hence, a brief discussion as to the connotations and meanings attached to these terms will precede the comparisons. This clarification would appear essential, since the relative dimensions of *openness* found in of each of the distance teaching universities are closely related to the dominant academic beliefs and practices in their respective national milieu.

Distance Education and Open Learning

Distance education and *open learning* are used synonymously by some scholars and practitioners. Others distinguish between them and even advocate the superiority of one term over the other (Fox, 1987; Guri-Rosenblit, 1993b). In Holmberg's view, today's usage blurs the distinction between the two terms because of "the strong influence of the British Open University and other distance teaching organisations that have adopted practices corresponding to and names containing this adjective (open)", and because "educators who find distance education a forbidding term may feel like replacing it by open learning" (Holmberg, 1995, 4, 6). Holmberg stated that *open* in itself has nothing to do with *distance education*, since if openness relates to flexible time schedules, entry policy, content of learning, etc., some of the distance teaching institutions might be regarded as closed.

Holmberg defined *distance education* as characterised by non-contiguous communication: "The term distance education... covers the various forms of study at all levels which are not under the continuous, immediate supervision of tutors present with their students in lecture rooms or on the same premises but which, nevertheless, benefit from the planning, guidance and teaching of a support organisation" (Holmberg, 1989, 3).

Holmberg's definition is somewhat limited in describing the practice of distance teaching institutions. It relates to a pure form of distance education, which does not involve physical face-to-face meetings between teachers and students. Yet, contiguous education and pure distance education are extremes that rarely exist. Many distance teaching universities, as well as other forms of distance teaching institutes, use face-to-face tutorials, summer schools, seminars and laboratory sessions. Likewise, many conventional education organisations utilise independent study and guided learning by tutors and through media. Tight (1987) argued that in reality a continuous spectrum exists between face-to-face and forms of distance education, the ends of which are never encountered in practice. Moreover, the advent of interactive media challenges Holmberg's definition from another angle. Nowadays, interactive computer networks, teleconferencing and interactive satellite sessions are used both by distance teaching universities and conventional campus-based universities.

Nevertheless, one of the major characteristics of *distance education* involves the physical separation of the learner from the instructor, at least at certain stages of the learning process. Keegan (1980a, 1986) defined the quasi-permanent separation of teacher and learner throughout the length of the learning process as one of the major characteristics of distance education. Keegan defined four additional characteristics (1986, 49–50): the influence of an educational organisation in the planning and the preparation of learning materials and in the provision of student support services; the use of technical media to bring together teacher and learner and carry the content of the course; the provision of two-way communication so that students may benefit from, or even initiate, a dialogue with their instructor; the quasi-permanent absence of a learning group throughout the length of the learning process—people are usually taught as individuals, not in groups.

Daniel's (1989, 1990) interpretation of the term *distance education* embraces all forms of instruction in which classroom sessions are not the primary means of education. Distance education is mostly homework, with occasional work in class, while conventional education is mostly classwork with occasional work at home. In conventional education, the teacher teaches; in distance education, the institution teaches. The primary challenge of distance education is then to set up institutional processes to carry out on a large scale the instructional functions that the classroom teacher performs on a small scale.

For Daniel the tendency to use the terms *distance education* and *open learning* interchangeably sprang from "an understandable desire to identify new institutions with the overall purpose for which they were established rather than the instructional means they intended to use" (Daniel, 1990, 106).

Rumble (1989a,b) attempted to clarify both terms and recommends appropriate uses for both. He concluded that the adjective *open* is both multi-dimensional and highly relative. Thus, the term *open learning* is confusing unless the context indicates the dimensions of openness that relate to it. Education can be *open* or *closed* in many different ways. The term *distance learning* is neutral in its connotation and describes a *mode* of educational delivery.

Bell and Tight (1993) linked *distance education* with opening up access to higher education. They offered the following definition: "Distance education refers to those forms of organised learning which are based on, or seek to overcome, the physical separation of learners and those (other than the learners themselves) involved in the organisation of their learning. This separation may apply to the whole learning process or only to certain stages or elements of it. Some face-to-face contacts may occur, but its function will be to supplement or reinforce the predominantly distant interaction. A good deal of private study will be typically expected of the student. Distance education offers one set of methods for opening up education to those who are unable or unwilling to regularly attend educational institutions" (Bell & Tight, 1993, 7–8).

Bell and Tight's definition perceived distance education as reflecting one dimension of *open learning*. But, diverse meanings attach to *open learning*. In the introduction to his book, Paine noted that: "There are many definitions of open learning including the association of open learning exclusively with open access, learning opportunities for adults, and the still prevalent confusion of learning at a distance and open learning as overlapping terminology. We prefer to define open learning as both a process which focuses on access to educational opportunities and a philosophy which makes learning more client and student-centred" (Paine, 1989, IX).

Paul pointed out that: "The use of the term *open* admits that education and learning have traditionally been *closed*, by various barriers—entrance requirements, time constraints, financial demands, geographical distance, and much more subtly, social and cultural barriers, as well as those of gender. An open learning institution is one dedicated to helping individuals overcome these barriers by further education" (Paul, 1990, 42).

Lewis (1989, 1997) claimed that open learning occurs when decisions about learning are taken by the learner or learners themselves. He argued that the misconceptions of the term open learning stem from the confusion of this term "with distance learning or (even worse) with correspondence courses. These terms imply thin educational experience delivered to isolated learners deprived of those interactions supposedly normal in conventional classrooms" (Lewis, 1989, 171). Rossetti (1989, 235–236) defined six major characteristics of open learning: open entry, individualised learning, self-assessment, learner support, self-pacing, and many start dates.

In Carr's view: "Overall, it is hard to escape the conclusion that there is a major gap between the rhetoric and the reality of open learning... Perhaps it would be best to abandon the term altogether. Or possibly, the most constructive step would be to confine its meaning to opening up of access" (Carr, 1990, 45).

Interestingly, Garrison and Shale (1989) defined *distance education* in precisely the same way as Carr (1990) proposed to define *open learning*. They argued that the distinguishing feature of distance education resides in its being a means of extending access to education to those who might otherwise be excluded from an educational experience.

From this plethora of definitions and interpretations, one would not be in error if one said that confusion still reigns among scholars as to the precise definitions of *distance education* and *open learning*, and most particularly in respect of the nature of the interrelationships between them. On one hand, it is clear that the terms are not synonyms, nor is one term a sub-group of the other. Open learning can take place either in a classical university or in a distance learning setting; and distance education can be either open or closed. On the other hand, it is not wholly clear what distinguishes them hither, since some scholars attribute similar characteristics to both of them, such characteristics as extending access to various educational frameworks, employing flexible schedules, enhancing self-directed learning (Guri-Rosenblit, 1991, 1993b).

One might surmise that it is not entirely accidental that universities which decided to adopt an open access policy have defined themselves as *open universities*, while most of those imposing entry requirements define themselves as *distance teaching universities*. Since the adjective *open* is qualitative and value loaded when compared to the descriptive nature of *distance*, I prefer the term distance teaching universities. That said, the dimensions of innovation and openness in each of the five distance teaching universities in its national setting are examined below.

Innovative Features—Parameters of Comparison

Distance Teaching at University Level

The degree of novelty in the concept of a *distance teaching university* in each higher education system is related to the history of distance teaching at university level in each national milieu. Both the UK and Canada have a long history of university correspondence education dating back to the nineteenth century. In Germany, Spain and Israel, however, the concept and practice of distance teaching at university level was novel and revolutionary until the late 1960s or the early 1970s.

(i) United Kingdom

Cerych and Sabatier (1986) claimed that the idea of the British Open University as a distance teaching university was not a break with tradition in the UK. The UK had long experience of post-secondary correspondence teaching, which provided a familiar context. Although none of its antecedents offered the precise mix of the British Open University, notably open admission at university level, nevertheless the notion of distance teaching at tertiary level was well-established and long-practised.

Bell and Tight (1993) argued that: "A number of British *open universities* have been extant during the last two centuries, and their provision has had an enormous impact, extending educational opportunities to hundreds of thousands of people who could not make use of more *conventional* courses" (*ibid.*, 1). Apart from the University of London, other British higher education institutions have also functioned, at least in part, as distance teaching universities during the last two centuries. The Royal University of Ireland and St. Andrews University in Scotland, for example, operated extensive distance examining systems, in a fashion somewhat similar to the University of London (*ibid.*).

In England, many professions, amongst which accounting, commerce, estate management, insurance, banking, rely on correspondence education even today. Glatter and Wedell (1971) in their extensive study on correspondence education estimated "that education by post has a following in Britain which numbers at least 284,000 enrolments annually. In any one time, the number of students taking a correspondence course is likely to be about 500,000" (*ibid.*, 3). In 1967/7 they reckoned that at least 100,000 correspondence students were studying for advanced qualifications (namely, degree level qualifications), and the great majority of these "were preparing for professional qualifications in commerce" (*ibid.*, 36). Bell and Tight (1993, 133) concluded that: "correspondence education remains a vibrant and valid model in the late twentieth century Britain".

(ii) Canada

Canada, as we noted earlier, also has a long history of distance education at university level dating back to the end of the nineteenth century. Given the sheer size of the country, distance education is widely practised, by departments and centres in numerous universities and colleges (Mugridge & Kaufman, 1986; Tight, 1994). Many Canadian universities work together in offering distance education under coordinating bodies. For example, universities in Ontario belong to the Council of Ontario Universities, which coordinates their activities in distance education. Similarly, the Atlantic province universities are grouped under the joint distance education committee of the Association of Atlantic Universities. In both cases, the coordinating body publishes a joint annual calendar summarising distance courses available in the respective provinces (Burpee & Wilson, 1995, 239). The University of Quebec operates the *Téle Université*, a constituent institution, established in 1972 and offering distance education to thousands of students, in diverse disciplines. Many other Canadian universities offer programmes entirely through distance education. Keegan and Rumble (1982) indicated that at the time the Athabasca University was established in Alberta, at least twenty other Canadian universities operated correspondence or distance education departments.

Distance education was so widespread in Canada that it is not surprising that the first meeting of the International Council of Correspondence Education (ICCE) took place in Vancouver, British Columbia in 1938, to discuss correspondence education from elementary school to university level (Daniel, 1995a, 6).

Although distance teaching at university level has a long history both in the UK and in Canada, even so the British Open University and Athabasca University were the first fully fledged, autonomous distance teaching universities, authorised to teach only at a distance. In this sense they introduced innovation into their higher education systems. None of the other universities in the UK or in Canada operated as a single-mode distance teaching university before the British Open University and Athabasca University were founded.

(iii) West Germany

In West Germany, distance teaching at university level was not practised at all until the 1960s (Bartels & Peters, 1986), though in the neighbouring East Germany 30 out of its 54 universities offered degree programmes at a distance during that period (Keegan & Rumble, 1982; Peters, 1965). "After the Second

World War," Peters has written, "Germany was one of those countries in which university-level distance education was virtually unknown. If it had been known, it would have been rejected by most people as absurd and the establishment of a distance teaching university would have been practically impossible at that time" (Peters, 1997, 53). When in the early 1960s, Otto Peters was asked by the Minister of Education of West Berlin, Carl Heinz Evers, to write a report about distance education, the latter was considered in West Germany as a new, unexplored field (Peters, 1994e). The report provided background material for preliminary discussions on distance education at tertiary level across 28 countries. Otto Peters was enthusiastic: "The more information I acquired from many countries all over the world, the more I learned about its techniques, its merits in educational emergency situations, its significance in the field of continuing and adult education, the more I was attracted by the new theme. This feeling was reinforced by the conviction that I had the rare chance of breaking new ground. I felt challenged by having entered a new field of educational research" (*ibid.*, 2).

The planning of a German distance teaching university began in the mid-1960s. It received a noticeable boost in 1965 when the Volkswagen Foundation founded a distance education research and materials development centre known as the German Institute for Distance Education at the University of Tübingen (*Deutsches Institüt für Fernstudien an der Universität Tubingen,* DIFF) (Keegan, 1994a, 244). The DIFF became a major promoter in developing a cooperative German distance teaching university, combining the DIFF, conventional universities, state and federal ministries of education, radio stations, television stations, and other interested parties. Negotiations ground on for years with no palpable result, a situation commented upon in Chapter 1. The innovative German distance teaching university—the FernUniversität—was established only in one of the West German Länder, in North Rhine-Westphalia.

(iv) Spain

Spain did not possess a distance education system until the 1970s, though it operated a framework of *independent study* within conventional universities. This path of study enabled working students to study by themselves and take the final exams, without attending the formal classroom sessions. García-Garrido (1988, 203) has observed: "The dropout rate of these external students was very high and conventional universities could do very little in order to help them". UNED's mission, among other goals, was to take over all external students, and provide them with a supportive environment of distance teaching.

(v) Israel

In Israel, as in West Germany and in Spain, distance teaching at university level, and at any other educational level, was totally alien to the educational culture and academic ethos of the early 1970s. Only foreign languages were offered by a few private correspondence schools in Israel prior to the foundation of the Open University of Israel.

Interestingly, the planners of UNED, the FernUniversität and the Open University of Israel, relied heavily on the British Open University model to convince their governments that university teaching via distance education was a liable concept. The British Open University itself could rely on a long tradition of university distance teaching in the UK. Its novelty lay in other features and dimensions, which will be analysed later. It could lay no claim to any primacy in introducing the idea of distance education into the British academia, however.

Access–Exit Requirements

Without any doubt whatsoever, the opening of access to university education at degree level without setting any entry requirements by some of the distance teaching universities, such as the British Open University, the Open University of Israel, and Athabasca University, broke drastically with the traditional, meritocratic concept of selective admission to university studies. In the context of the elite higher education systems of the UK and Israel it was particularly revolutionary. An open admission policy put the distance teaching universities employing it in a sensitive and vulnerable position.

Open entry is one of the main, if not the most important, pillar, of the British Open University's structure. The principle of open entry had been made explicit in Harold Wilson's speech of 1963; it was made explicit in the report of the Planning Committee; and reiterated yet more strongly in the report of the Advisory Committee. The Advisory Committee stated unequivocally that: "We take it as axiomatic that no formal academic qualification would be required for registration as a student" (Daniel, 1995b, 400).

Lord Perry admitted that the principle of *open entry*: "was a frightening one for most academics" (Perry, 1976, 55). It was by no means clear how to plan academic courses that were divorced from a certain entry behaviour and prior knowledge. The Advisory Committee suggested that the first year of the British Open University's courses should be foundation courses. Such courses in each study path would both reintroduce adults to serious study habits and provide the basic, substantive information in relevant disciplines required to proceed to second-level courses. In this, the British Open University drew on the previous experience of Keele University with its successful Foundation Year scheme (*ibid.*).

Perry has hinted that the suggestion for offering preparatory courses at pre-university level was examined several times, and in the end rejected. "If we were to do this, we would be seen by the outside academic world as admitting that the principle of open entry to universities was not a tenable one. We would be seen to be starting off at pre-university level and would therefore prejudice the possibility of achieving that status as one of the *family* of British universities that we were very anxious to achieve" (*ibid.*, 58). This account underlines the vulnerable position of the British Open University and its eagerness to gain acceptance on a footing of equality with its conventional counterparts. In order to achieve parity of academic status in the elitist British higher education system with an open admission policy, it was crucial to calculate the first moves very carefully, and to ensure that the exit requirements were of the same standards as of other universities.

One of the natural consequences of an open admission policy is a high drop-out rate at the beginning of studies. In a system where attrition rates were amongst the lowest in the world (Trow, 1974), it was important for the British Open University to show the lowest drop-out rates possible. The British Open University developed a unique registration system. It is the only distance teaching university that registers first-year undergraduate students on a provisional basis for the first three months of study—a kind of a trial period for the student. Students who do not finally register after three months are not considered as having been part of the University at all. At this early stage between 25% and 30% of the students drop out (Perry, 1976, 60). Such a system enables students "to test the temperature of the water before plunging into it" (*ibid.*, 59). It also affords them the trial period by paying a partial tuition fee. At the same time it helps the British Open University to show favourable retention rates.

Furthermore, the British Open University is the only distance teaching university with an open admission policy where applications to the under-graduate programme outnumber the places available, which are limited by staffing and resources (Open University, 1992; Perry, 1997). Generally, the admission to the University is based on a first-come first-served basis. For most foundation courses there was, until recently, a waiting list of between one and three years.

On the issue of exit requirements, it was relatively easy in British higher education to compare the level of the British Open University's graduates to the graduates of other universities in the framework of the external examiners system (Silver et al., 1995). After a short time the British Open University established its academic credibility up to national standards, as attested by external examiners from other universities (Perry, 1976, 1991).

The Israeli Open University has also adopted an open admission policy, but at the outset it did not create any special mechanisms to tackle some of the problems that such a policy entails, as the British Open University has done. The *open entry* policy of the Open University of Israel has placed it in a defensive position in the Israeli elitist-oriented higher education system even today. The Open University of Israel had not developed any special foundation courses for first-year students. Basically, most courses (except the seminar, third-level courses) are open to all students. It defines the open entry as an advanced student-centred admission policy. Anyone can enrol and test her/his capability to cope with high-level academic studies. Anyone is free to try again if he or she fails. The student is advised to register at the beginning only for one course (out of at least 18 courses required for a bachelor's degree), not for a whole academic year. This first course acts as a kind of *admission test*. Obviously, such a policy is less supportive or guiding compared with the foundation courses in the UK. The drop-out rate is indeed very high in the Open University of Israel—approximately 50% drop out of the first course (Guri-Rosenblit, 1990c).

For a short period, from 1982 until 1989, the Open University of Israel put on special preparatory courses tailored for the socially and educationally disadvantaged. One such programme was offered to community leaders from the most disadvantaged neighbourhoods in Israel; another was designed for the blue-collar workers in cooperation with the General Labour Federation (Guri-Rosenblit, 1989). Some of these students often had no more than eight years of formal study, but were characterised by an extremely high motivation and rich life experience. Interestingly, over 50% of them completed their studies successfully. Many indicated that the most significant feature that helped them persevere in their studies was the intensive tutoring provided once a week in the framework of a study group (*ibid.*). Currently, the Open University of Israel no longer offers preparatory courses, though nearly 80% of its students follow intensive tutorials where they meet with their tutors for two to three hours per week (President's Report, 1995, 1997). In addition, a special student support service has been established. Both the intensive tutorials and the student support system will be dealt with in more detail later.

Exit requirements are most stringent at the Open University of Israel, and its graduates are readily accepted for advanced degrees at conventional universities. Yet, since a small proportion of its students graduated during its first decade of existence (Guri-Rosenblit, 1989, 1990c), it took the Open University of Israel more than a decade to achieve academic credibility within Israeli higher education.

The Canadian Athabasca University, like the British Open University and the Open University of Israel, also exercises an open entry policy. Canada's admission rates are very high, second only to the USA. Since Athabasca University is a relatively small distance teaching university, the impact of open admission is somewhat limited. Canada, like the USA, has developed a system of mass participation in higher education. Participation rates were more than twice those of the UK in the 1980s and in the 1990s (Tight, 1991, 1994). Moreover, many community colleges in Canada admit practically anyone, without demanding any entry qualifications. Thus, open entry by its very nature does not constitute a radical departure from tradition. Athabasca University sought to be innovative in other respects and these will be presented further on.

As previously mentioned, the Spanish UNED and the German Fern-Universität decided to adhere to the same access–exit requirements as conventional, campus-based universities. From the outset, such a policy did not challenge their status and has enabled students to transfer in mid-study to other universities, and vice versa. UNED, as we have noted before, developed a special Admission Course for those aged 25 years and over, who do not meet the required entry qualifications. Since the 1970s, all Spanish universities have been required to admit persons over 25 who do not meet standard entry requirements, provided they pass a special examination of aptitude and capability (James, 1982, 149). The innovative step UNED took was to offer a whole-year course, rather than merely administering an examination. After passing the Admission Course at UNED, students may apply to other universities in Spain. In this sense, UNED had an impact on the Spanish higher education system at large. In 1993, over 20% of UNED's students were enrolled in the Admission Course (García-Aretio, 1995; Osborne, 1995).

The German FernUniversität admits students without formal university entrance qualifications for the purpose of continuing education; they cannot, however, be awarded a degree from the FernUniversität (Bartels & Peters, 1986).

Part-time Adult Students

Nowadays, part-time adult students constitute an important segment of the student body in universities worldwide. Part-time higher education is increasing in importance. In some higher education systems part-time students outnumber the full-timers (Tight, 1991, 1994; Davies, 1995; Silver & Silver, 1996). Part-time adult students are usually employed, have a family, and are engaged in social and/or community activities. Part-time provision is perceived as "the most pragmatic means for expanding access to higher education... enabling students to combine study with work, domestic and social responsibilities" (Tight, 1991, 52).

Though part-time higher education is widespread, many countries make no formal distinction between full-time and part-time students in their official statistics. Both the UK and Canada distinguish between part-time and full-time provision, but they define part-time in different ways. In the UK the distinction is based on financial calculations and support. Part-time students are funded on a different and a less generous basis compared with full-time students. In Canada part-time relates to the students' workload (Tight, 1994). In Spain, Germany and Israel no formal distinction is made between full-time and part-time higher education provision, but many documents show that large numbers of part-time adult students are studying in all three higher education systems, combining part-time discontinuous periods of study with full-time or part-time employment (Tight, 1991, 1994; Davies & Reisinger, 1995; Osborne, 1995; Council for Higher Education, 1995).

Distance education almost by definition is part-time. It is founded and structured on this basis. All of the distance teaching universities analysed here cater mainly for part-time adults. The extent to which such a policy was innovative in the 1970s in each national higher education setting varied from country to country. It was a most significant departure from the policy of conventional universities especially in the UK.

After the Second World War the reforms in British higher education placed a greater emphasis on full-time provision while decreasing the relative importance and availability of its part-time equivalent (Duke, 1967; Tight, 1991; Parry, 1995, 1997). The Robbins Report (Prime Minister's Committee on Higher Education, 1963) often perceived by many during the 1960s as a blueprint for the future of British higher education paid attention to part-time adults, but did not offer any substantial solutions. "Part-time higher education was actually outside the official remit of the Robbins Committee, although it did get brief consideration, mainly as a temporary safety relief valve to be used during the expansion of the system" (Tight, 1991, 17). In 1964 only 1.3% of all first-degree students in the British universities were studying part-time (*ibid.*, 18). In effect, there were few opportunities to study for degrees on a part-time basis with the single exception of Birkbeck College in London (Perry, 1997, 6).

The unique role of the British Open University in providing university education for part-time adult students is highlighted by Perry (1976). He replied to the criticism, sometimes voiced against the British Open University, that it was an unnecessary development, since what it had done could just as well have been carried out by other universities acting in concert. For Perry the idea in 1969 that other British universities "might seriously have contemplated moving either singly or collectively into the field of part-time adult education is unrealistic. It could not have happened. The overriding view in the academic community was that this problem did not concern them, it ought to concern somebody else. It was this view that perpetuated the gap in education provision" (*ibid.*, 5).

In his inaugural address on 23 July 1969, Lord Crowther, the British Open University's first Chancellor, underlined the basic need to establish a university "open to people", and especially to adults who had missed the opportunity to study earlier in their career. "The first, and most urgent task before us is to cater for the many thousands of people, fully capable of a higher education, who, for one reason or another, did not get it, or do not get as much of it as they can turn to advantage, or as they discover, sometimes too late, that they need. Only in recent years have we come to realise how many such people there are, and how large are the gaps in educational provision through which they can fall. The existing system, for all its expansion, misses and leaves aside great unused reservoir of human talent and potential... Wherever, there is an un-provided need for higher education, supplementing the existing provision, there is our constituency" (in Daniel, 1995b, 400).

The British Open University enrolled more part-time adult students than all of the polytechnics together, establishments that were also set up to maintain a strong part-time provision. In 1986/7 the British Open University enrolled 66,200 part-time first-degree students as compared with 6,100 in all of the other British universities, and 27,100 in polytechnics and colleges (Tight, 1991, 25). Part-time provision has grown rapidly in the UK since the 1980s, mainly in sub-degree and postgraduate programmes (Parry, 1995). In 1989/90 there were 1,086,300 higher education students enrolled in the UK. Of these 37% were part-timers, including post-graduate students (Tight, 1994, 185). At postgraduate level they constituted 47% of total enrolment (*ibid.*, 188). At the sub-degree level part-timers outnumbered full-time students, accounting for 67% of the total enrolment (*ibid.*).

The pattern of part-time provision in the British higher education system is of more than passing interest. Part-time students study within a limited number of higher education institutions: the British Open University; one university college (Birkbeck College in London which specialises in providing part-time face-to-face evening study); a group of large former polytechnics located in big cities, which provide a wide range of part-time courses, concurrent with full-time courses; a number of older university departments of adult or continuing education offering a range of part-time courses, but largely operating on the periphery of their universities; and a growing range of departments offering profit-making post-experience vocational courses (Tight, 1994, 186). In most British universities "part-time provision remains a small-scale or marginal activity" (*ibid.*).

Part-time provision in Canadian higher education has increased most sub-stantially since the Second World War. Between 1954 and 1979 the number of part-time students rose from 9,900 (13% of the total) to 229,000 (38% of the total). Between 1954 and 1964 part-time student numbers grew at an average rate of 50% per year (Belanger et al., 1982; Tight, 1994, 186; Andrews et. al, 1997).

Unlike the situation in the UK, part-time study for academic credits in Canada is integrated with full-time provision across many, if not all, universities. Part-time students form a major part of the enrolment of all the large city universities, and in some cases effectively outnumber full-timers (Tight, 1991, 1994). Part-timers are also evenly distributed between first-degree and postgraduate studies. Part-time students make up 37–38% of the total enrolment in community colleges, and at the undergraduate and graduate levels within the universities (Tight, 1994, 188–189).

Against this backdrop, Athabasca University by providing study opportunities for part-time adults follows a general pattern in other Canadian universities rather than introducing a breakthrough in existing patterns.

In Spain, Germany and Israel part-time provision is a common practice, though no official figures are available. Pedro (1988) indicated that a substantial proportion of enrolments in Spanish universities is made up of mature students. Usually, every university has two sessions of a given course per day. The first session in the morning is offered mainly to young full-time students. The second session in the evening is attended by part-time older students, most of whom work during the day. In many colleges and faculties evening course students outnumber the morning students particularly in the social sciences, law, business administration and humanities (*ibid.*, 132). UNED accounts for 10% of the total Spanish student body, and most of its students are in full-time employment (Tight, 1991,43). Clearly, catering for part-time, employed adults was not a break from tradition in the context of Spanish higher education.

German students are older than either British or Canadian students. The average age of graduation in Western Germany is 27.9 (Davies & Reisinger, 1995, 174). Given the length of study time and the later entrance into higher education, German students as a whole tend to lead *adult lives*, and part-time study is most popular. Ritter estimated that: "Already today more than 60% of the students are part-time students in our big city universities and up to 30% hold a full job" (Ritter, 1986, 119). Thus, the FernUniversität extended study opportunities for working adults, but by no means had it introduced a new development into the German university. Its major innovation lay in its contribution to continuing education. Around 40% of its total student body are enrolled in continuing education courses, a feature unique among German universities (Bartels & Peters, 1986, 110).

Likewise, Israeli students are older than most of their counterparts in other countries. Most enter the university at the age of 20 to 22, on completing military service. Many work full or part-time while studying towards their first degree. Courses at all Israeli universities are offered throughout the day, from the early morning until late evening, and every student can design her/his academic curriculum around flexible schedules.

A comprehensive study on the profile of Israeli students in humanities and social sciences from 1971 to 1976 found that 64% of the students had been working when they started to study, and in the course of their studies this percentage rose to 90% (Globerson, 1978, 14). Other enquiries show that the majority of Israeli students work either full-time or part-time while studying their first degree, and half of them are married (Iram, 1991). A background document on undergraduate studies in Israeli higher education, submitted in 1987 by the Planning and Budgeting Committee to the Council for Higher Education, noted that graduates are absorbed into the labour market without major difficulty, and explained that: "One reason for this smooth absorption is the gradual process of transition from studies to employment, which begins for many of them while they are still students, working to support themselves during their studies" (Silberberg, 1987, 50). Hence, the Open University of Israel was not a pioneer in offering university education to part-time working adults. However, it was a pioneer in allowing many adults with insufficient entry qualifications to pursue academic studies and to upgrade their professional training within a university.

Ethos of Academic Freedom

Academic freedom is that right granted to academics as professionals to pursue their research interests as they see fit, and to teach their areas of expertise as they wish. There are different attitudes towards the quality mechanisms that apply to research and to teaching. It is well accepted and recognised that scholarly work has to be submitted to peer review before publication. Some additional spheres are to be found in academic life, where evaluation and critical examination are common practice in most higher education systems. Menand (1993) spelt out some of them: "We decide who is to be permitted to enter the profession, requiring candidates to be admitted to and to complete satisfactorily doctoral degree-granting programmes... And we create permanent members of the profession by requiring junior professors to submit their work to the approval of senior professors before awarding them tenure" (*ibid.*, 13). Teaching in academia is rarely subject to thorough evaluation.

The concept that underlies academic freedom in relation to teaching departs from the view that what goes on in a particular course or classroom is the sole responsibility of the professional scholar concerned. This notion presumes that the academic, once granted the *venia legendi*, is "professionally competent over the full range of activities he undertakes, and his competence includes the necessary knowledge and skills to make or seek insightful and valid appraisals of his work and to act on these appraisals" (Adelman & Alexander, 1982, 15–16).

Some of the distance teaching universities presented a threat to the prevalent ethos of academic freedom in teaching within their national settings, by defining stringent quality assurance procedures to ensure the quality of the instructional materials and of the learning and teaching processes. In contrast to most of conventional universities, study materials written by academics in many distance teaching universities are evaluated and commented on by colleagues inside and outside the university. Clearly, the prevailing interpretation of academic freedom in particular national settings is an important variable which influences the nature of the quality mechanisms each distance teaching university employed.

The British Open University was the first to initiate the model of teamwork in preparing self-study courses (Perry, 1976; Harry, 1986). A team was formed of highly specialised staff, including subject-matter experts, educational technologists, television and radio professionals, editors, tutors and others as needed. Within the team framework, the writings of individual academics are evaluated both by other members of the team and by external counsellors. Scaled-down versions of the course-team approach have been adopted by the Israeli Open University and the Canadian Athabasca University.

Perry (1976) explained that during the recruitment of academic staff to the British Open University, it was made abundantly clear in the initial interviews that "conventional academic freedom would not, and could not, be available to members of the staff of the Open University. It is unarguable that team responsibility implies a loss of freedom of action on the part of the individual teacher in determining what is presented to students" (*ibid.*, 93). Perry claimed that an additional limitation on individual academic freedom at the British Open University stemmed from the fact that courses are not lectures presented in private behind closed doors, but are open to scrutiny by the general public. Perry reckoned that academics took the limitations on their freedom in different ways. Some found it relatively straightforward, while others had difficulties in coming to terms with these structures.

Arguably, the collegiate teaching tradition and the practices of external examiners in the UK eased somewhat the induction of an academic team approach (Guri-Rosenblit, 1996b). The external examiner system in the UK seeks to ensure comparability of standards across higher education institutions. By its very nature, it puts limits on academic freedom in teaching, by appointing external academics to evaluate, and even to modify, the content and the structure of the final exams, in courses taught by faculty members that possess a full *venia legendi*. In such an environment it might well have been simpler to implement the British Open University's course-team model, than in the higher education systems of Continental Europe.

In Germany and in Spain, where the ethos of academic freedom is highly prized and sacred, to develop formal compulsory quality assurance procedures for evaluating the study materials written by professors at UNED or at the FernUniversität (Guri-Rosenblit, 1993b) was virtually unthinkable. Both these distance teaching universities employ what has been termed the author/editor model (Smith, 1980). Under this arrangement, the materials written by a faculty member are edited by a professional editor. The work of the editor may be limited to proof reading and assisting with graphics and layout or it may involve substantial restructuring of the author's work. The employment of an editor at UNED and at the FernUniversität is not mandatory, but rather desirable and recommended. Academics may refuse. Learning materials are then subjected to minor corrections and quality assurance procedures.

Otto Peters—the first Rector of the FernUniversität—expressed unswervingly the deep-rooted commitment to the sanctity of academic freedom in Germany. While endorsing the weight of tradition in the design of the academic faculties at the FernUniversität, he admitted: "It would be wrong and unwise to conceal from our critical observers that the way in which these faculties develop their teaching is strongly influenced and conditioned by tradition. Although we are a young university, this tradition was carried over from the other universities of our country by our 56 Professors and partly also by their more than 20 assistants... Therefore, the importance of tradition is stressed—as far as the content of academic instruction and the organisation of research is concerned. This is also one of the reasons why the FernUniversität did not establish the course team in which, according to rumour, the subject matter specialists sit together with media specialists and experts in testing on equal terms how to develop a new course. We believe that this responsibility cannot be divided. Thus, it is the individual professor's obligation to plan, develop and evaluate his course. He is given the autonomy and authority to get his most important job done. His knowledge and intuition, his sagacity and inventive mind, his creativity and experiences give the course developed by him a personal quality, as well, of course, as his errors, mistakes and perhaps also dullness. He picks the fruits of his endeavours and has to take the blame for his failure which might spoil his reputation. This has caused our Professors to put all their professional skill and energy into course writing and course development" (Peters, 1988, 84). Such an explanation shows the enormous strength of prevailing norms which surround both academic freedom and the status of professors in Germany and which shape the roles of academic staff and define course production procedures at the FernUniversität.

Bartels and Peters (1986) stressed the pressing need for the Fern-Universität to shape itself and to develop as a *research university*. The Fern-Universität "is not a mere teaching institution nor a technological system for dispatching and spreading knowledge produced somewhere else. It is a research university in its own right. This, of course, is the very basis of its institutional self-confidence and self-assurance in relation to other universities as well as of the development of its academic identity" (*Ibid.*, 109).

The Israeli Open University faced a most complex situation. The ethos of academic freedom to teach is most jealously guarded and greatly valued in Israeli universities, perhaps even more so compared to conditions in Germany and in Spain. The Open University of Israel opted to lay down stringent quality measures in developing its courses. The Open University of Israel is based on a small nucleus of academic staff and relies heavily on outside contributors. Some scholars from campus-based Israeli universities were most reticent to submit to procedures of inspection and criticism of their teaching materials, and refused cooperation with the Open University of Israel. A few even proclaimed that such inspection mechanisms contradicted the very concept of academic freedom. Not surprisingly the Open University of Israel faced difficulties in recruiting external scholars for writing its courses. In addition, the insistence on strictly controlled procedures for evaluating the quality of the study materials has resulted in some 30% of the approved courses being abandoned in mid-production (Guri-Rosenblit, 1993c, 1997a).

The Canadian Athabasca University produces its own self-study materials, but also purchases some textbooks from the British Open University, whilst cooperating with a few Canadian and US universities in developing certain courses. Athabasca University put in place a scaled-down version of the British Open University's course team model. Instructional designers play an important role and take an active part in course production, course evaluation and course revision (Morrison & Saraswati, 1988). In Canada, where many mainstream universities produce special materials for distance study, it was easier for Athabasca University to draw up special quality procedures for developing its materials, without posing a real threat to the norms of academic freedom. Academic subject-matter experts are closely assisted by course managers, instructional designers, editors and visual designers in the course of developing materials. They are less subject to evaluation and criticism by other academics, especially external academics, than is the case in the Israeli Open University.

In summary, the British Open University, the Open University of Israel and Athabasca University employ special quality mechanisms to ensure the quality of their study material and the teaching process. To implement such procedures was easier in the academic cultures of the UK and Canada, and most fraught in Israel. UNED and the FernUniversität chose not to impose either limitations on the academic freedom of their staff or compulsory procedures, so as not to threaten or enter into conflict with what is the most central value in the academic community. Even so, they employ special, non-mandatory editorial procedures to ensure the quality and didactic clarity of their self-study textbooks.

Size of a Distance Teaching University

Distance teaching universities are, by their very nature, large universities, designed to take on large numbers of students. Obviously, they differ in size. Daniel (1995a, 1996a) defined distance teaching universities that enrol over 100,000 students as *mega-universities*. He argued that the absolute size of a distance teaching university is a key in analysing its policy and logistic planning: "Some of the key strengths and weaknesses of the mega-universities are due to their absolute size. For example, the financial base associated with their size allows them to make substantial financial investments in new technologies. Equally, the scale of their logistics creates an inertia not found in smaller institutions. Furthermore, some new technologies may lead distance teaching institutions to serve students beyond their national boundaries. Size may influence the international reach of individual distance teaching institutions" (Daniel, 1995a, 2–3).

Yet, the impact a distance education institution may have on the society it serves is not necessarily a function of its *absolute* size, but rather its size *relative* to the total population. The Open University of Israel, for example, is a relatively small university, but its penetration into the Israeli society which consists of around six million, is equal to some of the very large distance teaching universities. Nevertheless, Daniel's differentiation between mega-distance teaching universities versus regular ones is interesting. According to Daniel's classification the British Open University and UNED are mega-universities.

Another way to look at the size of distance teaching universities is to compare their relative size with the usual size of universities in their national higher education systems. Without a doubt, the size of the British Open University constitutes a radical departure from the traditional British concept of how large a university should be. The English do not like large universities (Ross, 1976). When the Robbins Report was published in 1963, apart from the University of London none of the English universities enrolled more than

10,000 students. In 1962 all of the British universities enrolled around 130,000 (Ross, 1976). The Robbins Report projected that British higher education would have to grow to around 350,000 in the 1970s. In the British context, the expansion required the establishment of new universities rather than a significant expansion of those existing.

The idea of a university bringing together tens of thousands of students was alien to the British academic culture. From this perspective, the British Open University brought revolution into the British higher education system. For the British Open University is by far the largest university in the UK. In 1991/2, when the University of London enrolled 51,392 students in all of its various schools, colleges and institutes, Oxford University enrolled 16,080 students in its 36 colleges and six permanent private halls, and Cambridge University enrolled 13,920 students in its 31 colleges (International Association of Universities, 1993, 918, 929, 905), the British Open University had over 100,000 students on its books.

The Spanish UNED is also a mega-university, but it is not the only mega-university in Spain. Complutense University in Madrid is larger still. In 1991/2 it had 127,000 students whereas UNED enrolled 110,802 (*ibid.*, 828, 829). Other Spanish universities cater for tens of thousands of students, amongst which are the University of Granada, the Technical University of Madrid, the University of the Basque Country, the University of Barcelona (*ibid.*, 825, 829, 822, 821). Although the size of UNED is monumental by any yardstick one cares to use, in the dimensions of size and scale it has not been so innovative in the Spanish higher education system as the British Open University has been in the UK.

The German FernUniversität is a large distance teaching university, but is far from being the largest university in Germany. In 1991/2 Munich University enrolled 63,888 students, the Free University of Berlin had around 62,000 students, Cologne University registered more than 54,000 students, and the FernUniversität had 49,395 students (*ibid.*, 358, 325, 331, 341).

Similarly, the Open University of Israel is a large university in the Israeli context, but it is not the largest Israeli university. The Hebrew University enrolled 21,600 students in 1992, Tel-Aviv University had over 19,000 students, and the Open University of Israel admitted over 18,000 students (*ibid.*, 485, 486).

Athabasca University is relatively a small distance teaching university and a small university in the Canadian setting. Even in the province of Alberta, where Athabasca University is located, the University of Alberta and Calgary University are larger. In 1991/2 the University of Alberta admitted 28,366 students, Calgary University 21,944, and Athabasca University 10,936 (*ibid.*, 125, 128, 124).

Modular Credit Accumulation

Some distance teaching universities have introduced innovations in the structure and content of their academic degrees courses. In particular, the

British Open University was the first English university to adopt a modular credit system (Tunshall, 1980, VII). Perry (1976) claimed that the English universities in the 1970s were out of step with the rest of the world in relation to credit accumulation. Hitherto, it was possible to study in one of the colleges of Cambridge or Oxford and take relatively few exams during the three-year study period; at the end of three years the individual student sat three to four weeks of examination and wrote papers, on the basis of which the degree was granted or withheld.

Today most universities operate some variant of the credit accumulation system. Considerable differences exist between credit systems across various higher education systems. The USA bases its system on *credit hours*. Each credit hour represents the equivalent of one hour of instruction per week throughout a semester or term. Most courses consist of three to four credit hours. Conceivably the elective credit system originated at Edinburgh University in Scotland in the early eighteenth century, where it was called the *voluntary system* (Rothblatt, 1991, 131). But it reached full flower in America. Thomas Jefferson who some historians credit with introducing the modular system to the United States, had a Scottish colonial teacher at the College of William and Mary in Virginia, and it is from there that several scholars trace the elective principle in the late eighteenth century. Evidently, it was introduced as a system by Jefferson in the University of Virginia founded in the mid-1820s (*ibid.*).

In the USA, the modular unit system was revolutionary indeed. Rothblatt has noted that: "The move to modules and student options was not an evolutionary process. It was a radical step, a sharp initial break with past practice, appearing first at the University of Virginia in the 1820s, but known better in its post-mid-century Harvard form" (Rothblatt, 1993, 48). The system of electives was associated with American consumerism, with the democratic ideology of giving students, as consumers of higher education, the choice to build their own academic curriculum. Thus, diversity and pluralism in the academic curricula replaced the *unity of knowledge*, inherent in the original idea of *liberal education* (*ibid.*). By the 1870s, modules were assigned an arithmetical equivalent "connecting the separate capsules of teaching to hours of instruction, thus creating the banking or trading-stamp system that characterises the administration of nearly all American modular arrangements" (Rothblatt, 1991, 132).

The Scottish credit system differed significantly from the American. Each module is much longer and equals approximately 15 USA credit hours. The British Open University opted for the Scottish pattern, of a large module, since it ensured that examinations would not be too frequent, that a fairly large and coherent area of study would be covered, and it had already operated in the British Isles. Both the Planning Committee and the Advisory Committee envisaged an arrangement which, by providing for examinations at the end of each course, allowed the student to obtain a credit in that particular course which could be carried forward as a mark of achievement, irrespective of whether the degree programme was completed or not. This provision was especially important for adults who might decide to terminate, without completing a degree.

The Scottish influence was undeniable. Both Jennie Lee, the leading champion of the British Open University, and Lord Perry, the British Open University's first Vice Chancellor, were Scottish. Both arrived at the conclusion that in developing the British Open University's credit system, the Scottish example was the most useful model for comparison and adaptation (Perry, 1976, 63). For the Ordinary degree at Scottish universities, students are normally required to take a minimum of seven courses. The British Open University's Planning Committee decided to require six course credits as minimum for the basic degree, and eight course credits for an Honours degree. Perry admitted he was somewhat unhappy that the British Open University required one course fewer than other Scottish universities, but he was unable to alter the decision of the Planning Committee. Since the British Open University teaches each course over 36 weeks compared to an average of 26 weeks in other British universities, it ensured that its degree was by no means reduced in length and vigour as compared to other universities.

The usual criticism against a modular system, is that teachers/tutors should determine the pattern of studies best suited to the individual student, and that tutorial supervision is the essence of university education. The proponents of this view believe that the Oxbridge tradition, which involves the whole of three years work being examined concurrently, gives the student a chance to display how far s/he has integrated all her/his studies, and that this is the best way, indeed the only valid way, of awarding a degree.

Opponents argue just as strongly that the student is the best judge of what s/he wishes to learn and that s/he should enjoy the maximum freedom of choice consistent with a coherent overall pattern. They hold that this is doubly true when dealing with adults, who after years of experience, ought to be in a better position to judge what precise studies they wish to undertake than a school leaver who has little or no experience outside the classroom. Since the early 1990s most British universities now embrace the principle of modularisation in the framework of Credit Accreditation and Transfer Schemes (Jenkins & Walker, 1995; Parry, 1997). In this sense the British Open University was a pioneer, which had envisaged the need to change the traditional concept of a unified and coherent curriculum, structured and monitored closely by a tutor, in the face of the rapid pace of knowledge growth, and the expanding pattern of adults studying part-time at a university.

Athabasca University offers, among its other degrees, a very special degree—a *Bachelor of General Studies*. What is particularly interesting about this degree, is that it might be earned without studying even one course at Athabasca University. Athabasca University acts in this sense as a credit bank: "Unlike the degrees offered by Athabasca University, the *Bachelor of General Studies* does not have a residency requirement and degree requirements may be completed in institutions other than Athabasca University" (Athabasca University, 1992a, 49). This degree programme provides a framework of individualised study within an Applied Studies or Arts and Science designation that gives the student great latitude to choose courses to meet career and educational goals.

The structure of the Open University of Israel's degrees differs from those offered by Israeli conventional universities. Its degrees were designed around 18 course modules. The underlying concept involved adapting the British Open University's credit system and dividing it into three (Ginzburg, 1995). The initial idea was to translate some of the British Open University's courses. Hence, it was important to bear in mind the British Open University's course structure and to align as close as possible to the credit system used at Israeli universities. At a very early stage of the Open University of Israel's operation, the idea of translation was abandoned after several unsuccessful trials. Nevertheless, the initial structure of the credit system remained, and only lately has it been slightly altered. Most courses equal six credit hours. Most other Israeli universities offer courses of three to four credit hours. Thus, their degree consists of more courses (24 to 36) as compared to that of the Open University of Israel. This difference created many misunderstandings especially when some of the Open University of Israel's students sought to continue studying at another university, and above all when the Open University of Israel designed discipline-centred programmes, which had to be approved and accepted by the other universities. Scholars from conventional universities argued that the Open University of Israel's degree was shorter. They had to be convinced that each of the Open University of Israel's courses was longer, broader and contained several subjects, normally offered in more than one course at a conventional university. Currently, the Open University of Israel is developing shorter, three to four-credit hours courses, in order to facilitate transfer arrangements with conventional universities.

Academic Year Calendar

Leaving aside the obvious differences in hemisphere, the academic year in higher education systems world-wide is quite similar: studies start in September/October and end in June/July. Some universities operate a semester system, others a term system. A few distance teaching universities have introduced new variations in the academic year, notably the British Open University.

The British Open University's academic year differs from the other British universities, in that it starts in February and lasts until October as a full year with no mid-terms. The idea behind this different academic year was to use the regular universities' facilities for summer schools when their grounds and campuses were vacant, whilst pointing out that the University did not wish to compete with them for high-school graduates. The British Open University was most careful not to enter into apparent competition with other universities. Many of its tutoring/teaching activities depend for their success on the support and the cooperation of other institutions in higher education to provide part-time staff and the space needed for study centres and for summer schools. The unique phasing of the British Open University's academic year facilitated the mobilisation of lecturers and other academics for counselling and tutoring the British Open University's courses (Perry, 1976; Smith, 1988).

The British Open University's academic year consists of 36 weeks with one week summer school compared with an average of 26 weeks teaching in a regular British university. The British Open University's academic year is longer by far.

Until 1976, UNED's academic year differed from the traditional universities, running from 1 February until 30 September of the same year, a pattern grounded on the British Open University (James, 1982, 162). This did not work well and it was decided to adopt the same phasing as the conventional universities, from October until June/July. The ease of student transfer in and out of UNED has been much enhanced.

The Open University of Israel developed longer semesters compared with the conventional Israeli universities—an 18-week semester instead of a 14-week one, thus allowing students longer time to submit written assignments. Furthermore, the Open University of Israel's summer term is most popular, and attended by many of its students (President's Report, 1995).

Athabasca University has a year-round continuous registration system. Anyone can start studying at any point in the year, except holidays (Athbasca University, 1992a). There are no terms, and admission is granted throughout the year. Many Canadian universities have a relatively short academic year from September until April (Ross, 1976); some offer a summer term from May until July or during July–August.

The FernUniversität operates the same academic year as other German universities—28 weeks divided into two semesters from October to July.

Use of Mass Communication

Distance teaching universities of the 1970s were regarded by many as the *open universities of the air*. Television in those days was queen of the media, and the new distance teaching universities were expected to harness the technology of mass communication to the purposes of higher education. Yet, only the British Open University went into official partnership with the BBC to co-produce academic courses. All four other distance teaching universities had recourse to radio and TV programmes only to a very limited extent.

In the UK, the whole concept of creating a new, single-mode distance teaching university reposed on the idea of mobilising mass communication media for the transmission of lectures throughout Britain. In reality, the British Open University had several forerunners which had adapted and practised this idea *de facto* in the early 1960s. In 1962 Michael Young wrote an article in which he proposed the creation of an *Open University* which would prepare people for the external degree of London University (Perry, 1976; Open University, 1992). He drew attention to the increasing use of broadcasting media for educational purposes in the USA. Young proposed the immediate creation of a National Extension College to help students gain degrees through London University's external system, by utilising television and radio. The National Extension College was effectively established in 1963 in Cambridge. Working with the Further Education Department of the BBC, it offered courses combining radio and TV broadcasts with education by correspondence. Another successful initiative was carried out by Harold Wiltshire at the Extramural Department of the University of Nottingham working with one of the independent television companies and putting on continuing education courses (Perry, 1976).

These initial trials of providing tertiary-level courses via radio and television provided a fruitful background for the partnership between the British Open University and the BBC. The BBC was keen to enter the post-secondary education field. In 1961 the BBC began negotiating with the Universities Council for Adult Education and other educational bodies to develop programmes for adult education (*ibid.*). During the latter part of 1968, the details of the educational partnership between the BBC and the British Open University were discussed at length and the Report of the Planning Committee stated that: "The radio and television programmes, required by the University and provided by the BBC, are to be planned on the basis of an educational partnership between the University and the BBC staff. In practice, this partnership will extend over the whole range from the conception of the course to the final production of the programmes... While the BBC recognises the right of the Open University finally to determine any such points that may be at issue, the University agrees that full participation of BBC staff in all discussions pertaining to these matters is a necessary condition of working effectively together" (in Perry, 1976, 49).

Such a close partnership between a distance teaching university and a high-prestige broadcasting company like the BBC was created only in the UK. It gave the British Open University an immediate and wide-ranging publicity. To date the broadcasts of the British Open University via the BBC are watched by hundreds of thousands of people, most of whom are not enrolled as Open University students (Bates, 1989a). None of the other distance teaching universities set up, nor could they have established, such relationships. In the four other countries it was neither feasible nor desirable.

In UNED, it was decided at the outset not to use television, on the grounds of expense. Instead it was decided to produce a limited number of video cassettes within particular courses. Limited radio transmission took place on Radio 3 some 15 hours per week (James, 1982, 156; García-Garrido, 1988, 207).

When the Open University of Israel was established, Israel had only one national TV channel. The Open University of Israel was allocated only five hours of broadcasting air time per week. Both the TV and radio programmes at the Open University of Israel were planned essentially for enrichment and not as an integral part of its courses (Seligman, 1982, 113). Ginzburg who was the Open University of Israel's President from 1975 until 1987 declared that: "We decided at an early stage that we could not afford to have extensive use of television support of our courses. Consequently broadcasting was very limited and consisted mostly of purchased films, translated for the Israeli viewer" (Ginzburg, 1997, 82).

Although Germany is a leader in communication technology, the Fern-Universität decided early on not to broadcast on television or radio, but rather to stay mainly with print technology, so as to be as similar as possible to other German universities (Keegan, 1982, 97). The FernUniversität developed some audio-tapes and video-tapes for some of its courses (Bartels & Peters, 1986, 97). Since 1983 it put out a 45-minute programme transmitted once a fortnight in cooperation with the West Germany Radio and TV Network. Peters argued that: "Close co-operation with broadcasting corporations (radio and television) was not be the goal. The only function of such co-operation was to spread the idea of education to the public and stimulate the desire to acquire a university education. Therefore the media structure of the FernUniversität was to remain rather conservative—mainly for legal, financial and institutional reasons" (Peters, 1997, 58). Bartels and Peters reveal the underlying justifications behind the decision of the FernUniversität to concentrate mainly on the print medium: "The deliberate choice of printed materials as a central medium is explained by the fact that a selection of media and the best media mix is not only a matter of technological development of know-how, but also of social acceptance, professional traditions and financial feasibility. There are experiments going on with teletext, the use of which might bring about interesting changes, but so far the principle of "Wait and see!" is a fair description of the attitude of the majority of the departments towards more advanced technological media for the delivery of courses" (Bartels & Peters, 109–110).

At the Athabasca University, television programmes are delivered through a variety of distribution systems, largely via cable. But also these are programmes mainly for enrichment. Athabasca University produced relatively few television and radio programmes of its own, despite its earlier and considerable interest in the multi-media approach. "The costs and difficulties associated with producing quality television were the major factors that led the University away from developing its own programmes" (Shale, 1982, 42).

Mass communication media are not the leading technologies of the 1990s. Obviously, the new information technologies have a deeper and stronger impact on all the distance teaching universities analysed in this study. The utilisation of the new, advanced media in each of the distance teaching universities will be discussed in detail in Chapter 5.

Distance Teaching Universities—Innovative Clusters

An analysis of the dimensions of novelty in each distance teaching university within its national higher education system reveals some interesting clusters. It reveals once again the peculiar importance of academic context in which each distance teaching university evolved, and the extent to which it tried to introduce new ideas and revolutionary practice into the prevailing culture of the broader academic community.

By far the most daring and innovative distance teaching university turns out to be the British Open University. In seven out of the eight parameters examined in this chapter it has revised common traditions and challenged long-standing assumptions in British higher education. It demanded no entry qualifications in a strongly elitist higher education system; it opened the university gates to part-time adults, virtually ignored by other universities; it challenged the ethos of academic freedom by inventing the course-team approach for developing courses; it was established as a mega-university contrary to the British tradition of relatively small universities; it was the first university in English higher education to adopt a modular system; it put in place a totally different phasing of the academic year; and from the outset it based its operation on a close partnership with the BBC, the better to mobilise mass media for the benefit of higher education. The only parameter in which the British Open University had not thrown tradition aside was distance teaching at university level. But even here, it was the first fully fledged university founded solely for teaching at a distance.

Tunshall remarked that: "The Open University breaks away from so many traditions of the British higher education that one should, perhaps, not be startled by the extreme nature of the attitudes expressed both for and against it" (Tunshall, 1980, VII).

Interestingly, UNED and the FernUniversität stand almost as a *negative photographic image* compared with the British Open University. The most radical and significant innovation they brought to their national higher education systems lay in providing university teaching at a distance. Prior to the early 1970s, no such practice existed either in Spain or in Germany. As to the other parameters, both UNED and the FernUniversität tried to be as far as possible similar to the conventional universities. They employed the same entry requirements as other universities; although they were oriented particularly to part-time adults, other universities also offered study opportunities for part-timers; they decided not to impose compulsory restrictions on the academic freedom of their professors; they are large universities, but not the largest in their countries; their credit system and academic year resemble those of other universities; and they did not form any special partnership to harness mass media for their purposes.

The Israeli Open University ranks second after the British Open University in its innovative cluster. It introduced both distance teaching at university level and an open access policy into the Israeli higher education system; and it has challenged the ethos of academic freedom by creating stringent quality regulations for developing its courses. In other parameters of comparison, it presented moderate changes in its credit system and the length of its academic year.

The Canadian Athabasca University was born in a diversified, mass-oriented higher education system with a prevailing openness to change and innovation and with a long tradition of distance teaching at university level. In such a setting it had to invent unique features in order to be innovative and special. It adopted an open admission policy, permitted registration all year round; and also decided to serve as a *credit bank*, and offer a special degree composed of credits gained partially or entirely at other Canadian universities.

The unique innovative cluster of each distance teaching university shows up clearly its special position within each system of higher education. It provides essential knowledge for a better understanding of the functional roles of each distance teaching university within its national milieu, and its relations and interrelations with its more traditional counterparts. Obviously, the more innovative a distance teaching university, the harder it had to work to build its credibility in the surrounding academic environment, and the more challenging its everyday operations turned out to be.

3

Students and Academic Faculty

Distance educators have struggled to define satisfactorily their activities and the major reason for this is the ambiguity as to paradigmatic assumptions regarding the teaching–learning process. The problem is that distinguishing characteristics of distance education too often overemphasise the separation of teacher and student.
Garrison (1993, 13)

The emphasis on instruction can be, and often is, so much greater in distance education where students are studying alone and at a distance. For them there is no peer group against which to judge themselves and their own personal reaction to the package of materials. The possibilities for instruction to the point of indoctrination rather than education are so much greater.
Sewart (1992, 238)

Introduction

The nature of the interrelationships between students and the academic faculty reflects the ethos and functional roles of different types of university throughout their historical evolution and development. Yet, marked differences existed even between the very first universities. The University of Bologna was organised in the eleventh century on the initiative of students who were mature, wealthy men, and who hired masters to teach subjects in which they, the students, were interested. From their early time, the Italian universities emphasised the practical professions—law, medicine, theology and administration (Ross, 1976). The universities of Oxford, Cambridge and Paris, on the other hand, were dominated by doctors of theology, clergymen called to service, who taught what soon became known as the seven liberal arts (*Septem Artes Liberales*). Here the masters took the initiative in organising the academic curricula and defining the students' roles; their view of what should be taught and what should be done in the university dominated.

Against this general background, it is worthwhile focusing on the development of the English academic ethos, since it had an overwhelming impact in shaping the learning and teaching system of the British Open University. That the British Open University acted as the lead model for most distance teaching universities means that the nature of its instructional system to a great extent influenced many other universities. Of most particular interest are the unique tutor–student relations that developed in the Oxbridge collegiate tradition.

At the centre of university life in England was traditionally the small college and a shared residential life of student and teacher. The attitude of the university was both paternalistic and authoritarian on one hand, and strongly individualised and student-centred on the other. The student was conceived as a ward of the university, which was responsible for guiding his development. The idea of *in loco parentis*, by which the university assumed responsibility as the parents' substitute for the care, discipline and all-round education of each student, dominated. The tutorial—the regular face-to-face meeting of student and tutor to explore and discuss the lessons and topics of the day—characterised the learning and teaching process. In the Oxbridge tradition, the tutors were, and still are today, responsible for examining the needs of individual students for suggesting the tutorials and the seminars they should attend and for advising on reading lists and the whole pattern of study for a degree. Tutors' involvement was not confined to academic studies. They also gave advice on how to live as an undergraduate in the environment of the college, how to overcome the psychological stress of examinations, and how to prepare for a future career. Such relationships often evolved into personal individual ties between tutors and students well beyond the strictly academic development of the student (Rothblatt, 1989, 1997; Sewart, 1992; Bell & Tight, 1993).

Until the nineteenth century it was generally assumed in most universities that a close relationship between professor and student should develop. In the mid-nineteenth century the idea of the *Humboldtian* German university gave impetus to a new interpretation of the student–professor relationship. The concept of *Lernfreiheit* stressed the freedom of the student to choose his own programme of study to live independently of the university, and to move from one university to another, following his particular academic interests. The concept of *Lehrfreiheit* by contrast highlighted the freedom of the professor to investigate whatever he chose to focus on and to teach the results of his research irrespective of utilitarian applications and without government influence. This was a different type of university, with students following their own academic inclinations and way of life. The university had no obligation or intention to be responsible for the general education of its students. The idea of the *Humboldtian* university had a profound influence on universities world-wide.

The external degree system of the University of London, which was analysed in Chapter 1, and all of other universities which adopted the external degree system, also initiated a new type of student–professor relationship. Students were isolated physically from academic staff and free to choose how they prepared themselves for the final exams.

The opening up of higher education in the twentieth century, especially after the Second World War, had no less an immediate impact on the student–academic faculty relationship. In today's world many of the long-standing assumptions about the nature of the face-to-face interaction in university settings are no longer tenable. Larger classes and a redefinition of the teachers' professional responsibilities have made the close ties between students, tutors or professors unrealistic, except at the wealthiest universities which can afford to maintain a low student–faculty ratio. The tutorial system is very expensive.

The move from the one-to-one tutorial or the small seminar group to lecture groups of dozens and even hundreds of students has ushered in wholly different forms of learning and teaching. Most undergraduate students nowadays attend lectures in large auditoria, follow a series of courses taught by specialists, and the overall learning process is both highly modularised and depersonalised. Sewart (1992) has argued that the most important change in mass-oriented universities as compared to small elite institutions, is the transition from *learning* to *being taught*. In mass higher education the professor lectures to a large audience. The educational process is reduced from a dialogue to a monologue; the professor is active and most of the audience is passive. The lecturer cannot take into account the large range of ability, learning styles, personal preferences and interests of an immensely diverse audience, drawing on students from every conceivable socio-economic class, age range and educational background. The traditional links between student and professor are today confined mainly to graduate-level studies.

Mass higher education has separated undergraduates from professors. In most universities, the latter are no longer responsible for the personal guidance, provision of an integrated pattern of learning and supervision of their students. Mass higher education has moved into a kind of industrialised mode in which the teaching process is fragmented between a wide range of specialists. Sewart argued that mass higher education has created "an assembly line approach in which the product representing studentship is assembled by a number of specialists, many in narrow academic disciplines, but some also in supporter areas which are at least as critical to the attainment of the final objective of successful completion of undergraduate studies" (Sewart, 1992, 235). Distance education takes the industrialisation of mass higher education a further step (Peters, 1983, 1994d; Sewart, 1992; Rumble, 1995a,b, 1996).

It has to be said that many comparisons between distance education and face-to-face instruction are often based on naive, generalist and even false assumptions about the interrelations between students and the academic faculty in most classical, campus universities. That a professor faces a student audience in a large auditorium by no means implies that lively discussion or interactive learning is taking place. Yet, it is both unfair and misleading to compare distance education with close encounters of the tutorial kind. However, an important element in studying in a campus setting is that students may relate to each other. Many distance educators tend to exaggerate the separation of teacher and student, and equally to overlook the profound implications that arise from the absence of peer interaction (Moore, 1989; Garrison, 1993; Mood, 1995). We will return to this issue later.

Both mass higher education and distance higher education separate students from academic staff in different ways. Both have been engaged over the past two decades in sustained efforts to find and put in place support systems to offset the depersonalisation of learning and teaching in academia, and to attenuate student alienation from professors and tutors (Mills & Tait, 1996).

In certain respects, distance education institutions have even surpassed conventional mass universities in initiating creative and well-founded measures to increase the level of exchange between students and academic staff. Distance teaching universities have been forerunners in setting up efficient and effective counselling support systems, experimenting with advanced technology for interactive purposes, and improving the didactic quality of instructional materials and the learning/teaching experiences.

In fact, distance teaching universities put more emphasis on teaching than most of their conventional counterparts, and by doing so revert to the long-standing traditional role of universities for over 800 years. Until the nineteenth century, teaching was the major concern of the academic profession. With the use of the *Humboldtian* interpretation of the university, teaching no longer enjoys the pre-eminence it once had. Nowadays the research function dominates. For most academics, research is far more important than teaching. They are promoted mainly on the basis of their research activities and products (Teichler, 1994a,b; Altbach, 1996). Paul claimed that: "As distance education becomes more and more established, the mainstream universities will once again pay more attention to the teaching function and the needs of the students, to the ultimate benefit of the latter" (Paul, 1987, 154–155). Arguably, distance teaching universities have the potential to revive the focus on teaching in higher education at large.

Moreover, by putting a major emphasis on teaching, distance teaching universities provide learning experiences that in several aspects are qualitatively superior to lectures in overcrowded amphitheatres. First, self-study materials that substitute for the lecture in conventional mass higher education are usually prepared by a team of experts and are subject to stringent quality assurance procedures (Guri-Rosenblit, 1993c, 1997a). Self-study packages are by and large better articulated, refined, clear and attractively presented than many face-to-face lectures. Second, in many traditional universities, the more renowned and senior academic faculty prefer to be engaged in graduate studies. Undergraduate teaching is frequently handed over to junior faculty and teaching assistants. Many undergraduates are rarely in a position to benefit from encounters with first-class scholars, whereas students at most distance teaching universities are exposed to the accumulated knowledge and expertise of the highest ranks of academic specialists, top experts in each field from different universities. These scholars contribute to planning and development of self-study materials either as authors or counsellors, and occasionally teach via video-conferencing techniques.

The advantages and disadvantages of studying at a distance compared to face-to-face encounters in classical universities are not self-evident, and cannot be reduced simply to the physical separation of students from professors. Physical separation is just one aspect of studying at a distance. The lack of a campus environment and a peer group interaction, the fragmentation of teaching responsibilities, the relatively high attrition rates and the potential danger of indoctrination are also problematic variables which deserve to be examined. Furthermore, the remedial mechanisms and support systems set up to overcome the difficulties and obstacles inherent in studying and teaching at a distance, are themselves important components to be considered when analysing the salient features of the learning experience at distance teaching universities. The discussion of the components that characterise the learning and teaching processes in the five distance teaching universities under scrutiny is preceded by an examination of the profiles and perceived roles of their students and the academic faculty.

Students: Profiles and Roles

Students have fulfilled various functions throughout the history of the university. The roles of students at different types of university in relation to the academic faculty are based on a number of distinct assumptions. Ross (1976) identified five major roles of students in higher education settings. Students can be: (1) an *apprentice*—working closely with a master, studying the master's ways and gradually becoming a master in their turn; (2) a *ward* of the university—placed by one's parents or society into the custody of the university, which is responsible for the student's welfare, and moral and intellectual development; (3) a *client* of the university—involved in a professional relationship in which the student seeks out professors to help in areas of interest and need; (4) a *customer*—who, having certain needs, seeks out places where services to meet these needs can be purchased; (5) a *member of the university*—and is therefore a citizen of that community with rights and obligations like those of other members. Silver and Silver observed that Ross' list "constitutes a kind of history, moving from the student as medieval apprentice to the student as late twentieth-century customer" (Silver & Silver, 1996, 164).

In distance education, as well as in most campus universities, students are nowadays viewed mainly as clients, customers and consumers of higher education, as individuals possessing an enormous range of inclinations, attitudes and perceptions (Mandell & Herman, 1996). To fulfil their academic and professional aspirations students look to institutions that best fit their style of life and social/family/work obligations. Viewing students as customers or consumers has led to formal regulation of the rights and services to which they are entitled from higher education institutions. In the UK, for example, the *Charter for Higher Education*, published in 1993 stated clearly that: "This Charter explains the standards of service that students, employers and the general public expect from universities and colleges and other bodies involved in higher education in England...The Government expects each university and college to set down and publicise the standards of service it provides... Customers of universities and colleges also have responsibilities and the Charter reminds you of some of them. But the focus is on the meeting of your legitimate needs. If you are not satisfied with the service you receive, the Charter explains what you can do to get it" (Department for Education, 1993, 2).

Distance teaching universities are customer-oriented establishments. Their *raison d'être* is to serve the needs of their potential clienteles, and to tailor appropriate programmes of study suitable to the interests and preferences of their students. Distance teaching universities are most attentive to labour market trends and to emerging demands of both old and new target populations. Many distance teaching universities invest efforts and resources to provide not only high quality learning experiences, but also supportive and friendly counselling and administrative services. They reach out to their student constituencies in a rich spectrum of ways. On May 25, 1993 a conference at Laurentian University in Canada discussed the institutionalisation of a *Student Charter for Distance Education*, in order to make the consumers of distance education aware of their rights (Tait, 1994c). A number of elements were suggested for inclusion in such a Charter: "Providing clear information as to what was expected from students; publicising a procedure for dealing with student complaints; guaranteeing that the mode of delivery would not affect the award or credit; guaranteeing timely and effective feedback and commentary on assignments; guarantees *re* provision of library services where these are necessary; provision of academic counselling pre-study before selection of courses; access to tutors on a regular basis; the publication of clear information *re* administrative regulations; the right to complete a programme of study within agreed time scales; the Charter should be related to the institution's mission statement" (*ibid.*, 64). Though no such Charter was finalised, it was widely agreed that student charters should form a valuable part of any distance education institution in the future and there was no appropriate option but to go forward in their establishment.

Table 3.1. Students' Distribution by Age, Gender, State of Employment and Purpose of Study at the British Open University, UNED, the Open University of Israel, FernUniversität and Athabasca University (1992)*

Variables	Distance Teaching University				
	British Open University	UNED	Open University of Israel	Fern-Universität	Athabasca University
Number of students	120,414	123,963	17,929	52,570	11,352
Age					
median	34	30	31	30	34
under 24 (%)	4.2	21.8	27.6	10.3	19.7
over 45 (%)	19.3	3.2	9.8	7.4	10.7
Gender					
female (%)	48.6	42.7	54.6	32.8	66.8
male (%)	51.4	56.9	45.4	67.2	33.2
Being employed (%)	70	71	82	80	80
Purpose of study					
degree (%)	78	74	77	80	32
other (%)	22	26	23	20	68

*Based on:
Athabasca University (1992b) *Demographic Profile of AU Students,* Athabasca University, Tables 2.21, 2.24.
Open University (1993a) *Pocket Guide to OU Figures,* The Open University Press.
EADTU (1993b) *Mini-Directory,* Herleen: European Association of Distance Teaching Universities, 18, 30, 38.
President's Report (1993) *The Open University of Israel 1992/93,* The Open University of Israel Press, 126–127.

Students choose to study at a distance teaching university for a variety of reasons that range from geographical isolation through family and work commitments to personal preferences to study at one's own pace and to benefit from a flexible academic programme. Cross (1981) and Wallace (1996) distinguished between barriers (negative reasons) and attractions (positive reasons) which draw students to study by distance education methods. Barriers may be situational (circumstances in the individual's life, such as family and work obligations); institutional (organisational policies and procedures); and psychological (attitudes towards oneself and towards learning). The main attractions of distance education are the ability to control the time, place and pace of study, as well as a flexible choice of curricula and a preference of printed materials over lectures. Most distance students are adults who are endowed with the autonomy to make choices, and are likely to be highly motivated and self-directed (Holmberg, 1995; Mood, 1995). Table 3.1 presents some basic variables relating to students' age, gender, state of employment and purpose of study in each of the distance teaching universities, under examination.

Age

In 1992, the median age of students at all of the five distance teaching universities ranged from 30 to 34, reflecting the fact that students at many distance teaching universities are older than students in conventional universities. For comparison, in 1994 the median age at conventional universities in the UK was 21 (Parry, 1997,14); in Israeli universities it was 24 (Herskovic, 1995, 99); and in Canada, 21 (AAUC, 1996, 10).

The percentage of the under-24 and over-45 age groups reveals some interesting differences between the five distance teaching universities. That only 4.2% of the British Open University's student population were under 24 years old, as compared with percentages that range from 10% to nearly 30% of this age group in all of the other distance teaching universities, reflects the fundamental policy of the British Open University since its inception, namely, to cater mainly to mature adults. The British Open University never viewed the younger age groups as a potential constituency. Woodley and McIntosh (1980) conducted a pilot study from 1974 to 1979 on the admission of the 18 to 21 age group, to meet the request of the Conservative Government to enrol high school graduates in the British Open University. The experiment failed in the sense that a higher drop-out rate was noticeable among the young compared with mature students. On the basis of this study, the British Open University's policy makers concluded that the loneliness of distance study was not for the very young. They would be far better off at a conventional university or polytechnic. The British Open University reversed this policy and from 1986 opened its gates to students of 18 years and above (Harry, 1986, 91), but it never really promoted its courses in the youth market. Nowadays, an increasing number of conventional, campus universities offer distance learning within their catchment areas. That 29% of part-time students in the UK in 1994 were under 24 years of age (Parry, 1997,14) shows that the new providers of distance education in the UK attract a younger segment of the part-time student population than the British Open University. The British Open University has also the highest percentage of the over-45-year age group compared with the four other distance teaching universities (nearly 20% versus less than 11% in all of the others). John Daniel, the British Open University's Vice Chancellor, proudly announced in 1996 that: "We have 800 students over 80 and 6,000 over 60" (Daniel, 1996, 37).

That between 10% and 30% of the student population at UNED, the Open University of Israel, FernUniversität and Athabasca University are under 24 years old is an important indicator, and suggests that most distance teaching universities also provide an alternative higher education option for young students. A natural outcome of this policy is the need to tailor different support mechanisms to accommodate the particular characteristics of the younger clientele. In some distance teaching universities such as UNED, the Open University of Israel and Athabasca University, cohorts of younger students have grown markedly since the late 1980s. As Lacasa and Padro de Leon (1990) commented: "Currently, our students differ from earlier cohorts of UNED students in several ways: students are younger than before, there are more women, and a large number are unmarried...these kind of students have similar needs to students from other universities, and perhaps their study motivation is different from the more classical distance education student. Young people need a different kind of help than adults" (*ibid.*, 85). Wallace (1996) in a comprehensive study on distance education students in Canadian universities revealed that noticeable changes had occurred in the demography and motivation of distance education students over the last decade. Whereas the mean age of students engaged in distance study in Canada was 32 years in 1984, it was 25 in 1995; and while the percentage of the under 26 age in 1984 was around 30%, it rose to 65% in 1995 (*ibid.*, 12). Younger students tend to take a heavier course load, to combine independent study with on-campus courses, and live not far from the university. In other words, during the last decade, many historically atypical students are enrolling in distance higher education.

The under-24 age group in the Open University of Israel in 1992 constituted nearly 30% of its student body, and in 1996 grew to 46% (President's Report, 1997, 119). This reflects the Open University of Israel's basic philosophy, in contrast to the British Open University, also to reach out to the very young segments of Israeli society, and more specifically to enable talented high-school students and young soldiers during their military service to study. Soldier students accounted for 14% of the Open University of Israel's student body in 1994 (President's Report, 1995, 106). The percentage of the young student body at the Open University of Israel has grown significantly since the late 1980s, due to a significant shift in the University's policy, to provide in addition a *first chance* to young high-school graduates (usually after completing their compulsory army service), most of whom were not admitted into departments in great demand in the conventional universities. This group of first chancers was added to the basic second chance student constituencies. The Open University of Israel initiated the establishment of municipal colleges which provide campus-like environments, so important for young students. The proportion of younger students at the Open University of Israel is growing constantly. In 1997, the under-25 age group constituted 59% of the newly enrolled students (Open University of Israel, 1997).

Gender

Table 3.1 showed that women constituted over 40% of the student population in both the British Open University and in UNED (43% and 49% respectively). In the Open University of Israel and Athabasca University they were the majority (55% and 67% respectively). By contrast, the FernUniversität had a dominant male student population with only 33% female students.

Christine van Prümmer (1994) attempted to explain why women students in the FernUniversität are proportionately fewer by comparison with other distance teaching universities, despite the fact that distance education is often considered especially suited to mature women who want to study while raising a family and being employed (Kirkup, 1996). On the face of it, distance education is per se a *women friendly* way of acquiring formal qualifications. There is little or no attendance requirement, at the same time as having a high degree of flexibility in learning schedules and time management. Van Prümmer identified "three areas of institutional factors affecting the enrolment and continuance of women distance students at the FernUniversität: range of subjects and degree programmes, teaching system and organisation, and the character of the institution" (van Prümmer, 1994, 5).

The relatively limited range of degree programmes and, until very recently, a strong emphasis on *traditionally male* subjects have been quoted as the major reason for the low level of women's enrolment at the FernUniversität. In 1992 the FernUniversität offered diploma programmes in four major subjects: economics and business administration (51.3% of its student body), computer science (13.5%), electrical engineering (6.3%) and mathematics (4.6%) which may be seen in Table 3.2. The FernUniversität also offered degrees in education, other social science disciplines, humanities and law (total of 23.3% of its students were enrolled in these areas in 1992). van Prümmer revealed that the lowest representation of women occurred in electrical engineering and the highest in education. She also argued that: "The emphasis placed by the FernUniversität on the self-sufficient and isolated learner has the effect of creating a hostile environment for women distance students who are more interested than men in elements of social interaction, in contacts with tutors and other students, and in cooperation with other learners" (*ibid.*, 6). These findings are born out by further studies by Gill Kirkup on the British Open University and by van Prümmer on the FernUniversität (Kirkup & van Prümmer, 1990, 1992; Kirkup, 1996). Women students in both the British Open University and FernUniversität made more use of study centres and the provision of support services than male students. They valued the range of services provided at study centres more highly than men, in particular the opportunity to meet other students. In other words, women went to more trouble to achieve what has been termed *connectedness* with other students.

Employment and Purpose of Study

The data in Table 3.1 show very clearly that most students (70–80%) at all of the distance teaching universities study while being fully or partially employed. Apart from the Athabasca University, the majority of students (around 80%) work towards an academic degree, with the rest studying for professional diplomas, certificates and continuing education courses. This finding sets out the main difference between fully fledged distance teaching

universities and other distance education providers, such as extension departments at conventional universities and small distance teaching establishments.
Mood (1995) reported that in the USA and many distance education institutions elsewhere most students take distance study courses with a short-term
intent, whereas in the single-mode distance teaching universities most students
pursue—or at least intend to pursue—a full course of studies towards an
academic degree.

Student Distribution by Fields of Study

Table 3.2 breaks down the student distribution across broad fields of study.
A more detailed analysis of the academic curricula in each distance teaching
university is provided in Chapter 4.

Table 3.2 shows that the student population in most of the distance
teaching universities does not divide evenly among the various fields of study.
The most even distribution takes place in the British Open University. Its
student population divides almost evenly between social science and arts
(48.4%) compared with science, math, computer and technology (47.7%). The
British Open University has more freedom to assign students to different fields
of study, since the number of applicants greatly outnumbers the places available. Only 41% of applicants to the British Open University in 1992 were
granted admission on the basis of "first come, first served", though some

Table 3.2. Registrations' Distribution by Fields of Study (%) at the British Open University, UNED, the
Open University of Israel, FernUniversität and Athabasca University (1992)*

Field of study	British Open University	UNED	Open University of Israel	Fern-Universität	Athabasca University
Arts	22.4	8.8	18.8	20.0**	20.7
Social Sciences + Education	26.0	31.9	59.5	51.3***	56.7
Sciences + Mathematics	29.8	4.3	11.4	4.6	18.8
Engin., Technology + Information Sciences	17.9	1.8	7.1	19.8	3.8
Law	–	25.9	–	3.3	–
Other	3.9	27.3	3.0	–	–

*Based on:
Athabasca University (1992a) *Athabasca University 1992-3 Calendar—Canada's Open University,*
Athabasca University.
Open University (1993a) *Pocket Guide to OU Figures,* The Open University Press.
EADTU (1993b) *Mini-Directory,* Herleen: European Association of Distance Teaching
Universities, 18, 30–31, 38.
Open University of Israel (1993) *Handbook of Courses,* The Open University of Israel.
**Includes arts and social sciences, except economics.
***Only economics.

quotas are employed to ensure courses are not oversubscribed (Open University, 1993a). The student distribution in the remaining four distance teaching universities portrays a more realistic distribution in student preferences. In 1992, around 60% of students in the Open University of Israel, FernUniversität and Athabasca University took social science courses. At UNED 26% of the students studied law, and 32% social sciences. The high percentage of students studying law at UNED may be explained by the civil service recruitment system in Spain, in which a law degree is a prerequisite for many administrative posts in government.

The distribution of the student population does not reflect the number of courses offered in each study domain, an aspect that will be examined further in Chapter 4. Relatively small numbers of students apply for science and maths courses in most of the distance teaching universities. Since the distance teaching universities by their very nature are designed to respond to demands both of the labour market and of students, student choice reflects the high demand of specific disciplines to which conventional universities are unable to provide an appropriate answer nor to accommodate the buoyant demand to study these disciplines. For this reason, students' distribution by study fields at distance teaching universities might well be an important element for policy makers and academics in conventional universities when planning the future priorities of their own universities.

Specific Student Characteristics in Each Distance Teaching University

In each distance teaching university, or group of distance teaching universities, there are certain specific student characteristics worth noting. The British Open University, the Open University of Israel and Athabasca University have an open admission policy. It is interesting on this account to examine the prior education level of their students. In the British Open University 39% of the student body in 1992 entered with fewer than two A levels, a necessary prerequisite for *application* to conventional British universities (Open University, 1993a). At the Open University of Israel only 25% lacked the *Bagrut* certificate, which is a formal requirement to apply to a regular university (President's Report, 1995, 108). In Athabasca University most students had the minimal entry qualifications to apply to a university— indeed 83% had more than 13 years of schooling or a university education when they registered (Athabasca University, 1992b). Some distance teaching universities, principally the British Open University and the Open University of Israel, provide a genuine alternative for students who lack the minimal qualifications to enter a conventional university. However, most of the students at distance teaching universities, even at those based on open entry, possess the minimal entry requirements to conventional universities. They are attracted to study at a distance teaching university for other reasons. They decide to study at a distance teaching university either because of work/family/

social/geographical constrains or because they are denied access to the field of study in which they would like to specialise.

The British Open University's student body extends to students beyond the UK. As from 1992, the British Open University offered its courses throughout the rest of Europe. In 1995 it had 5,816 students in EC countries and a further 10,430 students were taking the British Open University's courses through partnership agreements with institutions in Eastern Europe, the Far East and Africa (Open University, 1995). According to Daniel, in 1995 the British Open University had students sitting examinations in over 300 centres in 93 countries outside the UK (Daniel, 1996b, 37). Evidently, the British Open University is a highly international-oriented university.

The British Open University reaches out to students with a variety of physical disabilities. Around 3,000 such students—4.3% of its total student body—studied at the British Open University in 1995 (Open University, 1995).

From 1992 the British Open University took over responsibility for students studying at other UK colleges and higher education institutes the degrees of which it validates. Following the abolition of the Council of National Academic Awards (CNAA), the British Open University established in 1992 the Open University Validation Services (OUVS). It validates higher education awards in educational establishments, commerce, industry and professional bodies which do not themselves have a degree-awarding status.

Similarly, UNED teaches students in England, Germany, Switzerland, Belgium, Argentina, Venezuela and Equatorial Guinea (EADTU, 1993a). UNED set up a special access course for those aged 25 years and older, who do not possess sufficient entry qualifications. Those completing this Admission Course successfully, proceed to degree level studies at the University. In 1993, over 20% of UNED's student body were enrolled in the Admission Course (García-Aretio, 1995, 93).

The Open University of Israel draws an important distinction between students studying in organised groups at a variety of colleges and institutions, who meet their tutors in each given course once or twice a week, and *regular* students studying at home, who have the option to meet their tutor once every three weeks. Since *distance* is not a real problem in Israel, the majority of the Open University's students prefer to study in the intensive tutorials framework. In 1992 the Open University of Israel had 9,965 students in the framework of organised groups within institutions compared to 8,007 enrolled as regular home-study students (Levtzion, 1992, 31). The number of students in organised groups has grown continuously since 1990. In 1995, they formed 60% of the total student body, and accounted for 69% of total registrations (President's Report, 1995, 106). Thus, the majority of the Open University's students prefer nowadays both to study several courses concurrently in an attempt to complete their studies within three to four years, and to learn in a campus-like environment.

From 1992 onwards the Open University of Israel has been engaged in an interesting project in the former Soviet Union, offering studies in Jewish history and philosophy working with the Foreign Ministry of Israel. In 1997 around 8,000 students in nearly 300 cities across the former Republics of the Soviet Union were enrolled in these courses (President's Report, 1997, 43).

The FernUniversität admits students from out of State and foreign students from abroad to the extent that only half its student population are resident in North Rhine-Westphalia. It has centres in Austria, Switzerland and Hungary, and throughout Germany (EADTU, 1993a). The FernUniversität has four types of students: full-time (who constituted 14% of the student body in 1992); part-timers (54%); students from traditional universities (12%); and associate guest students (20%) without formal qualifications who follow individual courses for personal development or for job-related requirements. In Peters' opinion there: "Is no other institution in Germany which provides continuing education to such a large group of persons in all walks of life" (Peters, 1997, 72).

Students registered as full-time students at another German University may study at the FernUniversität either as *Studiengangszeithörer* or *Kurszeithörer*. *Studiengangszeithörer* enrol in a second programme of study which differs from the programme they are studying simultaneously elsewhere in Germany. Their aim is to earn an additional university degree. This programme is comparable with a part-time study as far as the number of courses and weekly study time is concerned. The *Kurszeithörer* study individual courses at the FernUniversität with the aim of completing studies undertaken at another German University. They may take part in the final examination of each course, but they are not eligible for final degree examinations (EADTU, 1994a, 42). This phenomenon of students from other universities studying at the FernUniversität reflects the long tradition of *wandering students and professors* in Germany (Teichler, 1986). In general, German students are encouraged to study at several universities, and follow their interests wherever the appropriate specialists are teaching. The German academic ethos also explains how important and crucial it was for the FernUniversität to take over all the rules of conventional universities in order to be considered on a par by them.

Most of the Athabasca University's students study for a variety of certificates and non-degree programmes. The profile of Athabasca University students is very similar to part-time students in other conventional Canadian universities (Shale, 1982; AAUC, 1996). Athabasca University also offers seminar-supported courses, in which the students meet their tutors face-to-face. Such seminar courses are usually based on 39 hours of group classroom contact (Athabasca University, 1992c). In 1992, 12.4% of Athabasca University's students were enrolled in seminar courses. Athabasca University also proposes a teleconferencing mode, which permits students from various locations to interact either with the instructor or between themselves (Morrison & Saraswati, 1988).

Academic Faculty: Profiles and Roles

The roles of academic staff in distance education, and within distance teaching universities in particular, are in some respects quite different from their counterparts in traditional universities. If we are to examine the major distinctions, it is important to refer briefly to the main roles that academic staff in mainstream universities are expected to play. Ross (1976) set out some of these expected roles. Students expect academics to be good teachers, knowledgeable, well prepared and articulate. Some parents expect lecturing staff to serve as guides and counsellors, as parent substitutes. Colleagues expect the individual to be a productive scholar engaged in research of some significance. The administration of the university requires academics to take part in committee work of their departments and bear their share of administrative work. The professional associations, to which they belong, expect their members to show interest, participate in their activities and adhere to their standards. The community and society expect academics to make their expertise available when it is required. The responsibilities of academics are truly very diverse. At distance teaching universities teaching roles differ sharply from those required in a classical face-to-face encounter, and are based mainly on writing and developing self-study texts. As for the other responsibilities in research, community work, administration and professional associations, academic staff in most distance teaching universities are by and large expected to fulfil the same tasks as their colleagues in conventional establishments.

The socialisation of lecturers into the academic culture differs in various national settings. Ross' foray into the evolution of the academic profession, noted that England and the USA, for example, imbued in their future academic staff somewhat different priorities and conceptions of the lecturer's role. In England, the emphasis was on the student, on the college and the tutorial. In the USA the academic staff concentrated on the graduate student and on research. English and American professors, he concluded, underwent rather different kinds of induction to a university career. Teachers in England cultivated much closer contact with undergraduates than their counterparts in all but a few universities in the USA.

These variations have important consequences when we examine the role of the faculty in distance teaching universities. That the British Open University served as the pioneering model for other distance teaching universities, and the fact that the English academic tradition placed a high priority on undergraduate teaching and on close relations between tutor and student, may to a great extent explain the considerable efforts invested by distance teaching universities, particularly in the British Open University, in founding intensive support procedures and tutorial services, in producing high-level study materials and in creating a close interface between students and tutors (Tait, 1996). The English academic tradition had a profound impact on shaping academic faculty–student relations in several distance teaching universities which operated in academic environments grounded in very different underlying principles in Israel, and to a lesser extent as well, on the Spanish UNED and German FernUniversität. In the Hebrew language the word *tutor* (Manhe) applies in academia only to graduate studies. It describes the role of a professor in counselling and guiding students who work on an MA thesis or a doctoral dissertation. No such role as tutor exists at undergraduate level, save at the Open University of Israel.

Teaching students and assisting them in learning through a broad spectrum of procedures is by far the major thrust of all distance teaching universities. Paradoxically, distance teaching universities provide both—on the one hand a highly industrialised form of higher education by breaking up the teaching responsibility between many actors, and on the other a close individualised exchange between students and tutors in learning and teaching. Such close interaction between tutor or personal tutor and students seldom exists in most mass-oriented universities.

A wide range of theoretical approaches has dealt with the roles of teachers in distance education settings. At one extreme, some scholars of distance education come near to a theory of complete student autonomy (Spear, 1989; Merriam & Caffaerlla, 1991). They believe that students should have autonomy not only to decide when and how to study, but also what to study, what time is required for completion, and what assessment standards should be set (Wedemeyer, 1981; Wedemeyer & Childs, 1961). Students should be self-directed. "Self-directed learning is a form of study in which learners have the primary responsibility for planning, carrying out and evaluating their own learning" (Morrison, 1992, 43). Moore (1986) classified distance education programmes as autonomous (learner-centred) or non-autonomous (teacher-determined), according to the following criteria: autonomy in setting the objectives; autonomy in methods of study; autonomy in evaluation. Some suggest that distance education does not perhaps need teachers at all. Carried to the ultimate, student autonomy would entail the end of teaching in distance education. For students with complete responsibility for their course, there is no need for teachers beyond preparation of study material. According to this logic, distance education would not be distance teaching, but rather true distance learning; teachers would be obsolete (Mood, 1995, 77).

However, most scholars and practitioners believe that teachers have a firm and central role in distance education, and particularly in the framework of fully fledged distance teaching universities. Evidently, lecturers in distance teaching universities need a variety of talents and abilities, beyond and in lieu of the traditional roles of professors, mentioned earlier. One of the main differences between academics at distance teaching universities and those in mainstream universities stems from what may be termed the *distributed responsibility of teaching*. The sheer size of distance teaching universities disconnects most of their teaching staff from the essential interaction of learning. Other less exalted ranks in academia are responsible for tutoring and counselling students and for monitoring their studies. In all of the distance teaching universities in this study the teaching responsibilities are distributed between senior academic staff and myriad other actors who participate in the design, development, and teaching of the academic courses, and in the students' ongoing evaluation. The roles of senior academic staff and other participants in teaching and learning in each distance teaching university are examined below.

Senior Academic Faculty

It is self-evident that the roles of academics in distance education universities depend on the setting in which they work. Thach and Murphy (1994) identified eleven roles for staff who teach at a distance. These roles, which might be assumed by one or more individuals, include: instructor, instructional designer, technology expert, technician, administrator, site facilitator, support staff, editor, librarian, evaluation specialist, and graphic designer. Although not part of the teaching in a traditional sense, such skills are necessary in distance education, and the degree of expertise with which each is exercised has a direct impact on students' learning. Obviously, in dual-mode universities which teach both on-campus and off-campus students, professors are likely to assume many of the roles mentioned above. In large distance teaching universities these roles are generally dispersed among many agents.

Distance teaching requires staff to devote far more time to the preparation of study materials than they would for a face-to-face classroom presentation. Furthermore, in some distance teaching universities academic staff have to work together in a team with tutors, editors, instructional designers, television producers, computer experts, graphic production personnel, etc. to develop and write courses (Gunawardena & Zittle, 1995; Rowntree, 1990, 1992, 1993). In the course team framework, their academic freedom in teaching is clearly reduced when compared with their counterparts in campus universities. Their main responsibility is vested in writing and composing self-study courses, and their performing skills as teachers are relegated aside. In truth, lecturers at most distance teaching universities form a new species of academic. Peters (1997) argued that the role of lecturers has been challenged drastically in all distance teaching universities. It is "a difficult task to switch from oral teaching to teaching by means of the written word and by merging traditional teaching techniques and modern technological ways of communication... The result is revolutionary in the sense that an academic teaching tradition of several hundred years had to be changed radically at once" (*ibid.*, 71).

Since all faculty members at distance teaching universities were socialised into the academic profession in regular universities, they have to undergo a demanding and challenging retraining while on-the-job, in order to adjust to their new expected roles. For instance, the academic faculty in the British Open University are expected to participate in writing self-study materials within a course-team framework. The course teams are composed essentially of three groups of staff: academics, educational technologists and BBC production staff (Perry, 1976). The size of the teams ranges from nine to over twenty members. Perry confessed that: "The concept of a course team is, I believe, the most important single contribution of the Open University to teaching practice at the tertiary level... I believe that the validity of the course-team approach has been proven by the quality of materials that the Open University has produced to date, which are second to none anywhere in the world" (*ibid.*, 91, 92). Some of the members of the large production team stay on as members of the maintenance team or caretaker course team in the teaching phase.

Scaled-down versions of the course-team system operate at the Open University of Israel and at Athabasca University. Teams at these two distance teaching universities are much smaller and generally include a few academics, an editor, a graphic or visual designer, and eventually an instructional designer or media specialists, if necessary. In Athabasca University either a full-time academic or a course coordinator supervised by a senior academic is responsible for the whole process of delivering courses. At the Open University of Israel, given the very small size of its senior academic faculty, academics are expected mainly to participate in developing courses and monitoring the development of courses written by external contributors. They are also responsible for supervising the quality of the final exams. Beyond that they do not participate in teaching the courses.

Academic staff at UNED and the FernUniversität are fully responsible for developing courses with the assistance of the lower ranks of academia. The senior academic faculty at both UNED and the FernUniversität are not subject to any compulsory quality assurance procedures in respect of their writings, though they are encouraged to do so. Working with an editor or an instructional designer is not mandatory, nor is the counselling by peer specialists, as is the case in the British Open University, the Open University of Israel and Athabasca University. In Spain academics may produce their textbooks outside UNED through other publishing firms. They get royalties from the sales of their books, if they develop them in UNED. This policy was introduced to encourage UNED's staff to use the editorial facilities and expertise accumulated at UNED in producing self-study materials (García-Garrido, 1993). UNED houses the University Institute for Distance Education (El Instituto Universitario de Educación a Distancia, IUED), which provides guidance and advice on methodological aspects of distance teaching and in particular to the appropriate use of various media, analyses of student characteristics, etc. UNED has also the Audiovisual Media Production and Design Centre (Centro de Medios Audiovisuals – CEMAV) which assists staff with the production of audio and visual materials (UNED, 1992b). The senior academic faculty of UNED composed of *Profesores Catedráticos* (full professors), *Profesores Titulares* (associate professors), *Profesores Ayudantes* (assistant professors), and *Profesores Asociados* (professional part-time professors, who are usually well established professionals outside the university, such as prominent lawyers), are normally known as "headquarters teachers". They are responsible for developing teaching materials, revising courses, correcting examinations, and offering direct assistance to students by correspondence, telephone and other means (*ibid.*).

At the FernUniversität lecturers are responsible for developing the academic courses. The heritage of the German university, characterised by the considerable autonomy of its faculty in matters of teaching and research, has also shaped the attitudes of the FernUniversität's teaching staff (Peraya & Haessig, 1995). Devising a course is the exclusive responsibility of the professor, who is free to delegate all or some of the tasks to external authors. It is the individual professor's obligation to plan, develop and evaluate his/her course. Materials written by academic staff are usually analysed by the Centre for Development of Distance Study Materials (*Zentrum für Fernstudienentwicklung*, ZFE) from the viewpoint of their didactic structure. This centre has qualified academics in each faculty area in addition to a technical production staff, which include video producers, computer specialists, graphics designers, and experts in didactics (Peraya & Haessig, 1995). It reports on the draft material to the lecturer who decides whether or not to modify his/her text (Keegan, 1982). The academic staff at FernUniversität are also responsible for setting and monitoring the final students' evaluation with lower rank academics.

An additional factor of importance to be considered when examining the roles of the senior academic faculty in each distance teaching university is their sheer size. In the British Open University both the Advisory Committee and the Planning Committee recommended the recruitment of a small nucleus of full-time academic staff to be assisted by a large number of *ad hoc* faculty members from other universities for short-term periods either as authors of study material or as consultants. Perry explained that: "The Advisory Committee envisaged that the University would require a central professional staff of between forty and fifty. This total included not only the academic staff but also the administrative and operational staff that would be required" (Perry, 1976, 77). From the outset, Perry dissented strongly from the idea of a small senior academic faculty: "Had this pattern been followed they would become inevitably *de facto* editors" he remarked. "In respect of course creation and course production, the university would have been little different from a conventional publishing house..." (*ibid.*, 97).

Perry fought vigorously from the very beginning to have at least four academics in each discipline. He admitted that: "This was a figure which I virtually drew out of the air. I knew that any smaller number could not provide for that cross-fertilisation of ideas through which academics maintain their drive and interest in their own subject" (*ibid.*, 78). At its start-up the British Open University received around 1,200 applications, approximately 50 applications for every post, coming from reputable candidates with an academic record comparable to, if not better than, that of applicants for jobs in other universities (Perry, 1976, 1997).

One central priority in the first decade of the British Open University's operation was to increase the numbers of full-time academic staff. Perry believed that the unstinting loyalty of full-time staff explains to a great extent the success of the British Open University: "The fact that the academics creating our courses are full-time members of the staff of the institution seems to me to be all-important. This factor of primary loyalty has often, I think, been overlooked. Many institutions across the world have tried to prepare multi-media courses by contracting very skilled, very distinguished academics on the staff of other universities to make the necessary programmes. On the whole, they have been failures.... I am quite sure that we were right to employ as our main course creators full-time academics of the Open University, and eschew the original idea of the Advisory Committee, and indeed of the Planning Committee, of using mainly consultants and people of secondment from other universities. Our success in creating courses, in other words, seems to stem from the fact that those who joined the Open University staff put their whole career at risk. Their success was contingent on the success of the Open University. This is never true of someone on secondment" (Perry, 1976, 92).

Perry was highly successful in reshaping the basic assumptions both of the size and functional roles of senior academic faculty at the British Open University. As Table 3.3 shows, in 1995, the British Open University had 863 academic staff, in addition to 938 academic-related personnel, including course coordinators/managers and project officers, administrative, computing and library staff involved in course production (Open University, 1995). Aca-

Table 3.3. Academic Staff at the British Open University, UNED, the Open University of Israel, FernUniversität and Athabasca University (1995)*

Staff	British Open University	UNED	Open University of Israel	Fern-Universität	Athabasca University
Academic staff: senior lower rank	863	910	34 (+198)	72 (+322)	66 (+170)
Tutors & Counsellors	7,621	3,341**	1,098	555**	224

*Based on:
Open University (1995) *Pocket Guide to OU Figures,* The Open University Press.
UNED (1995) *Memorio Curso Academico,* Madrid: Universidad Nacional de Educación a Distancia, 3.
President's Report (1995) *The Open University of Israel- 1994/95,* The Open University of Israel Press, 41–42.
O'Rourke et al. (1995) Distance education in Canada, In: D. Sewart (ed.), *One World Many Voices: Quality in Open and Distance Learning, Volume 1,* ICDE & The Open University, 29.
Schuemer (1997) *Personal Communication.*
**Most of the tutors and counsellors are not employed directly by the university.

demics at the British Open University were recruited on the same basis as in conventional universities. No special weight was placed on previous acquaintance with broadcasting, adult education or instructional design (Perry, 1997).

The planners of the Israeli Open University took on almost completely the basic ideas of the British Open University's Advisory and Planning Committees (Ginzburg, 1997). According to Table 3.3, in 1995, it had only 34 senior academic staff. It also employed 198 junior academic staff, including course development coordinators and course teaching coordinators. Naturally, the number of senior academic staff influences the range and nature of their responsibilities in both phases of developing and teaching the courses. Abraham Ginzburg, the Open University of Israel's president from 1975 till 1987, admitted that: "We exaggerated in keeping the size of the senior academic staff small... We should have had an academic staff of 70–80 by now" (Ginzburg, 1997, 85).

A distance teaching university like the Open University of Israel, which depended heavily on the employment of external academics from other universities, faced particular problems and had to establish totally different work routines for course production than a distance teaching university with a large staff, and with its materials developed mainly by its own faculty members. Given the small number of internal faculty members at the Open University of Israel, several hundred scholars from the seven conventional Israeli universities were—and are still—employed on short-term contracts to consult, write or re-write varying portions of its courses (Guri, 1987; Guri-Rosenblit, 1997a). The Open University of Israel's senior academic faculty members are expected mainly to write courses and to supervise the development of courses written by external colleagues. They are much less involved in teaching the courses or in setting and marking final exams.

The Spanish UNED had, in 1995, 910 lecturers of all ranks (UNED, 1995). Academic personnel in UNED enjoy a high status, and each post usually attracts between five to ten candidates (García-Garrido, 1993). That academics in Spain are civil servants, and can be posted to wherever the State deems necessary, explains to some extent UNED's appeal to well established academic faculty. Their stay in Madrid is ensured (*ibid.*). *Asignaturas* or *cursos* are developed both by the internal academic faculty and by external staff under the supervision of internal academics (James, 1982; García-Garrido, 1993).

In 1995 the German FernUniversität had 72 professors and 322 additional ranks of academic related staff (Schuemer, 1997). In the FernUniversität's early days many courses were contracted out to prominent academics in conventional universities. The amount of in-house development varied from department to department. The general goal was to have 50% of the courses written externally (Keegan, 1982). Like UNED, the FernUniversität has attracted excellent and well-known staff. Peters (1997) has argued that the FernUniversität benefited from the way the recruitment system of German universities operates. Convention requires that academics cannot be promoted if they remain at their university. They must be offered and have accepted chairs at several universities during their career, if they are to enjoy improvements of their working and living conditions, and gain academic repute. During the first years of the FernUniversität, about 5,000 applied for chairs advertised in newspapers, "of whom about seventy successfully survived a very painstaking screening procedure and were appointed by the Minister of Higher Education and Research. The FernUniversität can be certain of having recruited the best scholars available in each case" (*ibid.*, 70).

The institutionalisation of the role of academic staff in Athabasca University is a fascinating saga. Athabasca University in its early days, as an "institution in its search for an identity as a non-traditional institution, had decided against having a permanent faculty of its own" (Morrison & Saraswati, 1988, 26). The initial policy was to hire a minimum number of academics, called Senior Tutors and Tutors, whose primary responsibilities would be to design programmes and identify courses to be developed. It was envisaged that the main body of permanent staff would consist of instructional designers and editors. Sometime later, Athabasca University realised it had to recruit a reasonable number of academics to its staff to write and produce courses. Such academics were hired on a contract basis. This policy sparked off a mini-rebellion by those academics forming the Athabasca University Faculty Association. Athabasca University agreed to a permanent staff policy, but to emphasise its non-traditional nature academics were ranked as "full professor equivalent", "associate professor equivalent" and "assistant professor equivalent". By 1986 Athabasca University had migrated towards a traditional university structure. Academic units were called "faculties"; directors were changed to "deans", and academic staff accorded the regular titles of "full professor", "associate professor" and "assistant professor" (*ibid.*, 27). In 1995 Athabasca University had 66 professors, 50 professionals, assisting in course production, together with 120 full-time support staff (O'Rourke et. al., 1995, 29).

Other Ranks of Academic Faculty and Professional Staff

Highly innovative institutions like distance teaching universities were bound to require categories of staff which have no counterpart elsewhere. Distance teaching universities employ several ranks of academic faculty and professional staff which have been recruited to meet their specific requirements and special academic activities. Such new positions had no obvious career structures and career ladders, which raised complex professional definitions, obligations and problems. Several lower ranking academics at many distance teaching universities possess wider responsibilities and degrees of freedom than teaching assistants at most campus universities.

Specific professionals were essential for the development of courses. Several distance teaching universities have a *course development coordinator*, usually a doctoral student or person with a master's degree in the particular field of the written course. Such a person is in charge of the whole process of development from the initial stages of planning and designing, through its writing, drafting, evaluating, counselling, and finally editing, producing and printing. Such an individual requires efficient management skills, excellent communicative abilities and preferably a thorough acquaintance with a specific subject-matter. Over the years, these cadres of junior academic staff at distance teaching universities have developed a high expertise in developing self-study courses, an expertise which is non-existent at conventional universities, even those which offer distance teaching courses.

In the development phase many more professionals are participating: instructional designers, media specialists, editors, curriculum developers, education technologists, evaluation technicians, graphic designers. At the British Open University, for example, BBC representatives have for many years formed an integral part of any course team. During the first year of the British Open University's existence, BBC personnel produced 130 programmes (Perry, 1976). Several clashes had been reported between BBC producers and academics on questions of expectations and points of view. The production staff of the BBC expanded in parallel with the growth of academic staff. Educational technologists employed by the Institute of Education Technology (IET) are also integral members of a team, but their number has not grown in proportion to the number of the academic faculty. Perry admitted that he had entertained the notion that in the fullness of time academics would acquire expertise as educational technologists, so there would be less need for the latter. This had not turned out to be the case (*ibid.*). In Athabasca University, on the contrary, after a few years experienced academics were able to write and produce courses with a minimal involvement of instructional designers (Morrison & Saraswati, 1988).

Educational technologists or *instructional designers* are employed by most distance teaching universities. They are a new category of professional staff involved in preparing self-study materials. Parer (1989a) in a comprehensive book devoted to the examination of the roles of *educational developers* or *instructional designers*, posed the question whether these roles have already established themselves as professionals with clear academic career paths. Educational development covers, Parer argued, a broad spectrum of activities - "to assist with teaching strategies, to improve communication skills, to extend the use of group dynamics, to assist with appropriate assessment, to provide a role of a surrogate student, to ensure that technologies are appropriately used and to develop policies and practices through research and so illuminate activities within educational institutions" (Parer, 1989b, 12). Although educational developers play an important role in the production of materials in most distance teaching universities, there is still a lack of agreement as to their professional status. Many of them feel frustrated at not being appreciated or sufficiently recognised by other academics (*ibid.*).

In the teaching phase the British Open University employs a range of junior academic professionals as tutors, tutor counsellors, personal tutors, counsellors. As Table 3.3 shows, in 1995 the British Open University had 7,621 tutorial and counselling staff, most of whom were employed on a part-time basis. *Personal tutors* are a specific British Open University phenomenon (Sewart, 1992). They specialise in a particular discipline, but as part of their job description they have responsibility for a small group of students across the whole range of their academic studies. In other words, they are responsible for monitoring the individual student's progress throughout the whole study period. The creation of the *personal tutor* derived from the English tradition of providing close tutorial care to undergraduate students. This model was imitated and implemented at several other distance teaching universities, such as the Open University of Israel. It received throughout the years most positive reactions from tutees. Such a comprehensive and close tutorial supervision replicates the English tutorial tradition and creates close ties between student and tutor. Still, it is important to remember that the personal tutors at the British Open University and at other distance teaching universities are intermediate academic faculty, assigned to support and assist the students in their learning. Even in such a supportive capacity, the fact remains that academic staff who planned, designed and wrote the courses are physically remote from students.

Among their many duties of checking assignments, holding tutorials and being available for students' queries and questions, tutors, tutor-counsellors and personal tutors are also expected to act as motivators. A number of studies make the point that communication between student and tutor is necessary not only for monitoring students' level of understanding, but also for keeping students motivated (Mood, 1995; Tait, 1996). Baath, in a series of studies, revealed that in correspondence education the more frequent communication between student and tutor lead to an improved student attitude and to decreased attrition rates (Baath, 1979, 1984).

At Spain's UNED tutorial and counselling staff are employed by study centres which are autonomous from headquarters supervision in their funding and policies. Tutors arrange appointments with students, answer queries by letter, telephone or face-to-face meeting, mark assignments and send monthly reports on students' progress to the appropriate faculties. Tutors may arrange lectures, seminars and other activities in the centre. According to Table 3.3, UNED, in 1995, had 3,341 tutors and counsellors employed in its study centres. Most of their time is spent correcting assignments, on assisting students in subject-matter learning and guidance, counselling and giving students psychological support in their studies.

At the German FernUniversität several academic ranks take part in teaching. Each course has one or several *Kursbetreuer*, equivalent to teaching coordinators, who are responsible for monitoring the teaching phase and for setting assignments. Sometimes, the *Kursbetreuer* may be the course author (Schuemer, 1993). *Fachmentoren* are employed by study centres. They are somewhat akin to tutors. But, unlike the tutors in the remaining distance teaching universities, *Fachmentoren* at the FernUniversität are not responsible for marking or checking students' assignments. They are responsible only for tutoring and assisting students in learning (*ibid.*). Keegan noted that: "The mentor's role is a delicate one as he cannot infringe on the teaching rights of the professor and is unaware of the progress of students as the grades on assignments are confidential and are not communicated to him" (Keegan, 1982, 102). *Beratungsmentoren* are counsellors, usually academics from other universities hired for counselling on a part-time basis. The assignments are checked and marked by *Wissenschaftlichen Hilfskrafte* who are postgraduate students, or by *Korrektoren*, external academics hired from other universities for that purpose, under the supervision of full-time *Wissenschaftlichen Mitarbeiter*, who are "lecturers" working with the professor (Schuemer, 1993). In 1995 the FernUniversität employed 322 full-time and 555 part-time lower rank academic staff (Schuemer, 1997).

At Athabasca University the course coordinator, when s/he is not the senior academic who developed the course, is responsible for "all the aspects of course delivery. In fulfilling this role he/she may with the supervisor's approval, rely upon tutors, markers, instructors, seminar leaders or support staff" (Athabasca University, 1991). The tutor at Athabasca University is regarded as "the most important element in the University's academic support to students" (Shale, 1982, 43). Tutors usually have master's degrees. A large number also hold doctorates. Typically, tutors are full-time teachers at other higher education institutions. The tutors in Athabasca University also play a key role in course revisions and modifications (Morrison & Saraswati, 1988, 35). They are responsible for contacting students on a regular basis, evaluating and commenting on students' assignments, and maintaining students' records according to guidelines established by the course coordinator (Athabasca University, 1991). In 1995 Athabasca University employed 224 tutors (O'Rourke et. al, 1995, 29).

The responsibility for course teaching at the Open University of Israel is almost totally undertaken by junior academic staff, due to the very small numbers of its internal senior faculty. Senior academics are responsible only for monitoring the content and quality of final examinations. They do not participate in marking. The course co-ordinators are responsible for setting the examinations, assignments, ongoing revision of courses, recruiting and guidance of tutors and marking the final examinations. The tutors are responsible for either tutoring students on a weekly basis or on a once-in-three-weeks arrangement; for commenting and grading the assignments. Since most of the Open University of Israel's students currently study in the framework of intensive tutorials, the role of tutors at the Open University of Israel is much more weighty when compared to tutors at other distance teaching universities. They face the students. They are expected to be the elucidators or teachers, though the *venia legendi* is vested in self-study materials. In 1995, the Open University of Israel employed 1,098 tutors, as Table 3.3 makes clear.

Since most of the tutorial and counselling faculty at distance teaching universities are usually part-timers, they might experience loneliness just as distance students do. Mood claimed they are the ultimate part-timers (Mood, 1995, 80). They work without close support of colleagues, without convivial coffee breaks or shared lunches. Meeting other tutors, exchanging ideas and discussing problematic issues on an ongoing basis is important and essential for their professional well-being. Many distance teaching universities, such as the British Open University, the Open University of Israel and Athabasca University, have set up regular comprehensive professional training and development programmes for their part-time tutorial and counselling staff on an ongoing basis (Paul & Brindley, 1996).

Learning and Teaching: Problematic Variables

Learning experiences and teaching practices at distance teaching universities differ in many respects from studying at conventional universities. The lack of a campus environment and a sustained peer group exchange and contact, and dispersed teaching responsibility form two such crucial differences. Two additional problematic aspects should be considered when examining the particular features of studying in a distance teaching university: relatively high drop-out rates, and the dangers of indoctrination in self-study materials produced by a small central academic staff and which are destined for masses of students scattered across a country and even beyond national boundaries.

Lack of Campus Environment and Peer Group Interaction

A campus environment and peer group interaction are highly important variables in students' learning experiences, especially at the undergraduate level. The importance of the interactive togetherness of campus life was eloquently portrayed by Cardinal Newman when he attempted to highlight the advantages of a collegiate university like Oxford, compared to the newly emergent urban London University. In a famous passage in his discourse on the idea of a university he wrote: "If I had to choose between a so-called University which dispensed with residence and tutorial superintendence, and gave its degrees to any person who passed an examination in a wide range of subjects, and a University which had no professors or examinations at all, but merely brought a number of young men together for three or four years, and sent them away as the University of Oxford is said to have done some sixty years since, if I were asked which of these two methods was the better discipline of the intellect...if I must determine which of the two courses was the better discipline in training, moulding, enlarging the mind..., I have no hesitation in giving the preference to that University which did nothing, over that which exacted of its members an acquaintance with every science under the sun" (Newman, 1859, in Bell & Tight, 1993, 32).

Clearly, Newman regarded peer interaction and residential campus life as the epitome of undergraduate university learning and training, as ingredients far more important than the act of teaching. Though this position is an extreme one, it underlines the importance of campus life. The need for contact and exchange with others varies for individual students. It depends on their age, personal inclinations, previous level of education, purpose of study, and even gender. Students who are more self-directed or autonomous may want or need less interaction than others. Professionals and executives, for example, "tend to prefer less interactivity than younger students who by and large want a high level of interaction" (Mood, 1995, 84). Adult students from disadvantaged backgrounds badly need a supportive environment (Guri-Rosenblit, 1989), and it seems that women distance students need more connectedness than males (Kirkup & van Prümmer, 1990, 1992; Kirkup, 1996).

In distance education, students may often experience feelings of extreme isolation. For many, the greatest drawback of studying at a distance might be the lack of interactivity with peers, the missing out of the enjoyment of campus life. Mood most vividly described the variables of social interaction which distance students miss: "Yet, even the highly motivated students who register for distance education courses on their own initiative find the experience lonely, difficult, and sometimes daunting. Studying alone can be discouraging and can lead to failure... There are no chats over a cup of coffee at the student centre, no causal encounters on campus with either the professor or with fellow students, no contact with people who took the same course previously. There is no way for the distant student to check progress: Students in a classroom can hear others asking questions and realise that they are not the only ones confused on a certain point. Residential students can hear others talk about how hard a particular chapter is to understand or how difficult an assignment is; distance students do not have that chance. If a student is having trouble with an assignment, it is easy for that student to think that everyone else is doing fine" (Mood, 1995, 103). In short, distant students miss the social interaction which is integral to studying on a campus, and this situation has an impact not only on their social activities and experiences, but more importantly on the quality and essence of the their learning. Isolation from fellow students is a grave shortcoming of distance education, and is of no lesser effect than remoteness from the teacher.

Smith and Small (1982) pointed out that many distance education providers have been wrong to spend vast amounts of time and money trying to devise learning packages which would allow students to become completely independent of teachers and other students. They claimed that: "In these systems the notion of learning as a social experience has not received the consideration we believe it warrants" (*ibid.*, 139).

Several support services, such as study centres available for students gatherings, face-to-face tutorials and seminar meetings, summer schools, study tours, virtual classroom settings, etc., have been developed by distance teaching universities to provide students with opportunities of peer interaction. We present them further on. Certainly, developments in interactive communication technology have helped to mitigate the isolation of distant students. Interactive satellite classes, teleconferencing, audio conferencing, e-mail correspondence and computer-mediated communication are examples of providing distance students with multi-communicative channels for exchanging ideas, participating in class discussions, working together with other students, and holding informal, ongoing conversations both with fellows and with lecturers, course co-ordinators and tutors. Distance teaching universities, more than other distance education providers, have invested heavily in providing students with accessible and user-friendly interactive devices (Mills, 1996; Tait, 1996). One of the major thrusts of distance teaching universities in the coming decade will likely be in increasing both student–student and student–faculty interactivity, as opposed to the first two decades of their existence, when emphasis was put on student–text exchange.

Distributed Teaching Responsibility

One consequence of mass higher education has been to divide the usual practice of guiding students through an integrated study programme amongst a wide range of specialists. In conventional universities, each specialist is fully responsible for all the components involved in teaching a course on a particular subject, from its initial inception and design, through its teaching in classroom or auditorium, to the evaluation of the students' achievements. At most, the lecturer might be backed by several teaching assistants in large classes, mainly to check assignments and exercises. In distance teaching universities, full responsibility of teaching a defined course is divided between many actors, who not merely assist the lecturer in specific areas, but take over fully some of the responsibilities in the development, teaching and assessment stages.

Distributed teaching responsibility is not necessarily an inevitable outcome of distance education. Prof. Knight of St. Andrews University, whom we mentioned earlier in Chapter 1, single-handedly taught all women students scattered across many countries. In dual-mode universities, such as one finds in Australia, and in extension or continuing education departments, like those in the USA, senior academic staff are usually responsible for the whole array of activities involved in preparing and teaching a course from a distance. They may be assisted by editors, instructional designers, curriculum and technology experts or graphic designers. Still, it is they who are held fully responsible for the whole range of teaching any specific subject.

Distributed teaching responsibility is a natural outcome of teaching at large-scale distance teaching universities. Many scholars do not differentiate between teaching at a distance, and teaching within large-scale distance teaching universities. For instance, Mood (1995), in a comprehensive anno-tated bibliography on distance education, devoted a special chapter to "The Teacher in Distance Education". No differentiation was made between diff-erent teaching ranks. Indeed, the words "teacher", "professor", "faculty", "instructor", "tutor" are used interchangeably and synonymously.

Peters was the first to focus on the division of labour, inherent in large-scale distance education frameworks, as a basic ingredient of his industrialisation theory (Peters, 1965, 1983, 1994a,d). He focused mainly on the impact of the division of labour on the planning of courses, on management and admini-strative organisation, and on the control measures for teaching large quantities of students. He emphasised the techniques of assembly line, mass production, standardisation, objectification, concentration and centralisation, typical of the development of self-study materials and of the monitoring of students' learning in distance education. He also homed in on the differential functions of academics teaching at a distance compared with university teachers in conventional universities, a differentiation that stemmed from breaking up the "complete work process of teaching" into discrete functions. Peters identified a three-fold division between knowledge providers (curriculum designers, authors), knowledge elucidators and evaluators (tutors, assignment and exams markers), and advisors or counsellors. He suggested that tutors and counsel-lors do not act autonomously, as they are normally not expected to teach by themselves. Rather they perform well-defined functions in the process of teaching and learning. They are essentially a link in a chain. This analysis holds true for the German FernUniversität where tutors are not authorised to mark students' assignments, and are even forbidden access to information on stu-dents' progress and grades. But in all other distance teaching universities studied here, course co-ordinators and tutors have a more influential role in monitoring student learning. They are by no means considered mere instru-ments in the teaching process.

Distributed teaching responsibility is apparent not only when the students study independently wherever they choose to study, and are thus physically separated from a tutor. *Distributed teaching responsibility* also affects students who choose to meet their tutors quite frequently. For example, at the Open University of Israel—where most students currently meet their tutors face-to-face once or twice a week—they do not have contact with the academics who designed and developed the course. The course coordinator, not the academics who wrote the course, retains the main responsibility for setting assignments and exams, and for recruiting and guiding the tutors; and tutors who deal with students in class have neither had any impact on the course content, nor are they responsible for the final evaluation. They answer students' questions, discuss chosen topics, and affect the way students learn and oversee the subjects taught.

Here I must take issue with those who claim that distance education refers only to situations in which students are physically isolated from either lecturer or tutor during most stages in learning. Many distance educators argue that as interactive encounters between students and tutors increase the learning and teaching ceases to be distance education. One of the underlying principles behind distance education, and distance teaching universities in particular, has been to reduce costs per student, mainly through the ability to absorb large numbers of students using materials developed by a relatively small number of senior faculty. This rationale applies also to situations where students have easy access to study centres and can meet their tutors quite frequently. Tutors are not those who shaped the content and quality of the course taught, and their part-time employment is significantly less expensive than a full-time senior faculty member. Even in the framework of intensive tutorials, students remain remote from lecturers. Clearly, we must modify many of the definitions of distance education, some of which were already presented in Chapter 2, and especially those which emphasise physical separation between teachers and students as one of the most obvious characteristics of distance education. Such definitions do not distinguish between different parties who share differential parts of the teaching responsibility in distance education, and who conduct differential relationships with students. An alternative definition of *distance education* which applies as well to those situations where distant students have the possibility to meet their tutors frequently, might be: *"Distance education implies the physical separation of students from professors/teachers who planned, designed and developed the course content at most stages of the study process. However, students may obtain guidance and assistance from tutors and counsellors, whom they may contact via interactive communication technologies or by meeting them face-to-face, as frequently as possible in any given context".*

An important question which emerges from the issue of *distributed teaching responsibility* is: Who are perceived as teachers or instructors by students? Are they the lecturers who planned and developed the self-study materials with an appropriate didactic apparatus? Are they the course co-ordinators or the maintenance course team personnel (whenever they are other than the course developers themselves), responsible for monitoring the whole process of teaching, setting and checking exams and assignments whilst being available for students' queries and questions? Or are they the tutors or personal tutors who are in close and frequent contact with the students throughout the learning process? This question is neither trivial, nor simple to answer.

From the point of view of a distance teaching university as an organisation, self-study materials replace the lecture in conventional universities. Professional and lower academic ranks which participate in the development and teaching stages are seen as support staff, but by no means regarded as substitutes for lecturers. As we mentioned earlier, the *venia legendi*, the right to teach at a university, is vested in the written materials. But students, as well as the teaching and professional staff in distance teaching universities, have been socialised within conventional settings, where the person who is in direct contact and dialogue with students is perceived as the *teacher*, and all other means, such as books and additional media, are looked upon as auxiliary devices.

This basic and profound socialisation which evolves from early childhood through to adulthood gives rise to an interesting paradox in the distance teaching universities which offer their students ample opportunities for inter-action with tutors and other academic staff both in regular face-to-face tutorials, seminars or in virtual settings. The more interaction takes place between students and between tutors, personal tutors, counsellors and course coordinators, the less obvious is the responsibility of senior academic faculty in the real phase of teaching and learning. In the Open University of Israel, for example, where the majority of students study within intensive tutorials, tutors inevitably assume a much heavier and greater responsibility in influencing student learning compared to the *Fachmentoren* in the German FernUniversität.

The increasing responsibility of lower rank academics in distance teaching universities raises the dilemma of de-skilling (Peters, 1965; Campion & Renner, 1992; Rumble, 1995a,b). Peters believed that even professors at distance teaching universities were de-skilled, since their functions are reduced mainly to planning and developing study materials, whilst other professionals and assistants relieve them of many tasks of instructional planning. Thus, most phases in the teaching and learning process take place without the professors' intervention. Rumble disagreed with Peters' thesis of a general tendency towards de-skilling at distance teaching universities in the case of senior academic faculty. He argued that: "Far from seeing the emergence of a de-skilled job, we are witnessing the emergence of a new kind of skilled academic job" (Rumble, 1995a, 17). Technological advances in telecommunications and computing, however, may well make the occupation of academics in distance education more skilled compared with their fellows in classical universities.

Rumble's assessment distinguished between full-time and part-time temporary jobs. De-skilling, he reckoned, applied mainly to part-time staff. Peripheral workers, employed on non-standard contracts are subject to de-skilling. Many distance educators are employed part-time. In most distance teaching universities, tutors, student advisors and counsellors hold temporary contracts which enables the institution to dispense with their services if students numbers are sufficient to warrant their employment. The jobs are based on the number of students, number of tasks to be performed, and on the number of hours required to fulfil these tasks.

Since most tutors and counsellors in distance teaching universities are by and large part-timers, the de-skilling of academic labour continues to be an important issue. Tutors, it might be said, possess less knowledge and skills than traditional academics. And such a fact might affect students' learning. The tutors respond to students' questions, identify students' misunderstandings, and are responsible for whatever is included or left out of the written texts. It follows that close links between senior faculty, course-coordinators and tutors are essential for ensuring that students get the highest possible level of accurate disciplinary information and didactic guidance. De-skilling comes as an important additional issue that may well feature on the agendas of distance teaching universities in the next few years. It is also likely that conventional universities will have to consider how to distribute teaching responsibility for specific courses when dealing with issues of strategic planning. How to manage universal access and continuous cuts of government funding with deteriorating ratios of student–faculty, will become a central dilemma in the coming decade for most universities, both distance and campus-based.

Drop-out Rates

Drop-out in distance education is a complicated and delicate issue. Many scholars and practitioners regard it as a pathology (Keegan, 1980; Woodley & Parlett, 1983; Garrison, 1987; Powell, 1991; Peters, 1992b; Zajkowski, 1997). On the face of it, some students successfully complete their programme of studies and some do not. The latter are considered as drop-outs. Obviously, in distance teaching universities with an open admission policy, drop-out may be an unavoidable consequence of combining quality and equality in higher education (Guri, 1986, 1987; Guri-Rosenblit, 1993b). All who wish to pursue higher education studies are permitted to try. But, by no means does open access policy imply that exit requirements are lower than those of conventional universities. In general, studying at a distance teaching university demands a higher level of motivation and persistence on the part of students. The drop-out rate during the first year is the highest (Peters, 1992b; Guri-Rosenblit, 1993b).

Other terms analogous to drop-out are *attrition* and *wastage*. All of these terms are loaded and have negative meanings. They signify a waste of time, energy and resources on the part of students, education providers and society as a whole (Powell & Woodley, 1995). Drop-out rates reflect badly on particular institutions and they may even be critical to institutional survival. The British Open University, from the very start, initiated a registration procedure that reduces the statistics of drop-out. Operating in a system in which drop-out at conventional universities was very low, it was essential for the British Open University to provide favourable graduation statistics. Beginning students first register on a temporary basis. They can withdraw within three months of starting without their registration showing up on the University records. At this stage, attrition rates do not appear in the British Open University calculation of drop-out. Between 25% and 30% of registered students drop out at this stage (Perry, 1976, 60).

Powell and Woodley claimed that (1995, 283): "Much contemporary thinking about drop-out in distance adult education is misconceived. At least, the consequences imputed to drop-out, strike us as entirely too negative and the all-too-busy equating of student progress and leaving behaviour in open distance education with conventional education is inappropriate" (Powell & Woodley, 1995, 283). Much of what is normally considered as drop-out in distance education systems is an artifact of participation in adult distance education and is not analogous to leaving behaviour in conventional universities. The simplistic definition of drop-out amalgamates students who voluntarily withdrew from studying with those who were forced to leave because of academic failure.

Many distance educators claim that the basic issue which perceives the role of distance teaching universities as producing graduates in ways similar to conventional universities, rests on a deep misconception about the expectations and profiles of their student clienteles (Guri-Rosenblit, 1990c, 1993b; Peters, 1992b; Powell & Woodley, 1995). Many adults enrolled in distance education do not aim for degree-level certification but seek to pick up packets of knowledge and skills on their way to achieving other educational, personal or career goals (Powell & Woodley, 1995). Some intend to study a range of courses without intending to get a degree. Many students at the Open University of Israel during the first decade were teachers who sought a "senior teacher certificate", which required less than half of the study time of a full bachelor's degree. Student-defined programmes vary from one course to many courses. Those who intend to study only one, or a limited list of, courses either for professional updating or for general education are usually successful. By no means can they be perceived as drop-outs.

Others indeed aim for a degree. But, they may use the course credits obtained via distance education to gain entry to programmes at other post-secondary institutions. Some distant students simply suspend their studies, and re-start after a few years. Others withdraw from one institution in order to enrol at another, which many of the soldier-students do at the Open University of Israel. In Canada, in Germany and in Spain students can move easily between universities and programmes. The German FernUniversität regularly admits *guest students* from other universities. They amount to around 12% of its total student body. Bartels and colleagues (1988) reported, for example, that 23% of the FernUniversität students in 1987/88 indicated that they had not re-registered because they were already enrolled at other campus universities. Joint undertakings between distance teaching universities and other universities lead to combined degrees and diplomas. It is often not clear whose graduates they are considered to be. So, it is by no means straightforward to interpret the results of drop-out in distance teaching universities.

Students drop out or cease to study at various points in their career. Fritsch (1988) classified student *drop-out* into four categories: students who enrol, but who do not take up their studies in practice (*non-starters*); students who begin their studies, but abandon them after the first attempts (*draw backs*); students who sent in fewer assignments than requested, and for this reason were not allowed to sit examinations (*drop-outs*); and students who failed the examinations (*failures*). An analysis of some 1,900 FernUniversität students, enrolled for a Mathematics for Economists course, showed a very high attrition rate at all these stages. About 34% were *non-starters*, 22% *draw-backs*, 16% *drop-outs*, 12% did not show up for the examination, though they were entitled to, and 5% failed the examination. Only 9% were successful. Peters' analysis of academic faculty's reactions to the low success rates, remarked that some German professors think that high drop-out rates "are something like a seal of quality which points to a high level of teaching" (Peters, 1992b, 250)—a very different attitude compared with the British academic ethos.

The importance of support emerged clearly in a special project organised by the FernUniversität in 1987 for 1,134 teachers, studying for a Postgraduate Diploma in Special Education and Rehabilitation. The programme lasted for eight semesters (three years), and the teachers met weekly under the guidance of a moderator. Since 1987 the programme has been repeated four times. The pass rate fluctuated between 80% to 85% (Peters, 1997, 77).

There may be many reasons for dropping out, not directly related to success in studies. Mood showed that studying at home is generally difficult: "It is easy to procrastinate, easy to convince oneself that other duties must be completed before studying. Work can easily take precedence over study for many distance students. After all, it is work that pays the bills, including the tuition bill, and therefore many students believe it must come first. A sudden deadline at work can take precedence over a class assignment. An unexpected out-of-town trip can eliminate three evenings planned for study, and increased pressure and stress at work can make concentrating on textbooks difficult" (Mood, 1995, 104). Brindley (1987) studied reasons for drop-out at Athabasca University. Students stated that completion was helped by such things as the availability of a tutor and the motivation that resulted from receiving a high grade in an early assignment. But one of the major factors that hindered completion were changes in the student's time commitments and duties outside the distance education course or programme.

It is both complex and interesting to examine the success rates in graduation at different distance teaching universities. Several do not report graduation rates in their official statistics. The British Open University ranks highest. Notwithstanding an open entry policy, over 70% of its undergraduates successfully completed their first-year examinations. More than 30% successfully graduate four, five, six or more years later (EADTU, 1993b; Open University, 1997,1). From 1971 to 1994 the British Open University awarded 136,828 first degrees (Open University, 1995).

Powell and Woodley (1995) studied drop-outs at several distance teaching universities, including the British Open University and Athabasca University. They tracked student progress from 1987 until the end of 1992. At the British Open University, 72% of those enrolled in 1987 registered for a second course; 28% of the starters graduated by the end of 1992. At Athabasca University,

50% of starting students continued to a second course; just 6% of those starting graduated by the end of 1992. Evidently, there is a significant difference between the student constituencies of these two distance teaching universities. Most of Athabasca University's students from the start did not intend to study towards a degree, whereas most of the British Open University's students did. Graduation rates at the British Open University were examined in another study conducted by van Enckevort and Woodley (1995), which looked at the status in 1993 of students who entered in 1984. They found that 31% of the British Open University students had graduated. Another 3% were still studying. Thus, the graduation rates at the British Open University fluctuate around 30% (Daniel, 1996a, 195).

Doerfer and Schuemer (1988) carried out a worldwide comprehensive survey on distance education providers. Among the parameters they used was the success rate average for three courses with the highest number of enrolments in each establishment. In Doerfer and Schuemer's report the British Open University also displayed the highest rates of persistence and graduation, among all other distance teaching universities. Around 70% of its students succeed in passing all of the courses (Doerfer & Schuemer, 1988, 214). In the Spanish UNED, the German FernUniversität and Athabasca University the reported success rates for three courses were 30%, 30% and 46%, respectively (*ibid.*, 296, 196, 74). Peters (1992b) held that the drop-out rate at UNED was comparable to Spanish campus universities, where 50% to 70% of students drop out during the first and second years of study. This is not the case in Germany where only around 30% drop out from regular universities (*ibid.*, 295). It is a finding that puts the FernUniversität in a delicate position. Graduation rates at UNED and the FernUniversität based on *guesstimates* over a ten-year period, fluctuate between 4% and 7% (Daniel, 1996a, 196).

At the Open University of Israel around 55% passed the first course. In 1991, 29% of its students succeeded in completing at least four courses. But, graduation rates revolve around 4–5% (Levtzion, 1992, 16–17). It is likely in the coming decade that graduation rates will rise because of the young student constituencies which joined the Open University of Israel from the early 1990s, and whose study patterns resemble those of students at campus universities (President's Report, 1995, 1997; Herskovic, 1995).

On the Dangers of Indoctrination

The danger of indoctrination within distance teaching universities is very real. They have the capacity to disseminate widely ideas that have a powerful impact on their students. That distance teaching universities teach massive numbers of students, use mass media and additional interactive technology, gives them the means to place any concept before thousands if not tens of thousands of students. Their influence can shape both knowledge and attitudes. Perry (1976) remarked that already in the 1970s certain nondemocratic regimes were interested in the idea of a distance education university, mainly to prevent students from concentrating in campuses and thus posing a political threat. Paul and Brindley observed that one of the dangers of operating large distance education institutions was indeed indoctrination: "As has too often been the experience of distance education, technologies such as satellite television can easily be misused for one-way learning and indoctrination. There is tremendous scope for tyranny here... through manipulation of the system for corporate or political ends that are contrary to libertarian ideals of education. Hence, learning may become indoctrination, and diversion may increasingly supplant genuine enquiry and debate as technology becomes a form of drug to keep the masses blissfully preoccupied and conformist" (Paul & Brindley, 1996, 54).

Distance teaching universities in totalitarian countries can easily be put to use as a vehicle for propaganda. And, of course, in democratic countries too they can impart certain political views. The British Open University's staff, for instance, had from time to time been accused by the then Conservative Government as representing *leftists* and *anti-establishment* views. One infamous incident took place in the early years of the British Open University, and created a great deal of publicity and suspicion about political bias in the university as a whole (Perry, 1997). A course was planned by the Faculty of Education on "School and Society". The course team included "a bunch of young men of extremely left wing opinions" (*ibid.*, 10). The course was withdrawn after strong criticism from the public and the government. Perry (1976) argued that since many distance teaching universities were promoting change in society and enhancing egalitarian goals, it was natural for many of their academic staff to be more "left of the centre" (*ibid.*, 95). But, he emphasised, one had to distinguish between the views of individual academics and those of institutions as a whole. Open universities should be careful indeed not to take any obvious political stance, just as they should be extremely prudent when designing the content of their courses.

Evidently, part of the stringent quality assurance mechanisms at distance teaching universities serves to guarantee not only the quality of subject matter and the didactic clarity of the materials. It serves also to ensure that individual academics do not indulge in polemic and present biased views to a large audience. In such circumstances, the quality assurance procedures applied in developing teaching materials in distance teaching universities entail some loss of academic freedom on the part of the individual lecturer. One has to recognise then that within distance teaching universities the freedom to teach what one wishes cannot be total. There are no clear procedures and measures to guarantee that the danger of indoctrination can easily be bypassed. Yet, distance teaching universities have constantly to be aware of this threat and as far as is reasonable, to be vigilant.

That many distance teaching universities are both national universities and also internationally-oriented makes this issue of indoctrination if anything even more sensitive. They can disseminate any given political and social view with ease especially to students in globally dispersed locations. British Open University's materials are used in a wide range of countries, developed and developing. Even without intending to be *cultural colonisers*, some distance teaching universities may find themselves doing precisely that—imparting the political ideologies and social doctrines of a small group of teachers to large audiences of students from different nationalities and a variety of social strata (Roll, 1995).

Sewart has pointed out that the solitude of the distant student and the lack of peer group influence provide fertile grounds "for instruction to the point of indoctrination" (Sewart, 1992, 238). The provision of student support systems, which create opportunities for students to debate and exchange points of view with faculty, tutors and fellow students, has a particular importance for distance education in general, and in distance teaching universities most especially.

Support Systems and Services

All the distance teaching universities covered here have various types of support systems. Generally, they are intended to provide services which help and guide students as individuals. Whilst it is the headquarters of all distance teaching universities which are responsible for delivering course materials, assignments and exams to all students, it is at the regional or local level, where study centres, summer schools and other channels of exchange are designed to meet the needs of individual learners. The central place of support systems, in addition to the production of self-study materials, is nowadays accepted by all distance teaching universities and by other providers of distance education (Mills & Tait, 1996). From 1993, the European Association of Distance Teaching Universities (EADTU) working with the European Commission Task Force on Human Resources initiated a EuroStudy Centre Project to improve the provision of support services to distance students in Europe. In summarising the conference on "The European Open University Network: Course Delivery, Student Support and Study Centres", in February 1993, Tait remarked: "It has been widely if not universally accepted that students would not in the majority learn effectively if able to work only from home-based study materials" (Tait, 1993, 50). In short, appropriately designed and well-maintained support systems are key to successful distance education enterprises.

The tradition of individual support for students in higher education differs between different national systems, and thus the function of support services in different distance teaching universities varies accordingly. Sewart argued that it is possible to transfer elements which make up course production between countries. The same cannot be said for student support services. They: "must be constructed in the context of the almost infinite needs of the clients; are dependent on the educational ethos of the region and the institution; are dependent on the dispersal of the student body, elements of resource and the curriculum or product of the course production subsystem; are dependent on the generic differences in the student body which it has been set up to serve" (Sewart, 1993, 11). Tait agreed that marked differences exist between individual support services, but advocated a systematic and comparative study into national systems: "Deeper understanding of respective student support systems on the basis of comparative analyses and research will have the potential of leading towards change and improvement on the basis of examination of the best practice. Although the different academic cultures of institutions which reflect their national contexts...will prevent the adoption of entirely common approaches for the foreseeable future" (Tait, 1993, 52–53).

The tradition of individual support for students is extensive in the UK, as in the United States, Canada and Australia. But, it does not exist to the same extent in other countries, such as Germany and Spain, or even Israel. Student support has always had a warm place in the British Open University's provision. Scott (1995) argued that the ties between tutors and students were so strong in the English tradition that: "Even the Open University was obliged to construct mechanisms of intimacy, such as summer schools, and permit the construction of myths of intimacy, such as *Educating Rita*" (*ibid.*, 7). But support in the British Open University goes well beyond the holding of summer schools.

Tait (1996) pointed out that Robert Beevers, the first director of the Regional Tutorial Services at the British Open University, was greatly influenced in shaping the tutorial systems of the British Open University by Oxbridge practices and by English traditions in adult education: "The insistence on personal attention and small group teaching derive, it can be suggested, from two traditions: university education in the UK, especially the Oxbridge tradition of micro-group or individual teaching... and adult education with its emphasis on group discussion and participation on a democratic footing... Beevers' own background as an Oxford-educated historian and later a lecturer in adult education has been considered to have contributed to the sort of student support which he was so influential in creating" (*ibid.*, 61).

The other side of the continuum dwells in the German FernUniversität. According to Peters: "The active support of students to reduce the drop-out rate has no tradition in German universities... Because of the lack of funds it is at present impossible and will remain so in the near future, to carry out personnel-interactive structural and organisational changes. The FernUniversität support and care system, in particular the study centres, are not in a position to give further, more exacting assistance, for personnel and factual reasons" (Peters, 1992b, 258). A partial explanation of the relative lack of enthusiasm for support devices at the FernUniversität stems from the general attitude towards dropping-out in German academic culture. In Germany, a professor can pride himself that his course is excellent precisely because the drop-out rate from the course *is* the highest (Peters, 1992b; Sewart, 1993). A similar view applies to some degree to Spain. It is then scarcely surprising that all of UNED's study centres and part of the German FernUniversität's study centres do not come under the direct supervision of the headquarters. They are managed both financially and administratively by local authorities. Nevertheless, both UNED and the FernUniversität place high importance on the local study centres, and this underlines the influence of the British Open University in shaping the support systems of other distance teaching universities.

Student support services in distance education cover those elements in conventional education that relate most closely to teaching. Beaudoin believed that many distance educators have for decades felt "compelled to simulate the interactive features typically associated with classroom-based teaching and learning, assuming that good things happen in face-to-face instruction" (Beaudoin, 1995, 2). Many distance teaching universities from the 1980s began to move beyond this view and have been engaged in defining types of support systems and modes of interaction more appropriate to their particular environment rather than seeking to replicate the best and worst of classroom instruction. Clearly, the concept of interaction applied to distance learning is more complicated than has been conceded in traditional instructional theory or classroom teaching (Moore & Kearsley, 1996).

Sewart (1993) took the view that distance teaching universities are basically a service industry rather than a *manufacturing industry*, and thus *sin generis* have to provide student support. He listed the major support services which distance teaching universities employ: class teaching at study centres; individual tutorials at study centres or elsewhere; annual residential schools (compulsory or optional); study or self-help groups; social events; counselling sessions at study centres; correspondence with tutor and counsellor; telephone contact with tutor and counsellor; group telephone tutorials; radio tutorials; audio cassettes "correspondence"; computer-mediated communication; student newspapers. The list he hinted is by no means exhaustive. At different distance teaching universities, student support services include part of these components. In examining support systems in the five distance teaching universities under scrutiny, discussions will focus on three major elements: study centres, tutor–student relations, and counselling services.

Study Centres

The concept of study centres in distance education has been analysed in many publications (Timmons & Williams, 1990; Sewart, 1993; EADTU, 1993a; Fage, 1995; Watts, 1995; Mills, 1996). The EuroStudy Centre project of the European Association of Distance Teaching Universities (EADTU) in its first stage collected data on 875 study centres managing distance education in Europe (EADTU, 1993a; Tait, 1994c). Study centres are formed at all distance teaching universities. The relations and links between headquarters and study centres differ significantly from one distance teaching university to another. Some are owned by local authorities and enjoy total autonomy. Others are closely supervised by headquarters (Mills, 1996). The administrative structure and the organisational arrangements between study centres and headquarters in each distance teaching university are discussed in detail in Chapter 6.

All of the study centres, whether based on a temporary renting of existing facilities or in permanent establishments, provide physical layouts for face-to-face tutorial meetings. Most employ counselling staff for initial orientation and for handling special target groups. They possess a library with appropriate literature; and technological media suited to the study process, such as video-tapes, audio cassettes, film screening, computers, virtual classrooms for satellite interaction whenever needed, etc. In all distance teaching universities, including the British Open University, attendance at, and activities offered by, study centres is optional, save for a few obligatory sessions in certain courses.

Study centres provide individualised linkages to students enrolled in distance teaching universities. They reflect the rationale of a *service industry* (Sewart, 1993), designed specifically to tailor programmes and services suitable to the needs of very different clienteles, and to be attentive and responsive to the individual student. Although most of their services are optional, many distance students make use of the wide range of support mechanisms on offer. In countries in which distance is no barrier, Israel for example, most students prefer to attend study centres, which offer campus-like facilities on a regular weekly basis. The demand for social interaction will in all likelihood grow in the future, and the role of study centres will extend accordingly, even in countries whose academic tradition is not positive towards personal student support. Such a move has become apparent in the past few years at the German FernUniversität. It is examined in the next section. Furthermore, the evolution of new technologies and their integration into learning and teaching have changed considerably earlier roles of study centres in many national settings (Mills, 1996). This theme is taken up fully in Chapter 6.

Tutor–Student Relations

The role of tutors in different distance teaching universities varies, as we have seen. In the German FernUniversität, the *Fachmentoren* have an entirely optional status for the student, unrelated to assessment or credit, which contrasts with all the other distance teaching universities, where tutors have an important and essential link with students, and are wholly responsible for marking assignments. Some even participate in checking final examinations. Tutors inject an individualised dimension to learning and teaching. In many cases, the tutor is the only person with whom the distant student has contact. Moore and Kearsley provided a systematic overview on distance education worldwide. They summarised the main roles of tutors as: discussing course content; providing feedback on progress; grading assignments/tests; helping students plan work; motivating students; answering administrative questions; supervising projects; teaching face-to-face seminars; keeping student records; intervening with the administration on behalf of students; evaluating course effectiveness (Moore & Kearsley, 1996, 248).

Close rapport between students and teachers or tutors is important both in campus and distance universities. A study conducted by Weston and colleagues (1996) on "How outstanding professors view teaching and learning" at US campus universities, found some "unexpected concepts" relating to the importance of caring about students, about counselling, reducing anxiety and providing a safe environment. Both students and professors viewed these variables as most important for improving student learning.

John Cowan, a tutor of the British Open University, argued vehemently that student–tutor exchange does not differ whether conducted in classical universities or in a distance teaching university. He pointed out to those responsible for tuition: "I ask them to set aside all thoughts of distance learning being different, as far as quality is concerned. As a learner, I have experienced both face-to-face and distance tuition. In each situation, support (for me) could be described in virtually the same terms. Sometimes, it was the explanation provided when I found I could not understand, and had asked for help; sometimes it could be the prompting from which I benefited, when I had been unable to make progress with a problem or task, yet wanted to do so in my own strength. Sometimes, it could be the encouragement which generated or sustained my (at times uncertain) motivation; sometimes it was the welcome feedback which advised me when I was uncertain about the soundness of my learning, or of my work; on occasions it was the facilitative interventions which prompted further and possible personal development, though I was otherwise autonomous. In each and all of these examples, I have found effective support in both modes to be the same in principle, although often very different in form" (Cowan, 1994, 59).

A number of research projects examined different student perceptions of effective and efficient tutorials. Since the 1990s, procedures for student feedback have been discussed within the British Open University and in other distance teaching universities. Tutorial and counselling staff were encouraged to use feedback forms in conjunction with their own dialogue with students (Watts, 1995). Stevenson and colleagues (1996) conducted a survey at the British Open University into the "Tutor's role in distance learning". Drawing upon the most frequently made comments during pre- and post-course in-depth interviews, which were supported by responses of pre- and post-course questionnaires, they found that students appreciated the following ingredients most in their interaction with tutors: mixture of teaching methods; definite aims and targets; advanced notice/programme; encouraging feedback on assignments; exam preparation opportunities. Students, they found, liked: tutors to come prepared; a well delivered lecture with opportunity for questions; tutors to be encouraging and supportive; tutors to have humour and dialogue in marking; day schools to be well planned and useful to justify the effort made to attend (*ibid.*, 28).

Another study carried out by Morgan and Morris (1994) into students' attitudes towards face-to-face tutorials, during education courses provided by the British Open University in Wales, noted that in general students reacted most positively to tutorial provision. Among the factors listed as most favourable and pleasing were: provision of notes, schedules and synopses, a well prepared presentation, humour, knowledge, guidance given on assignments, generally "being helpful", meeting with other students and opportunities to discuss with other students. Students were critical towards tutorials with: a loose structure, dominated by one student, tutorials rushed through because of lack of time; insufficient class discussion, particularly in the case of small groups of students; sessions dominated by the tutor; and too few tutorials with insufficient continuity between them (*ibid.*, 32).

An interesting study was conducted by van Prümmer (1994) on the communication preferences by German FernUniversität students. The data she collected did not support two of the FernUniversität's underlying assumptions about the communication requirements of distant students. Van Prümmer's study showed that, contrary to initial assumptions, adult distant students did not prefer to study by themselves. They favoured even less written communication. Most of the students in the survey "have marked preference for personal interaction with academic staff and other students. They are less interested in forms of written communication, including electronic mail, a number of students even rejecting them outright" (*ibid.*, 293). As far as their stated communication preferences were involved, FernUniversität students wanted a much higher degree of personal interaction than it is currently possible for the institution to provide. Ninety-four percent of the respondents had a decided preference for face-to-face talks, 86% for telephone interaction and 69% for group discussions and seminars. The telephone, though without face-to-face facilities, was seen as a vehicle of personal interaction allowing simultaneous exchange and direct conversation with a live person (*ibid.*, *ibid.*).

Van Prümmer revealed a large discrepancy between the communication preferences of FernUniversität students on one hand, and the types of communication supported by the institution on the other. Van Prümmer's study may reflect the impact that globalisation and internationalisation in distance education might have in some national circumstances on rethinking and revising long-held beliefs, particularly if such practices are effective in reducing drop-out and improving student persistence. Research by some FernUniversität faculty into the attitudes of their distant students towards social learning might bring about some alteration of the FernUniversität's support services and a redefinition of the tutor–student relations.

Most distance teaching universities which use tutors extensively, provide orientation workshops and printed manuals to outline responsibilities and lay down guidelines for effective tutoring. The British Open University, the Open

University of Israel and Athabasca University monitor their tutors closely and provide continuous in-service professional training. Such training is highly important given that most tutors are usually part-timers, and have neither the knowledge nor the expertise expected of a full-time lecturer.

Counselling Services

All distance teaching universities employ a varied combination of counselling services which include: pre-registration information; continuous counselling throughout the period of study; professional orientation; special support and counselling systems for students with special needs.

The major key features of the British Open University's counselling services include: pre-entry educational and vocational guidance, including diagnostic help, advice and information on a wide range of educational, financial and practical areas; guidance for open learning methods; basic preparation and development of study and learning skills and confidence through preparatory and learning skills materials, packs, tutorials and workshops, which cover areas such as time management, essay writing, note-taking, examination techniques and numeracy; comprehensive educational and vocational guidance on credit accumulation and transfer and vocational qualifications is also available (Fage, 1995). The Open University of Israel and Athabasca University employ counsellors for functions comparable with those of the British Open University. The Student Services Unit at Athabasca University and the Dean for Students' Affairs at the Open University of Israel also advise students on the availability of student loans, scholarships and financial matters (Morrison & Saraswati, 1988; President's Report, 1995). At the German FernUniversität and Spanish UNED counsellors are responsible mainly for academic and professional orientation.

Some distance teaching universities provide counselling services for students with special needs. In 1994, the British Open University had over 3,000 disabled students enrolled in its courses—more than in all other UK universities (Open University, 1995). It offers extensive support to such students and for those with other special problems, be they examination anxiety or geographical remoteness (Fage, 1995). The Open University of Israel employs also specialists to assist students with learning disabilities (President's Report, 1995). In 1986, handicapped students account for about 20% of the FernUniversität students. They receive special treatment from counsellors and tutors at local centres (Reddy, 1988b).

Disadvantaged students need a great deal of support. As we mentioned earlier in Chapter 2, the Open University of Israel embarked in 1982 on a special project of training community leaders from particularly disadvantaged neighbourhoods in Israel. In 1985, it initiated, together with the General Labour Federation (*Histadrut*), a project to raise the general level of education amongst blue collar workers (Guri-Rosenblit, 1989). Students in both programmes were ill-prepared for academic study and had an average of 9–11 years of formal study. The Open University of Israel provided them with intensive tutorials. Thus, the concept of "intensive tutorials" was born at the Open University of Israel. The perseverance of these students was found to be comparable to that of regular Open University students. By 1988, over 50% completed their courses successfully. Most of the special students indicated in an evaluation study, that group cohesion and frequent face-to-face meetings was the most important factor to account for their persistence (*ibid.*).

In a comprehensive paper on counselling distance learners, Carol Carter (1992) discussed ways to implement counselling services. She recommended that an institution prepare packets of information about issues of shared concern—stress management and communication skills—and distribute them as needed. Carter believed that difficulties and stress in a student's personal life, such as moving house, the birth of a child, multiple home duties, lack of family support, could affect students' success. She recommended increasing counselling facilities for distant learners, whether face-to-face, by telephone, or by correspondence.

The place of counselling services within distance teaching universities will most certainly expand over the coming decades, as more diverse student clienteles pursue higher education studies. More unprepared students from disadvantaged backgrounds will enrol at both distance teaching universities and classical universities, and such students will most assuredly need sophisticated and elaborate counselling and support.

4

Academic Curricula

By and large, the curriculum of open universities is routed squarely within the traditional notions of knowledge within universities.

Morrison (1992, 52)

What one has learned—not where or how, in what sequence, at what institution, or in what period of time—is the only criterion of supreme importance.

Wedemeyer (1983, 136)

Greater social openness of the mass university encourages academic closure. Openness increases the pressure for much tighter control over the structure of academic programmes.

Scott (1995, 161)

Introduction

The establishment of a new type of university naturally generates expectations for change in academic curricula. Nearly all innovations indirectly influence the university curriculum in its widest sense. They may affect the programmes' content, structure, teaching methods, delivery media, and forms of assessment. When examining the study programmes proposed by different distance teaching universities, one should distinguish between *what* is taught and *how* it is taught. The initial hopes of many were that distance teaching universities would be innovative and original in answering both the *what* and *how* questions. Yet, most distance teaching universities have been somewhat conservative in their choice of courses, and have not dared to wander too far from the programmes offered by their conventional counterparts whatever their national setting. Their *revolutionary* impact has emerged mainly in altering the delivery systems and formal structures of the study programmes (e.g., dividing up courses into modules or units).

The distinction between the *what* is taught and *how* it is taught is not always clear or self-evident. John Daniel, for instance, when he attempted to explain that Spain's UNED's costs per student were, over the years, about one-third those of the British Open University, speculated that perhaps: "It appears that definition of the curriculum by government makes course development and production much cheaper" (Daniel, 1996a, 187). But the content of the programmes at the British Open University and UNED affects the costs of their courses far less than the way they are produced. Clearly, the development of a course within a team model and the application of stringent and lengthy validation procedures during the phases of approving, designing and writing the study materials are substantially more expensive than a course written by a single author assisted by an editor.

It is highly complicated to compare academic curricula across several countries: "Curricular rationales vary strikingly according to disciplines and occupational areas, according to types of higher education institutions, and according to the historical goals of higher education in each country" (Teichler, 1994a, 10). Study programmes, study frameworks and exit requirements vary greatly between countries, between institutions, and within institutions. The academic curriculum of any given university can, for instance, be strongly research-oriented or directed towards vocational and professional training; programmes can be based on disciplinary lines or on inter- and trans-disciplinary principles; they can be short or very long. Teaching at most universities is grounded mainly on the delivery of discipline-based knowledge. Universities have historically employed discipline-directed learning as a way of ushering students into the accumulated knowledge of the sciences and of the humanities. Distance teaching universities have also taken on discipline-directed learning, with special attention paid to the structures of knowledge through instructional design (Morrison, 1992). Disciplinary knowledge is complex. The underlying values and principles of academic disciplines vary immensely, and are shaped by prevalent research norms and conventions in any given field (Clark, 1983 1987, 1993; Messer-Davidow et al., 1993; Usher, 1993; Nicoll & Edwards, 1997).

Gibbons and his colleagues (1994) recently made an interesting distinction between two types of knowledge generation, which they labelled as Mode 1 and Mode 2. Mode 1 is grounded in disciplinary structure, is hierarchical in nature, and is based on established research conventions ruled by scientific academic communities. Research in Mode 2 is carried out in a context of application, is trans-disciplinary in nature, and is conducted by *ad hoc* teams, gathered from various institutions within and outside universities, teams which dissolve when a problem is solved. "Members may then reassemble in different groups involving different people, often in different loci, around different problems" (Gibbons, 1997, 5).

Mode 2 is already practised by research universities and research institutes outside universities. The assumption is that Mode 2 will become the leading research model for most universities in the future. Yet, to this day teaching is still conducted predominantly within the confines of Mode 1. How to inject the products of Mode 2 research into teaching practice is one of the intriguing issues for the future development of universities. Interestingly, knowledge generation within Mode 2 resembles, in certain aspects, the process of course preparation at many distance teaching universities. It is based on an *ad hoc* team of internal faculty and outside experts, which dissolves when the course development is completed. In this sense, distance teaching universities, by their particular organisational infrastructure, may be better equipped than conventional universities to translate the products of Mode 2 research into a teaching discourse. However, this potential has been realised to a very limited scale in their first decades of existence due to strategic constraints discussed later. The overall programmes at most distance teaching universities may be designed on an inter-disciplinary base, but the individual courses are largely discipline-grounded.

Amongst the hopes for distance teaching universities, as well as for many new universities born in the 1970s and the 1980s, was that they would develop inter-disciplinary courses and curricula broader than those of traditional universities. The belief flourished that more general-type programmes will grow and expand, and would better suit the study preferences of new students. In reality, the opposite happened. Scott, examining the trends of mass higher education in the UK since the 1960s, concluded that: "Most universities have retreated from their early inter-disciplinary ambitions. Most hopes were exposed as naive... Disciplinary and professional specialisation intensified as the university system grew. Most staff and students had more pragmatic and less radical ambitions as compared to the founding fathers" (Scott, 1995, 55–56).

The situation in distance teaching universities was more complicated and perhaps delicate than that in large, new campus-universities. Pragmatic considerations aside, distance teaching universities had to establish their academic credibility, and could not have embarked too hastily on drastic change. It might have damaged their standing and labelled them as very different and idiosyncratic institutions. Perry revealed with customary candour the underlying principles behind the British Open University's decision to follow the academic programmes of conventional universities as closely as possible: "The question that remained was: what would the subject matters of these courses be and how innovative could we afford to be in designing them? Here we made a clear decision not to innovate but stick to the traditional fields of study typical to conventional universities, and I suppose that we could therefore legitimately be charged with having had *cold feet*. The decision was in my view, determined by our overriding need to achieve academic respectability. Had we embarked on a series of courses that broke too far with tradition... we would have achieved nothing at all. The other universities, our colleagues throughout the country and throughout the world, would have regarded the degree of the Open University as something so different as to be second-rate, even if the standard of the courses themselves was acceptable. We were not, after all, dealing with students who were simply anxious to achieve a degree of equivalent standard; they also wished their degree to be recognised by employers as of equivalent content. This was especially significant in those lines of study as science and technology, where the courses were regarded as *vocational*" (Perry, 1976, 66–67).

The standpoint voiced by Perry was not untypical of all distance teaching universities in this study. The Spanish UNED and Germany's FernUniversität openly sought to align their curricula as much as possible on those of conventional universities. The Open University of Israel and Athabasca University experimented on a restricted scale with designing inter-disciplinary courses of an innovative type, but gave up after a short while (Hughes, 1980; Shale, 1982; Daniel, 1997; Ginzburg, 1997). Nevertheless, the breadth, duration and foci of the curricula in each distance teaching university vary considerably. Some decided to offer broad and comprehensive programmes. Others focused on limited and restricted areas of study. Some set out a full range of academic degrees from the bachelor level to graduate research degrees. Others taught mainly towards first degrees. Some provided a wide range of vocational and continuing education programmes in contrast to a limited range of such courses at *sister* distance teaching universities. For some programmes the duration is as long as eight years whereas others are quite short. Some administer extensive transfer schemes with conventional universities, while others require the major part of studies towards a degree or diploma to be followed within their own institution.

In this chapter we examine the range of academic and continuing education curricula in each distance teaching university. The different degree requirements and prevailing norms underlying the various types of degrees in each national system and some dimensions of *closure* and *openness* of distance teaching universities' delivery practices are analysed.

Fields of Study

The diversity in academic curricula in different distance teaching universities originates to a great extent from deep-rooted academic traditions in each nation (Teichler, 1993a,b, 1994a,b). For instance, engineering schools are near the top of the academic hierarchy in Germany, Spain, France, USA, and Japan—indeed in most industrialised countries. In the UK, most especially in the 1960s and 1970s, they were subterranean. The best students went into humanities and pure sciences. They knew that such fields carried higher status, and would provide them with a better opportunity of highly paid posts with long-term prospects than if they chose a "more useful" subject (Perkin, 1987). Comparing the professional orientations of the British and German higher education systems, Teichler concluded: "British industry and private services employ a higher proportion of graduates from fields of study not directly linked to business careers" (Teichler, 1993b, 4). Such an acute difference between subject hierarchies accounts for the relatively marginal status the British Open University accorded to professional faculties in its early days by comparison with the FernUniversität and UNED. This is just one example. In addition, disciplines are grouped into different faculties in different countries. They enjoy—and sometimes bitterly lament—differential academic and professional standing.

To set out the essential differences between academic curricula of the five distance teaching universities on the basis of generally accepted categories of faculties or fields of study is a thankless task. For example, Geography figures in the Social Science Faculty at the British Open University. It is grouped as a separate faculty with History at UNED. In the Open University of Israel, Geography sits within the Natural Science Department, as is the case in Athabasca University. Social Sciences are a large faculty/department in the British Open University and at the Open University of Israel. At Athabasca University they are part of the Faculty of Arts, the FernUniversität groups them together with Education and Humanities into one faculty, with Economics singled out as a separate faculty. In Spain's UNED, Social Sciences are split across three different faculties (Psychology, Economics and Business Studies, Political Science and Sociology). Any general categories fail to show the different underlying philosophy in the overall curriculum of each distance teaching university. Rather, we will analyse briefly the main programmes in each distance teaching university and focus on the innovative and specific features in each institutional setting.

British Open University

The British Open University offers several study routes: undergraduate, continuing education and post-graduate programmes. Overall, the curriculum reflects the three remits in its Charter: to provide an opportunity for adults to study for BA (Open) and BA honours degrees; to offer professional and technological updating, through such institutes as the Open Business School, the Department of Health and Social Welfare and such MSc level programmes in "Computing for Commerce and Industry" and "Manufacturing Management and Technology"; and finally to design programmes for the educational well-being of the community, for example, courses on "Parents and Teenagers" and "Health Choices" (EADTU, 1994a, 125).

The largest group of British Open University students study for BA degrees. The British Open University teaches around 10% of all British undergraduates each year, and produces around 8% of the graduates (EADTU, 1994a; Daniel, 1996a,b; Perry, 1996, 1997). Students may choose from a range of courses at foundation, second, third and fourth levels, available at the University's six faculties and schools: Arts, Social Sciences, Education, Mathematics, Sciences, and Technology. To gain an ordinary BA (which is called Open) students must complete six credits. Attainment of honours depends on results at third level. Until 1993, the BA honours required eight credits, modelled after the Scottish system, where an ordinary first degree is based on three years of study and an honours degree on four years. In English universities, both BAs, ordinary and honours, may be obtained in three years (Jablonska-Skinder & Teichler, 1992). Between 1971 and 1976, British Open University students required ten credits for an honours degree (Open University, 1993b, 2). From 1993 onwards, following the translation of polytechnics into universities, the abolition of the CNAA and the setting up of the new Higher Education Funding Councils, of which the British Open University is now part, the latter changed its BA honours requirements to six credits by adopting a common, nationally-agreed standard of 360 points for BA degrees (each credit at the British Open University equals 60 points) (Platt, 1997).

The decision to focus from the outset on building solid and respectable first degrees, was part of the British Open University's drive to win academic prestige. From a 25-year retrospective, Perry justified the initial decision to start with, and concentrate on, the undergraduate programme: "At the very start of my term as Vice Chancellor of the Open University, I said that I believed that the most important function that it would serve in the long term would not be the production of more graduates, but the provision of both graduates and non-graduates of continuing education for the refreshment, updating and retraining that all kind of workers would require regularly during their careers in the new technological world. I was, however, very sure that we could not start with that. We had to prove ourselves first; we had to gain respect amongst academics by offering a high quality first degree. I am quite certain that this was the correct decision" (Perry, 1997, 18–19).

As has been pointed out earlier, the British Open University's basic subject matter of courses is consistent with other British universities. Table 4.1 describes the distribution of teaching to each courses at undergraduate level of the British Open University's six faculties, the breakdown of registered students by faculties, and the main disciplines and subjects in each faculty. Both courses and registered students are quite evenly distributed between arts/social sciences and science/math faculties. The low percentage of students at undergraduate level in the School of Education, is due to the fact that most teachers in the UK already possess first degrees. The British Open University played an important part in raising the academic qualifications of teachers. During its first decade, teachers accounted for 17% to 20% of its undergraduate student

Table 4.1. *Academic Courses at the British Open University Distributed by Faculties, 1992* (at the undergraduate level)*

Variables	Arts	Soc. Sciences	Education	Mathematics	Sciences	Technology	Post-experience courses
Number of courses (total = 132)	22	21	11	22	25	26	5
Breakdown of regist. students by faculties** (total = 91,161)	22.4%	22.1%	3.9%	16.9%	12.9%	17.9%	3.8%
Disciplines & Subjects	Art History History Hist. of Scien. Literature Music Philosophy Religious Stud. Europ Humnt.	Geography Economics Government Psychology Sociology Social Policy Social research Methods	Curriculum Educ. Policy Soc. Research Human dev. Language & curriculum Youth & Adult Studies Educ. Manag.	Mathematics Applied Math. Computing Statistics	Biology Chemistry Physics Earth Science Science Educ.	Electronics Engin. Mechanics Materials & Manufact. Information Techn. Mangmt of Technology	Health Social Welfare 'U' courses***

* Based on: Open University (1992) *An Introduction to the Open University*, Fact Sheet, Number 1, The Open University Press.; Open University (1993a) *Pocket Guide to OU Figures*, The Open University Press; International Association of Universities (1993) *Universities Handbook*, New York: Stockton Press, 2978.

** Number of registered students differs from the total undergraduate body because students may register for more than one course.

*** 'U' courses are cross-faculty.

body (Perry, 1976). Nowadays, many teachers pursue MA degrees at the British Open University. The relatively small number of courses (132 in 1992) is attributable to the duration and breadth of each course. One credit course amounts to a sixth of a first degree. This credit system was based on the Scottish degree system, as we discussed in Chapter 1. Indeed, the British Open University's modules are mostly condensed large chunk courses as compared to courses at the other distance teaching universities in this study. A full credit course at the British Open University presumes 450 to 600 hours of study (ICDL, 1997).

The British Open University was the first to introduce the modular system into English higher education. Previously no system existed for cross-accreditation through which individuals who had obtained credits towards part of a qualification in one institution could transfer that credit to another. Here, the British Open University acted as a catalyst for credit transfer in England. Clearly, *credit currencies* modify transactions that take place in higher education. Employment of modular courses encourages flexibility of study programmes and broadens student choice. It also provides the basis for designing inter- and trans-disciplinary programmes. Most British universities today employ credit accumulation and transfer schemes.

The design of the overall curriculum is reflected not only in existing courses, but also in the disciplines and subjects that were deliberately left out. Some subjects were considered not suitable for distance education—medicine, dentistry, veterinary science, forestry, agriculture, aeronautical engineering (Harry, 1982; Perry, 1976, 1997). Others, such as law, were excluded because it was held that provision for part-time study in this field was already adequate at other universities and higher education institutions (mainly polytechnics). Interestingly, the decision of the British Open University not to teach law saved the external degree programme of the University of London. Bell and Tight (1993) reported that London University decided to cancel many of its external subjects following the British Open University's establishment. In 1961, 27% of the new external registrations at London University for first degrees were in economics, 20% in law, 19% in arts, and 15% in other subjects, by 1986 the subject breakdown had become highly skewed, with 79% of all new external registrations in one subject, law (*ibid.*, 108). Bell and Tight argued: "This was partly a reflection of the growth of alternative study opportunities in Britain resulting from the CNAA and the Open University (indeed, if the latter had decided to offer a law degree, the University of London external system might not have survived)" (*ibid.*). The British Open University intends to open a Law School in 1998 in collaboration with the College of Law, as well as a new School of Languages (Daniel, 1997; ICDL, 1997). English and French were added as subjects in the Arts Faculty from 1995. Over 2,000 people studied French in 1995 (Open University, 1995). German is offered from 1997, with Spanish to follow in 1999 (ICDL, 1997).

Not only the credit system, but also foundation courses were an innovative feature of the British Open University's undergraduate programme. Foundation courses were designed in response to the open admission policy. With no entrance qualifications, enrolled students evidently commanded very different levels of background knowledge. It was decided to require all undergraduates to take a foundation course, which assumed no previous knowledge of the subject and provided a broad introduction to a range of subjects and study skills. Each foundation course is multidisciplinary. In Arts, for example, it covers English, History, Philosophy, Music and Fine Art; in Science it includes Chemistry, Physics, Biology and Geology. After successfully completing a foundation course in a chosen area, students can choose courses from any level, though naturally they are encouraged to move on to more demanding higher level courses. Students are even encouraged to take two foundation courses to broaden the scope of their degree, if they do not wish to focus on a particular subject or field. Until 1990, students were required to take two foundation courses (Open University, 1993b).

The agreement between the British Open University and the Government was for the latter to subsidise the cost of undergraduate education, but continuing and postgraduate education would be self-supporting. Thus, either the fees for such courses would be very much higher or the university would have to find sponsorship for such courses from potential employers or other well-wishers (Perry, 1997, 18). This was undoubtedly one of the reasons why it took so long to develop the continuing education programme to a reasonable size. The Department of Education and Science, which up to 1992 sponsored the British Open University directly, determined how many students would be admitted each year to undergraduate programmes (currently the quotas are set by the Higher Education Funding Council of England). Quotas are drawn up for each foundation course, which maintain a reasonable balance between applications and places for each region and for each sex, precedence being given to those who applied in previous years.

Undergraduate courses are also available to those wishing to study without registering for a degree. The associate student programme is designed for adults who want to extend knowledge relevant to their career or acquire knowledge of a field for in-service or general interest purposes without embarking on a full degree programme. Associate students pay higher fees than undergraduates do on the same course. In 1992, for example, associate students paid £ 425 for a full credit course and £ 275 for a half credit course, compared with tuition fees of £ 244 and £ 163 respectively, for regular undergraduates (Open University, 1993b). Many courses taken by associate students carry credits which may count towards BA degrees if they decide later to register in the undergraduate programme. In 1992, 11,581 associate students enrolled in undergraduate level courses (*ibid.*). Students who complete the course work and pass the final exam receive a *Course Certificate*, and a *Letter of Course Completion* is sent to students completing the course satisfactorily, or not sitting the exam or failing it. The *Letter of Completion* was discontinued from 1991 on (*ibid.*).

In addition to courses selected from the undergraduate curriculum for associate students, the British Open University developed, and continues to develop, a wide range of continuing education courses and study packs. Continuing education programmes provide courses for community education, in-service teacher training, health and social welfare, technological updating materials, management education, etc. The British Open University offers a range of courses in the latest manufacturing techniques and computer applications to help engineers and managers stay at the leading edge of new technology. Some of these courses, funded by the Science and Engineering Research Council, are structured, modular courses, leading to a postgraduate diploma or MSc degree. Others are self-contained packs. The University also produces a wide range of study packs and courses on community and family issues, others on cultural subjects. Most are intended for use by people who wish to study on their own. Some are linked to *tutor packs* to allow employers or community groups to set up study groups and training sessions. In 1992, for instance, 21,161 students were enrolled in short associate courses; 15,346 of them were registered in the Open Business School. In that year, the British Open University sold 74,338 packs of learning materials (*ibid.*).

The Open Business School was set up in 1983 and established as a fully-fledged faculty of the University in 1987. It offers a range of management training opportunities at different levels. Short, practical courses for existing or newly promoted managers are available to individuals, groups and organisations. For those who want to acquire some form of qualification, taking a series of these courses can lead to the professional Certificate in Management and Professional Diploma in Management. The upper tier is a distance-taught Masters in Business Administration (MBA), for which either the Diploma or a good honours degree is the normal entry requirement. The British Open University's Business School is currently the largest in Europe.

From the very beginning the British Open University developed post-graduate and research degrees. The normal minimum entrance requirements for postgraduate students are identical to those in British mainstream universities. Masters degrees are awarded through courses taught in mathematics, literature, advanced educational and social research methods, industrial applications of computers, manufacturing, management and education. 6,707 students were enrolled in taught master courses in 1992 (*ibid.*). The University also provides opportunities to take research-based degrees of BPhil, MPhil, MSc, MA and PhD, full or part-time: 193 full-time and 562 part-time research students were registered in such programmes in 1992 (*ibid.*).

Universidad Nacional de Educación a Distancia

Spain's UNED provides five different study tracks: 16 academic degree programmes (*carreras*) are offered by its nine faculties, leading to the degree of Licenciado; third cycle studies toward doctoral degrees and other post-graduate courses; an *Admission Course* for people over 25 who lack sufficient entry requirements; vocational programmes, such as a diploma of *Asistente Tecnico Sanitario* for hospital nursing, a special course for teachers in business administration, etc.; and open distance learning programmes (*Matricula Abierta*), which are free enrolment courses, for those who want a university education without completing the whole cycle leading to a *Licenciado* degree. In the Open Programs students can choose any course or combination of courses they like (García-Garrido, 1988, 205–206; EADTU, 1994a, 140–141; ICDL, 1997).

Basically, UNED offers the same academic curricula as other Spanish universities and shares common degree categories. Most study tracks are of a five-year duration with the exception of Engineering which takes six years and Computer Science (systems engineering and computer assisted management) which requires only three years. A typical five-year programme consists of approximately 25 courses (asignaturas). However, study duration as it is specified above, is only a minimum for full-time students. Even at campus universities, studies frequently last longer than officially specified. Clearly, for part-timers the study period towards a *Licenciado* degree could last even longer! The structure of the long degree in Spain, which is typical in many European countries, may account for the low completion rates in Spanish universities; less than 50% of enrolled students graduate (Teichler, 1993a, 28). It is far harder to keep on studying over six to ten years, than it is over a three-year bachelor degree. Table 4.2 shows the distribution of academic courses at UNED according to its nine faculties, the breakdown of registered students by faculty, and the main disciplines and subjects in each faculty.

Table 4.2 shows nearly 36% of UNED's students were enrolled in the Law Faculty in 1993. The popularity of law studies in Spain is explained by the fact that most civil service posts require a degree in law, and most law students do not intend to become practising lawyers. Law schools are large schools in conventional Spanish universities as well. Over 40% of UNED's students were enrolled in social science faculties, which underlines the relatively high demand for social science programmes in Spanish universities, a trend notice-able in other countries. Although 133 courses, out of the total of 605 courses in 1993, were in sciences, only 6% of the student body enrolled in science. Furthermore, the percentage of students in humanities (geography & history; philology; philosophy & education) was quite low, altogether less than 15%. In addition to the Engineering Faculty, UNED runs from 1994 onward a Techni-cal School of Computer Science, providing short-cycle three-year degrees in *Information System Technical Engineering* and *Management Systems Technical*

Table 4.2. Academic Courses at UNED Distributed by Faculties, 1993*

Variables	Faculty								
	Law	Geography & History	Philology	Philosophy & Educat.	Psychology	Economics & Bus. Stud	Sciences	Engineering	Politics & Sociology
Number of courses (total = 605)	25	33	45	100	51	67	133	86	65
Breakdown of students by faculties (total = 105,649)	35.7%	6.5%	2.1%	6.3%	13.9%	19.2%	6.0%	3.1%	7.2%
Disciplines & Subjects	Law	Geography History	Spanish Philology	Philosophy Education	Psychology Research Methods	Economics Business Administ.	Physics Maths. Chemistry Adaptation courses	Industrial Engin. Electronics Energy	Political Studies Sociology

* Based on: UNED (1992b) *Past and Present*, Madrid: Universidad Nacional de Educacion a Distancia, 5–6; EADTU (1993b) *Mini-Directory*, Herleen: European Association of Distance Teaching Universities, 30–31; UNED (1993) *Información General*, Madrid: UNED, 200–239.

Engineering (UNED, 1996). Formal requirements for short-cycle courses are identical to long course programmes in Spain, unlike the situation in Germany, for example, where entry requirements to universities and *Fachhochschulen* differ (Teichler, 1993a).

UNED offers a broad spectrum of 58 doctoral programmes built around 790 courses in different faculties (UNED, 1996); 2,250 students were registered in doctoral programmes in 1995 (*ibid.*). UNED sets a great store on research and is highly ranked in this aspect in Spanish higher education. Apart from doctoral programmes, UNED also offers two-year postgraduate pro-grammes, where students acquire a basic grounding in different research fields. During these two-year taught courses, the student has to obtain 32 credits, at least 12 and no more than 24, to be obtained in the first year. Some postgraduate courses lead to a master's degree. Postgraduate courses are offered in: foreign trade; financial auditing; the national taxation system; adult education; human sexuality (leading to a master's degree); environmental education (leading to a master's degree); behaviour therapy (leading to a master's degree). These postgraduate courses, registered 2,076 students in 1995 (*ibid.*).

The *Admission Course* for students over 25 years prepares adult students for the University entrance examination. This exam is available at all Spanish universities, though only UNED offers a special preparatory programme. The course is inter-disciplinary in nature, and covers the following disciplines: Spanish language, basic mathematics, philosophy, literature, world history, art history, biology, and additional special courses for entry to a specific faculty. For instance, to enter the Economics Faculty, the *Admission Course* includes an introduction to economics; for the Science Faculty, students have to study physics and further advanced mathematics (UNED, 1993, 193–199). 23,553 students enrolled in the *Admission Course* in 1993 (García-Aretio, 1995, 93).

UNED created special programmes for further study, cultural advance-ment or professional improvement. Continuing education courses cater for professionals who require or seek updating in their work. A very high demand exists for this type of course, which is offered in three broad areas: health sciences, nursing assistants and physiotherapists; education, especially for in-service training for primary and secondary school teachers; and economics, coordinated by the Faculty of Economics and Business Studies. Many courses are drawn upon academic programmes. Some are developed specifically for update and training. Special teacher training programmes enrolled 8,041 in 1995 (*ibid.*).

The *Open Distance Learning Program* opens up avenues to study academic subjects which remain outside conventional syllabuses, involving personal interests or hobbies (comparable to the associate student programmes at the British Open University). In 1995, the programme included some 40 courses. No academic requirements are needed for entry. The programme is run by the Vice Rectorate of Continuing Education. Courses are supervised by UNED academic staff and other recognised experts. Courses are offered in law, science, engineering, education, philology, philosophy and economics. In 1995, 5,135 were enrolled in the Open Courses at UNED (*ibid.*).

The Open University of Israel

The Open University of Israel provides academic studies, leading to bachelor degrees; professional training in technology through the School of Technology; special translated courses for study abroad; and continuing education in the fields of: management, teacher training, cultural enrichment, community studies, film and video production, and language studies. Until 1996, the Open University of Israel was authorised to teach only towards bachelor degrees. In 1996, it was granted permission to teach towards an MSc degree in Computer Sciences. Two additional master level programmes in the areas of *Democracy Studies* and *Curriculum and Management in Education* were submitted in 1997 for the approval of the Council for Higher Education, and are currently under consideration.

No faculties or departments existed prior to 1997, when a structural reform assigned the various courses into seven disciplinary departments: Literature, Music and Arts; History and Judaic Studies; Psychology and Education; Sociology and Political Science; Management and Economics; Computer Science and Mathematics; Sciences. Until 1996 two main administrative organs existed—one responsible for the development of courses, the second for instruction. Courses were, and are, developed by *ad hoc* course teams. A bachelor degree is conferred after completing at least 108 credit points (equivalent to a three-year bachelor degree at other universities). Most courses are worth six credit points (the equivalent of six taught hours per semester). Of the 108 credit points, no more than 36 may be at an introductory level and no less than 24 credits must be at an advanced level (equivalent to third and fourth level courses at the British Open University). Introductory courses are generally basic, and provide a broad overview of a field. Unlike the British Open University, specific introductory courses are not compulsory for beginning students. Students may choose as a first course any of the introductory or intermediate level courses that do not impose specific entry requirements. Students register for each course separately. Some take only one course per semester. Others, mainly those enrolled within a group framework, study up to five courses per semester. All students pay the same tuition fee—approximately $ 350 for a six-credit course. No differentiation is made between those who declare that they study towards a degree and those who take a course for any other reason.

Courses were divided from the very start into four broad areas: humanities; social sciences and education; mathematics and computer science; life and natural sciences. Students are not obliged to choose a certain study programme, although if they are to get a degree they must follow certain guidelines and requirements. Students pursuing humanities and social sciences must complete 84 of the 108 credit points in the humanities and/or social sciences, and 18 of the 24 advanced credit points required for completion of a degree, in the broad chosen field of study (e.g., social science and humanities). Students pursuing sciences and mathematics must accumulate at least 84 points of the 108 credit points in sciences and/or mathematics, and at least 24 of the 84 points are required in advanced courses in these areas. Students may construct a modular degree of courses in several disciplines. Or, they may concentrate on one or two subjects, such as mathematics, economics, psychology, etc. In the last decade, growing pressure came from students to have more discipline-focused programmes, clearly named in their BA degrees. Since 1994, the Open University of Israel grants more focused degrees specifying two majors, such as: Economics and Administration, Sociology and Administration, Psychology and Sociology, Education and Psychology, Education and Sociology, Sociology and Political Science. Table 4.3 sets out the distribution of academic courses at undergraduate level according to the Open University of Israel's four fields of study, the breakdown of registered students by fields of study, and the main disciplines plus subjects in each field.

As Table 4.3 makes clear, the 466 courses are distributed reasonably evenly across the four fields of study, but the number of registered students is highly skewed towards courses in social sciences. This reflects a general trend in Israeli higher education and elsewhere, according to which applied social sciences, business and managerial studies are highly attractive with a better market pay-off. It is extremely difficult and highly competitive to be admitted to departments of economics, business administration and psychology at regular Israeli universities (Central Bureau of Statistics, 1997, 34). High demand for social science studies is reflected in the concentration—nearly two thirds of the Open University of Israel's students—in this area. Though 126 courses were offered in 1993 in Life and Natural Sciences, only some 7% of Open University of Israel students followed courses in science disciplines.

Israelis and Hebrew speakers living abroad wishing to take Open University of Israel's courses can do so by mail. For speakers of English, Spanish and Russian, the Open University of Israel has translated a limited number of academic courses, mainly in Jewish studies. These courses are either studied for credit or for general knowledge purposes, both by individuals and organisations. In 1997, some 8,000 students were enrolled in such courses in the areas of the former Soviet Union (President's Report, 1997, 43).

The School of Technology of the Open University was established in 1984 in cooperation with the Center for Educational Technology. The study programme was developed to educate and update professionals in the rapidly advancing fields of technology. Initial courses designed by the School of Technology focused on computer software and electronics. Completion of a one to two-year study programme, in addition to a final practical project and government-authorised exams, leads to three levels of professional diplomas,

Table 4.3. Academic Courses at the Open University of Israel Distributed by Fields of Study (1993)*

Variables	Faculty			
	Humanities	Social Sciences & Education	Mathematics & Computer Sciences	Sciences
Number of courses (total = 466)	133	127	80	126
Breakdown of registered students by field of study** (total = 41,546)	17.1%	64.3%	11.8%	6.8%
Disciplines & Subjects	History Judaic Studies Philosophy Literature Music Arts	Sociology Psychology Economics Administration Political Science Education Statistics & Research Methods	Mathematics Computer Science	Physics Chemistry Biology Geology

*Based on: Open University of Israel (1993) *Handbook of Courses*, The Open University of Israel Press, V–XIII.
President's Report (1995) *The Open University of Israel, 1994/5*, The Open University of Israel Press, 106.
**Number of registered students differs from the total student body because students may register for more than one course.

ranging from technicians to applied technical engineers in electronics and computers. In-service programmes tailored to the needs of industry and manufacturing plants are also available in such fields as microprocessors, television, data communication, computer graphics, and computer programming languages. In 1993, around 850 students enrolled in the School of Technology (President's Report, 1993, 78).

The Open University of Israel offers a range of in-service teacher education courses working together with the Ministry of Education and Culture in fields such as curriculum planning and evaluation, alternative evaluation methods, computer technology in education, educational administration, special education, language acquisition, implementation of new disciplinary curricula. In 1993, around 3,000 students were enrolled in continuing education courses for teachers (*ibid.*, 51–53).

The Open University of Israel runs a special Unit for Continuing Education for Executives (*Tafnit* in Hebrew), geared to professional updating and upgrading for executives and managers in a broad range of activities. Study programmes include individual courses through to diplomas and certificates in management, accounting, tax, financial investments, etc. In 1993, 2,243 participated in *Tafnit's* programmes (*ibid.*, 90).

A special department is responsible for developing enrichment courses of a general nature in a variety of subjects: theatre, music, cinema, literature, philosophy, science, international relations, geography excursions both within Israel and abroad, ethnic cultures, etc. Cultural enrichment courses enjoy an immense popularity with the public, with over 6,000 students enrolled for these programmes in 1993 (*ibid.*, 91).

The Media Division which is responsible for producing audio and video programmes, also operates a School for Film and Video Production, that awards diplomas and certificates. Over 500 students were enrolled in this School in 1993 (*ibid.*, 109).

The School of Language Studies is another popular school and offers a compendium of courses with special focus on the English language. A graded programme from elementary English to academic level English allows students to improve their English proficiency to the level required by the Open University of Israel for a bachelor's degree. The English courses are open to the general public. Other languages taught within the School of Languages include French, Arabic, Spanish, German, Italian, Russian and Chinese. 4,140 students studied within the School of languages in 1993 (*ibid.*, 84).

FernUniversität

The FernUniversität is one of the six Gesamthochschulen in North Rhine-Westphalia. The purpose of the *Gesamthochschulen* was to combine both academic subject matters usually taught at universities, with vocationally oriented courses, found in *Fachhochschulen*. In general, high status is accorded in Germany to professional and vocational education, even in its elitist universities. The academic curriculum of the FernUniversität is unambiguously tied to a professional/vocational bias.

Peters, the FernUniversität's founding Rector, looking back over some twenty years, admitted that several important faculties were still absent at the FernUniversität. The issue was a delicate one to solve. "Should it become an institute of continuing education or limit itself to higher continuing education or should it become a conventional university teaching at a distance? This discussion was nourished by political convictions, progressive and conservative views on education, strategic and tactical considerations, and naturally also by sound interests. The academic faculty preferred a traditional structure, since it was more suitable to their becoming recognised in their scientific communities, whereas a new and experimental organisation would probably mean the end of their academic careers. Students in the various bodies of the university's self-government demanded a more practical orientation for the courses, open access and more weekend seminars, and emphasised the importance of continuing education. Between these two positions there were also a number of mediating and integrating points of view" (Peters, 1997, 64).

Finally, it was decided that the FernUniversität should first seek an academic reputation. Only genuine scholarly achievements in research and teaching could ensure recognition both by the public and by the academic world. Thus, it was decided first to develop degree courses; second, postgraduate courses; and third, continuing education courses. Such an order of priorities was announced by Peters to the Senate in April 1977 (ibid., 65).

The main guideline for choosing which academic fields of study should be included at the FernUniversität centred on subjects for which a noticeable lack of places existed at conventional universities, or, as a second consideration, where it was highly probable such a shortage would loom in the near future (Schuemer, 1993). The two subjects chosen were economics and computer science. Since it is impossible to teach computer science without some mathematical background, it was decided at the start to provide mathematics and computer science in a joint faculty (later divided into two faculties). As all subjects selected were also to contribute teacher training (*Lehrerausbildung/ Weiterbildung*), a faculty for educational and social sciences was also founded. Later, faculties of law and electrical engineering were added (Peters, 1988, 1997).

Currently the FernUniversität has six faculties: economics; mathematics; computer science; education, social sciences and arts; electrical engineering; and law. They have developed and organised research and teaching in the same way as other universities in Germany, except that the courses are delivered by distance teaching methods. This extends to doctorates as well. *Habilitations* are also possible (EADTU, 1994a, 40). Students in Germany can easily transfer from one university to another. Tuition is free in Germany. FernUniversität students have to pay a charge for course materials.

The six faculties are subdivided into 85 subjects (ICDL, 1997). Each subject is usually the responsibility of one professor with two to four lower rank staff (EADTU, 1994, 40). The first degrees granted are either *Diplom I* or *II*, or *Magister Artium*. The underlying principles of each degree are explained later. Table 4.4 sets out the distribution of academic courses at the FernUniversität by its six faculties, the breakdown of registered students by faculties, and the main disciplines and subjects covered by each faculty.

As Table 4.4 suggests, the academic curriculum of the FernUniversität consists mainly of professionally oriented courses. In 1992, over 50% of the students were enrolled in the economics faculty, which from the very start was perceived as having high priority. Although more than half the courses (736 out of 1435) were in the fields of education, social sciences and arts, only 20% of the students were enrolled in these courses. The fact that all the subjects and disciplines of the arts, social sciences (except economics) and education are grouped into one faculty reflects the marginal place these subjects occupied in the FernUniversität's overall curriculum.

With the exception of the diploma in Industrial Engineering, degree programmes are offered either as of three-year duration for full-time students (six-year programme for part-timers, *Diplom I*) or of four-years' duration (eight years for part-timers, *Diplom II* and *Magister Artium*). Students are advised to allow an additional six months for writing the dissertation (*Diplomarbeit*). In reality, studies last much longer, as is the case in UNED. They are divided into two stages: the initial stage (*Grundstudium,* stage I studies), and the main or advanced stage (*Haupstudium,* stage II studies). Foundation studies take two years full-time. After eight semesters (four years for part-time students), and before being admitted to the stage II courses, students pass an intermediate exam known as *Diplom-Vorprüfung* or *Zwischenprufung*. All students must pass this examination before being allowed to continue with the next stage.

All courses developed for academic degrees are multi-purpose courses and are also used for continuing education programmes. The FernUniversität also offers specialist continuing education courses such as: introduction to the profession of a lawyer; introduction to Japanese civil law; scientific advanced further education; forms of psychotherapy; computer science; philosophy of economics. Special entrance requirements are imposed for some of these individual courses. Special fees are charged in continuing education courses.

Supplementary study programmes and postgraduate programmes help graduate applicants to earn a further professional or vocational qualification. Supplementary study programmes in Electrical Engineering are targeted at students who have successfully completed a course of study in Electrical Engineering at a *Fachhochschule*. The duration is five semesters of full-time studies. The final qualification is *Diplom-Ingenieur*.

The Department of Law was originally conceived to train lawyers and teachers of law. Together with Düsseldorf University, the FernUniversität

Table 4.4. Academic Courses at the FernUniversität Distributed by Faculties (1992)*

Variable	Economics	Mathematics	Computer Science	Education, Social Sciences & Arts	Electrical Engineering	Law
Number of courses (total = 1,435)	272	118	81	736	104	134
Breakdown of students by faculties (total = 52,759)	51.3%	4.6%	13.5%	20.0%	6.3%	3.3%
Disciplines & Subjects	Economics Business Administration	Mathematics Systems Analysis	Computer Science	Education Sociology Philosophy German Literature History Political Economics Psychology Political Science	Electrical Engineering	Law

* Based on:
FernUniversität (1992) *Das Studium an der FernUniversität: Informationen zum Studium*, Hagen: FernUniversität, 25-32.
FernUniversität (1993) *Personal und Kursverzeichnis: Hinweise für Studierende*, Hagen: FernUniversität.
Schuemer, R. (1993) *Personal Communication.*
EADTU (1994a) *Universities Membership 1994*, Herleen: European Association of Distance Teaching Universities, 43-47.

currently offers a complete curriculum in law. About 80 courses in law are available, and they are available at both universities.

FernUniversität also offers orientation programmes. Study units selected from the first semesters explain the demands of studying at a distance and the performance level required. Such orientation courses are available in the departments of economics, education, social sciences and arts.

Athabasca University

Athabasca University set out to develop a new and radical curriculum (Hughes, 1980). John Daniel who served as Athabasca's Vice President for a brief period, from 1977 till the end of the decade, claimed that in reality it: "concentrated more on the distance delivery of a fairly standard curriculum" (Daniel, 1997, 9). In the context of Canadian higher education, it contains elements of a *standard curriculum*, but it is a curriculum quite different from the programmes in the four other distance teaching universities, examined here. Julia Kwong (1993) who analysed the shift of programmes in Canadian universities during the 1980s towards a "business model" concluded: "The proportion of course offerings in humanities declined, whereas those in professional schools increased. Commerce and business administration grew from 5.8% of the student population in 1967 to 12.9% in 1984... New courses and programmes were addressing issues of great concern to powerful lobby groups. Others were offered simply because these could attract students... Expansion of courses in certain areas in a period of retrenchment had ramifications for traditional and less *popular* disciplines" (*ibid.*, 71). These general trends, typical of most Canadian universities, are clearly reflected in Athabasca University's programmes.

At the beginning, Athabasca University had two faculties: the faculty of arts and sciences, and the faculty of administration studies (Hughes, 1980; Morrison & Saraswati, 1988). Currently it has three: a faculty of arts, a faculty of sciences, and a faculty of administration studies. The faculty of arts covers both arts and social science courses. Athabasca University courses fulfil five distinct purposes: studies towards bachelor and master degrees; certificate studies geared mainly for professional upgrading and training; transfer programmes providing courses for degree requirements of other universities (mainly in education, nursing and social work); professional recognition (specialist courses entitling the students to obtain professional qualifications recognised by accounting associations, the Institute of Canadian Bankers, the Canadian Institute of Certified Administrative Managers, etc.); and courses for professional development and recreational purposes (Athabasca University, 1992a, 7).

Table 4.5 describes the distribution of academic courses at Athabasca University according to faculty, the breakdown of registered students by faculty, and the main disciplines and subjects in each faculty.

*Table 4.5. Academic Courses at Athabasca University by Faculties (1992)**

Variables	Faculty of Arts	Faculty of Sciences	Faculty of Administration Studies
Number of courses (total = 262)	177	45	40
Breakdown of registered students by fields of study** (total = 18, 175)	48.3%	22.6%	29.1%
Disciplines & Subjects	English, French, History, Humanities, Philosophy, Human Geography, Economics, Native Studies, Political Science, Psychology, Anthropology, Sociology, Labour Studies, Women's Studies	Biology, Chemistry, Mathematics, Computing Science, Geology, Physical Geography, Environmental Studies, Nursing, Nutrition, Science	Accounting, Administration Applied Studies, Commerce, Finance, Legal Studies, Industrial Relations, Tax, Marketing, Management, Organizational Behaviour, Public Administration

*Based on:
Athabasca University (1992a) *Athabasca University 1992–3 Calendar—Canada's Open University*, Athabasca University, 136–142.
Athabasca University (1992d) *Registrations by Discipline*, Athabasca University, Table 2.3.3.
**Number of registered students differs from the total student body because students may register for more than one course.

The bulk of Athabasca University's curricula is concentrated on social sciences and administration. 28% of the student body, enrolled in social science disciplines in the faculty of arts. Courses divide into three levels: preparatory courses, introductory level courses, senior level courses. Currently, Athabasca University organises six undergraduate degrees in administration, arts, commerce, nursing, science, and general studies. Degree programmes last between two to three years of full time study. From 1994, Athabasca University has also taught two master degrees: in distance education and business administration (Crawford & Spronk, 1995).

In the *Bachelor of Administration* degree programme students concentrate on one of three areas: business administration, public organisation, or organisational behaviour. In the *Bachelor of Arts* programme, students must choose a major from one of seven areas: Canadian Studies, English, French, History, Information Systems, Psychology, or Sociology. The *Bachelor of Commerce* degree is a limited enrolment programme available to full-time or part-time students in Calgary and Edmonton. Applicants must have completed two years (equal to 60 credits) of course work at another recognised post-secondary institution. Students are required to study full-time and attend courses at the learning centre. The *Bachelor of General Studies* degree affords students the most flexibility to create a programme to suit their individual needs. The *Bachelor of Nursing* degree caters for Registered Nurses. It provides nurses with the intellectual, technical and cultural components of both a professional and a liberal university education. The *Bachelor of Science* degree dispenses a general science education. In 1992, 3,597 students out of a total 11,352 were enrolled in degree programmes (Athabasca University, 1992d).

Athabasca University also organises eight university certificate programmes in accounting, advanced accounting, administration, French language proficiency, health development administration, information systems, labour relations, public administration. 1,086 students studied for various certificates in 1992 (*ibid.*). Interestingly, almost 60% of Athabasca University's students followed non-programme courses (*ibid.*). In this sense, Athabasca University stands out from the other four distance teaching universities, where the majority of students are enrolled for academic degrees.

A unique study format at Athabasca University is the *capstone* programme. The University's courses are taught on college campuses. This allows graduates of two-year "university transfer" programmes in the colleges to complete their degree while remaining in their own community (Paul, 1990). Such courses are often taught by community college instructors backed by local facilities, such as the registrar's office, a library, and a student-services unit. Athabasca University exercises control by hiring the instructors, monitoring the curriculum through its course packages, setting and marking the final exams. The programme began in the late 1980s, and in 1992, 96 students were enrolled in the *capstone* programme (Athabasca University, 1992d).

Degrees and Diplomas

Degree and diploma requirements in different countries show great variety and variation. Even specific terms have different meanings. For instance, a *Diplom* in Germany denotes an academic degree in science, engineering, social sciences and economics, whereas a *Diploma* in Israel describes a qualification awarded after completion of short-cycle non-degree programmes, usually following a first degree (Jablonska-Skinder & Teichler, 1992). The length of studies toward a degree, the accumulation of credits, accreditation for prior learning and programs' composition have an immense effect both on access and completion rates in each national setting. So we may grasp more fully those variations between different distance teaching universities in respect of their degree and diploma programmes, a brief outline is provided to clarify the particular definitions and degree structures in each of the five national cases.

United Kingdom

The ordinary and honours degree system in the UK is well nigh unique and certainly complicated to grasp to external eyes. Jablonska-Skinder and Teichler (1992) in a comprehensive *Handbook on Higher Education Diplomas in Europe*, wrote: "The system of higher education diplomas in the UK is much more complex and more difficult to understand for both British citizens and foreigners than any other system of diplomas in the European community" (*ibid.*, 266). The term *degree* refers to the successful termination of what is considered to be a complete course programme at universities or a complete university-level programme at other institutions of higher education. There are possibilities, however, for concluding higher education courses with an award, which is formally called a *degree*, but which is less demanding in standards and qualifications required. It does not open access to advanced courses, and is named in a way that hints at a lower level. The lower level might be called a *Pass*, or *Ordinary* or a *General Bachelor* or a similar name. In all cases, the absence of the phrase *honours degree*, points out a level somewhat below the usual university standard. A holder of a general degree would not be admitted to research training and in all likelihood not to a taught master's course of one-year duration either (Neave, 1997).

An honours degree indicates a complete qualification of a university standard. In it are four levels: First Class Honours; Second Class (Division I) Honours; Second Class (Division II) Honours; and Third Class Honours. In the case where the term *honours* is not appended to the title of the first degree, its holder might have taken part in a lower-level programme or have been performing less well than is considered the university standard in a regular *honours* programme. Principally, the main difference between ordinary and honours degrees is the level of specialisation during the third year of studies (*ibid.*).

In Scotland, ordinary degrees involve three-year programmes, while honours degrees require four years to complete. The British Open University adopted the Scottish system. Six credits (equivalent to three years full time study) counted as an ordinary degree, and those opting for an honours degree needed two more credits at third and fourth level courses. This division was abolished in 1993, when the British Open University adopted a standard common to both regular and honours degrees as in other British universities. One may obtain an ordinary degree without taking any courses at third level or fourth level (Platt, 1997). Tracking into ordinary or honours degrees depends to a great extent on students' achievements in first and second year courses.

Most of the British Open University's graduates are awarded ordinary degrees. Daniel reckoned it to be misleading to compare the British Open University's graduates to graduates of most distance teaching universities. Referring to the relatively low number of graduates at UNED at the celebration of its tenth anniversary (3,000 graduates out of 60,000 student registrations), Daniel argued: "Given the nature of the Licenciado degree, its output of graduates should be compared to the 2,000 honours graduates rather than to the 40,000 ordinary bachelor degrees approved by the British Open University at its first decade" (Daniel, 1996a, 186).

Even so, the number of British Open University's graduates is impressive, and is clearly higher than in other distance teaching universities analysed here. Over 30% of enrolled students graduate compared with 4–7% in other distance teaching universities (Daniel, 1996a). In 1992, 24% of the BA graduates (1,768 out of 7,230) obtained BA honours degrees. The accumulated total of honours degrees produced by the British Open University up to 1992 was 23,398 out of a total of 122,552 graduates (Open University, 1993a).

Originally, the British Open University decided to award only the BA as a first degree, to encourage students to build a profile from a variety of courses and fields. Currently, the British Open University also awards BSc degrees. Bachelor's degrees are given in broad fields, such as *BA in Social Sciences*. Students may request a certificate to show that the majority of courses taken with grades were in a specific discipline. In the past decade, students pressed for named degrees in specific discipline to be added, e.g., *Bachelor in Psychology*. In April 1997, the Senate approved a motion to introduce named British Open University degrees. A group has been formed to implement this decision (Platt, 1997).

A further bemusing feature of the British degree system is for some bachelor's degrees to be awarded for advanced study. A BPhil certifies an advanced in-depth study of a single field or a combination of fields. Some bachelor's degrees designate advanced study, the BLitt and BD (Bachelor of Divinity), for instance. Masters' degrees are awarded after one or two years of advanced study. The British Open University's first taught postgraduate course was a BPhil in advanced educational and social research methods. Its research degrees include BPhil, MPhil, and PhD degrees awarded on completion of a programme of research and advanced study and after the submission of a dissertation or thesis. In 1992, the British Open University awarded 58 PhD diplomas, 11 further research degrees and 1,295 taught master degrees (Open University, 1993a).

At the British Open University, students can obtain up to four credits for previous educational experience, out of the six needed for a degree. Thus, the minimal *residency* requirement for a first degree at the British Open University is two credits. Teachers gain three credits for their professional studies prior to enrolment. Thus, the British Open University could award its first degrees in 1973, just two years after opening.

Spain

Two clearly distinct types of first degree programmes exist in Spanish universities: course programmes of long duration (five or six years of full-time study), and course programmes of short duration (three years). Faculties (*facultades*) teach the *Licenciado* degree. There are 26 possible titles of the *Licenciatura*, generally referring to broad fields of study. Higher technical schools (*escuelas técnicas superiores*) confer the degrees of *Arquitecto* and *Ingeniero* after six years of study. Medicine and veterinary studies also last for a minimum of six years. The titles of *Diplomado* or *Arquitecto Técnico* are conferred after a short three-year course offered by university schools (*escuelas universitarias*), run by universities. Spanish universities teach both long and short degrees. UNED functions an *Escuela Técnica Superiore* for engineers in the fields of industrial, electronics and energy engineering with programmes of six years, and an *Escuela Universitaria de Informatica* with programmes of a three-year duration.

Postgraduate studies lead either to certificates or to master degrees. The highest academic degree is the *Doctorado*. Doctoral studies require a minimum of two years of study, after which a thesis must be submitted. The average time spent on doctoral studies is about five years (Jablonska-Skinder & Teichler, 1992, 226).

UNED provides the full range of degrees up to doctorates. At present, UNED has the highest number of postgraduate and doctoral students, of other distance teaching universities in this study. 2,250 students were enrolled in doctoral programmes at UNED in 1995, and a further 2,076 in other post-graduate courses (UNED, 1996). Those who finish UNED degrees have no problem in having their credentials recognised. Students may obtain credit exemptions and transfer credits to other universities. Accreditation regulations apply to all Spanish universities including UNED.

Israel

In Israel, first degrees are earned in most disciplines after three to four years full-time study. Master degrees are awarded after two to three years of further study after the bachelor degree. Most students at Israeli universities study for specialised disciplinary degrees (e.g., Bachelor in Physics, Bachelor in

Literature). The field of study is usually stated on the BA document. The Open University of Israel, from the start, organised around broader degrees, such as a Bachelor in Humanities and Social Sciences, Bachelor in Natural Sciences and Mathematics. Yet, many students, and most particularly the younger ones, preferred discipline-focused degrees. Such specialisation makes their admission to postgraduate studies at other universities less difficult.

As we have pointed out, permission to grant a master-level degree was conferred upon the Open University of Israel only in 1996. That the Open University of Israel for nearly twenty years awarded only first degrees undermined its status as a university in Israel. One of the major distinctions between universities and non-university institutions is that the latter (with only two exceptions) are entitled only to confer first degrees. Abraham Ginzburg, the Open University of Israel's president from 1975 to 1987, was of the opinion that: "We should have started to develop master's programmes in various subjects much earlier (and this is closely linked to the smallness of the senior academic faculty). It should be noted that, in Israel every such programme must get approval from the Council for Higher Education" (Ginzburg, 1997, 85–86).

The Open University of Israel accredits previous studies at other universities or tertiary education institutions up to a maximum of 60 out of the total 108 needed for a degree. Teachers have a much less generous accreditation for their three-year professional training when compared with the British Open University. Their exemption may range from 18 up to 36 credits, depending on their training profile.

Germany

In Germany, as in Spain, study toward first degrees is relatively long, requiring an average of six years to complete (Jablonska-Skinder & Teichler, 1992, 125). Peters, the founding Rector of the FernUniversität, made an important rider: "One must bear in mind that there are no *colleges* in the Federal Republic and that our diplomas and master's degrees have definitely no parallels with bachelor's degrees abroad with regard to the prescribed contents and levels of aspiration of the corresponding courses of study and their sequence" (Peters, 1997, 75).

Earlier we noted that the term *Diplom* in German denotes an academic degree in science, engineering, social science and economics subjects, conferred mainly by universities and *Fachhochschulen*. It is a full academic and professional qualification and entitles its holder to work independently in the corresponding professional field. During the diploma course programme, students must pass an interim examination and receive a *Vor-Diplom* certificate. The final *Diplom* examination entails the completion of a thesis within a period of six to nine months (at universities) or within three to six months (at *Fachhochschulen*), in addition to a comprehensive set of written and oral examinations. The examinations are administered by the professors of the respective institutions (Jablonska-Skinder & Teichler, 1992).

The *Magister Artium* is an academic degree in the humanities and social sciences. It is conferred only by the universities or by institutions of equivalent standing. The degree of *Magister*, contrary to that of *Diplom*, is not related to any particular professional field. Corresponding course programmes must be completed either in two major subjects or in one major and two minor subjects. Examinations are set and administered by the professors of the university. The *Magister* is not preceded by any other award, as, for instance, the Bachelor in Anglo-Saxon universities. It represents a level of education equivalent to the *Diplom* and the *Staatsexamen*.

Staatsexamen are equivalent to the *Diplom* and the *Magister* degrees, the difference residing in the purpose and formal organisation of the examination rather than in the content and structure of the study programme. Course programmes and examinations are set by state laws and regulations, while the responsibility for the academic quality and substantive contents remains with the university. The award of the *Staatsexamen* entitles the recipient to be admitted to a doctoral programme. It is also considered to be an entry qualification to civil service positions or the professions of medicine, pharmacy, law and teaching.

The official duration of studies in Germany is eight semesters (four years full-time study) for most fields. It is shorter in certain areas of teacher training and longer in the field of medicine (12 semesters). In reality, a full course of study implies a much greater investment in time than the officially stipulated duration.

The German system of higher education stresses uniformity of quality and standards in institutions of equal status. The difference of prestige among German universities is small when compared to certain countries where a clearly defined hierarchy has prevailed for decades (Teichler, 1986; Peters, 1997). Transfer arrangements exist between all German universities.

In the fields of study that the FernUniversität has chosen to teach its degrees are comparable to other German universities. The FernUniversität covers the following programmes: integrated *Diplom* degree (*Diplom I* and *Diplom II*) in electrical engineering, mathematics, computer sciences, economics; *Magister Artium* degree programmes in education, history, modern German literature; philosophy; sociology, political and social sciences. Subsidiary subjects include: education, law, mathematics, modern German literature, philosophy, psychology, quantitative methods of economics, political science, social sciences, statistics and data analysis.

Canada

In Canada, universities exercise complete and final control over the programmes they teach (Jablonska-Skinder & Teichler, 1992, 75). Hence, undergraduate diplomas and certificates may be as varied as the institutions that award them, both as to content, duration and designations used. Programmes normally range from one to three years' duration, while the requirements of a special certificate programme may be fulfilled in less than a year. Diploma and certificate programmes may also be taught in cooperation with occupational and professional institutes and associations, an arrangement that enables individuals to gain credentials in such fields as banking and real estate. This unique situation explains the large number of students at Athabasca University enrolled in short diploma and certificate programmes.

Two types of bachelor degrees are to be found in Canada: the general (*pass*) degree and the *honours degree*. The general degree requires a minimum of three years of study, though some universities have both three- and four-year general degrees. An *honours* degree requires four years of study and a prescribed amount of specialisation in a stipulated subject. Unlike the situation in the UK, an *honours* degree is not a prerequisite for all postgraduate level studies, though it is recommended in many. Many universities and colleges have cooperative programmes: two-year colleges have joint agreements with universities, so their students may go on to complete a degree at a university, after a two-year programme at the local college.

Athabasca University supports both three and four-year BA programmes. It also organises a programme found nowhere else, namely the *Bachelor of General Studies* (BGS). It can be earned without taking a single course at Athabasca University. In effect, Athabasca University acts as an *accreditation bank* for studies conducted at other higher education institutes. Students may also study toward the whole or part of, the BGS degree at Athabasca. The BGS programme gives "students maximum freedom to develop their own intellectual and academic interests. This does not mean that course selection should be casual; students are expected to ensure that their vocational or personal needs are well defined. Evaluation of the degree for further academic work or by prospective employers usually requires an assessment of the programme as recorded on the student's transcript" (Athabasca University, 1992a, 49).

Athabasca University is also most liberal in its *residency* requirements for its five other bachelor degrees. The *Bachelor of Administration* is a three-year programme (= 90 credits), of which 45 must be taken at Athabasca. *Bachelor of Art* degrees are four-year programmes (= 120 credits), of which only 30 credits are to be taken at Athabasca University. And for the four-year *Bachelor of Commerce*, similarly 30 credits have to be obtained there. The *Bachelor of Nursing* is a two-year programme (= 69 credits) designed for students holding registered nurse diplomas. Only 12 credits must be taken at Athabasca University. The *Bachelor of Sciences* is a four-year programme, in which 30 credits of science courses have to be taken on site. These collaborative degree schemes are unique to Canada, and demonstrate the very special type of degrees Athabasca University organises.

On Closure and Openness of Academic Curricula

Distance teaching universities are often referred to as *open universities*, even if they are not called an *open university*. They maintain a principle of openness towards access requirements, choice of study tracks, composition of individual academic programmes, place and pace of study. Arguably, most distance teaching universities are more student-centred in their overall educational approach than many traditional and veteran, campus universities. The opportunity to study part-time, to accumulate credits over a long period, to leave and re-enter studies when convenient, to build up a multidisciplinary or focused curriculum based on one's individual interests, to study with high-level learning materials specially developed to be user-friendly and self-guiding, these are amongst the most attractive features of distance teaching universities. They explain their very substantial contribution to the democratisation of higher education.

Yet, some features in the working of distance teaching universities reflect "closure" rather than "openness". *Closure*, as related to academic curricula in distance teaching universities, emerges in three domains: in the range of courses; in tightly structured (and sometimes over-structured) learning materials; and in highly uniform study requirements.

Distance teaching universities are deeply committed to subject-based teaching. One of their major contributions to distance higher education and to higher education at large, lies in the development of demanding yet student-friendly materials, produced by teams and/or conjointly with external experts, instructional designers, editors, media producers, etc. They invest large amounts of money in designing and developing their courses. Only large numbers of students may justify the high cost of such courses. Distance teaching universities cannot afford to cover the full range of courses as large campus universities do, most particularly highly specialised courses aimed at very low numbers of students. In such fields, they may sometimes organise small seminar-based or computer-conferencing courses. All the distance teaching universities in this study develop part of their courses, mainly at advanced levels, from existing textbooks, backed by study guides. Most distance teaching universities decide upon the format to develop different courses, by combining both academic considerations—the substantive content of each study field—and economic factors, potential clienteles for each course, sources of funding. Patterns of development vary considerably between distance teaching universities, between faculties and departments within each distance teaching university, between different level courses, and between continuing education and courses leading to academic degrees. Generally speaking, the range of courses organised by distance teaching universities is more restricted compared to those on offer at large classical universities.

One of the unavoidable consequences of large numbers of students in universities is closer control over the curriculum. In Scott's views: "Greater social openness of the mass university encourages academic closure. Openness increases the pressure for much tighter control over the structure of academic programmes" (Scott, 1995, 161). Furthermore, one of the paradoxes of greater student choice, for many universities, has been an over-regulated curriculum, more detailed prescriptions of aims, objectives and more stringent quality assurance procedures (Guri-Rosenblit, 1993c; 1997a; Tait, 1997). Rigidly structured learning materials govern the transmission of a uniform content to large numbers of students scattered across the nation. The principle of *uniformity* is both the strength and weakness of such a model (Morrison, 1992). Its strength is that the same product, structured in the same manner, is provided to everyone, no matter where one lives or how s/he prefers to study. Hence, it is possible to underwrite both the *quality* and *equality* principles. Its weakness is that it does not take into account the varying needs and learning styles of students. Often, the major response to the diversity of students is to define yet again and structure the objectives, assignments and content of study materials. A tight and logical content structure is often seen as conducive to equally tight and efficient learning (*ibid.*). Cerych and Sabatier (1986) went so far as to see the *sameness* or *universal* principles at the British Open University as *equal deprivation* and *shared misery*. In short, if a service cannot be provided to the whole highly diverse, student body, it should not be offered at all. The British Open University, for instance, remained obdurate to the plea of many students for more frequent tutorials, on the grounds that students in remote areas lacked the necessary transportation to attend study centres frequently. Thus, tutorials remained optional or remedial in nature.

García-Aretio (1995) from UNED observed that the distribution of teaching materials to large numbers of students entails the application of mass production: "This can detract from the flexibility of the organisation as the system must be rigidly programmed and relations among course designers, tutors, etc., and pupils highly structured, this is detrimental to flexibility and attention to personal needs" (*ibid.*, 93).

Over-structured materials may enhance passive learning, though all distance teaching universities devote much thought to the interactive dimensions in their texts. Thus, the limitations inherent to distance learning technologies served as catalysts for the development of original methods in instructional design to increase interactive learning (Parer, 1989a,b; Moore & Kearsley, 1996). Holmberg, for example, developed the notion of *guided didactic conversation* in self-study texts. The principle underlying this concept is that simulated interaction, through the presentation of subject-matter in pre-produced courses, should replace part of the interaction of a regular face-to-face meeting, by forcing students to consider different views, approaches and solutions and generally interact with the course content. Course writers should then *converse* with students through special techniques inserted in the written discourse (Holmberg, 1986, 1995; Ortner et al., 1992).

Scott (1995) claimed that in many mass universities there is also an intriguing sub-text. Students in a mass system, although formally empowered as customers, often lack the cultural traits needed to make genuinely autonomous intellectual decisions. Hence, the increasing preoccupation with guidance and counselling, which may empower students but can also serve as a discreet form of academic surveillance. Highly specific guidelines, directions and counselling are expressions of academic control. Certainly, courses, as well as teaching and learning, at distance teaching universities are highly structured and controlled. Their students may enjoy considerable latitude to devise their overall curriculum, but once enrolled in a particular course, they are subject to stringent requirements and to the principles of *uniformity* and *sameness*.

Academic quality is naturally a prime concern of distance teaching universities. All our case study institutions insist that the standard of their courses and degrees should be at very least comparable in every way to the degrees offered by other universities in each nation. Distance teaching universities, it may be said, pay greater attention than conventional universities to the quality of study materials and teaching. All put in place special quality procedures to monitor the design of their materials, to evaluate tutoring and teaching, and to assess students. Their courses are subject to the unwavering scrutiny of the outside world, as much because of their widespread availability to the public as on account of their transparent nature.

To achieve high quality learning materials, each distance teaching university drew up special quality assurance procedures for course approval, for course design and development. As already pointed out in Chapter 1, the particular interpretation of *academic freedom* in individual states was crucially important in determining the nature of procedures for verifying quality. The British Open University developed the course team model, and scaled-down versions of it operate in the Open University of Israel and of Athabasca University. The author/faculty contract is used by many distance teaching universities, which engage external writers to develop a course or part of a course. It is a usual arrangement at the Open University of Israel, which has a very small number of senior faculty. Spain's UNED and the German Fern-Universität established special institutes to help lecturers design and develop courses, though they are, in effect based on the author/editor model (Smith, 1980). In this arrangement materials written by a faculty member are edited by a professional editor. The work of the editor may be limited to proofreading and assisting with layout or graphics, or it may involve substantial rewriting of the original. Clearly, the course team model is more expensive and slower to produce materials, but the final products are often more refined and better expressed. Differences between distance teaching universities in course production methods explain the variable variation in costs and in course production time. The FernUniversität covered nearly 80 courses in its first year, based mainly on existing books (Peters, 1997). Course production within teams can take between three and five years (Guri-Rosenblit, 1997a).

This lengthy and expensive process built around a team risks producing outdated materials. One of the criticisms of the British Open University made by the Funding Council's teaching assessment programmes, whilst rating the British Open University's teaching as excellent in many disciplines, was that: "Courses took too long to produce, and risked becoming dated during their lifetime" (Daniel, 1996a). It is tremendously difficult indeed to amend, change and revise materials produced over several years. Advanced technologies, and desktop publishing as one of them, bring some remedy by substantially reducing the length of course production and by making the updating of materials less fraught.

Similarly, and alongside quality assurance procedures applied to the design and development of courses, equal rigor applies for course delivery, to the marking of assignments, of final examinations and to tutorials. Desired standards in setting and marking examinations are ensured by elaborate quantitative and subjective analyses and reviews. Most distance teaching universities employ stringent course assessment and evaluation which applies to all students.

Under normal circumstances, the individual lecturer or tutor in any classroom may alter and redefine set assignments and study tasks in the light of the dynamic in teaching. However, teaching faculty in distance teaching universities, both senior faculty and tutors, do not have any latitude whatsoever to make such alterations. The principles of *sameness* and *uniformity* apply to assignments and exams as they do to content. To uphold equal standards, prescribed assignments are the same for all, without any built-in flexibility to accommodate individual differences. Though a variety of support services assist students in their study, learning requirements cannot be modified or changed to meet the preferences of individuals.

The brief presentation of certain aspects of *closure* in the dissemination of academic curricula within distance teaching universities sought to pinpoint some limitations and restrictions inherent in training masses of students by distance teaching methods. Such limitations are offset by the considerable achievements of distance teaching universities in producing first-class teaching materials for use by both their own students and those at conventional universities. Distance teaching universities have raised instructional design in academic study materials to unprecedented heights, and have led the way in introducing formal criteria of excellence and close control into academic teaching. Some have become the largest academic publishing houses in their countries. Since their courses are written in the spoken idiom of each national tongue, many distance teaching universities, the UNED, the FernUniversität and the Open University of Israel, have an important role in helping first degree students to overcome some of the difficulties when assigned to read in English. Most distance teaching universities' courses are delivered through various forms of media. The range of media employed for instructional purposes is analysed in the next chapter.

5

Technologies in the Service of Distance Teaching Universities

Technology's the answer—but what is the question?
Paul (1990, 119)

There is no "right" or "wrong" technology for distance education. Each medium and each technology for delivering it has its own strengths and weaknesses. One of the worst mistakes an organisation or an instructor can make is to become dogmatically committed to delivery by a single medium.
Moore and Kearsley (1996, 99)

Introduction

The quest for appropriate technologies to improve the quality of distance teaching and to offset the lack of interactive social learning which is inherent in a regular classroom setting, lies at the heart of the development of distance education in general, and distance teaching universities in particular. In many respects, distance teaching universities were pioneers in experimenting with a variety of media for producing and delivering high-quality texts and study packages, and for increasing the level of interactivity between student–teacher and student–student in distance learning environments. In the early 1970s distance teaching universities, taken as a whole, were characterised in the mind of the public with the use of broadcasting media, and more generally with a multi-media approach. Distance teaching universities were anxious to adopt a new, innovative image to distinguish themselves from the first generation correspondence institutions (Perry, 1976; Rumble & Harry, 1982). Indeed, the objectives of many distance teaching universities specifically required them to make use of, and experiment with, new media and technologies to improve educational opportunities for adults. Since the late 1980s almost all distance teaching universities have been engaged in investigating the utilisation of inter-active communication and information technologies. New advanced techno-logies have the potential of increasing the efficacy of course production and delivery by developing more portable and effective media. They can produce study materials and dispatch them far more quickly and more cheaply than before (Christoffel, 1986; Paul, 1990). Interactive computer-mediated commu-nication and teleconferencing technologies have the power to improve inter-action between the distant learner and remote databases and knowledge resources as well as to strengthen the interpersonal dimension in distance education. Van Seventer argued that the full-scale use of information tech-nology in education is central to the work of distance teaching universities and other distance education providers. It constitutes a "fascinating challenge, because in this matter we have to perform far better than many traditional counterparts have done and are doing" (van Seventer, 1990, 13).

Self-evidently, we live in a period of transition between an industrial society and an information society. New information technologies affect most spheres of life, including education in its conventional settings (Tifflin & Rajasingham, 1995). As industrial societies become information societies, conventional com-munication systems are becoming information systems. From depending on transport systems to get people and paper to the places where business is done and education is performed, society depends more on telecommunications to move information to where it is needed. The intense experimentation of distance teaching universities with varieties of media and telecommunication technologies for nearly three decades ought to be of prime interest to mainstream universities as well as to other educational establishments, es-pecially when it bears on the potential advantages, obstacles and shortcomings associated with the introduction of different technologies for teaching/learning purposes.

Utilising new and advanced technologies is central to the evolution of all distance teaching universities. It is part of the core business of their everyday workings. However, many expectations which first attached to the potential impact of various technologies over the last two decades have not been met. Paul has pointed out that: "The case for adapting new technologies to the development and delivery of educational materials is a strong one, but, in almost every milieu, the actual experience of implementation has been far less successful than expected" (Paul, 1990, 119–120). In summarising the appli-cation of media in European distance education, Bates noted that: "Some people may perceive from the literature on educational technology and dist-ance education, from Governmental and European Commission initiatives, and from promotional activities by commercial information technology suppliers and manufacturers, that there is a major revolution taking place in distance education, based on advanced technologies. Nothing could be further from the truth... in practice the use of technology in any one institution is in most cases limited to just one or two main media, with perhaps some experimentation with new technologies on one or two courses, or with small numbers of students" (Bates, 1990d, 285).

Such was the state of affairs in 1990. Since then the development and utilisation of interactive teleconferencing technologies and computer-mediated communication have accelerated both within distance teaching universities and classical universities, as well as in business and industry settings. The Internet is nowadays a world-embracing enterprise, affecting education, research, communication, politics, trade, commerce, etc., and abolishing national borders and institutional boundaries. Unquestionably, its impact on both distance teaching universities and campus universities in the very near future is going to be immense. No university can allow itself today to ignore its existence.

Several typologies of technologies exist, most of which are based on historical stages (Garrison, 1985). Soren Nipper (1989) identified three generations of technologies: the first was correspondence teaching; the second multimedia teaching—integrating the use of print with broadcast media, cassettes, and to some degree computers; and the third generation was identified with new interactive technologies. Nipper's main unit of analysis was the feedback process that characterises each technological generation. He claimed that the main objectives of the first and second technology generations were the production and distribution of teaching/learning materials to learners. Communication with the learners was marginal, and communication amongst the learners was more or less non-existent. The technologies offered one-way and very restricted two-way communication. Nipper argued that these technologies effectively excluded underprivileged populations since they "mostly appealed to groups of educationally already privileged learners, and it has to a certain extent expelled the educationally or socially weak learner" (Nipper, 1989, 64). Nipper's perspective is provocative in the sense that it attacks one of the declared missions of the second-generation distance teaching universities, namely, to attract students from socially and educationally disadvantaged backgrounds. According to Nipper, autonomous, self-directed study does not suit the needs of such students, unless intensive support systems are provided, as discussed earlier (see Chapter 3). Third-generation technologies focus on communication, and on learning as a social process. By their very essence they are student-friendly and supportive.

Tifflin and Rajasingham (1995) also divided the technological media into three historical generations: print and postal services; television, film, radio and telephone; information technologies which focused in the 1980s on computer-assisted learning and from the 1990s on telecommunication technologies.

For my own part, I prefer to group technologies in the service of distance teaching universities into two categories, which are not based on historical generations, so much as on distinct functional roles: on one hand, production and delivery technologies; and on the other hand, interactive communication and information technologies. Production and delivery technologies include all media that shape the form and symbol systems of the materials which are posted or shipped to students or which are delivered via mass communication media, such as radio, television and satellites. Delivery and production technologies include: printed textbooks, readers, study guides, audio and video cassettes, radio and television programmes, video discs, experimental portable laboratories, special study kits, as well as sophisticated electronic publishing, and pre-prepared computer programmes. Interactive communication and information technologies include: correspondence, e-mail and fax, the telephone, interactive satellite sessions, teleconferencing (both audio conferencing and video conferencing), and computer-mediated communication. This two-fold categorisation is not based on the age of various media, nor on the extent to which they are *novel, modern* or *advanced*. Advanced electronic publishing modifies and refines print outputs. In this sense, it belongs to technologies that are brought in to assist and improve print products. Likewise, video discs, CD-ROMs and additional sophisticated multi-media, are used to package academic curricula and study content in distinct ways. But, they do not necessarily enhance interactive social learning with other learners or with tutors and professors. All production and delivery technologies, both old and new, are designed to package and wrap information, values and attitudes to be taught in specific forms and unique shapes. Interactive communication media provide channels for interpersonal exchanges or for access to remote databases. Neither the content nor the end-products of the interactive processes are pre-designed. The interactive vehicle merely provides grounds for creating endless final outcomes. The ancient correspondence technique has been utilised for interactive communication, and so has the old and reliable telephone medium. Clearly, the new communication technologies bear a tremendous potential to expand the boundaries of both conventional and distance education and open new avenues for rewarding and exploratory learning journeys. Computer technologies, more than any technology before, have the potential to combine both production and delivery functions with interactive communication possibilities.

Production and Delivery Technologies

A wide range of production and delivery technologies has served distance education since ancient times. Certain materials and media were used for communication between religious, educational and political leaderships and their followers. For instance, in the days of St. Paul, scribes wrote his words on a papyrus, which is a tough and flexible medium that can survive long and difficult journeys (Tifflin & Rajasingham, 1995). Delivery of those papyri was made by messengers who travelled by sea and by foot to the early Christian colonies around the Mediterranean. The invention of print, the advent of postal services, the development of efficient means of transport and professional publishing houses have stimulated and broadened the use of written texts for correspondence education purposes. Mass communication media make it possible to reach out to huge audiences by air. The development of electronic publishing increases the sophistication of printed materials and the speed of delivery. The use of print and electronic publishing; radio and audio cassettes; television, video cassettes and tutored-video instruction; and computer-based pre-developed programmes in the five examined distance teaching universities are discussed below. In addition to these technologies several distance teaching universities also produce special study devices, such as portable laboratory kits, games, geological stone samples as part of study packages required by certain courses.

Print and Electronic Publishing

Print-based materials constitute the oldest and most prevalent technology in distance education, and are to date the main medium of instruction at most fully fledged distance teaching universities (Bates, 1989a,b, 1990a, 1995; Curran & Wickham, 1994; Moore & Kearsley, 1996). In an extensive international study, Perry (1984) found that printed texts were being used by 94% of the distance education institutions he surveyed. The choice of print as the principal medium for developing self-study materials at distance teaching universities was not accidental, and apart from practical reasons was also based on academic and political considerations. Most distance teaching universities' planners and leaders felt that broadcast media as the main means of delivery would not be taken seriously by the academic community. The British Open University's Planning Committee made clear at the outset that it was neither practically possible nor pedagogically sound to rely on broadcasting as the major or exclusive means of teaching at university level (Rumble & Harry, 1982). Perry argued that one of the main obstacles he had to overcome in the first stages of setting up the British Open University's infrastructure was to convince colleagues from conventional universities that the *University of the Air* was not going to be based on television: "Most academics still thought of the new institution as one that would teach primarily by television and, quite justifiably, refused to believe that anyone could get a degree just by watching the telly... Consequently people were very surprised when I told them that television would make up 5% of the teaching programme. The whole concept of The *University of the Air* had properly been regarded as a gimmick, as an unrealistic idea" (Perry, 1976, 32–33).

Otto Peters, too, stressed the academic value attached to the print technology: "The main means of communication for the teaching Professor is the printed course material. Fortunately, the printed book has been a well accepted medium at our universities for centuries. Furthermore, you can also argue that the abstractness of the written language might lend itself more easily to the teaching of abstract scientific contents than, for instance, the image on a TV screen which presents concrete phenomena and live situations. The more abstract you get in your academic teaching, the more adequate the printed word might become and, hence, the more conducive it might be to the learning of abstract thinking" (Peters, 1988, 85). Keegan (1982) suggested that the choice of print-based courses by the FernUniversität was influenced by the long debate that took place in Germany during the 1960s and the 1970s as to the relative advantages of media. The debate ended with "the inherent superiority of print-based materials over the audio-visual media generally accepted" (*ibid.*, 98). Thus, in a highly advanced technology-oriented society, such as Germany, it was decided to base distance education mainly on print as a consequence of a strong academic conviction rooted in the long-standing university tradition. The main technology for material development at the Spanish UNED, the Open University of Israel and Athabasca University is also print.

The distance teaching universities of the 1970s were caught in a delicate dialectical situation. On one hand, in order to gain an innovative and a *breakthrough* image, they stressed that they were *multi-media* institutions. On the other hand, to establish their academic reputation and credibility they relied heavily on print technology and tuition by correspondence. Evidently, the quality of print materials varies considerably. Distance teaching universities have not merely utilised print technology. They have also refined the print products, improved their quality and reputation, and elevated the status of the study materials to methodological and didactic heights. Special efforts were employed to turn curricular materials into more *student-friendly* formats. Print takes such forms as textbooks, study units, readers, literary works, study guides, manuals, assignments, newsletters. Print can be distributed via public mail services, private delivery, or via electronic devices.

In addition to factors both academic and of status, print possesses some obvious advantages. Moore and Kearsley (1996) listed several of its major virtues: it is a relatively inexpensive technology to develop and distribute; it is reliable; it can carry dense and large volumes of information very efficiently; and students can read the materials whenever and as often as desired, i.e., print enables a high level of learner-controlled use. The biggest weakness of print-based study materials is the relatively low level of interaction they enable between student and teacher. Also the didactic guided conversation (Holmberg, 1995) which characterises many of the self-study texts produced by distance teaching universities, supports only restricted levels of dialogue.

The development of electronic publishing technologies has a tremendous impact on the efficiency and quality of producing print materials. Previously, printing required the work of typesetters, illustrators, graphic designers and layout experts. This process usually took months, and the packing and distribution of materials consumed additional precious time (Bacsich, 1990; Paul, 1990; Moore & Kearsley, 1996). When the process is done electronically, the text plus all the visual demonstrations and illustrations may both be developed and revised much faster, and sent directly for print.

Bacsich (1990) reviewed various arrangements for electronic publishing in distance teaching universities: traditional publishing enterprises based on special computerised typesetting systems; desktop publishing systems, which are software systems running on a standard office computer, and oriented to the layout of pages rather than to their initial drafting; corporate publishing systems which are layout systems running on an industry-standard Unix workstation, and oriented mainly to the production of technical documentation, such as technical manuals and textbooks; and Word processing systems, capable of producing high-quality documents and study materials. With electronic publishing it is possible to cover the stages of material production and dispatch, from the author's first draft to access by student (Bates, 1989b). Electronic publishing can both reduce costs and increase the speed of producing a text. It allows texts to be continually updated—a difficult, time-consuming and expensive endeavour in traditional print technology. Electronic publishing increases authors' control over the shape and form of the final products. It facilitates joint productions and the sharing or adaptation of materials among different institutions (*ibid.*). Electronic publishing can be used both for production and distribution. The final product can be distributed by traditional mail and shipping delivery systems, or the texts may be sent directly to students' home computers. The delivery of materials to large audiences via electronic devices depends obviously on the access of students to computers. Currently, most distance teaching universities' students do not own computers. Thus, electronic publishing is utilised mainly for production, and delivery is performed by more traditional means.

Interestingly, Bacsich (1990) reported that despite a great deal of talk about the effect of electronic publishing on the productivity of authors, very little effect has been found in reality, unless the text writers type their own manuscripts. Yet, anyone with a personal computer can nowadays turn out high-level text material. Electronic publishing alters the processes of text production, storage and dispatch. All ranks of academic faculty should be trained to use the technologies currently available for print-based materials, if only to improve the quality and visibility of the materials they develop, and stimulate revisions on an ongoing basis.

Computer-based printed materials may be used to help disabled students. In the FernUniversität, for instance, some eighty courses in German language and literature, psychology, social science and law are provided in Braille for the blind and partially sighted (Curran & Wickham, 1994, 17). Programmes are available on a computer disk either in short-form Braille files for visually impaired students with access to a computer with Braille display, or in long-form Braille files for computers with a synthetic voice device.

Paul (1990) has observed that electronic publishing also allows for electronic rather than physical storage of materials, and *just in time* inventory systems can print out course materials as required. It saves storage space, and means that there is no need to have recourse to outdated study materials or to postpone courses because unexpected demand has exhausted the materials available.

Radio and Audio Cassettes

Radio broadcasting in education has a respectable history and can be traced back to as early as the beginning of the twentieth century. Radio has been used most successfully in primary education in Africa, Latin America and Asia (Potashnik, 1996). Given its generally low cost and wide availability, it was "assigned second place in importance behind print as a medium for delivering distance education" (*ibid.*, 8). Radio has also been deemed an appropriate tool for adult education (Robinson, 1982), but not to the same extent as at lower levels of education. Perry (1984) found in his worldwide survey that radio was used by 15% of the distance education institutions he investigated. The British Open University started broadcasting via radio in cooperation with the BBC during its first year of operation. The initial agreement provided for up to 15 hours of radio broadcasting per week to be available for the British Open University on BBC national channels (Perry, 1976).

Newport (1990) sought to explain the merits of radio programmes, relying mainly on the British Open University experience. First, by its public nature radio helps create an image of the University, and appeals to far broader circles than the University's students. Second, it can be used for recruitment, allowing potential students a *taster* of the material before enrolling in a Faculty and in the University. Third, radio is essentially a flexible medium. The nature of the production process of radio programmes may allow rapid updating of materials. The advantage of immediacy allows for updating or the transmission of news from course teams about assignments as well as a demonstration of the relevance of current events and issues to certain study fields. Fourth, it allows graduates to keep in touch with developments in the University. Fifth, there is an economic benefit for distribution to large numbers. It was calculated that for course populations greater than 1,000 it is better to broadcast rather than distribute cassette material. Newport concluded that: "Properly targeted radio can be a valuable asset to distance learners. The important thing is that radio complements audio cassettes and is used for its own strengths. It is the most flexible of all media" (Newport, 1990, 100).

Since the late 1980s the British Open University has initiated some new-type radio programmes of appeal to a wide variety of students. These programmes include subject presentations, talks, discussions, phone-ins.

There has been a rise of a new type of *faculty-wide radio*. *Arts Review* and the *Math Faculty Radio* broadcast to all students who are studying or who are interested in the faculties concerned. There are several special programmes such as: *Open Forum on the Radio* which is a weekly programme with two well-known professional presenters; *Into the Open* is a series of four programmes designed to be an introduction to the study skills needed for distance learning. *Information for Associate Students* is a parallel programme to *Into the Open* for short course non-degree students. In 1987 a new radio channel was opened in the UK (Radio 5) for sports and educational programmes. It has given the British Open University better transmission times and more air time. Concurrently with developing new programmes and new conceptual frameworks for radio utilisation, the major trend of the last decade within the British Open University has been to rely increasingly on audio cassettes. Many functions initially fulfilled by the radio broadcast have been taken over by audio cassettes.

UNED also used radio transmission from its early days. Radio programmes are broadcast for two and a half hours every weekday between October and June on the national radio station and other stations (James, 1982; UNED, 1992b; Curran & Wickham, 1994, 36). The first hour is used for broadcasts relating to specific courses. The second hour is used for more general programmes designed to appeal not merely to UNED students, but also to a wider audience. The final half-hour is used for the open access courses. Lacasa and Padro de Leon (1990) reported that very few of UNED students actually listen to the radio broadcasts. Only 4% of UNED students in 1987 reported listening to UNED's radio on a regular basis, and an additional 7% had listened occasionally, compared to 50% who said they had never listened to the radio. The main reasons for not listening were inconvenient broadcast times, poor reception, programmes were too general, and radio was not considered as a good medium for distance learning. Lacasa and Padro de Leon listed the main advantages for using radio in the UNED context as: reaching large audiences; low cost and easy preparation; up-to-date information; providing a suitable teaching content; and allowing easy and indirect contact with teachers. The major problems associated with radio programmes at UNED were: programme objectives not always clear; too many introductory programmes; little information for students on use of the media; and sparse didactic information. Lacasa and Padro de Leon noted that these shortcomings are easily corrected with careful planning.

The Open University of Israel used radio programmes until 1994, when it decided to discontinue them, given the low student numbers listening to them. Most programmes consisted of lectures, discussions and symposia keyed to various courses, and were transmitted for two hours every weekday, one in the early morning, the other in the late afternoon. All the functions the radio had served were placed on audio cassette. At Athabasca University, radio programmes were broadcast over private stations and a station run by ACCESS, the provincial education media corporation in Alberta (Shale, 1982). Athabasca University uses radio programmes to a limited extent. The Fern-Universität does not use radio.

The audio cassette is used by all five distance teaching universities, and its importance has grown throughout the years. Perry (1984) reported that 40% of the distance education institutions he surveyed used audio tapes as compared to only 15% using radio. Bates (1990c) claimed that the most widely used technology in the British Open University, after print, is not television, computers or radio, but audio cassettes. Each year, the Open University mails to students more than 750,000 hours of cassette materials. The introduction of audio cassettes has been the most important technological innovation in the twenty-year history of the British Open University, in terms of numbers of students and courses affected, and the impact on learning. Bates concluded that: "It is clear that audio cassettes are a success story at the Open University, and indicate that in distance education, media need to be simple, widely available in students' homes, low-cost to produce, easy to design well, interactive, and integrated with other media. Now there's a challenge for satellites, hypertext, and intelligent computer-assisted learning!" (*ibid.*, 104).

There are important functions that audio cassettes can fulfil from a pedagogical perspective: talking students through parts of the printed material; talking students through practical procedures, such as home experiments; analysing human interaction, such as decision making and personal experiences; collecting views of specialists, experts, or personal experiences; discussing different views or alternative explanations; providing feedback on student activities; providing aural experiences of music, foreign speech, sounds (*ibid.*, 102).

There are also practical advantages in their usage: everyone has the equipment for replaying audio cassettes; production costs are the same or lower than for radio. Audio cassettes are extremely cheap to deliver. In the British Open University the cost of audio cassette distribution was reduced to less than two transmissions of a radio programme for courses with less than 1,000 students (*ibid.*, 102). Furthermore, the audio cassette reaches virtually all students, unlike radio programmes that are transmitted in a given timeframe, which may be inconvenient for many. Students can control the interaction with the audio cassette, stop it as often as they wish and use it when convenient. Audio cassettes are also *user-friendly* to teachers, not only to students. Teachers feel they retain more control over the design of an audio cassette than over a radio programme. They are free to determine its length according to the content taught. British Open University experience suggests students greatly welcome the personal, friendly approach of professors on audio cassettes. As one student put it: "It is like having the professor in the room, talking to me over the shoulder" (*ibid.*, 103).

The German FernUniversität decided to adapt the usage of audio cassettes in 1975 (Peters, 1988), a decision based on both practical and academic considerations. Most, if not all, of its students owned a tape-recorder, "a medium which was and still is technically perfect and relatively cheap. We considered it as an additional, supplementary medium which is used only where it can carry special teaching functions" (*ibid.*, 86). For instance, special audio cassettes were developed to assist students with the pronunciation of foreign language terms or Greek symbols in mathematics. Studies at the FernUniversität revealed that: "Lectures and discussions sounded more authentic when recorded on an audio or video tape" (*ibid.*). Audio cassettes in the FernUniversität are employed in approximately 100 courses. About 80 courses provide audio cassettes for students with visual handicaps (Curran & Wickham, 1994, 16).

Spain's UNED produces audio cassettes as an integral part of some courses, such as for language teaching. In addition, all radio programmes are automatically recorded and sent to study centres where students may borrow them (*ibid.*, 36). At the Open University of Israel and Athabasca University audio cassettes forming an integral part of a given course are delivered directly to students, whereas cassettes for enrichment are distributed to study centres.

Television, Video Cassettes and Tutored-video Instruction

The extent to which television is used in distance education varies. Some systems are centrally based on television, such as the Television Universities in China, and EuroPACE in Europe (Curran, 1990). Some use television as an integral part of their programmes, as in the British Open University. Others use it on an occasional basis as is the case of the remaining four distance teaching universities in this study. Television programmes can be delivered through a variety of techniques: via landline, cable, satellite, and digitally (Potashnik, 1996). Bates (1989b) suggested that it is important to distinguish between television as a medium and its delivery technologies, which differ across various national contexts. A particular television programme can be terrestrially broadcast in the UK, delivered by cable in Belgium, by satellite in Spain, and by video disc in the Netherlands (*ibid.*, 30).

Perry (1984) reported that 14% of distance education institutions which he surveyed worldwide used television for instructional purposes. Nevertheless, the distance teaching universities of the 1970s as a whole have long been identified with the television more than with any other medium. This is due to the initial planning of the British Open University as the *University of the Air*. Television was the major instructional technology envisaged by Harold Wilson who had been greatly impressed by the emerging educational television in the USA. Television was politically attractive and has helped gain the distance teaching universities support from planners and policy makers at the national level, while helping them throw off the "correspondence image" (Perry, 1976; Bates, 1984). The British Open University achieved rapid visibility by broadcasting its video course components on the BBC networks, which helped sustain the public presence of the University (Granger, 1990; Radcliffe, 1990).

In the 1960s, television seemed to hold great promise for education. It was described as a window to the world for the classroom; a way to bring new experiences and new presentation techniques to learning (Tifflin & Rajasingham, 1995). Part of the enthusiasm of educational broadcasting stemmed from the general interest that surrounded a number of educational television and radio projects in the 1960s (Chu & Schramm, 1967; Schramm et. al., 1967). Yet television never really worked in and for schools and universities. Bates (1984) already in the early 1980s detected a clear move away from using broadcasting in distance learning systems. Television proved to be of less significance in teaching systems and more difficult to use than was originally expected. With a few exceptions, educational television in its first incarnation as a medium for broadcasting instruction was never able to establish its claim to be a more effective or a less expensive way of teaching (Curran, 1990). Various television projects around the world did not attract student numbers that would have made them an economically viable alternative to conventional education. If it has become the great educator of our time in social and political domains, it was not, however, in the way anticipated by educationists.

Tifflin and Rajasingham argued that: "Broadcast television is the medium par excellence for the grand event; for creating the global village with its fêtes and fairs and sports events and its preachers and politicians...When the best of the educational and television worlds come together, as sometimes happens in educational documentaries, we realise that television is a powerful medium for lecturing to large groups of people... Television is attractive to those who see teaching as explanation. It is the technology of the lecture. It has the potential for presenting education at the national, pan-national and global levels. These are the macro-fractal levels where learners are masses, problems are things that societies face and knowledge is a conjunction of common sense, pseudo-science and the sweet voice of reason in the presenter" (Tifflin & Rajasingham, 1995, 96–97).

Television by its very essence is a rich medium, combining most of the manifestations of human symbol systems: words, visual displays, sound, movement. It possesses the ability to present real-time and up-to-the-last-minute events, and to reach huge masses. Radcliffe (1990, 118) reported that late night viewing on BBC2, included about 200,000 people watching the British Open University's broadcasts. Only a small minority of them were British Open University's students. Bates (1989b) has pointed out that the representational qualities of television are particularly important for non-academic learners and students from disadvantaged backgrounds, who often require concrete examples or demonstrations to comprehend a given topic rather than an abstract theory. Television can help students to understand by watching, when words are not enough to comprehend the study material. It can provide powerful audio-visual concrete examples of abstract principles and be of particular assistance to students who are struggling with difficult concepts. But programmes of quality exploiting the representational richness of the television medium are extremely expensive to produce. Their distribution costs are high as well. To reduce production costs many distance education providers use television to relay a lecture, to present students with a so-called talking head (Bates, 1995; Potashnik, 1996).

Perry (1991) criticised strongly the *talking head* practice in educational television. In addressing an American audience at Indiana University in 1991 he confessed that unlike the enthusiasm of Harold Wilson for the potential merits inherent in the USA television: "I was myself less impressed when, a few years later, I studied what was being done in this country. I found that there was a wealth of extremely sophisticated and versatile hardware—including systems of two-way link-up—which had cost millions of dollars to develop; but there was an accompanying dearth of software of any quality... I saw some of the most sophisticated systems being used to show an inept lecturer writing simple algebra on the blackboard! The dollars were not being spent on the programmes; they tended to take a camera into a traditional classroom. One reason for this was—and there still is—a belief that TV can be used as the main medium of instruction. I think that there is already good evidence that this is a fallacy" (*ibid.*, 7).

Perry focused on an additional weakness of the television as an instructional medium apart from its being either highly expensive to produce and broadcast or poorly utilised, i.e. its *ephemeral* nature: "I believe its message to be ephemeral—evanescent, if you like—unless it is almost immediately reinforced by reading" (*ibid.*, *ibid.*). An additional shortcoming of television is limited or non-existent learner–teacher interaction (Bates, 1995; Tifflin & Rajasingham, 1995; Moore & Kearsley, 1996). Currently, some interactive television programmes try to improve interaction in tele-learning situations by allowing learners to interact with a television teacher. There are various ways of doing this, but how far viewers can respond is always limited.

One particular variant for relaying lectures is tutored-video instruction (Bates, 1989b, 1995). By contrast to broadcast television, it is narrowcast to few designated locations. It relays classroom lectures by cable, satellite or video cassette to different sites, where local face-to-face tutors handle questions and discussion following the viewing of a programme. The lectures are usually given by leading experts in a field, specially brought in for the programme. Tutored-video instruction is a very low-cost form of television, and allows experts, with little extra preparation, to bring their latest work to a wider audience. The justification for tutored-video instruction lies in the low cost and convenience, and its distributional characteristics, rather than in the presentational use of the medium. It does not exploit the special representational characteristics of television or the control characteristic of cassettes and discs. Bates claimed that tutored-video instruction is best used when students already have a good conceptual grasp of the subject matter, and where presenters are of high status and good lecturers. Tutored-video instruction is already used in Europe, whether it is distributed via satellite for in-house company training in scientific and technical updating, via the EuroPACE programme, or via video-cassettes to companies by the British Open University and other institutions. Several satellite systems are available for such programmes (ASTRA, EUTELSAT, Olympus) all with European-wide coverage. After the lecture, the presenter is available for questions by telephone from local centres. The EuroPACE programme in Europe used satellites for tutored-video instruction distribution (Bates, 1989b). The Open University of Israel transmits via satellite 200 broadcast hours of tutored-video instruction per month with a provisional availability of a simultaneous interaction between students and lecturer(s). The satellite project *Ofek* (Horizon in Hebrew) started in February 1995 (Guri-Rosenblit, 1996c).

Many of the roles first assigned to television programmes were transferred to video cassettes. Bates estimated in 1989 that almost 80% of homes in the UK and more than half the homes in several European Community countries had a video recorder (Bates, 1989b). Video cassettes, like audio cassettes, are also a powerful tool. Video is especially effective in conveying attitudinal or emotional aspects of a subject, something that is difficult to do with other media. Video is a good medium for teaching interpersonal skills. Video cassettes exploit both the unique representational qualities of television, and the interactive potential of stop–start facility. Unlike audio cassettes, the production costs of an original video cassette are very high. Hence, video cassettes might constitute an efficient medium in courses targeted at large numbers of students. Collaboration on an international level may allow for the co-production of video cassettes in several language versions.

The British Open University is the only distance teaching university, in this study, to base its operation from the outset on close cooperation with a national broadcasting enterprise like the BBC. The partnership between the BBC and the British Open University was established in 1969. The British Open University was allocated up to 30 hours a week of television time on the BBC's national networks (in addition to radio programmes). A special department was created and was housed till 1980 in Alexandra Palace in North London. Since the early 1980s, it has moved to the British Open University's campus in Milton Keynes in a specially built Production Centre, which designs television, radio, as well as audio and video cassettes (Radcliffe, 1990). The BBC set up special professional teams to work with each of the academic faculties. The British Open University broadcasts many television programmes: documentaries, lectures, art programmes, geological expeditions, and visits to various locations.

Increasingly, video cassettes are used to replace or as an alternative to, live broadcasts. Crooks and Kirkwood (1990) analysed the advantages of video cassettes in the British Open University context. Originally video cassettes consisted of a taped television production. Since the 1980s the use of video cassette has grown and intensified. There are some obvious pedagogical advantages in designing a video cassette from the start. Students reported more extensive usage than watching television programmes, and usually viewed it more than once. A study carried out in the British Open University (*ibid.*) discovered that students replay video cassettes as many as five or six times to make sure they have got what they needed from it. In addition, non-broadcast material has been prepared for residential schools, where such materials are integrated with face-to-face and other teaching methods. As with audio cassettes, the video cassette frees both students and teachers from fixed study schedules. It enables them to discuss its content in a group session.

UNED at its start-up neither produced nor purchased television programmes for broadcasting. Television programmes were considered an expensive investment for supplementary purposes only. In 1991 some experimental television programmes were broadcast. In 1994 two television programmes were introduced: a scientific programme related to academic courses, and a programme designed specifically for direct access courses which are open to the broader public (Curran & Wickham, 1994, 36). More than 60 video cassettes have been produced. They are used for two main purposes: to support regular courses and to develop direct access courses (*ibid.*).

At the German FernUniversität, audio-visual production started in 1977/ 78 as a pilot development (Laaser, 1990). In 1983 a small-scale transmission by regional public television was undertaken on an experimental basis, every two weeks for 45 minutes. Since the 1990s two educational television programmes have been introduced at the FErnUZFE television *FernU im Dritten*. The programmes are broadcast 12 hours per week in cooperation with the German Television/West 3 (Curran & Wickham, 1994). Target groups are Fern-Universität students and the general public. Video cassettes are used to support course material for approximately 120 courses. This represents around 10% of the total number of courses provided. FernUniversität participates in the JANUS project (Joint Academic Networks Using Satellites); it is a prime contractor of FernU TEMPUS JEP- Satellite Distance Learning in Hungary and Poland, and is also a programme provider to EUROSTEP, European Distance Teaching via the EUTELSAT II/F# Satellite (*ibid.*).

With more than 50% of FernUniversität's students studying economics, audio-video production focuses mainly on this field (Laaser, 1990). The pro-grammes are jointly produced by academics, by the Centre for Distance Education Development and by audio-visual specialists. The entire production is directed by academic staff at the University. Occasionally, technical assist-ance is supplied by private firms. Video copies may be borrowed free of charge by students, and they can use video-players at local study centres. Laaser advocated the relaying of lectures. He claimed that the professor explaining "live" enriches the illustration of various abstract themes and assists in grasp-ing economic problems. Video cassettes are used more extensively than television programmes at the FernUniversität. Fixed time schedules are a basic disadvantage of live broadcasts. A survey conducted in the late 1980s found only 10% of students studying economics at the FernUniversität watched television, compared to 20% using video cassettes (*ibid.*, 125). Television is preferred mainly for publicity effects.

The Open University of Israel, too, uses television programmes mainly as a supplement and not as an integral part of its courses. From its inception a special contract was signed between the Open University of Israel and Educational Television. The Open University of Israel was given only two broadcast hours per week. From 1995 the Open University of Israel signed a further contract with Cable Television, Channel 8, the Science and Education channel. The Open University of Israel now has 38 hours of weekly air time. On weekdays it transmits six hours per day, and on weekends four hours a day. Its programmes include supplementary films and television productions both for academic and continuing education courses. Video cassettes are used in around 100 courses, and constitute an integral component for 17 courses. A few attempts have been made to make original productions, for a course on the "Opera", and "The Representation of Israeli Literature in the Israeli Film Industry". Most television and video programmes are imported, and subtitled in Hebrew.

At Athabasca University television programmes are delivered through a variety of distribution systems, mainly by cable. At the start, Athabasca University experimented with developing original programmes, but very rapidly the costs and difficulties in producing quality television led the University away from developing its own programmes (Shale, 1982). Athabasca University purchases television programmes and tele-courses from other universities or commercial companies. All television programmes are available to Athabasca University's students on video cassettes.

Computer-based Pre-developed Programmes

Computer-based pre-developed programmes have a variety of names, such as CAL (Computer-Assisted Learning), CBT (Computer-Based Teaching), CAI (Computer-Assisted Instruction), CBL (Computer-Based Learning). All these acronyms refer to any form of teaching where the learner is directed by, and interacts with, pre-developed and pre-programmed study materials contained in computer software. The distinction between computer-based teaching and computer-mediated communication, which is discussed further on, is that the latter involves interaction through a computer terminal but with other sources, such as another learner, tutor or administrator, or with remote data-bases, but not with the computer programme itself. In addition, computer-mediated communication requires a modem and a telephone line to link the student either with other people or with information resources. Clearly, computers are gaining ground in distance education as well as in conventional settings (Kurland, 1986; Kaye, 1990; Rossman, 1992). Computer technologies are changing at a rate probably faster than ever in history, and it seems certain that in the near future they will have a major impact on teaching/

learning practices in education in general, and in distance education settings in particular.

The attraction of computer-based programmes is their ability to combine the strong interactivity of computers with the powerful representational qualities of television. Computers nowadays are able to take over many functions of correspondence education and educational television. However, there are distinct differences between the educational goals and instructional functions of television and computers. Tifflin and Rajasingham (1995) portrayed these basic differences in a colourful manner: "Education on the television uses a broad brush. Computers applied to learning use a fine pen" (Tifflin & Rajasingham, 1995, 98), implying that television is an efficient medium for lectures delivered to mass audience whereas the computer, by contrast, is a medium for individualised learning and interpersonal interaction on a small scale. The computer functions as the student's ever-patient, and responsive *partner*. Computers allow students to work at their own pace and to obtain feedback on their progress. The computer technology is also utilised for testing students' knowledge and for identifying areas where further study, practice or explanation are needed.

Until the 1990s computer-based instruction was often criticised for using poor graphics, and no colour and voice input. Heavy emphasis lay on drill and practice, passive page-turning and limited responses. High quality courseware was very expensive to produce, and frequently required on-line access to a mainframe. Since the mid 1990s the products of pre-developed computer programmes have become highly refined and sophisticated, combining high quality visual displays, colours and sound. Such programmes are delivered by floppy discs, CD-ROMs and also on video discs. The latter provide the highest representational and operational qualities, but are both extremely expensive to develop and exceedingly hard to access, since only a tiny number of people currently own a video-disc player. Video discs can either be used in a stand-alone form, in the same way as a video cassette, only with more precise and convenient control, or combined with a computer.

For the first time since the distance teaching universities' inception in the early 1970s, computer technology now offers a real challenge and potential to supplement existing technologies and to provide new exciting possibilities to enrich and improve the quality of learning in distance education. It forces distance teaching universities to decide on a substantial redesign of their infrastructure, delivery and production systems. Bates (1990b) compared distance teaching universities to public telephone companies. Both already invested heavily in well-tried *older* technologies and services. The new technologies, computers, fibre optics and satellites open new horizons and prospects, but they require a major change in the overall operation, if adopted on a large-scale basis. Such decisions are not easy. Thus, at all the distance teaching universities in this study most computer-based programmes to this date function on a very limited and experimental basis.

A significant step in the implementation of computers in the British Open University came in 1988 with the requirement for 1350 students and 65 tutors in the "Technology Foundation Course" (T102), to use a home computer (Bates, 1989b; Curran & Wickham, 1994). Students' use of home computers at the British Open University, though subsidised in a number of ways, is not seen as realistic in extending the current scheme to widespread use across the university. In the early 1990s some 14,000 students (10% of the total British Open University student body) owned home computers (Curran & Wickham, 1994). Computers are currently a requirement for a number of courses, originally in the core area of informatics, but also in other areas of mathematics, science and technology. The use of computers continues in summer and residential schools and allows the use of more sophisticated programmes and systems.

Yet, computer programmes are expensive to develop. Part of the difficulty in design and delivery is the absence of standard hardware. A number of different types of computers exist, and programmes need to be developed in different versions for each type of machine (Moore & Kearsley, 1996). Bates (1990b) reported that even where a very restricted specification for home computer equipment, including a single operating standard, were required and used in one of the British Open University's programmes, software had to be developed in seven versions to accommodate differences between just two hardware manufacturers, and between colour and monochrome screens, and hard discs and floppy discs. Such problems multiply when national borders are crossed. Even the keyboard layout is different for different languages.

As in the British Open University, computer-based programmes are used at all four distance teaching universities, but experimentally. Most computer-based learning takes place in courses on computer science, mathematics and technology, and to a lesser extent in science courses (Curran & Wickham, 1994; President's Report, 1995). The advent of computer-mediated communication through the Internet is likely to hasten the use of computer-based instruction in the coming decade both at distance teaching universities and in mainstream higher and continuing education.

Interactive Communication and Information Technologies

Interactive communication and information technologies enhance social learning, by interaction with other learners and with instructors. They provide access to additional information sources which, stored at databases and Internet locations, were not included in the learning package delivered to students. Such technologies have revolutionary implications for distance education: they provide the means to free students from centralised control of pre-packaged and constricted curricula, strengthen the social dimension, the lack of which has been the *Achilles heel* of distance education for centuries.

Until recently, traditional correspondence and the telephone were the main means of communication for distance education. The major shortcoming associated with them is the limited interaction they permit, and the hiatus between students' queries or assignments' submission and the reply they receive. Some new advanced technologies allow for a two-way communication in distance education, in both synchronous and asynchronous modes, and at relatively low costs. Synchronous communication takes place when transmitter and receiver operate in the same time frame, for example, in a face-to-face discussion or in a telephone conversation. Asynchronous communication is when transmitter and receiver do not act in the same time frame, as in correspondence education. Communication in a conventional classroom switches easily between synchronous and asynchronous modes. Correspondence, fax, e-mail, computer conferencing provide opportunities for asynchronous communication between learners and teachers in different places. Telephone, audio conferencing and video conferencing are based on synchronous transmission systems that bring teachers and learners together in real time. They provide students with an experience analogous in several respects to a traditional classroom. They create a virtual classroom environment (Tifflin & Rajasingham, 1995). The virtual classroom uses telecommunication instead of transport to gather students together. Tifflin and Rajasingham argued that the possibilities of a virtual classroom are particularly attractive at tertiary level education since the catchment areas of elementary and high schools are usually small and the distance their students have to travel to school may not constitute a problem: "It is at a tertiary level that the distance between where people live and work and where they go to study may become a serious matter for many students. Universities offer a wide variety of specialist subjects which attract people from around the world.... It is people seeking tertiary education who are most likely to have travel problems, but students of any age group can have travel problems if they live in remote places or are disabled, house-bound or incarcerated. Therefore, it is in distance education and tertiary education that the development of the virtual classroom is likely to make its first advances" (*ibid.*, 161–162).

Advanced communication and information technologies are extensively under essay in classical, mainstream higher education, and contribute to blurring of the boundaries between distance and campus universities. How the main communication technologies are employed in our five distance teaching universities is presented below.

Correspondence, Fax and E-mail

Letter writing as a means of communication has served distance education from the most ancient times to the present. Tifflin and Rajasingham (1995) suggest that today's transport and mail costs are artificially low and telecommunication costs tend to be artificially high. Governments subsidise transport systems and perpetuate an industrial society, while telecommunication companies, which often have a monopoly, make handsome profits. This is likely to change in the near future. Furthermore, in countries that possess insufficient or problematic transport and mail systems, delivery of course materials via post is not easy. When the British Open University, for instance, started to operate in the former Eastern European bloc in the early 1990s, in some locations it was difficult, and sometimes impossible, to send student materials by mail. Some packages never reached students' homes. Many developing countries do not have sufficient or effective transport systems to provide distance education by correspondence. New telecommunication technologies may speed up correspondence, bypass transportation obstacles, transcend local and national limits and provide education on a global level. Transport systems, roads, railways, shipping and airways respect national boundaries. Electronic communication via fax or e-mail slips across them.

Fax and e-mail overcome the major weakness of traditional correspondence, which is its slowness and delayed feedback. Delivery technologies allow convenient communication between tutors and students. Facsimile communication is broadly used for administrative matters, and for instructional purposes to a lesser extent. It is convenient for sending letters, timetables, corrections and amendments to texts, leaflets. Its use is still limited to short messages, and to a few pages. It is not suited to transmitting large amounts of text. It is expensive. Electronic mail combines the advantages of correspondence with a more or less immediate feedback. Compared with fax, it is much more convenient for teaching and learning interaction. Turnaround time of response and feedback to students may be dramatically reduced from weeks to days and even hours. It is not the technological sophistication so much as the opportunities for untrammelled person-to-person communication which makes this medium so educationally important (Holmberg, 1990). Obviously, personal computers with modems are required, and if possible printers, for e-mail communication to take place; and to send faxes one must own or have access to fax machines.

Paul (1990) claimed that e-mail is a very powerful tool not only for tuition by correspondence, but also for management and for inter-faculty discussion. It is ideal for quick information dissemination or consultation on simple decisions between faculty, course team members and administrators.

All the distance teaching universities in this study possess fax machines in their headquarters and in most of their study centres. Most fax communication is used for information and general exchange between students and various university authorities. Only the FernUniversität uses fax for students to send assignments in (Curran & Wickham, 1994, 17). Obviously, fax communication is not convenient for sending multi-page documents. E-mail is used in all distance teaching universities for communication between academic and administrative staff within and outside the universities, and experimentally for instructional purposes. In the FernUniversität, for example, a special system called PORTACOM has been developed combining both e-mail and computer conferencing facilities (*ibid.*, 16). Students in some courses, mainly inform-ation sciences, use e-mail to send in their assignments to be corrected by tutors and returned via e-mail. The Spanish UNED uses the IRIS network for e-mail communication between faculty, and to a limited extent between students and tutors (*ibid.*, 36–37). The British Open University, the Open University of Israel and Athabasca University use e-mail in teaching a limited number of courses (Curran & Wickham, 1994; President's Report, 1995; Athabasca University, 1992c).

Telephone and Audio Conferencing

Communication by telephone and audio conferencing allows students to hear and converse either with an instructor or with fellow students at a given instant. Audio conferencing is the most common and least expensive form of telecommunication. In most countries, it is based on analogue telephone technology. It can link individuals or groups. Individual participants use their regular personal phones. To link more than two parties requires a *bridge* (Robinson, 1990; Moore & Kearsley, 1996). The *bridge* may be supplied by a telephone company or by the organisation conducting the audio conference. In small groups, telephones with a speaker are adequate. For large groups, linked push-to-talk microphones or voice-points are used. However, sound quality constitutes a major problem in using audio conferencing (Tifflin & Rajasing-ham, 1995). Classical telephone systems were not designed for more than two links. Echo formation and acoustic coupling in analogue telephone systems increases with the number of parties connected.

All the distance teaching universities in this study use telephones as an integral part of the regular communication between tutors and students. In several documents tutors are referred to as *telephone tutors*. Students may telephone their tutors at specified times. The use of telephones is to help students learn from their printed and other materials, to resolve their difficulties, and to give access to a tutor or counsellor on issues or queries students wish to raise. One-to-one telephone tutoring develops a relationship between tutor and student. It provides a human *real voice–real person* element in distance education (Robinson, 1990). Tutors are encouraged to phone students from time to time, especially when the latter "cut" tutorials or if written work hints at particular difficulties.

Robinson (1990) examined the benefits and drawbacks of using audio communication at the British Open University. There, telephone teaching takes two forms: one-to-one telephone tutoring and small-group audio conferencing. Neither is used to deliver course content. Audio conferencing at the British Open University is conducted on a small scale, as a small-group activity with a maximum of up to nine participants, unlike large-scale, audio-delivery-based systems in the USA. Audio conferencing is used in eleven out of the Open University's thirteen Regional Centres. That telephone costs are higher in Europe, explains in part why audio conferencing is less used compared to the USA.

For Robinson, the advantages both of one-to-one telephone communication and audio conferencing at the British Open University were: "The telephone, or two-way audio, is an effective communication medium for linking people together for purposes of conversation, for saving time and travel, for quick feedback and resolution of problems and for humanising otherwise impersonal systems... audio conferencing is used for two reasons: to save travel costs and time and to provide educationally desirable interaction for widely dispersed groups who would not otherwise be able to meet" (*ibid.*, 107–108). Telephone contacts in the British Open University proved ineffective for lecturing, for passing on lengthy and detailed instructions, or for courses that require the exchange or construction of spontaneous and dynamic visual materials. Effective use of the telephone, as with other media, lies in recognising its strengths and weaknesses, and in developing to complement other media (*ibid.*, 108).

In the case of the British Open University, poor telephone technology hampers greater use of telephone teaching, and audio conferencing has declined there since the early 1980s (Curran & Wickham, 1994, 41). Factors that have contributed to this decline include high telephone costs, outdated and inadequate technology, and the requirement of synchronous communication, which is not convenient for many distance students.

Van Prümmer (1994) found that the telephone was held to be a most important means of communication by FernUniversität students. Many looked to the telephone to provide the closest element of personal contact, when face-to-face meeting is ruled out. The FernUniversität has not employed audio conferencing, and the same applies to the Open University of Israel, where one-to-one telephone communication is used extensively, but audio conferencing has never been tried. Both telephone and audio conferencing are used at Athabasca University as important means of communication between tutors and students.

Generally, the telephone is used less for instructional purposes in Europe than in North America or Australia. Rather, its potential seems to be undervalued. This situation may change given developments in telecommunication technologies, and the policy currently under way in Europe. However, once digitalised systems are in place, communication is largely trouble-free. The control and organisation of national telecommunication services differ as to standards, type of equipment, cost structures and tariffs. Access to voice and data networks via satellite may resolve some of the difficulties mentioned, whilst Integrated Services Digital Networks (ISDN) hold out considerable promise for distance teaching (Robinson, 1990). Moore & Kearsley (1996) have suggested that the most significant development in communication and information technologies in the late 1990s is the ISDN—a new generation of telephone lines based on fibre-optic cable instead of on copper. Fibre-optic cables can carry a massive amount of information. Information is transmitted in digital form rather than analogue. Information can be compressed, which further increases transmission capacity and speed. With such increased capacity, it becomes possible to transmit a very wide range of information along telephone lines, including audio, video, images, data voice, and facsimile and that simultaneously on a single phone line. With an ISDN connection, any home or office has the capability to send and receive multimedia information.

Tifflin and Rajasingham (1995) argued that telephone costs are currently distorted. Satellites can reduce the price of long distance calls substantially, and consequently could intensify the use of audio conferencing in distance education. That an international call today costs much more than a local one, they pointed out, makes perfect sense to a "transport-based mindset", in other words, the greater the distance, the more one expects to pay. But this reasoning does not apply to satellite communication. The cost of a satellite link on an international call across the world is no different from the cost of a local call. It is a small fraction of the real costs to the telephone company. Advances in telecommunication technologies may well increase the usage of audio conferencing for distance learning.

One special variant on audio conferencing is audio-graphic conferencing in which audio communication is combined with transmitting graphic information via facsimile machines or computers (Tifflin & Rajasingham, 1995; Moore & Kearsley, 1996). Copies of documents can be sent to all participants. Electronic boards can also be used, which transmit anything drawn at one site to television monitors elsewhere. Computers may also be used to facilitate the delivery of visual presentations and graphic data from one computer screen to others. Of the five distance teaching universities, only the British Open University has experimented with audio-graphic conferencing through the CYCLOPS service though only in one region. The experiment was discontinued in 1983 after three years (Curran & Wickham, 1994, 41).

Video Conferencing

Video conferencing allows those engaged in distant exchange to see one another, whilst conducting a discussion. The exchange can be either one-way or two-way video-based. One-way video conferencing involves participants (or students) seeing the presenter/s or other participants at a distance, but inter-action is based on sound alone. A two-way video conferencing involves all participants seeing, listening and conversing with each other at a given time. Video conferencing is the closest one that comes to a *virtual classroom*, of being with other people without actually meeting them. As its name implies, it is based on the use of video cameras and monitors to show both the participating parties and any other visual devices, pictures, slides, pre-selected video clips, film strips, transparencies, text quotations, electronic boards, computer presentations. Video conferencing may be transmitted via satellite, cable, slow-scan or compressed video through digital telephone lines, videophones and computers (Moore & Kearsley, 1996).

It is still in its infancy and the basic infrastructure is highly expensive. Tifflin and Rajasingham (1995) believed that: "Video conferencing is where television was fifty years ago. This is a virtual class where the tele-presences have their eyes open, but are myopic" (*ibid.*, 112). Some problems with video conferencing are technical: cameras need light whereas projected images need darkened rooms; most participants forget to look at the camera, not at the monitor, when addressing people, which results in a lack of eye contact—so important in a face-to-face discussion. Personnel employed at video conferencing centres do not always have the professional and artistic skills a high level presentation demands. The high costs of video cameras and of employing professional technical staff to operate the equipment are, at the moment, a major barrier to implementing widespread video conferencing by distance teaching universities and by other providers of distance education.

Yet, in the very near future, the development of sophisticated compression techniques, and the advent of the desktop video will allow computers to join video conferences on a broader scale. It will result both in a noticeable improvement in the quality of video communication, and a lowering of running costs, thus making it accessible to many users and participants. If such a scenario is realised: "An individual can join a video conference from the desk in their office or home and can see, hear and write to other people in the conference. They can also send or present files of multimedia materials they have previously prepared. The synchronous and asynchronous modes mesh as easily as they do in a classroom" (*ibid.*).

Video conferencing experiments have been carried on a limited scale by the British Open University, German FernUniversität, Athabasca University and the Open University of Israel. The *Ofek* satellite project at the Open University of Israel services both video-based instruction, where the emphasis lies on delivering lectures of experts in a range of disciplines, and for communication between presenter and audience the latter scattered across the country. Video conferencing is used mainly for in-service teacher training courses (President's Report, 1995; Guri-Rosenblit, 1996c). Currently, students can view the presenter, but interaction is achieved by regular telephones tied in via satellite. The phone keypads serve as a keyboard for data communication, and voice communication is handled by a phone handset. Students in all participating classes can listen to a conversation between any student and the presenter through television speakers at all connected sites. This arrangement allows students to engage in a between-school or between-site dialogue, which has been found most effective in implementing new curricula. The planning team can converse concurrently with participating teachers spread throughout the land. Teachers reported they found it to be most beneficial and rewarding to see and listen to leading experts, to be able to ask questions and hear the replies as well as the questions of their fellow teachers (Guri-Rosenblit, 1996c).

Computer-mediated Communication

Computer-mediated communication (CMC) relies on a mainframe computer with appropriate software, connected via telephone and data networks to users with terminals and microcomputers. CMC covers a range of different facilities: e-mail, which allows messages to be sent to electronic letter-boxes for named individuals, and can be accessed when the named user logs on; computer conferencing, which allows messages to be shared "openly" by all "members" of a teleconference; access to remote data-bases, such a bibliographic sources, sets of abstracts and Internet locations, from which students can download data into their computer and store it for later use (Mason, 1990). To use CMC, students need a computer, a modem connected to the public telephone system, appropriate word-processing and communication software, and preferably, though not necessarily, a printer. CMC does not entail production costs, comparable to the high costs associated with developing computer-based programmes. But, it is unpredictable. It is unpackaged, and the "paths to learning" may result in very different final outcomes.

E-mail is a technology easily understood and mastered, since it closely resembles traditional forms of correspondence in purpose and conception. Computer conferencing is the most common use of CMC in distance education (Bates, 1989b, 1995; Potashnik, 1996). One of the advantages computer conferencing has over e-mail is the possibility for extensive group interaction and the creation of collective intelligence by an on-line community (Mason, 1990). It fosters many-to-many group communication at a time convenient to each. Students, tutors and central staff are linked together by a telecommunication network to a common space for discussion, exchange of ideas and collaborative group work. Computer conferencing allows students to raise queries and questions, to receive replies and suggestions from other students and from the tutor. Central faculty and support staff can also answer questions and offer help, and thus provide students with support broader than has ever been available before.

Computer conferencing holds out great promise for enriching learning and teaching practices for distance education. Computer conferencing can substitute for other means of communication, such as the telephone, face-to-face meetings, mailed letters and print-based materials. It can also complement on-line educational material, as for instance remote databases and computer pre-developed programmes. CMC may be employed for discussing printed material, previously delivered to students by mail, and as means for sustaining educational activity between face-to-face meetings. In short, computer conferencing can be easily integrated with other delivery modes, while providing a strong interactive dimension in distance education. Computer conferencing is an asynchronous form of communication, and thus there are no constraints of time and location as in audio and video conferencing; i.e., computer conferencing combines the benefits of human interaction with the advantages of being independent in time and space—crucially important parameters for distance learners. The asynchronous nature of the medium enables students to prepare their messages carefully on a word processor, and taking as much time as necessary to correct errors before uploading for others to read. The written record of all messages is always available for summarising, revision or simply for rereading (Mason, 1990; Bates, 1995).

CMC holds major implications for course design and development. It might change radically both the role of the academics in distance teaching universities and the structure and content of courses. A course can be developed around a dynamic database made up of bibliographies, case studies, laws and access to Internet locations. At the advanced and graduate levels, it is possible to create very different courses injecting far more student–tutor and student–remote resources communication, and to have far less emphasis on specially pre-prepared self-study materials. In the future, students at distance teaching universities and mainline universities will be able to access programmes virtually from an infinite number of providers around the world. They will be guided by hypermedia interfaces that make the database easy to access and search, and are useful as a learning tool.

To monitor and moderate successful CMC, academic staff at all levels will have to learn how to handle such electronic communications. Moderators will be called on to ensure high quality exchange among learners, between themselves and the learners and between learners and remote databases. CMC requires a good deal of training for both teachers and students if it is to be used effectively. These skills are not simply taken over from face-to-face learning and teaching. Much support deftness and encouragement is needed in the early stages, by technical and tutoring staff, to exploit the potential of this medium. Tutors in particular will need a good control of the subject, and more precisely be knowledgeable about the relevant and available sources of information (Mason, 1990; Bates, 1989b, 1995; Potashnik, 1996).

The major limitation of CMC in most distance teaching universities at present is its cost. CMC ingurgitates quite amazing sums of money. In addition to purchasing the hardware and software needed, on-line telephone charges are very high for students. Not all learners have access to a telephone line, and even if they do, the telephone cannot be used for voice communication at the same time as it is used for computer communication (Mason, 1990). Nor are solutions for students to have access to computers at study centres entirely adequate. Yet, it is a medium that thrives on ease of access. It is perhaps currently best applied in fields where students require a computer for other reasons—computer science, business administration, technology, mathematics. After experimenting with CMC at the British Open University, Mason (1990) concluded that the difficulties that arose from introducing this technology are outweighed by the advantages it offered. Students who use it appreciate easy access to colleagues, the ample opportunities to discuss course issues with tutors and fellow students, and—to use the obvious *jeu de mots*—to overcome the isolation of learning at a distance! CMC is used in British Open University courses as an optional tutoring method; as tutorial support for all students; for discussion of one part of a course; and for fully on-line courses. Graduate-level courses, especially reliant on discussion and exchange were ideally suited for transfer to on-line delivery. The CoSy system at the British Open University has been used to create an *electronic campus* for several thousand students on a limited number of courses (Kaye, 1990).

CoSy was purchased in 1986 from the University of Guelph (Ontario). It includes: e-mail; computer conference facilities which can be "read only" or "read/write" for joint discussion; open or closed; confidential or public; "conversations" for informal communication on a given topic; a "scratch pad" for preparing and editing message texts on-line; directories of users, containing personal resumes of conference participants. The CoSy system was first used in the DT200 Information Technology course (Curran & Wickham, 1994, 40). No other course has taken up CMC on a compulsory basis although there are some, run by the Open Business School and the Faculty of Technology, which are using CMC. It is currently used by many central and regional staff, by some students in other courses on a supplementary basis, and by several people external to the British Open University. Kaye believed that CMC, if effectively implemented, could give rise to a similarly creative atmosphere of expression, discussion, and self-discovery throughout the year, as residential schools manage to do during their short week-long existence (Kaye, 1990, 228).

CMC is used experimentally at all four other distance teaching universities, for instructional purposes in low-population specialist courses, and for special support for particular groups of students—the house-bound or institution-bound, the geographically remote, and those overseas. The Open University of Israel developed a special experimental CMC programme for junior-high science teachers. It has been running since 1995. Over 100 teachers converse with each other and with eight experts across a computer network. Discussions focus on assignments, ways to teach issues in science, everyday implementation problems in class, and for gauging reactions after face-to-face meetings.

Choosing the Balanced Mix of Media

The search for a right and balanced mix of media for each distance teaching university is a most complex and delicate task. As Moore and Kearsley (1996) remarked: "There is no 'right' or 'wrong' technology for distance education. Each medium and each technology for delivering it has its own strengths and weaknesses" (*ibid.*, 99). The selection of media should be made for each course and each programme separately. Each curriculum has distinct requirements depending on its formal objectives, the structure of the subject matter, the background of the student population for which it is intended, and the particular characteristics of the learning environment. A combination should be selected which meets the diversity of discipline-oriented programmes and the variability of learners.

Several attempts have been made to create a standard taxonomy, setting out specific functions and applications for each of the media available, with the idea that a natural, logical choice may be made for each part of a course of study (Holmberg, 1989, 73). No taxonomy has yet been either generally useful or applicable. From the time Wilbur Schramm published his classical study on *Big Media, Little Media*, it has been generally admitted that any claim to superiority by one medium over another has limited relevance. Schramm (1977) argued vehemently that: "There is no cookbook of recipes for media selection that can be applied automatically in every education system" (*ibid.*, 263). While serving as the head of the Commission to explore the feasibility of an Open University in Israel, Schramm and his colleagues emphasised that: "More television, more radio, more films, more instructional tools of any kind have never solved basic educational problems anywhere in the world. Solutions lie not in the media, but in the instruction for which they are used and instructional systems for which they are a part" (Schramm et al., 1972, 40–41). Rowntree (1981) recommended making media choices according to the functions they perform in learning. Some media are better suited for learning at home; others for learning with other students at learning centres and a third for learning at work. Bates (1989b, 1990a, 1995) made a telling point that in selecting media it becomes rapidly apparent that new or advanced technology is not necessarily better or more relevant than established media of text, audio cassettes, television and radio. Newer technologies still have to prove themselves in terms of educational effectiveness and cost. The apparent cost-effectiveness of some of them may yet prove illusory.

Bates laid down seven criteria for selecting media which he presented in the form of an acronym ACTIONS: Access and availability to students; Costs; Teaching functions; Interaction and user-friendliness; Organisational constraints; Novelty; Speed of course development/adaptation (Bates, 1989b, 1995, 1997).

The degree of student access to technological equipment is highly important in deciding whether to use any given medium in a course. If the access policy of the distance teaching university is built around open entry it must consider the technologies available for every potential student. It must calculate the costs of providing students with the media required. For open access distance education, there are, at the moment, relatively few technologies available for large-scale use, such as print, audio cassettes, and to a lesser extent, video cassettes and television, plus the telephone. Neither satellite reception nor home computing is universally accessible. Video-discs, for instance, are unlikely to be feasible for home-based distance learning in the near future. On the other hand, distance education focused on specific professional groups, managers or teachers, either at the place of work or at local centres, can use more sophisticated and expensive media; hence, the choice is less limited. Satellite transmission and computer-based learning become reasonable propositions for individuals at their work-place, or gathered together in "virtual" classes. Even video discs become viable for local centres, when and where they can be shared by several users.

It is important to distinguish between *capital* and *recurrent* costs. Technologies such as television and computing require high initial capital expenditure to purchase a mainframe computer or a television studio and equipment. Recurrent costs are those that are needed each year to keep the system going. These include staff required to service equipment, money to be spent on production or on the purchase of teaching materials, and the cost of delivering courses.

There is also a difference between *fixed* and *variable* costs. The cost of a television programme is fixed: it will be the same for one or for one thousand students. The likely enrolment on a course in terms of sheer numbers is crucial in determining the choice of technology. Joint productions allow for the sharing of fixed costs among several institutions and collaborating groups. Technologies vary considerably in fixed and variable costs. Audio and radio productions, for instance, have low fixed and variable costs. Face-to-face teaching and video-based instruction have low fixed costs but high variable costs. Good quality television programmes have very high fixed costs and relatively low variable costs (Curran, 1990). Sparkes (1984) compared the amount of academic input demanded by different media to produce one hour of teaching material. He found that audio cassette, radio, teleconference and face-to-face instruction require one unit of investment (= one hour of preparation); a video-delivered lecture and computer-mediated instruction, two to five units; print-based materials, two to ten units; high quality television programmes and computer-based pre-programmed learning, twenty to fifty units; and computer-controlled video-disc production fifty to hundred units. In truth, the variability of time invested in preparing study programmes by different media is great indeed.

Curran (1990) also pointed out that politicians tend to believe that an increased use of technology automatically leads to increased cost-effectiveness in educational systems. However, this is not necessarily true in many learning settings, and most particularly so in distance teaching universities, where staff student ratios have been historically far lower than in conventional universities. At best, new technologies are likely to throw out old technologies, rather than leading to major reductions in labour costs. Quite often implementing new technologies increases costs, since most of them serve as supplementary media, and not as substitutes for existing production and delivery technologies. Most distance teaching universities examined here made serious attempts to introduce advanced technologies, such as CMC, computer-based programmes and video conferencing. But by no stretch of the imagination can it be said that these media have become central teaching media. To date, rarely have they even replaced existing technologies. Yet, they have indeed led to increased costs to institutions, and in some cases to the student, and to boot have added an extra burden to the student workload.

Effectiveness in teaching is considered by many to be the main reason for turning to the media technology. "If the technology is not effective, then no matter how cheap, or how convenient it may be for access, it should not be used. However, it is much easier to discriminate between technologies on the basis of access or cost, than it is on teaching effectiveness" (Bates, 1989b, 10). Media vary in the extent to which they can represent different kinds of knowledge and different substantive structures of taught disciplines. And, furthermore, teachers differ considerably in their teaching preferences. Until recently, media selection has not been a major issue facing academic staff. Bates suggested that for many academics in distance education: "Media and technology are gimmicks which at best merely distract academics from their research and teaching, and which at worse interfere with the student–teacher relationship or even add to cost and time in producing courses" (Bates, 1990b, 17). Even so, it takes a great deal of time for a new technology to work its way into a central teaching role. It is likely in the coming decade then that more academics will be taken up with defining criteria to choose appropriate media for producing and delivering their courses, and that more research will be carried out into the effectiveness and merits of different technologies. New developments in this area provide real opportunities for distance education. Computer-based technologies and other forms of interactive media open up nowadays opportunities too tempting to be ignored by the academic community, both in distance teaching universities and at mainstream universities.

User-friendliness and the availability of interaction are additional important criteria of importance which influence the choice of media for instruction. Bates (1989b, 1995) claimed that the control a student has over any medium greatly influences its instructional efficacy. Research has indicated that learning from ephemeral media, such as lectures, radio, television and satellite broadcasting, is more difficult than learning from permanent materials, such as books, audio and video cassettes, discs and computer-based programmes. Being able to stop, re-read or re-listen to study materials increases efficiency in learning. The ability of students to interact with both their fellows and teaching staff is a highly important variable to be seriously considered when choosing media appropriate to distance learning.

Organisational arrangements of distance teaching universities also affect to a high degree the application and installation of new media. As we have already noted, Bates (1990b) argued that distance teaching universities, like public telephone companies, have already made heavy investment in well-tried *older* technologies and services. They currently face new competitors, new governmental and inter-governmental initiatives, and thus further pressures from the growing availability of new technologies. For large-scale distance teaching universities, the shift to new technologies demands a major overhaul of their whole operation and another huge investment in setting up a totally new infrastructure for developing and delivering courses. Such major decisions are not easily taken nor can they be taken quickly. Yet it is evident that if distance teaching universities do not take up positively the challenges of emerging technologies, they may well lose students and government support (Bates, 1990b). It is possible, however, that international joint ventures, financed by global networks, will help to speed up the adoption of new technologies by distance education on an even wider scale.

Bates (1989b, 1995) views novelty as the least important consideration when choosing media. Still, decision-makers in distance teaching universities cannot avoid the fact that, at the moment, it is easier to obtain funds to implement *new* technologies than it is to order *old*, low-cost and reliable media, such as audio cassettes. So, the "novelty value" of a particular medium is not beyond influencing funding agencies to back its use and its take-up.

The speed of course development/adaptation is an important element too, when considering the choice between different production and delivery media. Technologies should be chosen with an eye to the frequency with which the study materials they disseminate require updating. Development of courses at most distance teaching universities takes a long time. It consumes large amounts of money and not inconsiderable human effort. Difficulties in up-dating courses are a major shortcoming of the *old* print technology. Which technology to choose should be determined by the relative ease it affords in the revision of study materials. Developing courses speedily with the possibility constantly to update them are amongst the substantial advantages of computer technology.

In fine, the quest for a balanced mix of media for distance teaching universities stands as an important challenge to their future development. The take-up of new technologies, as also their integration with already proven media, will shape to a large extent the function of distance teaching universities and their effective profiles in their respective national environments.

6

Governance, Funding and Organisation

In organising the universities one clearly sees the impact of the conventional universities. This is mainly because the planners are accustomed to conventional universities, and in the case of open universities they would not like to make bold and unknown experiments in their organisation.

Reddy (1988b, 14)

Bringing down the costs of education and training has usually been an aim of distance learning systems. That is their relevance to the search for a more cost-effective model of mass higher education for the 21st century.

Daniel (1996a, 60).

As for study centres, as students demand a wider curriculum and more opportunities to take courses from other institutions, perhaps in other countries, it will be increasingly difficult to provide local or even regional tutorial support.

Mills (1996, 86)

Introduction

The key to successful management of any university, distance teaching universities included, lies in efficient and effective planning, organisation and leadership. *Governance* is a term used mainly in the context of higher education to describe management, administration and leadership (Middlehurst & Elton, 1992). Birnbaum (1988, 1989) claimed that there is no single definition of *governance*. A *governance* system is at its broadest meaning an institution's answer to the enduring question: *"Who is in charge here?"* Universities in general do not have a steep hierarchical structure of government.

Essentially, they are cellular in nature, each cell representing one academic discipline or department (Perry, 1976).

Cohen and March (1986) developed the model of *organised anarchy*, in an attempt to show that governance of higher education institutions cannot be explained by business models. In universities, the administration is based on the principle of *academic freedom*, combined with the responsibility to co-ordinate all of the university activities and management. For this model to work requires an efficient information system, which makes the anarchy organised, where information flows freely vertically, both up and down, as well as horizontally.

Going beyond the work of Cohen and March, Birnbaum (1988, 1989) suggested the *cybernetic model* as most suitable for describing the governance of higher education institutions. He claimed that, despite the total absence of tight structures of management in traditional universities, they have proved remarkably stable institutions. He pointed to the fact that "something has brought a reasonable degree of stability and order to a system so complex that outcomes cannot be predicted even by most powerful computers" (Birnbaum, 1989, 240). According to Birnbaum, such stability depends on constant adjustments and responses through the cybernetic working of self-correcting mechanisms operating at a micro level. Nowadays, governance systems of many universities have become more managerial and business-oriented, transferring more power to decide at the macro level (Neave & van Vught, 1991; Trow, 1994, 1996b; Groof, et al., 1998).

Distance teaching universities, by their very nature, are more hierarchical in their structure and organisation, compared to most mainstream universities. Most distance education systems are endeavours of a sizeable scope with myriad interconnected parts. Each part of the distance education organisation relies on excellent communications and appropriate control over the various organisational components (Schlosser & Anderson, 1994). Because of the inherent complexity and interdependence of their parts, distance teaching universities require tighter management than conventional higher education institutions (Snowden & Daniel, 1980; Verduin & Clark, 1991; Rumble, 1992a).

The need for tighter management is natural to distance teaching universities, in the sense that the administrative and management units of distance enterprises need to retain a higher degree of control and must command a greater measure of knowledge on the inner workings of their organisation than normally would be used in a non-distance institution. Effective coordination of personnel at numerous levels and multiple sites requires excellent communication among all elements of the enterprise (Verduin & Clark, 1991). As the number of students grows and expands beyond national boundaries even, the intricacies of operating distance education systems on a daily basis become proportionately more complicated.

This chapter examines various *governance* models of the five distance teaching universities in the context of the norms prevailing within their national settings. It explains funding arrangements for each distance teaching university and discusses the management centralised versus decentralised of their regional and local study centres.

Governance

Neave and van Vught (1991) drew an important distinction between higher education systems where universities are conceived as a state service and those where a university is held to be a free standing corporation whose administration is carried out in the name of an independent body, be it a *Board of Trustees* or a *University Council*. UNED and the FernUniversität function as part of a state service framework, whereas the British Open University, the Open University of Israel and Athabasca University operate as autonomous corporations.

There are different governance systems in different national settings, and even within national boundaries (Neave, 1995; Groof et al., 1998). Some terms are confusing. They denote different meanings in various places. For example, a *Vice Chancellor* is the head of the university in most British universities, equivalent to a President in American universities. In the Open University of Israel a *Vice Chancellor* is mainly a ceremonial title, who acts as the chairman of the Council in the absence of the Chancellor and Deputy Chancellor. A *Chancellor* in the UK, in Canada and in Israel is a ceremonial title, while in Germany a *Kanzler* used until the Reform Act of 1976 to be the Head of the Central Administration, representing under close supervision of government, the government's legal obligations in the university. From 1976 on, the *Rektor* or *President* of a German University combined the headship of both legal and academic parts of the university. The *Kanzler* no longer reports on legal and financial matters to the state government but rather to the *Rektor* or *President*. An additional example, a *Senate* in most universities acts as the supreme academic authority and a *Council* is responsible for the financial matters, while in Germany's universities the function of the *Council* falls to the *Senate*, which is responsible for both the academic and financial matters (Frackmann, 1994; Frackmann & De Weert, 1994; Groof et al., 1998). The size of a *Senate* varies greatly in different institutions, and comprises from a few dozens, as in the case of the Open University of Israel, to over 1,000 members, as in the case of the British Open University. Table 6.1 sets out the basic variables of the governance, funding and organisation of each distance teaching university.

British Open University

As Table 6.1 shows, the main governing bodies of the British Open University are the *Council* and *Senate*. The Planning Committee decided that the government structure of the British Open University should be of the traditional kind with the *Council* as the main financial controlling body of the University,

Table 6.1. Governance, Funding and Organisation of the British Open University, UNED, the Open University of Israel, FernUniversität and Athabasca University*

Variable	British Open University	UNED	Open University of Israel	FernUniversität	Athabasca University
Governance	Council Senate (bi-cameral)	Consejo Social Claustro Universitario Junta de Gobierno	Council Academic Committ. Executive Committ. (bi-cameral)	Senate Kuratorium	Governing Council (uni-cameral)
Head	Vice-Chancellor	Rector	President	Rector	President
Academic Units	Faculties Course teams	Faculties Departments	Departments Course Teams	Faculties Departments	Faculties Course teams
Operating Budget**	$300 million	$129 million	$51 million	$70 million	$20 million
State Funding	60%	40%	27%	95%	57%
Student Numbers	157,450	136,480	28,771	54,430	10,974
Study Centers	13 Regional 250 UK 21 Europe	96 57 local 27 sub-centers 8 overseas	108	63 29 NRW 29 FDR 5 abroad	3 regional
Control of Study Centers	Centralised	Decentralised	Centralised	Mixed	Centralised

*Based on:
Open University of Israel (1986) *Statutes and General Regulations*, The Open University of Israel.
EADTU (1993a) *Directory of Study Centers in Europe*, Herleen: Europ. Assoc. of Distance Teaching Universities, 24, 50, 70.
Daniel, J.S. (1996a) *The Mega-Universities and the Knowledge Media*. London: Kogan Page, 31.
Schuemer, R. (1997) *Personal Communication*.
Patten, P. (1997) *Personal Communication*.
**1995 figures.

and the *Senate* as the supreme academic authority (Perry, 1976). The British Open University's government structure resembles the bi-cameral model of conventional British universities (Eustace, 1992; Bull, 1994). The *Council* is a relatively small body on which members of academic staff are in minority and the lay membership, as defined in the Charter, in the majority. Usually, it is composed of about 30 members, 20 of them lay people and 10 members of university staff. There is a lay chairman who is usually called a Pro-Chancellor. The Pro-Chancellor is non-executive (Perry, 1997), by and large elected for two-three years. Chancellors and Vice Chancellors are ex-officio members of the *Council*. The British Open University's *Council* includes representatives of the Privy Council, Committee of Vice Chancellors and Principals, local authority associations, Royal Society, BBC, Senate, students, graduates, tutorial and counselling staff. The *Council* is responsible for the university's financial affairs, confirms the *Senate's recommendations on academic appointments in consultation with the Senate*, and appoints the Vice Chancellor.

The principal responsibility for academic affairs in British universities resides in the *Senate*, a fairly large body composed wholly of University staff, and chaired by the Vice Chancellor. *Senates* often include all professors ex-officio, additional selected academic members, and usually the registrar and chairmen. The Vice Chancellor is ex-officio the chairman and serves as a link between the *Senate* and *Council*. The Senate's powers extend to coordinating the work of faculty boards and making recommendations on professional appointments, the award of degrees, student discipline and teaching Programmes. The British Open University's *Senate* comprises full-time members of the University's central and regional academic staff, representatives of part-time and tutorial staff together with BBC representatives and student representatives. Senate membership in the British Open University during the 1990s went over 1,000 members.

Daniel (1996a) perceived the large *Senate* as one of the British Open University's strengths: "Students and staff have a large role in a participative governance structure that includes a 1,000-member Senate. Most British Open University people see this as a strength. They would argue that although it may take longer to reach decisions with such structures, those decisions are carried out faster and more effectively because they are widely owned" (*ibid.*, 194).

Obviously, *Council* and *Senate* delegate everyday work to boards and committees. The Academic Board, Validation Board, Senate Agenda Committee, Honorary Degrees Committee, General Assembly and Quality Assurance Panel report directly to *Senate*. The Strategic Planning and Resources Committee reports to both the *Council* and the *Academic Board*. Building Estates and Accommodation Committee, Finance Committee, Audit Committee and Staff Policy Committee operate under the *Council's* auspices (Open University, 1992; Platt, 1997).

There are different patterns of governance in the UK for civic and new universities, Oxford and Cambridge, and for federal universities (London and

Wales). In civic and new universities, the chief administration officer is the *Vice Chancellor*, who usually holds office until retirement. The Chancellorship is a ceremonial position held for life. At the second échelon, there are one or more Pro-Vice Chancellors, who are professors holding office for limited terms. *Registrars* handle academic registrations, and the *Bursars* or *Treasurers* are concerned with university finance. Normally, *Vice Chancellors* are drawn from the ranks of professoriate. Until recently, unlike the situation in the USA, there has been very little interchange between government, industry and academic life in the UK (Eustace, 1992, 764–5).

The executive head at the British Open University is the *Vice Chancellor*, assisted by several Pro-Vice Chancellors, each with a responsibility for a specific policy area, such as Strategy; Resources; Programme Development; Presentation and Student Support; University Relations and Research (Rumble & Harry, 1982). Walter Perry, the first Vice Chancellor of the British Open University, has pointed out that to operate a hierarchical structure where responsibility is assumed by an individual head within a system with two separate governing bodies, was a most difficult task, particularly given that the detailed infrastructure required both to support the statutory bodies and to implement their policies and decisions were not laid down in the Charter, and have emerged, developed and changed over the years (Perry, 1976, 1992, 1997).

On the academic side, the British Open University made a significant break from the normal pattern. Within its six (seven from 1987) faculties, responsibility for individual teaching Programmes is vested not in departments or disciplines but in course teams, created for that purpose. The academic structure of the University is a much smaller part of the total university operation than in conventional universities. Organisationally the British Open University is divided into five major areas: the faculties; the Centre for Continuing Education; The Institute of Educational Technology; Regional Tutorial Services; Operations responsible for course production; the Administration (International Association of Universities, 1993, 929).

The operational divisions of the university, its regional structure and its relatively complex administration are hierarchical rather than cellular in nature. The sheer size of the British Open University and its unique operation turned up a whole range of administrative problems. The University's administration is headed by the University Secretary. It operates on a large scale and includes divisions of: student administration, academic administration, finance, management services, and estates.

Universidad Nacional de Educación a Distancia

UNED is an integral part of the national system of Spanish higher education. It operates under central governmental authority, which lays down a national curriculum for higher education and employs university staff within the civil service (James, 1982; García-Garrido, 1988). The Spanish higher education system is based, as in France, on the *Jacobin State* model, in which the state control is ensured through close oversight and standardisation of the curricula, hours to be taught and assigned to each subject, conditions for appointment and criteria for advancement (Neave, 1995).

When democracy was restored in 1978, the new constitution of 1978 reorganised the entire political fabric of the country, creating 17 regions of autonomous communities (García-Garrido, 1993; Neave, 1995). There was a move from total centralism to regionalism. According to the Spanish law on university reform (*Ley de Reforma Universitaria*), issued in 1983, UNED is the sole national university, depending directly on the Central Ministry of Education and Science. Other Spanish universities depend on committees within their autonomous regions.

UNED has a bi-cameral academic and administrative structure. As Table 6.1 sets out, its main governing bodies are: the *Claustro Universiatrio*, the *Consejo Social* and the *Junta de Gobierno*. The *Claustro Universiatrio* (as in any other Spanish University) is the main collegial or corporate body. It is a monumental body of 235 members, of which 106 are permanent or tenured professors, 45 non-tenured academic staff, 60 students and 20 administrative staff (García-Garrido, 1994). The main responsibilities of the *Claustro* are the preparation and approval of the *Statutes* of the University, the election of the Rector, and the approval of general lines of actions in the university (García-Garrido, 1988, 1993).

The *Consejo Social* represents society within the university. It is composed of about 20 members representative of employers, trade unions, local corporations and academic and non-academic staff of the University. It approves the University's budget, as well as provides a link between society and university. The Chairman is a person external to the university generally a prominent public figure or a high-rank person from the corporate world. Unlike universities which operate as autonomous corporations, where the *Council* has solid standing (like in the UK), the *Consejo Social* in Spanish universities is neither very important nor a very efficient body. The *Claustro Universiatrio* appoints the Rector, not the Council, which is the case in the UK. Three fifths of the *Consejo Social's* members are non-university members, the remaining two fifths include representatives of the *Junta de Gobierno*, elected by the latter from among its own members, which necessarily include the Rector, General Secretary and the Chief Administrator (García-Garrido, 1994).

The *Junta de Gobierno* is a small governing body of the University, which discusses ongoing academic and organisational matters. It is chaired by the Rector and composed of Pro-Rectors, General Secretary, deans and directors of faculties and schools, plus representatives of professors and other staff. In 1994 it included 45 members (*ibid.*). It meets once a month (James, 1982, 165). Faculties have also *Juntas*.

The main executive head of UNED is the Rector. Amongst other important decision-makers are: The Pro-Rector of Academic Affairs and Academic Staff; the Pro-Rector of Research; the Pro-Rector of Study Centres; the Pro-Rector of Continuing Education; the Pro-Rector of Finance. The second tier of governance includes the deans of the faculties, the Director of the Institute of Educational Sciences (Instituto de Ciencas de la Educación); and the General Secretary who is responsible for the administrative bodies of the University (García-Garrido, 1988, 204).

Apart from its special features which derive from its particular nature, UNED's headquarters organisation is very similar to that of traditional Spanish universities. Within the faculties, the core of academic life revolves around departments. The departments, each under the control of a full professor (*Catedrático*), are responsible for the preparation of study materials, examinations and assignments; staff mobilisation; contact and coordination with the study centres; and the counselling of students (James, 1982). The Institute of Educational Sciences and Technical Division for audiovisual Materials carry out research on student characteristics, motivation and performance, study at a distance, use of media, study centres etc. The warehouses are also located at headquarters.

Open University of Israel

Section 15 of the Council for the Higher Education Law of 1958 guarantees the autonomy of Israeli universities, both in their academic conduct and in their administrative and financial affairs. Though higher education institutions are financially dependent on government support and are required to submit to the Planning and Budgeting Committee their budgets for approval, each institution is free to conduct its academic and administrative affairs as it sees fit, within the confines of approved budget.

Most Israeli universities have two heads: a *President* and a *Rector*. The supreme authority of each university is vested in its *Board of Governors* and *Executive Committee*, drawn from prominent Jewish individuals outside Israel in academia, business and management. The *Board of Governors* appoints the *President*, whose main responsibility is for the administrative and financial affairs. The president is assisted by a Director-General and/or a Vice President.

The supreme authority in academic affairs is the *Rector*, who is a full professor, elected for a two–three year term, by the *Senate*, in its turn, composed of all full professors and representatives from other academic ranks, plus few representatives from the student body. *Senates* of the large universities are quite extensive with several hundred members. The power of the *Rector* and of *Senate*, and its committees, extends beyond academic affairs to administrative matters as well. The Israeli university is basically grounded on the principle of a loose coalition of self-governing departments (Ben David, 1986, 126–127).

The Open University of Israel developed its main governance on somewhat different bodies compared to its conventional counterparts. As Table 6.1 reveals, its main governing bodies are the *Council*, the *Executive Committee*, and the *Academic Committee*. The *Council* is the supreme authority of the University and acts as the University's Board of Trustees. It is composed both of lay and academic representatives, and apart from the Chancellor and the Deputy Chancellor, who come from the UK, all other representatives are from Israel. It is headed by the Chancellor of the University. The Deputy Chancellor acts as chairman if the Chancellor is absent; and the Vice Chancellor acts as chairman in the absence of the Chancellor and Deputy Chancellor. The *President* is an ex-officio member of the Council. In 1995 the Council was composed of 36 members (President's Report, 1995, 9). The Council lays down the policies of the University and oversees their implementation. The *Council* supervises the affairs of management, business and property (Halperin, 1984; Open University of Israel, 1986).

The *Executive Committee* is elected by the Council from among its members to fulfil planning, guidance and follow-up operations specified in the Regulations, and is responsible to the Council. It is composed of eight members (President's Report, 1995, 9).

The *Academic Committee* is appointed by the Council. It is responsible for drawing up the academic regulations and Programmes and with maintaining the academic standards of the University, including the range and structure of the academic Programmes. It is a modified and scaled-down version of a *Senate* in conventional universities, and is composed of both full and associate professors of the Open University of Israel as well as from other universities. Professors from other universities were invited to become members of the Open University of Israel's *Academic Committee* due to the limited numbers of its internal academic faculty. In the early days, external professors constituted a majority of the supreme body of the Open University of Israel (Ginzburg, 1997, 83). In 1995 the *Academic Committee* was composed from 35 members, of whom 15 were representatives from other universities (*ibid.*, 10). The Chairman of the *Academic Committee*, is the President. Following broad disciplinary lines the Committee has appointed four sub-committees in: Humanities and Judaic Studies; Social Sciences and Education; Mathematics and Computer Science; Natural and Life Sciences.

The *President* wields the academic and administrative responsibilities, is the Head of the University, and is assisted by a Vice President for Academic Affairs and a Director General. It is important to remember that in three conventional universities the roles of President and Rector were unified *de facto* in the last decade, and are carried on by one person.

There is also a *Faculty Council*, composed of all the Open University of Israel's senior academic faculty. It meets once a month and is closely involved in discussing various issues pertinent to the Open University of Israel's operation. Yet, the role of the *Faculty Council*, is not defined in the Statutes and General Regulations of the University, and thus the *Faculty Council* has no decision-making power. It can merely advise the *Academic Committee*. In reality, most of its proposals are adopted.

As we have seen (Chapter 4), the Open University of Israel had neither faculties nor departments until 1996, but rather three administrative divisions responsible for course development, teaching and student affairs. In its early days, the Open University of Israel's President explained the rationale behind the relatively lean structure of its governance and overall academic organisation: "We did not follow the traditional division into faculties and departments. The university functioned as one unified academic body. We had also been very careful to establish as few committees and other statutory bodies as possible. This saved us a lot of time and bureaucracy and enabled straightforward and fast decision-making" (Ginzburg, 1997, 82). This rationale differs substantially from those underlying the organisational infrastructure of most other distance teaching universities, whose organs of governance resemble closely those of conventional universities in each national context. It definitely differs substantially from the large senate found in the British Open University. In this respect, the Open University of Israel is unique. Clearly, the *smallness* of its faculty has some administrative advantages, but also bears many heavy disadvantages, which were discussed earlier in Chapter 3.

From 1996 on, the Open University of Israel divided its faculty and courses into seven departments: Literature, Music and Arts; History and Judaic Studies; Psychology and Education; Sociology and Political Science; Management and Economics; Computer Science and Mathematics; and Sciences. But still the course teams constitute the main units of operation at the Open University of Israel, and are constructed on an *ad hoc* basis.

The *Director General* is directly responsible for the administration of the University, which includes six organs: personnel; finance; purchasing, supply and construction; computing services; maintenance; and the library. The publishing, course design and teaching assessment units operate also at the headquarters.

FernUniversität

Universities in Germany are public corporate bodies. Higher education institutions are governed by a three-fold system: the legal acts of the federal government; those of the relevant Land; their own statutes. The 1949 constitution of the Federal Republic of Germany gave jurisdiction over education and culture to the 11 Länder (after the German re-unification there are currently 16 Länder). The Länder governments influence university affairs through their approval of university statutes, and appointment of permanent teaching staff (from among the nominees of the faculties). The *Wissenschaftsrat* (Science Council), established by the Länder in 1957 is a federal advisory body, and is the highest consulting body for higher education

(Teichler, 1986). The *Wissenschaftsrat* consists of academics appointed by the President of the Federal Republic, and state government and federal state government representatives. It makes general recommendations in respect of the institutions' and the state investment plans.

The individual states have their own laws and regulations concerning higher education but with certain shared features agreed upon in a Framework Act, jointly passed by the states and the federal state (Teichler, 1986; Frackmann, 1994). The Framework Act of 1976 abolished the dual administration, which consisted of the head of university central administration (*Kanzler*) and the *Rektor*, elected only for two years, and who represented the so-called academic self-government (Frackmann et. al, 1994). The 1976 Framework Act extended the role of the President from four to eight years and set him over both parts of the higher education governance, legal and academic. The 1985 Framework Act re-introduced the role of a *Rektor* as an alternative option for university administration. Thus, there is either a *President* or a *Rektor* as the head of a German university.

The *Senate* is the highest and most important body of the self-governance, assisted by commissions and committees which prepare recommendations. The *Senate* deliberates issues of coordination and planning in research and teaching, as well as the distribution of the budget. The *Rektor* is elected either by the *Senate* or by a *Konvent* (Council) (Groof et al.,1998) After election, however, the Minister of Science and Research of the Land has to confirm the elected person and officially appoint the new *Rektor* to his post. There have been a few instances where the Ministry refused to confirm the elected candidate (Frackmann, 1994).

The Framework Act of 1976 gave middle-level academic teaching and research staff, students and non-academic staff between one quarter to one third of the votes on self-governing bodies at central institutional level. A court decision in 1973 has guaranteed a majority of 51% for professors in regard to all important issues of research, and a 50% majority at least where issues concerning teaching were involved. Representatives of the public were never admitted as members of these bodies (Teichler, 1986; Bartels & Peters, 1986).

Like the traditional universities in the Federal Republic of Germany, the FernUniversität is autonomous in its academic teaching and research. The FernUniversität's *Senate* comprises the *Rektor*, four Pro-Rectors, *Kanzler* (responsible for financial affairs), four representatives of professors, three lower rank academic staff, two administrative staff, the secretary of the university and three students (Peters, 1981; Keegan, 1982). Clearly, the Senate of the FernUniversität is substantially smaller than its British Open University counterpart, and both its composition and functions differ. In addition to the *Senate,* there is a standing advisory board in the FernUniversität (*Kuratorium*) made up of representatives of other universities, of higher education ministries of other states, of radio and television, and of employers' organisations and unions (Bartels & Peters, 1986, 98). Four committees operate under the

Senate's oversight: the Committees on Academic Affairs, on Research, on Continuing Professional Education, and on Construction and Finance (Keegan, 1982).

The head of the University is the *Rektor*, who is responsible both for academic and administrative issues. Elected by the *Senate* and appointed by the State Minister of Science and Research of North Rhine-Westphalia, he is assisted by Pro-Rectors for Academic Affairs, Research, Continuing Education, and Structure and Finance, as well as by the Secretary of the University (Peters, 1981, 1994c, 1997).The *Rektor* is the chairman of the *Senate*, and chairman of the *Rektorat* which is the central governance committee of the University, similar to the *Junta de Gobierno* in Spain. The *Rektorat* is composed of the *Rektor*, four Pro-Rectors and the Secretary of the University. It is the main executive body responsible for all matters not officially assigned by the university statutes to other bodies (Keegan, 1982, 104).

German higher education is based on a deeply rooted tradition of confidence in the individual researcher and in the chair holder rather than a strong departmental organisation. Professors are civil servants with life-long tenure. Universities that were originally centred on the full professor, moved to a more faculty-oriented structure in the course of the 1970s. The old and rather large faculties were divided into departments. Compared with the old faculty, the department is smaller in size and discipline-oriented. The department or faculty is headed by a dean, who is supervised by the *Rektor*. As in traditional German universities, the faculties and departments of the Fern-Universität are responsible for the curricula, research and tuition; they plan and develop the study materials, and design and conduct examinations.

The central administration provides services and takes care of enrolment and materials delivery. There are five administrative divisions: organisation, student affairs, personnel, technical production and study centres. The central institutions include the Centre for Development of Distance Study Materials (ZFE); the Central Institute for Distance Education Research (ZIFF); the Library; the Computing Centre; and the Student Counselling Services (*ibid.*).

Athabasca University

The provinces in Canada are vested with the authority of their higher education systems (Jones, 1997). The Universities Commission in Alberta was created in the 1966 Act as an intermediary body between Government and universities. Alberta boasts a Universities Coordinating Council consisting of the president and senior vice president of each university, appointed to it by the General Faculties Council of the university. In addition, up to three other members of the academic staff of each university may be appointed by the Universities Coordinating Council. The Council has the authority to approve the admission standards for first year students, has jurisdiction over the conditions of entry to certain learned professions and callings, and may take forward to the Minister any matter it considers to be related to university issues.

In traditional forms of governance in Canada (except the French-speaking universities) authority over academic affairs rests in the *Senate*, whereas authority over non-academic affairs lies with a lay governing board, known as the *Board of Governors, Trustees or Regents*, which appoints the President, deans and department chairmen, decides on faculty promotion, controls the property of the institution, approves the recommendations of the Senate on academic matters; and has financial responsibility for the institution. Until the 1970s, these boards were composed solely of laymen. Statutes and provincial universities barred academic staff from membership. The board of provincial universities includes a considerable number of government officials, as well as representatives from business and the professions (Andrews et al., 1997).

Academic *Senates* normally include deans and some additional elected or appointed faculty representatives, students' representatives, alumni, provincial government appointees, and other outside persons with special interests in higher education. *Senates* may have as many as 200 members. Their jurisdiction extends over academic policies including admissions, degrees and students' discipline. Like *Governing Boards*, they function through a number of committees.

Following a special report of a commission on higher education in the 1970s, it was recommended to increase the number of faculty representatives on governing bodies; to diversify membership of governing boards; to limit the size of *Senates* to 50 members; to empower *Senates* to make recommendations to the *Governing Board* on any matter whatsoever; and to represent students on *Senate* committees.

French-speaking universities in Canada combine the Governing Board and the Senate in an overarching governing body called the *Conseil d'Administration*. Furthermore, the University of Toronto created in 1972 a new government structure with a single governing body. The University of Toronto stands as a fascinating test case for the practice of uni-cameral government (Groof et al., 1998). As shown in Table 6.1, Athabasca University has also adapted a uni-cameral system (Andrews et al. 1997, 72). Athabasca University and Laval University are the only English-teaching Canadian universities to follow the uni-cameral governance model of the University of Toronto. Athabasca University established a corporation—*The Athabasca University Governing Council*—which combines the duties of a Board of Governors, General Faculties Council, and Senate. The maximum number of members on the Governing Council is being set at 27 (Shale, 1982, 47). This uni-cameral body is headed by a chairman appointed by the Lieutenant Governor in Council of Alberta, in addition to whom are the president and three vice presidents of the University, one student, one non-academic staff member, five academic staff members, a tutor, and 14 further members representing the general public. Athabasca University adapted the uni-cameral governance structure "in the belief that concentrating the responsibility and authority for both academic and administrative affairs in one body would allow the institution to respond in a more timely and concerted manner to services demands placed on it" (*ibid.*, 52). In reality, the *Council* "has experienced a corporate schizophrenia because of its divided responsibilities and membership" (*ibid.*). To remedy this, the *Academic Council* has been established as a subordinate committee of the *Governing Council* (Rawlence, 1994).

The chief academic and administrative head of Athabasca University is the *President*. There are three vice presidents, each of whom heads one of the three operational divisions: Learning Services, responsible for the academic functions; University Services, which provides administrative services in support of the University's academic operations; and Finance and Facilities, responsible for financial affairs and facilities planning (James, 1982). Like the British Open University and the Open University of Israel, Athabasca University does not have departments within its faculties. Course development is planned and written within course teams. There is a Centre for Distance Education which, from 1994 onwards may be considered as a quasi-faculty and is primarily responsible for the development and delivery of Athabasca University's MA in Distance Education (Rawlence, 1994).

Units that provide support services to students are: Regional and Tutorial Services, which administers the system of tutors and coordinates the delivery mechanisms; the Student Development Service, which disseminates information and advice on career and educational planning to students; and the Registry which is responsible for student administration and student records. The Library, Computing Services, Media Services, Editorial Services, Instructional Development Unit provide administrative and instructional support to instructional activities of course preparation.

Some Observations on the Distance Teaching Universities' Governance Systems

An examination of *governance* systems of the five distance teaching universities reveals two interesting phenomena. First, a clear distinction exists between large and small distance teaching universities in their overall approach to their governing bodies. Small distance teaching universities, like the Open University of Israel and Athabasca University, try to maintain their administrative organs as small and as compact as possible. The Open University of Israel's Academic Committee is very small, compared with the Senates of conventional universities, and its organisational infrastructure is "lean" in the extreme. The Athabasca University adopted a uni-cameral model of governance so that decision-making, both in financial and academic matters, would be more efficient and less time consuming, compared to the traditional bi-cameral arrangement. The rationale behind the "slimming down" of the governance structure is mainly financial. Small distance teaching universities, by their very nature, have to struggle harder than the large ones, to achieve economies of scale. They cannot afford to support heavy governing bodies. Large distance teaching universities, on the other hand, have no such problem. Thus, the British Open University, UNED and the German FernUniversität have *governance bodies* comparable in most regards to those in traditional universities. In the case of UNED and the FernUniversität this policy is tied in with their overriding desire to resemble on nearly everything their conventional fellows.

A second noteworthy development relates to the organisation of the academic units in distance teaching universities. The British Open University, the Open University of Israel and Athabasca University, which officially adopted an *open access* policy, and sought to provide different and innovative curricula, moved away from the departmental structure—the core organisational feature of classical universities—and placed the course development and course teaching on a *course team* arrangement. The course team unit allows greater flexibility in developing inter- and trans-disciplinary programmes. It encourages cooperation between academics and other professionals in designing innovative-type curricula. UNED and the FernUniversität however cleared to the traditional organisation of faculties and departments. This thrust clearly underlines the tremendous impact which the initial mission goals of each distance teaching university, and the unique prevailing academic ethos in each national setting both had upon the shaping of organisational and academic structure of each university.

Funding

Although funding policies and methods vary greatly among countries, most distance education institutions are funded somewhat differently from conventional higher education establishments, and are reckoned to provide substantial economies of scale (Wagner, 1977; Perraton, 1988, 1993; Mugridge, 1994a,b; Daniel, 1996a). Due to their specific nature, the majority of distance teaching universities are expected to show a high degree of fiscal accountability, and to be cheaper per student and per graduate when set against their conventional counterparts.

In examining the funding arrangements of the five distance teaching universities we will focus on the differences within them, and on the differences between them and traditional universities in each national context.

Comparing the Distance Teaching Universities' Operating Budgets

Table 6.1 shows that the British Open University commands the largest operating budget. In 1995, this was around $300 million (with 157,450 students) compared with $129 million budget for UNED (with 134,480 students) (Daniel, 1996a, 31; UNED, 1996). However, additional parameters should be considered if reality is to be presented with great precision. The UNED budget, for instance, excludes 80% of the operation costs of its study centres whilst the salaries of part-time tutors, are borne by local authorities. This is discussed further on (García-Garrido, 1988; UNED, 1993, 1995). The same applies to the FernUniversität, which does not finance its study centres outside North Rhine-Westphalia.

When we take into account all the relevant parameters, course production cost in the British Open University is the highest of all distance teaching universities. Even in the early 1970s, the cost per course (which amounted to one sixth of an ordinary degree) ranged from £500,000 for an Arts based course to double that amount for a Science based one, which required a home experiment kit and a higher component of television time. In the 1970s, BBC productions accounted for around third of the total operating budget of the British Open University. Later, the proportion of funds devoted to broadcasting was reduced considerably (Perry, 1997, 16). By contrast, in the Open University of Israel the production of a course (which equals approximately one third of a British Open University's course) ranges from $100,000 to $200,00, despite the fact that stringent quality assurance procedures for course production also apply at the Open University of Israel (Guri-Rosenblit, 1993c, 1997a).

Variations in the process of course development, choice of media, number of courses, and the nature of the support systems are the main variables which explain the relative differences between the operating budgets of the different distance teaching universities. The more quality assurance measures employed in course production, the more expensive media involved, the more generous and more intensive the support systems, the greater the fixed and variable costs for each distance teaching university. The number of students is an additional important variable for explaining variability both within distance teaching universities, and between distance teaching universities and campus universities. A more detailed explanation as to the cost structure of distance teaching universities follows further on.

A particularly interesting variable involves state participation in the distance teaching universities' budgeting. As may be seen in Table 6.1, state participation varies greatly. It ranges from 95% in the case of the German FernUniversität to less than 30% in the case of the Open University of Israel. Initial differences between national budgeting conventions and regulations, the substantial variances in the proportion of state funding also reflect a differential attitude of each government to the role of its national or provincial distance teaching university. In Germany, universities are fully financed by the governments of the Länder in which they reside (Teichler, 1988; Frackmann, 1994). FernUniversität is basically funded on the same formulae applied to classical universities, taking into account its unique characteristics. In reality, FernUniversität was requested by government to charge for its study material (from 1983 on), the exception rather than the rule in Germany. In Israel, universities derive around 70% of their operating budgets from government through the Planning and Budgeting Committee (Pazy, 1994). Thus, the relatively low participation of the state in the Open University of Israel's budget reveals the underlying assumption by the Israeli government that a distance teaching university should be highly cost efficient, base its operation mainly on its own revenues, or risk closure. This basic policy explains to a great extent the very lean organisational infrastructure of the Open University of Israel and the limited numbers of its academic faculty.

Funding arrangements for some distance teaching universities have been subject to several revisions over the years. The British Open University is the most interesting case. After a quarter century of separate and special funding, from 1993 onwards, the British Open University has been placed on the same footing as other universities, and now receives funds direct from the British government (Daniel et al., 1994). From its genesis in the 1960s, the British Open University was funded directly by the Department of Education and Science (DES) rather than by the Universities Grants Committee (UGC). The UGC, established by the Treasury in 1919 to advise on the financial needs of universities and allocate to universities the money voted by the parliament, was replaced by the Universities Funding Council in 1989.

The British Open University was the only university to be funded by the Department of Education and Science. The University's grant was determined annually in the light of the British Open University's own statement of requirements, and from the 1980s as the recommendation of an Advisory Committee of independent persons appointed by the DES Secretary. Further, the fear that the UGC would not devote sufficient funds to an innovative institution, resulted in the decision to put the British Open University directly under the ambit of the DES. The arrangement had certain advantages: the government could examine the funding requirements and make whatever provision it judged necessary to support the particular needs of a growing distance teaching institution. This consideration was particularly important during the university's formative years. However, it also meant the government was able to fund the British Open University on a UK-wide basis, since it operated across 13 regional centres all over the country.

Clearly, the funding of the British Open University posed a unique set of financial challenges. The cost of producing high quality multi-media courses using full time academic staff and BBC production staff was extremely high; initial expenditure was exactly the same for one student as for a million students (Perry, 1997, 17). In normal circumstances, exact figures in estimating the budget of an innovative institution are essential for its success. In the case of the British Open University, a gross miscalculation of its actual operating budget saved it from extinction. Twenty-five years later, Perry revealed that the first estimates made by Lord Goodman turned out to be wrong. Lord Goodman based his estimates of the annual running costs on a figure of £3.5 million: "In doing so he made one of his rare misjudgements for the figure turned out, quite soon after, to be a gross underestimate. Many years later, in the House of

Lords, he quite openly admitted his error and boasted that it had been a vital factor in the creation of the University, since a correct estimate almost certainly would have led the Treasury, already scared by an apparently open-ended financial commitment that was implied by having no entrance qualifications for the new university, to abort the embryo institution" (Perry, 1997, 7).

From the late 1980s, the disadvantages of separate funding began to outweigh the advantages (Daniel, 1993; Daniel et al., 1994). The Funding Councils of the universities and polytechnics introduced funding methodologies and special schemes to promote and reward growth, innovation and encourage competition. The British Open University was unable to take advantage of these new opportunities nor to play its full part in the expansion of educational opportunities that they encouraged. Its rate of growth began to lag. Both Government and the British Open University recognised this major problem and in the early 1990s jointly examined the possibility of new funding arrangements. The government paper "Higher Education: A New Framework", was published in May 1991, proposed a major revision to the complex funding patterns of universities and polytechnics. It recommended the abolition of the so-called *binary system* composed of universities and polytechnics and its replacement by a unitary system of higher education (*ibid.*).

From 1993 the British Open University became integrated with new funding arrangements for higher education in the UK, which followed the upgrade of 38 polytechnics and colleges to university status. The British Open University now operates "alongside and in competition with other providers of higher education" (*ibid.*, 13). Its core grant comes from the Higher Education Funding Council of England (HEFCE), though it is the only national British university, which, in principle, is entitled to be part of the Funding Councils of Wales, Scotland and the special office for Northern Ireland. It was decided that the HEFCE should fund the British Open University for teaching and research throughout the UK. Other funding councils sponsor special projects and activities undertaken by the British Open University outside England.

These new arrangements allowed the British Open University to manage its finances in a more conventional manner, and put it on an even footing with other universities. The British Open University has not lost from this reform. Its budget for the academic year 1992 was 152 million pounds. Of this, almost 90 million was funded through the DES. In 1995, its budget exceeded 200 million pounds, with the same proportion as 60% funded by the HEFCE. The evaluation of the British Open University by the same criteria as other universities, also facilitated comparison with conventional universities in relation to the quality of its teaching, its research and its cost efficiency. In a report, issued by the HEFCE in 1995 as its first round of quality assessments, the British Open University figured as one of only 13 universities out of 70 to offer a comprehensive curriculum and to receive excellent ratings in more than half the subjects assessed, despite the fact that public expenditure per full-time equivalent student was the lowest in the UK (Daniel 1996a, 9).

Funding of the British Open University may even improve given possible changes in the funding of full-time versus part-time students. Hitherto, full-time students were supported by government and local authorities, whereas all the British Open University being part-time students had to pay for their courses. The Report of the Dearing Committee, published in July 1997, recommended introducing tuition fees in all universities (National Committee of Inquiry into Higher Education, 1997). In 1995, the cost of an undergraduate course of 60 credits (out of 360 required for a first degree) at the British Open University was £279 for regular students and £485 for associate students (Open University, 1995). There are additional costs for residential schools and other items, which bring the average cost of a BA or BSc degree at the British Open University to about £2,900.

UNED is funded on grounds similar to other universities in Spain. Public universities in Spain are financed by the state. On average, 70% of public universities' income comes from the state, but with large margins of difference. For instance, Universidad of Extremadura received in 1987 81% of its total budget, whereas Universidad Autonoma de Madrid received only 61%. The public university which has received least state aid was UNED: of the 1987 budget, only 37% came from the state, with the remaining 63% coming from academic fees and other sources (UNED, 1992b). The government sets the fees charged to students for all universities. No discretion is allowed. In 1994, fees per head per annum were approximately $500 (76,680 pesetas) in science-based faculties and $350 (54,300 pesetas) for the remainder (UNED, 1996).

As Table 6.1 makes plain, the Open University of Israel gets the smallest proportion of government participation in its budget, compared to other distance teaching universities. It gets also the smallest participation compared to all other Israeli universities. The finance of regular universities ranged from 65% to 75% in the 1980s and 1990s (Pazy, 1994, 3), whilst the Open University of Israel's grant equalled 22–28% throughout the decade (Open University of Israel, 1995, 2–3). During its first seven years, the Open University of Israel was financed as an experimental project by the Rothschild Foundation (see Chapter 1). Only after demonstrating it was able to generate its operating budget mainly from its own revenues, did the government assume the responsibility of providing less than a third of its budget.

The tuition of a full first degree at the Open University of Israel is the same as the tuition cost of a first degree at conventional universities. A six credit course costs about $300. A full degree requires the equivalent of 18 such courses. Thus, a full undergraduate degree at the Open University of Israel costs about $5,400 to $6,000, roughly similar to campus universities. However, unlike conventional universities, the Open University of Israel does not require a minimum payment for three residential years. Hence, students who get accreditation for studies prior to joining the Open University of Israel pay only for the courses they study at the University, which makes the price of its degree lower. This regulation is particularly attractive to teachers who may be exempted for upwards of a full year of studies, even if together they have to pay the equivalent of two years to complete a full degree.

The particular funding arrangements of the Open University of Israel place it in a situation of continued precariousness, facing growing competition from the Israeli higher education system over the last decade, and the fear of a fall in overall student numbers: "The Open University of Israel's great reliance on income generated by its own activities makes it extremely vulnerable. The financial reserves at our disposal are small and a quick adjustment of expenditure to revenues is essential... Every 1,000 registrations lost would mean a loss of $190,000 of income, which is equivalent to 7.6 positions" (*ibid.*, 4–5), a 1995 report noted.

In Germany, higher education institutions receive 95% to 100% of their funds from the state (Frackmann, 1994). Tuition fees do not exist. The Rector negotiates the budget with the Land's Minister of Education and Science. Each university's budget is highly differentiated. Peters (1981, 1997) tells how, on several occasions, the FernUniversität had to notify the ministry that the university would have to halt the dispatch of study materials unless additional funds were forthcoming. The FernUniversität requires students to pay a symbolic sum for the postage of study materials which the government required from 1983 onwards. Each course consists of anything from one to seventeen units. Students pay DM15 per course unit. On enrolment students must pay for at least 10 units (= DM 150). The average charge per student is about DM 300 (Schuemer, 1997). This fee is applied only to the FernUniversität and in 1996 drew 10 million DM (Peters, 1997, 74).

In Canada, higher education institutions receive their main operating funds as an annual grant from the provincial government. From 1976 a system of block grants has been in force. Universities are free to decide how to spend their income. Whilst institutional revenues come from government grants, other sources including fees, are important. Provincial operating grants vary substantially among different types of institutions. In 1994/95, one university obtained 71% of its operating budget, as against 54% of a college (Andrews et al., 1997, 79–80). The operating budget Athabasca University in 1991 was $18 million (Canadian dollars), of which 80% was granted by the Alberta government (Archer, 1992, 1,051). In 1995 its operating budget reached $28 million (Canadian dollars), with 57% came from government coffers (Patten, 1997). In 1995, tuition fees per a three credit course were $358 for Alberta residents; $408 for Canadian citizens out-of-Province; $458 for foreign nationals residing outside Canada; and $634 for foreigners residing in Canada (*ibid.*).

Costs per Student and per Graduate at Distance Teaching Universities versus Campus Universities

As we have seen, some distance teaching universities are financed more generously by their governments than others. In theory, it is possible to make a distance teaching university as expensive or as cheap as the planners wish

(Wagner, 1977, 1980). The key economic variables which distance teaching universities can manipulate are: the media employed, the number of courses taught and developed, the cost of producing and maintaining such courses, the quality assurance mechanisms employed, the number of students, and the extent of tutorial support. Despite the considerable variance in operating budgets between different distance teaching universities, the study cost at all of them is cheaper than at traditional universities in their national milieu. While techniques of examining and comparing costs have been developed, only a small number of cost studies have been undertaken.

Over the years, a number of studies have helped to establish a methodology for estimating cost and have demonstrated the cost advantage of some distance teaching universities (Wagner, 1977, 1980; Snowden & Daniel, 1980; Perraton, 1993, 1988; Rumble, 1993; Daniel et. al., 1994; Mugridge, 1994a,b). One purpose of such cost studies was to provide a basis for comparison between distance and conventional education, and to demonstrate their relative cost efficiency. To make such comparison, it is important to differentiate between *capital* and *recurrent* costs. Generally, distance teaching universities and conventional universities require different mixes of *capital* and *recurrent* costs. And because they perform different tasks, comparison is difficult (Perraton, 1993; Mugridge, 1994,a,b). Obviously, distance teaching universities have less call upon some forms of *capital* expenditure, such as school buildings, classrooms, lecture theatres, laboratories, student facilities and residential accommodation. Yet, effective distance education exerts its own demand for resources. It needs more time to prepare self-study materials than to prepare a classroom lesson covering the same ground. Distance teaching universities need premises and equipment for developing, storing and dispatching their courses. *Recurrent* costs, as the term implies, refer to the ongoing expenses of operating the system, such as the cost of postage or radio broadcasting in each given year or semester.

A further distinction made in the literature is between *fixed* and *variable* costs. Most *capital* costs are likely to be *fixed*. They are unchanged regardless of the number of students. But certain costs that are sometimes treated as *recurrent*, for example, staff costs for the production of materials, are likely to be *fixed* in just the same way: the cost is the same to write and edit materials for 100 students as it is for 10,000 students. In practice, some costs are *semi-fixed*: the same computer may accommodate from 100 to 10,000 students but a larger one may be needed for 1,000,000 students (Perraton, 1993, 381). *Variable* costs are influenced primarily by the number of students. Student numbers have an impact on the number of part-time tutors and counsellors, on the cost of copies of teaching materials, examinations, records keeping, postage, etc. Cost analyses to take account of these distinctions, can be expressed in the simple formula below (*ibid.*):

$$TC(n) = F + V(n)$$

where TC = Total Cost, n = number of students, F = fixed costs, and V = variable cost per student.

Some claim that the only realistic way in which funding for conventional and distance teaching universities may be compared is in terms either of cost per full-time equivalent student or of cost per graduate. Distance teaching universities can be cost-effective, because they can enrol extra students for a modest additional cost. Once materials are written and an administration put in place, the marginal cost of teaching one more student is quite modest. Distance education is less costly than conventional classroom education when the numbers of students are large. The critical question is, *how large*? After organising a number of cost studies, Rumble arrived at the general conclusion that small distance teaching universities with 10,000 to 20,00 students are probably critically balanced, in as much as their unit costs are on a par with, or below those of, campus institutions. Larger distance teaching universities, with more than 20,000 students evidently enjoy economies of scale (Rumble, 1982, 138).

Wagner (1977) showed that the average cost per full-time student at the British Open University in the 1970s was a third the cost of a regular university, and the cost of a British Open University graduate was less than half. Nearly two decades later, Daniel and colleagues (1994), using a different type of analysis, showed that costs comparisons were strongly in the favour of the British Open University. In 1991, a government review of the British Open University compared its costs per graduate with those of three other institutions. The British Open University's costs were significantly lower: between 39% and 47% of the other universities' cost for ordinary degrees, and between 55% and 80% of honours degrees (Daniel, 1996a, 39)

García-Aretio (1995, 94) calculated that costs per student at Spain's UNED in 1990 were 41% of those at conventional universities and costs per graduate, 53%. UNED is even more efficient when comparison was made with British universities. James (1982) found that UNED's costs per student in the 1970s were about one third those of the British Open University. This proportion has remained steady over the years (Daniel, 1996a, 187). This result serves to underline the considerable variances between student costs in different countries.

Yaari (1995) calculated that with 10,000 enrolments, the cost per student at the Open University of Israel was approximately 50% that of conventional Israeli universities. Snowden and Daniel (1980) analysing the cost of Athabasca University, found that with 2,000 full-time-equivalent students (8,000 course enrolments) its costs were within the range set by comparable programmes at Alberta's three conventional universities.

Perraton, reviewing many cost studies, reached the conclusion not without some expressions of caution: "The cost data are consistent and robust enough for us to look next at the findings on the effectiveness with confidence that there is a reasonably firm economic case for the use of distance education" (Perraton, 1993, 389).

Centralised versus Decentralised Control of Study Centres

The management of regional offices and/or local study centres, dotted across the country and beyond national boundaries, the supervision of part-time, off-campus tutors, counsellors and administrative staff, constitute the sharpest differences between the organisational infrastructure of distance teaching universities set against campus universities. It entails major management problems. *Centralised* versus *decentralised* dimensions which are classic in the literature of organisational theory apply naturally to the administration of the distance teaching universities' study centres (Paul, 1990; Rumble, 1992a). The challenge has been to strike the right balance between their relative advantages, in defining regulations for managing efficiently far-away branches, which are responsible for the core activities of each distance teaching university. To define clearly the jurisdictions and responsibilities of regional or local authorities in full coordination with the headquarters has been an issue of the utmost importance.

Some distance teaching universities, like the British Open University, the Open University of Israel and Athabasca University, opted for a centralised control over their study centres; the FernUniversität chose a mixed approach, by financing fully the study centres in North Rhine-Westphalia and collaborating with local authorities in other Länder; whilst the Spanish UNED from the very start conferred the authority over its study centres to local authorities.

The main headquarters of the British Open University are located at Walton Hall in Milton Keynes with a network of 13 Regional Centres covering the UK. The Regional Centres are financed 100% by central headquarters (EADTU, 1993b). Two centres supervise students in continental Europe and in the Republic of Ireland (Watts, 1995). Benelux countries are served by the North Region Office, and other European countries by the East Anglia Region (Tait, 1994b). Altogether, there are about 250 study centres located throughout the UK, with 21 on mainland Europe (EADTU, 1993a, 70). Regional Centres vary considerably in size. The South East Region, for instance, in 1994, catered for 17,000 students, had a network of 26 study centres and recruited over 800 part-time tutors and counsellors. It employed 80 secretarial, administrative and academic personnel (Watts, 1995). Recruitment of tutorial and counselling staff is the major task of the Regional Centres. They are also authorised to move the site of study centres when appropriate. Staff development programmes are arranged for all categories of staff, both from Walton Hall and the Regional Centres.

From the first, UNED decided to operate a network of study centres in full collaboration with local authorities. Altogether, UNED has 92 study centres: 57 full study centres (*Centros Asociados*) located mainly in towns where there is no other university, 27 additional sub-centres located in large cities, and 8 overseas centres: in London, Paris, Bonn, Geneva, Brussels, Rosario

(Argentina), Caracas (Venezuela), and Equatorial Guinea. The overseas centres are connected to the Ministry of Labour, except in Guinea, and are reserved for Spanish expatriates only (EADTU, 1993a, 50). It is through the centres that students elect their representatives and participate in all university decision-making committees, including staff meetings. Students obtain materials at the study centres, since UNED distributes materials in bulk to the study centres for handing out.

UNED's study centres serve as cultural foci in the city or village where they are located (Popa-Lisseanu, 1986). They are established through the initiative of corporations or private agencies, which provide buildings, equipment, materials and the salaries for all personnel, including part-time tutors. Tutors get differential salaries, based on resources available to each study centre (García-Garrido, 1993). The average number of tutors in each study centre is around 60 (EADTU, 1993a, 50). Study centres are autonomous in regard to their organisation and budget management. They are managed by a Trust (*Patronato*) which includes representatives from local authorities, such as town halls, provincial councils, local savings banks, and in some cases private firms, insurance companies and business corporations; plus representatives from UNED's headquarters. The Trust is in charge of fund raising for each centre. UNED's central headquarters contribute on average about 20% of the centre's annual budget, with great margins of variation which range from 5% to 40% (*ibid.*, 51). The remaining budget is split between the various parties that share the responsibility of running the local centre. UNED's study centres are responsible for organising their academic activities, provided they are in keeping with the minimum requirements set out by headquarters. The coordinators in charge of study centres, work closely with the academic staff of UNED. Together with departments and the rectorate at headquarters, they provide tutorial support, counselling services and organise summer courses. The choice of courses in each study centre is determined partially by its "own geographic, social and cultural surroundings" (*ibid.*).

In 1997, the Open University of Israel had the large number of 108 study centres throughout the country. Study centres constitute a most vital part of the University's activities, since more than 80% of students currently study within a framework of *intensive tutorials*, where they meet once or even twice a week with their tutors. Students undertaking four to five courses, attend study centres several days per week. The Open University of Israel controls centrally both the academic activities and the organisation of each study centre, and recruits all of the tutors centrally. Study materials are mailed directly by the Open University of Israel's headquarters to students. Tutors are assigned to study centres by the headquarters, which is located in Ramat-Aviv.

Nevertheless, in the last decade, following the expansion of the intensive tutorials framework, the Open University of Israel signed some agreements with private trusts which undertook the physical management of some study centres. In reality, some of these private enterprises operate municipal colleges, which provide, by and large, campus-like environments. One such establishment, Ramat-Gan College, grew massively over the past few years to more than 7,000 students in 1997. Municipal colleges charge special fees (of about $350 to $400 per year) in addition to the tuition fees paid to the Open University of Israel. The campus-like environment appears so attractive to many young students that they prefer to pay a higher tuition fee and to be enrolled in a municipal college (Levtzion, 1992; President's Report, 1995, 1997).

In addition to the study centres in Israel, the Open University of Israel operates some 30 study centres in the former Soviet Union, which coordinate studies in 260 cities and locations (President's Report, 1997, 95). The cost of administration of these overseas centres is borne by the Israeli government.

The German FernUniversität has 63 study centres, of which 29 are located in North Rhine-Westphalia, 29 in other Landër of Germany, and five in other European countries (three in Austria, one in Switzerland, and one in Hungary). The FernUniversität's study centres are controlled by a mixed mode. Those in North Rhine-Westphalia are centrally organised. Most of them are fully financed by the FernUniversität. The personnel numbers in the FernUniversität centres are usually very small. A typical study centre employs one part-time administrator, one counsellor and several tutors (Mentoren) (EADTU, 1993a, 24). We noted earlier (see Chapter 3), tutors at the Fern-Universität have the most restricted and limited authority of distance teaching universities. Study centres in other states, operate on the basis of cooperative contracts between the FernUniversität and other universities, private firms, and municipalities. The number of staff in study centres of the other Landër varies.

The FernUniversität has established highly productive links with industry, firms and business corporations. The latter recognise that cooperation with the FernUniversität opens up avenues for research, technology transfer and efficient professional upgrading. The FernUniversität uses cooperation with the corporate and industry worlds to extend research activities, to increase the standing of its graduates in the employment market, and to strengthen the political lobby for distance education (Groten, 1992). One example of a successful collaboration between the FernUniversität and several companies is to be seen in the Cologne study centre of North Rhine-Westphalia. Together with several companies in the field of communications technology, a Media Park has been established. Another example is the cooperation with the BMW firm (a leading company in the German car industry) to establish study centres in Münich and Upper Bavaria. The agreement between the FernUniversität and BMW includes tailor-made learning programmes and training for BMW employees. In 1992 over 500 BMW workers were enrolled as FernUniversität students (*ibid.*, 54). BMW provides the rooms and facilities rent-free and pays maintenance fees for the FernUniversität activities.

Athabasca University has three regional offices at Calgary, Edmonton and Fort McMurray. They are controlled and financed centrally (Rawlence, 1994).

The Athabasca University's regional centres enjoy a high degree of autonomy in organising both academic and support activities. They offer almost all of the University's student services in the local community: information, advice and counselling, on-line admission and registration, course material pickup, examination supervision, seminars and teleconferencing. The regional model at Athabasca University has been overhauled four or five times in the past two decades, although most of the changes involved reporting procedures (Paul, 1990).

One interesting dilemma turns around the physical location of study centres, and the ownership or renting arrangements between the distance teaching universities and the parties owning the facilities (Mills, 1996). In some institutions study centres are owned by the distance teaching university and run by its staff. At the other extreme, study centres may be suites of rooms in another institution's building, usually rented during evenings or on Saturdays. Some centres are run in thriving adult community centres, schools or public libraries. But, all too often, they "are dreary, poorly equipped schools or Colleges of Further Education" (*ibid.*, 75). In the British Open University and the Open University of Israel most study centres operate in rented rooms, typically in a school, college or community centre, increasingly on a charge-by-hour basis. In Spain and Germany they are usually located in public buildings like town halls and commercial premises.

After a thorough examination of study centres in the British Open University and some other distance teaching universities in Europe, Mills concluded that there was a huge waste of: "educational plant and resources because of the inability by institutions to think creatively about the joint use of premises during evenings and weekends, an increasing emphasis on competition, and because of the lack of national and local leadership on educational issues" (*ibid.*, 77).

Mills highlighted a dilemma crucial for the future operation of study centres. Developing communication technology poses the need to review the roles these centres have played. He claimed that if pursued to the extreme, it was arguable that: "Today, with the rapid development and availability of information technology in the home, at least for some students in richer countries, it could be argued that the future for study centres is clear... extinction!" (*ibid.*, 73). Students will be able to access information banks, to contact tutors, course authors and fellow students studying in the same course anywhere in the world. In such a situation there may be no need for study centres.

The centres at the British Open University, for example, began as Listening and Viewing Centres to VHF radio and BBC2 in the days before large numbers of students had such access at home. Study centres also provided replay devices through audio and video cassettes, plus counselling and tutorial sessions. As more students had access to radio, television, audio and video players, study centres focused on providing access to computer terminals, to tuition and counselling. This too has changed. Today, most study centres are simply rented rooms where face-to-face tuition, together with some individual and group counselling take place in ordinary classrooms. Still, many students find face-to face meeting as most valuable to their studies (*ibid.*, 80). They complain about poor facilities, but enjoy greatly meeting fellow students and tutors. The British Open University Business School uses hotel suites as study centres. One of the more fraught questions at the British Open University is nowadays whether to move study centres to hotels, conference and company training centres. It might increase expenses substantially. And it might well harm the relations with some local authorities.

A clear definition of the expected roles of study centres is essential for their smooth functioning and for adequately adapting teaching and learning to the new technologies. My prediction is that study centres will not disappear. On the contrary, their role in strengthening social interaction in distance education will become if anything more important in the future. Distance teaching universities will redefine the mission goals of their regional and local study centres and create new contracts with local communities. We will deal with this aspect in Chapter 8.

A further development and one of considerable interest, is the EuroStudy Centre network, which started to develop in the early 1990s. Today, it en-compasses leading study centres across Europe. The network was set up to improve the cross-national delivery of courses between European distance teaching institutions, to speed up the application of new technologies, to diffuse information about open and distance learning facilities into regions of Europe where it was previously little known, and to allow students across Europe to have access to distance education providers (EADTU, 1994b). We are likely to witness in the future the strengthening of local study centres endowed with larger margins of freedom to match their activities to the profiles of their student clienteles. Trans-national and global networks of study centres will grow and provide students with broader and more flexible study opportunities across institutions and across countries.

7

Distance and Campus Universities: Scepticism, Collaboration and Competition

To found a university is always risky. To found a distance teaching university is incomparably more risky.

Peters (1997, 68)

There are almost limitless possibilities for fruitful collaboration between distance and conventional institutions.

Hayduk (1994, 44–5)

Single-mode distance teaching institutions will find fierce competition from the traditional systems on their doorsteps, and will need to change in order to have a role to play at all in the future. If open universities become fixed and unchanging, we will only have two styles of obsolete universities, each with its own outmoded approach.

Roll (1995, XIII)

Introduction

On a general level, the relationships between distance teaching universities and their conventional counterparts in each national setting can be described as evolving over the years from a widespread scepticism of the latter towards the former in the 1970s, through growing cooperation in the 1980s, to increased competition in the 1990s. All three elements of scepticism, collaboration and competition, each at various degrees of intensity, still co-exist and even today characterise the intricate relations between distance and campus universities in nearly all national settings.

Following the birth of the distance teaching universities in the early 1970s, the early years were marked, by and large, by strong criticism and opposition. The degree of opposition related directly to the innovative cluster of each distance teaching university, as Chapter 2 noted. The more innovative the distance teaching university aspired to be, the more likely it was to attract arrows of suspicion and negativism. In essence, the academic communities in most countries regarded the new distance teaching universities as special institutions catering for *second chance* students, and thus having little, if any, consequence for mainstream undergraduate studies. Many distance teaching universities, such as the British Open University, the Open University of Israel and Athabasca University, strongly emphasised their claim to be unique universities, operating as complementary higher education institutions rather than being antagonistic to, or competing with, traditional universities. The British Open University, for example, adopted a wholly different academic calendar, starting in February, and limited access to students aged 21 years and older, in order to make clear from the very start its intention to cater for a very different student clientele compared to conventional universities.

Although distance teaching universities have cast aside the stigma of that attached to the first generation of correspondence schools and have endowed distance education with a new legitimacy and pride, many distance teaching universities are still not yet fully accepted as fully fledged universities. Even nowadays when growing numbers of campus universities teach via distance education methods, and with issues once tackled mainly by distance teaching universities moving from the margins to the centre stage of higher education, still many traditional educators, employers, and even potential students of distance teaching universities see distance education as a trifle *second-class*, not quite as good as *real* education (Perry, 1986; Morrison, 1992).

Apart from being targets of ongoing criticism, antagonism and scepticism, all the distance teaching universities studied here established from the very first fruitful collaborations with academics from campus universities, both on personal and institutional grounds. External experts were recruited for counselling, writing and evaluating self-study courses; for tutoring students and for monitoring or checking assignments and examinations. They were recruited on a part-time *ad hoc* basis on the grounds of personal merits and expertise. Small distance teaching universities, such as the Open University of Israel, rely heavily on scholars from traditional universities.

Apart from personal ties with individual academics, most distance teaching universities invested considerable energy and effort to establish academic credibility and reputation by ongoing dialogues with members from conventional universities, and by their emphasis on providing high quality study experiences. Throughout the years, particularly from the 1980s onward, several inter-institutional projects and agreements have grown up between distance and campus universities, in the use of facilities of regular universities during summer breaks, credit transfer and collaborative course production. Some of the inter-institutional agreements were successful. Others failed.

The massification of higher education and the emergence of advanced technologies in the 1990s created pressure and provided incentives for universities, both distance and campus-based, to change. Teaching by distance education methods is accelerating at an amazing pace in traditional universities across the world. The higher education market in the last decade has become more international and competitive. Readjusting universities to the needs of higher education in the third millennium is crucial to their very existence, as Roll stated: "It is going to be dangerous to be stuck in old, outmoded ways of doing things. This is true not only for powerful corporations and military organisations, but also for powerful distance teaching universities as well as for traditional ones" (Roll, 1995, XIV). Clearly, distance teaching universities are no longer very new universities. They have to rethink their mission goals and redefine their strategic planning in the light of new developments. The future scenarios of single-mode distance teaching universities, as well as of mass universities, are discussed in Chapter 8. This chapter examines the particular ties between the five distance teaching universities and mainstream universities in each national milieu as they have developed over nearly three decades.

Scepticism and Opposition

Organisational theories teach us that no change takes place without opposition. Profound and large-scale innovations, such as the establishment of distance teaching universities, naturally generate waves of opposition. All of the distance teaching universities in this study were initiated and put forward to operate by high-ranking politicians. In most countries, the regular universities were not consulted during the planning, but merely informed after the event. In some instances part of the hostility of classical universities towards the newborn distance teaching universities stemmed from their exclusion from the deliberative process that gave birth to the new-type universities. Even universities with a wealth of experience in distance education were left out. In the UK, for example, the University of London was neither consulted during, nor involved in, the hectic planning activity which launched the British Open University, despite the fact that the external system of the University of London had operated since 1858, and relevant and important lessons might have been learned from its long experience in providing distance education. Bell and Tight claimed that as a result: "The University of London external system and the Open University have both had a massive effect and influence upon the development of education in Britain and overseas, they might just as well have been on different planets (rather than based about 50 miles apart) so far as their relations with each other over the last 20 years have been concerned" (Bell & Tight, 1993, 128).

Most of the distance teaching universities met with suspicion and hostility, emanating from academic circles, politicians, media commentators, various educational establishments and corporations. Most, but not all, encountered strong hostility. UNED, for instance, was born in a period of a total reorganisation of the Spanish education system from the nursery level to university studies (see Chapter 1). Apart from offering its studies by distance education methods, it mimicked conventional universities in nearly everything else. Thus, it did not evoke waves of opposition. Two special institutes of distance education were established in Spain in the 1970s to offer studies at the elementary and high-school levels (CENEBAD, Centro Nacional de Educación Básica a Distancia; and INBAD, Instituto Nacional de Bachillerato a Distancia). In the massive overhaul of the whole educational system, the establishment of a distance teaching university constituted just one element in the overall reform. Furthermore, UNED's location in Madrid attracted highly reputed scholars to its faculty, which ensured it a high academic status (García-Garrido, 1976, 1993).

Not only did conservative distance teaching universities, such as UNED, avoid large doses of antagonism. A highly innovative distance teaching university such as Athabasca University, which from the very start proposed to depart from practices of conventional universities as far as possible, was integrated into the higher education system of Alberta with relative ease. Clearly, the surrounding national context and the prevailing academic culture are crucial determinants in shaping the nature of relationships between distance and campus universities in different national settings. A distance teaching university, such as Athabasca University, would have been considered as a most radical university in German, Spanish and even Israeli higher education systems. Athabasca University adopted an open admission policy, a year-round enrolment scheme, highly flexible accreditation rules, demanded minimum *residency* requirements for completing its degrees, and even enabled students to get a Bachelor of General Studies based solely on studies carried on at other universities. In the Canadian context, which encourages institutional diversity and exercises a universal access, the *newness* of Athabasca University was neither striking nor threatening.

As we have already seen in Chapter 1, Athabasca University was nearly cancelled when the Progressive Conservative Party returned to power in Alberta in 1972. The new government immediately suspended all physical facilities planning (Shale, 1982). But this suspension had nothing to do with distance education or with the innovative nature of the new university. On the contrary, Athabasca University was initially planned as a campus university. Only later did it take on the identity of a distance teaching university. In effect, its conversion to a distance teaching university saved Athabasca University from extinction. Assuming tasks that were not taken on by Alberta's campus universities gave it a unique mission and justified its status as an experimental project.

The British Open University, the Open University of Israel and Fern-Universität drew strong opposition and criticism during their first decade. It stemmed from different sources, and came from different directions. The British Open University was attacked by many parties, and was surrounded by profound scepticism garnished with ridicule and hostility (Perry, 1976, 1997; Young, 1995). Lord Perry, its first Vice Chancellor, recalled that nearly everyone who knew about the plan to found the British Open University was sceptical as to its prospects. Even Michael Swann, the Principal of Edinburgh University where Perry was a professor, was generous in allowing him to leave the University to become the British Open University's Vice Chancellor, but was not a little dubious "about my future and the future of the Open University" (Perry, 1997, 8). The Conservative Party came out against the British Open University, since it was a creation of the Labour Party. The Conservatives promised their voters that, once in power, they would not sustain it. A very senior Conservative Shadow Chancellor of the Exchequer "described the embryonic plans for an Open University in Britain as "blithering nonsense" and vowed to axe it as soon as his party took over government" (Moran & Mugridge, 1993a, IX). Luckily, they did not keep their promise.

Comments in the press were uniformly sceptical and often scathing, describing it as "a pipe dream", "an untimely caprice", "a cosy scheme showing Socialists at their most endearing but impractical worst" (Perry, 1997, 8). Many articles questioned whether the use of television was justified, whether costs could be contained, and whether there would be any demand for such studies. The world of adult education regarded it as "a diversion of resources". The university world looked on the idea as a gimmick, very unlikely to survive (*ibid.*). Bell and Tight suggested that the use of the television focused the main source of opposition from the academic world. The links between television and entertainment were too close for many "delicate academic stomachs in the early 1970s" (Bell & Tight, 1993, 156).

As a matter of fact the British Open University's milieu was conceived by most academics as a separate world, which had no relevance to the normal anticipation of higher education needs (*ibid.*, 152). This attitude was manifest until 1993 by excluding the British Open University's statistics from most reporting on the British higher education system, and by confining its existence to brief footnotes, if at all. Furthermore, in reviews describing and forecasting future developments of British higher education, the British Open University was often omitted from the general analysis, such as in Perkin's review (1987), and that of Trow (1993).

Scott, in an extensive overview of British higher education remarked that: "The Open University has done more than any other university to reshape popular attitudes to higher education in Britain. Yet cross-fertilisation with other universities has been limited. In terms of research and scholarship the

Open University and its staff have been fully accepted. But, as a teaching institute, the Open University has been kept at arm's length, and seen as one of a (very special) kind. As a result, other universities have dabbled in distance learning, though without recourse to the Open University's quarter-century of experience" (Scott, 1995, 47).

Perry voiced most poignantly the dialectic relations between the British Open University and mainstream universities, even after it has proved its academic credibility beyond any doubt: "Academics all over Britain, he writes, accept that the Open University has succeeded, that distance learning works and that the Open University graduates are as good as any others. They (these graduates) have been accepted by every other British University in postgraduate courses without any question. The quality of the courses is seen and is commended by the academic world. The quality of the students, the quality of the exams—they are all recognised by the academics in other universities. But emotionally, many of them don't accept it at all. Emotionally there still is a strong feeling that on-campus teaching in the face-to-face situation is the one way of actually teaching and that this is the vital thing in order to train scholars of the future. It may take decades rather than years to overcome this emotional reaction. You have to remember, I suppose, that every advance in education has been resisted for years" (Perry, 1986, 15).

Hopefully the inclusion of the British Open University under the same funding guidelines applied to other British universities from April 1993 on, will help to integrate it more fully into the fabric of British higher education. Currently, parameters for evaluating both teaching and research have become most transparent. The British Open University scored in the upper third of all British universities in the first round of quality assessments held by the Higher Education Funding Council of England in 1995 (Perry, 1997, 11). Its teaching received excellent ratings in more than half of the subjects assessed (Daniel, 1996a, 9).

The Open University of Israel faced—and still faces—copious opposition and scepticism from most campus universities. Abraham Ginzburg, its president from 1975 to 1987, claimed from a twenty-year perspective that: "I do not need to describe the amount of scepticism and often sheer disbelief amongst the academic community about a new university, especially one based on distance teaching. Israel reacted like other countries did to distance education universities, especially as there was no tradition of correspondence studies in the country" (Ginzburg, 1997, 84). Here, an important distinction has to be made between personal and institutional relations. From its earliest moments, the Open University of Israel had no problem in mobilizing academics from traditional universities to write, consult and evaluate its courses. But these academics were recruited on a very personal basis, and this situation reflects reality up to the present.

Official circles in conventional universities greeted the Open University of Israel glacially, and perceived it principally as an *outsider*. The Open University of Israel has not been accepted as a member in the Council of the Universities Heads, which includes the seven campus-centred universities and institutes (five comprehensive universities, the Technion and the Weizmann Institute). It has no representative in the Council for Higher Education, as do all other universities. One of the ostensible reasons for this exclusion has been that the Open University of Israel is not a full-fledged university, since it teaches only undergraduate degrees. The situation has not changed, even when the Open University of Israel was granted the authority to confer master-level degrees in 1996. Like its British counterpart, the Open University of Israel was kept apart from official statistics and future projections of Israeli higher education. If its statistics are included, they are provided separately (Herskovic, 1995).

Furthermore, the *outsider* status of the Open University of Israel was clearly reflected in a vigorous campaign against its campus-like provisions, which expanded noticeably since the late 1980s. Conventional universities claimed that the Open University of Israel had deviated from its original mandate to operate as a distance teaching university. They demanded that the Council for Higher Education appoint in 1992 a special committee to explore whether the Open University of Israel had remained true to the framework of its mission goals. The Committee set strict limits to the maximum number of hours permitted for intensive tutorials at the Open University of Israel. The attraction of the Open University of Israel for a growing number of young students, and the provision of campus-like grounds threatened to change its position as a very special and different-type university, catering mainly for *second chance* clienteles. Yet, despite the fact that the Open University of Israel is not yet accepted by most conventional universities, its graduates are highly regarded and readily admitted to graduate level studies at all mainstream universities.

The German FernUniversität faced assault mainly for taking the lead as a solo operator of a distance teaching university without having given any prior notice to other Länder or to other universities in North Rhine-Westphalia. Peters, its founding Rector, noted that the first criticism of the German FernUniversität came from the Christian Democratic Union of North Rhine-Westphalia, particularly the parliamentary group which had to reply to the bill establishing the FernUniversität. They were opposed in particular to the setting up of an autonomous distance teaching university. They argued rather that distance education should be organised by existing universities. They demanded that North Rhine-Westphalia refrain from founding this new university and that it should participate solely and exclusively in the joint project of the Länder to create a distance education consortium which had started experimenting on a limited scale at four universities in the early 1970s (Peters, 1997, 59). At the time political parties faced new elections in North Rhine-Westphalia. The Christian Democratic Union promised to abolish the FernUniversität as soon as they returned to power. In part, they gave tongue to the opinions of many professors at traditional universities.

Minister Rau, the champion of the FernUniversität, began a political manoeuvre to nuzzle the Christian Democrats' criticising the FernUniversität. He negotiated with 26 mayors of communities, promising the FernUniversität would establish study centres in their communities. Community administration considered this a most welcome improvement to their educational infrastructure. It would benefit students living there. It would be a significant cultural enrichment. Many mayors, though belonging to the Christian Democratic Union, became unexpected defenders of the FernUniversität. And so, "local Christian Democrat members of parliament also became interested in the FernUniversität and were disinclined to vote for its abolition" (*ibid.*). After some time, Christian Democrat leaders not only tolerated the FernUniversität, but were ready to support it in some instances.

More important was the opposition of governments in those Länder run by Christian Democrat governments. They refused to cooperate with the FernUniversität, to establish study centres in their regions, or to support them. As a result of such obstinacy, students in Bavaria and Baden-Württemberg, about 20% of FernUniversität's student body, remained without study centres.

Peters (1981, 1994c, 1997) remarked that in the early years of the FernUniversität's saga the universities of North Rhine-Westphalia were not pleased with its foundation either. They feared it would affect their operating budgets: "So, when I paid my first visits to the rectors of these universities, I sensed sceptical reserve nearly everywhere" (Peters, 1997, 61). The situation changed, however, when the FernUniversität started and slowly gained status. Before long, the Rectors' Conference in North Rhine-Westphalia and the West-German Rectors' Conference voted the FernUniversität to full membership of these bodies, which helped a great deal in achieving recognition.

Additional support for the FernUniversität came from the Scientific Council (Wissenschaftsrat). The Council reported on the FernUniversität; a procedure necessary if the FernUniversität was to be included on the list of university buildings jointly financed by the Federal Government and the respective Land together on an equal basis. The report, approved on 11 June 1975, stated that the FernUniversität was "a significant experiment of great importance in higher education policy" (*ibid.*, 63). As the Scientific Council was an opinion leader in the scientific community, such an opinion on the beginnings in Hagen was invaluable. Afterwards it became much easier to defend the goals of the FernUniversität against critics from without, as it was those from within the FernUniversität.

The Chamber of Commerce and Industry for South Westphalia was eager to establish connections with the FernUniversität, which was equally useful. The Chamber paved the way towards recognition of the FernUniversität by many industrial companies. It helped in raising financial support by establishing *the Friends of the FernUniversität*, which provides the FernUniversität with funds to support students and professors in special projects. It helped found and run the *Technology Park* mentioned in Chapter 6. It became the driving force in negotiations with many administrative and industrial representatives which sought to found the *House of Science and Continuing Education*, for students to stay when in Hagen attending seminars or sitting examinations.

The brief account of the opponents and critics of distance teaching universities in their early days brings out once more the unique situational variables in each case. Opposition in the UK, Israel and Germany originated from different quarters. The British Open University had no need to justify being a *distance teaching university*, since distance education at university level had a long history in the UK. But it did have to defend its *open admission* policy and its teaching via *television*, which was stressed more in its early plans than was practised in reality. In Israel and Germany the notion of *distance teaching* itself was one of the main targets of division and scepticism. The idea of *open access* was never considered as applying to the German and Spanish contexts. It constituted the pillar in the educational rationale of the British Open University, the Open University of Israel and Athabasca University. The idea of *open access* has with difficulty been "digested" by Israeli academics. To this day, *open access* is looked upon by many Israeli scholars as a populist idea, and as a vulgarisation of higher education. Since Israel has no external examiner system, unlike the UK, and since it produced small numbers of graduates in its early years, it faced a far more complicated situation than the British Open University to prove the legitimacy and viability of its basic rationale. In addition, the restriction of the Open University of Israel to teaching, for over twenty years, only at undergraduate level has deeply undermined its academic status in Israeli higher education system. Athabasca University offered its first master degrees in the 1990s, but this has not prevented it from becoming a full member of the Universities Coordinating Council of Alberta.

In spite of marked differences between the contextual background variables in each country, some arguments against the distance teaching universities are found across all national settings. In the early 1970s, many academics from traditional universities were sceptical of the need to establish a single-mode distance teaching university. They claimed that the functions fulfilled by distance teaching universities could have been equally met by existing universities. Once the distance teaching universities were established and started operating, the reactions of many scholars changed. The distance teaching universities' successes and the huge numbers of students, which most of them had attracted, the active participation of many professors in the distance teaching universities' activities, led them to reconsider the inherent merits present in the possibilities of working together.

Collaboration

By their very nature, and from the outset, distance teaching universities had to seek out creative ways of collaborating with their more conventional counterparts. Design and development of study materials have been based, in varying degrees, on cooperation with external scholars in all five distance teaching universities. Part-time tutors and counsellors were recruited principally from the ranks of junior and senior academic faculty of traditional universities. The campuses of classical universities served as sites for summer schools and residential schools during vacations, weekends and holidays. The vested interest of distance teaching universities in encouraging credit "portability" between higher education institutions was an essential element in their overall mission to democratise access to higher education and to enable their students to move easily between higher education institutions and to advance freely in their studies over time. Paul has argued that distance education institutions are ideally suited to collaborate with each other, and with conventional higher education institutions. Not only are they suited to collaborate, but it is in their sheer interest to do so: "In fact, this collaboration is often essential to their effectiveness, as they are often not, in themselves, the whole answer to a student's requirements" (Paul, 1990, 143). Thus, distance teaching universities were highly collaboration-minded from the very start, as opposed to the prevailing ethos of classical universities, which have over years cherished and guarded the concept of institutional autonomy.

Throughout their long history, traditional universities always sought to maintain their specific identity. By and large, they have been wary of extensive cooperation with other institutions. distance teaching universities clearly took the lead in initiating various inter-institutional ventures with conventional universities (as well as with other organisations and establishments). Rarely had they been approached first. distance teaching universities invest considerable imagination and effort to forge the particular links they wished to create with campus universities. Collaboration with their conventional counterparts has been a most demanding task early in their existence, above all when it had to be developed in the face of intense criticism and opposition, which most of them encountered.

Partnerships, if successful, create greater strengths. The basic rationale behind cooperation is that the *whole* may be greater than the *sum of its parts*. The synergy created by collaboration often yields benefits well beyond those originally hoped for. Failure to collaborate, however, may result in unnecessary duplication of effort and ineffective investment of scarce resources. Yet, successful collaboration is immensely difficult to achieve and sustain. Many failures are reported (Coffey, 1989; Paul, 1990; Moran & Mugridge, 1993a; Thorpe, 1995; Moore & Kearsley, 1996). A handful of collaborative ventures were more wind than rock. Those that were implemented did not always turn out as intended. In truth, most collaboration produces something different from the goals originally stated, sometimes for the better, sometimes for the worse (Paul, 1990).

Since the 1980s inter-institutional collaborative ventures have proliferated among distance teaching universities and between distance teaching universities and conventional higher education institutions. Moran and Mugridge

(1993a) conducted an extensive review of collaborative projects and programmes in distance education, and concluded: "There are signs, that for political, educational, and financial reasons, collaboration is becoming a central feature of distance education at local, regional and international levels" (Moran & Mugridge, 1993c, 151). But, soberly, they noted: "The fact remains, however, that inter-institutional collaboration is an extremely difficult and complicated undertaking, even in its simplest forms" (Moran & Mugridge, 1993b, 4).

Clearly, there are important differences in the cultures of various organisations which complicate the management of collaborative projects (Paul 1990). Collaboration requires an unusual degree of self-confidence and openness. Still, the rewards can be considerable if the *fit* between participating institutions is good. Coffey (1989, 288) suggested five basic pointers for ensuring successful collaboration: to state clearly what the joint venture is; to keep it simple, complex arrangements are fine on paper but difficult and expensive to set up and sustain; to define exactly what the role of each partner is; to be clear about money; and to maintain review procedures over all aspects of collaboration. Moran and Mugridge (1993c) believed that for a collaboration to succeed it required: accommodating institutional cultures; building trust and perceiving the mutual benefits to be had. Paul, humorously, reached an interesting insight on the deteriorating intensity of cooperation as it moves from top-down decisions to the practical, operational levels: "Inter-institutional agreement is more likely the higher one goes in the organisation. Hence, presidents will agree almost anything with each other, vice presidents will usually find a way through, while deans are much more sceptical. Faculty are strongly resistant, and academic secretaries don't want to know" (Paul, 1990, 148).

Cooperative frameworks for producing courses, tutoring, counselling and monitoring exams, were discussed in earlier chapters. Here, we focus mainly on inter-institutional agreements for credit transfer and accreditation purposes across various national settings. Credit transfer and the tying together of studies and credentials bring many advantages both to individual students and to the participating institutions. Collaborative ventures in accreditation offer new opportunities for students, which would not otherwise exist. Credit "portability" allows students to earn credentials from using courses completed at a number of institutions. This is particularly advantageous to those who work in highly mobile professions. The consolidation of the European Union and growing globalisation of the 1990s have already increased substantially the number of such mobile professionals. Credit transferability facilitates career changes and provides the basic elements for a lifelong-learning society, and helps students to plan programmes suited to their professional and personal needs (Brindley & Paul, 1993). Important gains are also embedded in accreditation agreements for the institutions involved. Successful collaborative credit arrangements raise cost effectiveness, and increase the flexibility of the academic programmes each institution offers.

The Spanish UNED and the German FernUniversität had no problem whatsoever in establishing accreditation regulations with conventional universities. Distance teaching methods aside, their academic programmes resemble those of campus universities, their students can move freely to other universities and vice versa. UNED established good relations with other Spanish universities, with other distance teaching universities in Europe and in Latin America (EADTU, 1994a). Adult students who complete successfully its special Admission Course, designed for those 25 years and older who do not possess the minimum requirements for university enrolment, are entitled to continue to study at any Spanish University and not just at UNED.

The FernUniversität had to put greater efforts than UNED into establishing collaborative links with campus universities, due to the latter's initial resistance to its very creation. Peters set great store by creating friendly relations with all educational experts in parliament and conventional universities. Parity between higher education institutions is very important in Germany (Peters, 1981, 1997). Soon after the FernUniversität's founding, Peters invited local and regional leaders and individual members of parliament to visit the FernUniversität and to discuss problems of distance education. He made a special effort to woo those who belonged to the opposition. In winter semesters during the early days, regular meetings were organised "in front of the open fire in the Rector's office. This proved to be very useful in many critical situations the university had to face in subsequent years" (Peters, 1997, 71). Peters also visited the rectors of conventional universities to discuss joint ventures and analyse the missions of the FernUniversität. Peters claimed that the FernUniversität focus on research from the first "was the reason for the early acceptance of the FernUniversität by other universities; ... it helped considerably to build the reputation of the FernUniversität in the national and international scientific community" (*ibid.*). Over the years, around 12–15% of the FernUniversität's student body have been *guest students*, studying simultaneously at the FernUniversität and at a conventional German university.

Compared to the relatively smooth path hewn by the UNED and FernUniversität, it took the British Open University, the Open University of Israel and Athabasca University more efforts and negotiations to establish accreditation procedures with their traditional counterparts. The British Open University was the first in England to introduce a credit system. At first, it opted to provide a general credit exemption, unrelated to particular courses at the British Open University. Each year of study at another tertiary institution would count as one credit unit. For example, teachers trained in three-year teacher training colleges were accredited with three credits (half of an ordinary degree) for their previous study. The accreditation of four units was only granted to students who studied at other British universities or at institutions awarding CNAA degrees.

The first accreditation agreement with a university brought together the British Open University and Lancaster in the early 1970s (Perry, 1976). For the study of a full-year equivalent at the British Open University, Lancaster University gave two credits, and vice versa. The Lancaster agreement was a real and major breakthrough. It was the first case of a bi-lateral agreement between two English universities in the area of credit transfer. Here, the British Open University has been a catalyst to the development of credit transfer in the UK (Perry, 1976; Wagner, 1984). Obviously, the credit system provides considerable flexibility. In other English universities, no credit was given for study partially completed. Students often found themselves after one or two years of study without any record of credit to fall back on. As we have seen (Chapter 4), Credit Transfer and Accreditation Schemes (CATS), currently exist in the UK and following the 1992 Education Act define credit transfer among most British universities.

The validation role the British Open University undertook, after the abolition of the CNAA is especially striking. Once the polytechnics became universities, after the 1992 Education Act, responsibility for the so-called *associated institutions* by the CNAA, was taken over partly by the British Open University, which set up the Open University Validation Services (OUVS), staffed by administrators, many of whom transferred from the CNAA. In 1994, 71 universities and colleges, including the British Open University, provided external validation, and all of them were members of the Council of Validating Universities.

The terms *validation* and *accreditation* are sometimes used interchangeably, though the former applies primarily to the approval of *courses* and the latter to the approval of *institutions* (Silver, 1996). The Council of Validating Universities defined the term *validation* as embracing the full range of partnership arrangements. It involves a degree awarding body judging whatever a programme of study offered by another institution (or organisation) is appropriate for a qualification of that degree-awarding body (*ibid.*).

In terms of student numbers, the British Open University is not the largest accrediting institution, though it has the largest number of associated institutions. Some institutions taken over for accreditation by the OUVS were large and experienced enough to obtain undergraduate degree awarding powers through the Higher Education Quality Council and left OUVS. For instance, The London Institute of Schools of Art once under OUVS auspices, became autonomous within a year (*ibid.*). New institutions accredited since 1994 have tended to be small, and thus the number of students for whom the OUVS is responsible, has declined. The total OUVS accreditation in 1995 involved some 8,000 students (Daniel, 1996a, 35). As for what are termed by the Council of Validating Universities as *validated programmes*, these covered 203,144 students in 1994, of whom 180,392 were British residents and 22,752 were located overseas (Silver, 1996). Some former polytechnics have been especially keen to build up partnership arrangements, often they have large numbers of *accredited* students (*ibid.*).

In view of the range of institutions involved (nearly 50 campus-based tertiary institutions), the OUVS is the largest accreditation unit in the UK, and is seen as the premier in the field (*ibid.*). An important feature of its work is the *turnover* of institutions, those newly joining later to become degree awarding. It also has the largest number of institutions seeking to negotiate accreditation. In addition, the British Open University inherited from the CNAA what is now called the Quality Support Centre. Among other things, it supports the OUVS and its institutions, issues publications, and offers consultancy services. The OUVS provides also an accreditation service for higher education qualifications to institutions outside the UK. The fact that the British Open University became the main successor to the CNAA, serves to emphasise its established reputation as a dynamic university. It also makes the point, that the British Open University is better equipped than conventional universities to deal with a wide range of various-type higher education institutions, and successfully negotiate accreditation arrangements with them.

Generally, there are no official accreditation schemes between Israeli universities. At campus universities, each faculty or department has a Teaching Committee, responsible for accrediting prior studies from higher education institutions. Substantial variations exist between different departments and faculties. The Open University of Israel established a special Accreditation Committee to evaluate students' previous studies undertaken at other universities and tertiary level institutions both in Israel and abroad. It is the sole Israeli university to have an institutional accreditation policy. In addition, the Open University of Israel has a Curriculum Committee. It approves students' academic programmes that lead towards undergraduate degrees. Officially it also has the responsibility to consider students' requests to study toward a degree concurrently at the Open University of Israel and at another university or college.

Few accreditation agreements have been signed between the Open University of Israel and conventional universities. In the late 1980s, two bi-lateral agreements were reached between the Open University of Israel and Ben-Gurion University in the south of Israel, and Haifa University in the North, dealing with collaborative academic programmes in regional colleges. Twelve regional colleges operate in peripheral areas under the auspices of universities. Teachers at these colleges possess the *venia legendi* from the university, which has oversight for the teaching in a given college. Students study in the college for two years, and then move to the mother university in their third (or fourth) year. Agreements passed with the Open University of Israel allow students to pursue courses simultaneously at the Open University of Israel and at the campus university in the framework of the local college. They may decide in the third year where they would wish to complete their degrees. Such an agreement enhances the academic curriculum, which is relatively narrowly restricted in regional colleges, due to the fact that only several hundred students enrol in each college. The collaborative programme also opens the way for students to complete the full range of studies towards a bachelor degree in their local communities, which makes it easier, especially for working adults to obtain an academic degree. Since the start of these collaborative agreements, several hundred students have taken advantage of these arrangements. Most participating students decide to complete their degree at the Open University of Israel.

In addition, to these agreements with the two universities, since the mid 1980s, the Open University of Israel established several interesting collaborative programmes with nine teacher training colleges (Guri-Rosenblit, 1994a,b). According to the terms of these agreements, future teachers study concurrently toward a teaching certificate for elementary and junior high school, awarded by the teacher training college, and, at the same time, towards an undergraduate degree awarded by the Open University of Israel. Other agreements were under negotiation in 1997, one with the Technion and the other, the Hebrew University, aimed at soldiers studying at the Open University of Israel, during their compulsory army service. The new agreements provide for students who, after completing several Open University of Israel courses with high average grades, will be entitled to register at certain departments at the Technion and/or the Hebrew University. They will be exempt both from the psychometric entrance tests and from corresponding courses, studied at the Open University of Israel. Though official accreditation agreements are very rare in Israel, experience suggests that high-school students and soldier students who began studying at the Open University of Israel, and who wished later to transfer their credits to a conventional university, had no problem getting their credentials recognised.

Since the late 1980s, Canada has seen a strong push for system integration and rationalisation. It reflects a tendency by government to see universities not as autonomous institutions but "as the apex of a coherent and integrated educational system, in which each level and each institution has its specific role, one which complements all the others, so that the best possible range and quality of educational provision is made to society" (Paul, 1990, 143). Part of this effort took the form of provincial governments initiating policy bursts that stressed the liberalisation of credit transfer and lifelong learning. Formal provincial bodies have been set up to negotiate and develop credit transfer arrangements across institutions. Alberta has a detailed and efficient transfer scheme, both between universities and between colleges and universities. The largest transfer group moves from colleges to universities (Andrews et al., 1997, 78).

Student constituencies in Canada have changed substantially, both in campus and distance-oriented universities, over the last two decades (*ibid.*). Athabasca University was originally conceived of as an alternative educational provider for adults, aged 25 years and older. From the early 1990s, an unprecedented growth has taken place in the numbers of 18–24 year-old students. The number of visiting students (students concurrently studying at another post-secondary institution) has grown markedly. In 1986, visiting students amounted to 14% of Athabasca University's student body, in 1992 31%, and in 1994 over 40% (Powell & McGuire, 1995, 455). The percentage of students enrolled simultaneously at Athabasca University and at one of the other region's conventional universities virtually tripled in less than ten years. Regular students from conventional universities take Athabasca University courses for a variety of reasons: some to accelerate the pace of their studies; others are unsatisfied with the range of courses at their institution; and some to fill gaps in their programme and to proceed more slowly.

The number of students studying at Athabasca University and graduating from other universities has also grown rapidly. In 1989 some 350 graduates from other Alberta universities had been former Athabasca University students. In 1993, the corresponding statistic was about 1,100 (*ibid.*).

Powell & McGuire (1995, 458) raised an interesting argument. Paradoxically, so they argued, the special features of Athabasca University initially designed to set it apart from the conventional universities, led to its integration within a more broadly conceived structure of educational provision. Originally, Athabasca University was planned to meet the needs of a geographically dispersed constituency of adult learners, unable or unwilling to achieve their higher education goals through the conventional system. In effect, its flexible policy attracted many conventional students. This development was not planned; it happened: "Athabasca University's structure of openness, flexibility and ease of credit transfer, put in place to serve an adult education constituency, were to suit the emerging needs of a conventional higher education student population whose characteristics and behaviours have become more and more unconventional" (*ibid.*, 458). More than 60% of Athabasca University's students do not intend to complete a full degree programme, but transfer credits to other universities.

Three frameworks are used by Athabasca University for accreditation: block-credit-transfer, bridging programmes, and capstone programmes (Paul, 1990; Brindley & Paul, 1993; Hayduk, 1994). *Block credit transfer* denotes that students who have completed a given credential at a conventional institution are assured in advance that they will be given a specified advanced standing towards an Athabasca University degree. A *bridging programme* provides a university course to students at present in non-university educational settings. For example, senior high-school students may study one or more introductory university courses via distance education and then transfer the credit to the university they will eventually attend. By studying Athabasca University courses, high-school students improve their chances of admittance at a conventional university through having demonstrated successful study at a university level. They may also *bank* a few university course credits in their prospective programmes, and thus lighten future course loads. *Capstone programme arrangements* allow students at two-year colleges to complete the final year/s of senior courses in a degree programme from Athabasca

University via distance education, while remaining at their home college. These accreditation alternatives offer highly flexible study tracks to students.

Over the last decade, global partnerships have developed rapidly. The new electronic superhighways made them ever more feasible and effective. We live in societies of mergers, take-overs, and networks as the world moves closer to a global economy. Changes are no less dramatic in education (Paul, 1990; Tifflin & Rajasingham, 1995; Daniel, 1996a). Since the 1990s, most universities have been compelled by a variety of forces—economic, social, technological and educational—to move "towards a higher degree of interdependence that earlier might have been considered neither desirable nor possible" (Moran & Mugridge, 1993b, 2). Most universities around the globe are coming to realise they can teach and conduct research more effectively by working together. Across the European Union, evidence is growing of cross-national cooperation in education, despite long traditions of institutional autonomy in most countries. International consortia and organisations are flourishing.

Distance teaching universities, it may be suggested, are clearly better equipped than classical universities to move fast into joint undertakings. "The techniques and approaches familiar to distance educators lend themselves well to cooperative projects" (*ibid.*, 3). Distance teaching universities will be important leaders in starting inter-institutional schemes for cooperation within national boundaries, and perhaps more so in promoting the establishment of international consortia and in advancing globalisation. The trends of globalisation are further discussed in Chapter 8. Side by side with the increased cooperation between universities, the last decade has witnessed also the spread of competition. One of the particularly complex issues that the future of higher education systems poses, lies in the balance between competition and cooperation among universities and other higher education establishments (Daniel & Marquis, 1979; Moran & Mugridge, 1993a,c; Roll, 1995; Tifflin & Rajasingham, 1995; Moore & Kearsley, 1996). Both collaboration and competition will co-exist dialectically in all higher education systems.

Competition

The emergence of new technologies, the massification of higher education and continuous budgetary cuts have led to a growing convergence between distance and conventional education in many national settings. The boundaries between distance education and classroom-based teaching, erected so carefully in the 1970s, started disappearing in the 1990s (Mugridge, 1993a,c; Roll, 1995; Daniel, 1996a,b). Many campus universities are moving towards distance education as a mechanism for teaching more and more students for fewer and fewer resources. Over the last decade, many governments have introduced competition between universities, in an attempt to bring to a greater accountability of their higher education systems (Tifflin & Rajasingham, 1995).

Rumble (1992b) highlighted the vulnerable position of large-scale distance teaching universities as conventional institutions increasingly moved into the market sector hitherto dominated mainly by the former. Rumble (1992b, 1994, 1996) believes the future belongs to small-scale dual-mode institutions which are likely to thrive in the coming decade. In the current distance education literature there is an ongoing debate over the future prospects of distance teaching universities, and this theme is addressed further on in Chapter 8. As alternative, cheaper and more flexible models of distance education and open learning have developed, it has become an imperative for single-mode distance teaching universities to rethink their missions and restructure their overall operation (Bell & Tight, 1993; Guri-Rosenblit, 1996b, 1997b).

Of the five distance teaching universities in this study, only the British Open University and Athabasca University currently face strong competition from their conventional counterparts. During the 1990s, only a few campus universities in Spain, Germany and Israel, have experimented with teaching via distance education technologies and that on a very restricted scope (Keegan, 1994b; Guri-Rosenblit, 1996b). Furthermore, the two countries, the UK and Canada, both with a long history of distance education at university level dating back to the nineteenth century, and well before the British Open University and Athabasca University, also provided tangible incentives for conventional universities to move into new modes of distance education from the late 1990s onwards. Obviously, the expansion of distance education in those national settings, which possess a wealth of experience in this domain, may proceed at a much faster pace, compared with countries that, until the founding of distance teaching universities in the early 1970s, had no history of distance teaching at university level at all.

In the UK the number of universities planning or offering part-time distance education has grown substantially in the last decade. Nationally part-time registration grew by 50% between 1983 to 1993, from 90,000 to 132,00 (Rickwood, 1995, 17). Evidence also suggests there is a growing push towards, and a marked increase in, the provision of distance learning courses in British campus-based universities since the late 1980s (Bell & Tight, 1993; Pritchard, 1994; Bayliss, 1995). The Open Learning Foundation, for instance, which started as the Open Polytechnic is a consortium of about 20 universities which jointly produce self-study materials (Thorpe, 1995). New initiatives like *FlexiStudy* by the National Extension College in conjunction with further education colleges combine varied elements of distance education and face-to-face education (Coffey, 1989). Competition in the UK is more evident than ever since polytechnics became universities in 1992. There is scarcely one of them which has not underlined distance learning for their growing numbers of part-time students. Many of the old civic universities are moving in this direction as well. Competition between distance education providers in the UK is currently most intense. Not only are institutions treading on each other's heels in terms of course provision, but also in terms of catchment areas.

Distance education, by its very nature, makes it easier for institutions to compete against each other for students. There are no geographical constraints on where they operate (Moore & Kearsley, 1996).

Young, the father of the idea of an *Open University* in the early 1960s (Perry, 1976, Tait, 1994a), claimed that: "As the Open University has helped to spread open learning around the world, so it has increased the number and effectiveness of its competitors" (Young, 1995, 6). Young suggested that, in the face of the new developments, one alternative option for the British Open University might be to open its own campus and intensify residential teaching. Bell and Tight (1993, 138) argued that as an educational institution the British Open University appears to be stuck firmly in the 1960s with a particular model of distance education. It remains wedded to a heavily structured programme of first degree courses offering a restricted range of subjects and options for general qualifications. Bell and Tight proposed that to compete with new emerging forms of distance education, the British Open University should become more flexible in its overall approach and consider working together with other higher education institutions.

Distance teaching at university and post-secondary levels is widespread in Canada. O'Rourke and colleagues in an extensive review of distance education there reported that in 1994, 29 out of the 69 universities, 51 of the 75 colleges, and 100 of 280 private sector organisations, were active in that field (O'Rourke et al., 1995, 29). There are many networks, consortia and collaborative ties between different distance education providers in Canada.

Distance teaching universities can adopt three major strategies in response to growing competition emanating from conventional universities: strengthen their relative advantages and demonstrate excellence in specific areas; collaborate with other competing institutions and reduce the competitive risk; extend their operation beyond local and national boundaries to international markets. All of the distance teaching universities in this study had recourse at least to one of these three, in bid to secure their position in the emerging and highly competitive market for higher education.

Jennings and Ottewill (1996) reckon that: "Competitive advantage can be gained either by being the lowest cost provider of a service or by differentiating a service from that of competitors in a way that is demanded by the customer" (*ibid.*, 17). As we have already seen (Chapter 6), large-scale distance teaching universities can easily provide high-level study materials, combined with substantial economies of scale. To gain clear competitive advantage in the particular fields on which they decided to concentrate, it is important for distance teaching universities to differentiate their provision.

Johnstone (1997) argued that future higher education systems will be much more diverse with many alternative forms of teaching, learning and scholarship. The virtual university, distance education and self-paced learning will figure in higher education, though less to revolutionise the traditional universities, which will continue to be the dominant provider of higher education to the traditional age rank of well-prepared and academically able young adults. Distance teaching and new organisational forms of higher education delivery will include growing and vast arenas of continuing, professional and corporate education, as well as recreational and personal enrichment education. Hence, that distance teaching universities should strengthen their curricula in fields, in which they already possess a clear advantage. And, as we noted earlier, in the past decade most distance teaching universities have moved into new domains, catering for potential new student clienteles.

The competitive aspect of distance education will place increasing weight on the quality of programmes under offer. The best courses or programmes will establish a reputation and are likely to be sought out by growing numbers of students. As a consequence: "Marketing will become a major preoccupation of educational institutions in a full-fledged distance learning environment" (Moore & Kearsley, 1996, 242).

Another strategy to strengthen the distance teaching universities' position in the market involves joining forces with other distance education providers. For instance, a special agreement was signed between the British Open University and the National Extension College to provide support services to each other for cost efficiency reasons (Paul, 1990). The past decade has seen the establishment of many distance education organisations and consortia, both within national borders, and more on an international basis. The European Association of Distance Teaching Universities was established on the initiative of the British Open University in 1987 (Tait, 1994b). It is actively engaged in planning, diffusing and implementing open and distance learning across Europe. Its members include single-mode distance teaching universities, dual-mode universities and distance education consortia. For its part, the International Council of Distance Education concentrates on change and partnership building, to increase the opportunity for educational institutions and networks in both traditional and single-mode distance teaching institutions, and to cooperate not only among themselves but also with representatives of major agencies leading the information transformation of the world (Tifflin & Rajasingham, 1995).

Between distance teaching universities and other higher education institutions, many different kinds of alliances are possible. Moore and Kearsley claimed that: "Eventually, the increased opportunity that distance education provides for competition between educational providers is likely to result in greater collaboration among potential competitors" (Moore & Kearsley, 1996, 240). The dialectical relations between collaboration and competition will continue to feature in most higher education systems in the coming decades. Alliances will be constructed and broken up in keeping with the relative gains or losses of those participating.

The third strategy to meet growing competition from conventional universities invites expanding distance teaching universities operation beyond national borders, and to identify attractive potential markets in other countries. This has been the declared strategy of the British Open University since the late 1980s. The British Open University's strategic plan sees its future as a European, distance teaching institution, with greatly expanded student numbers (notably at postgraduate level) (Bell & Tight, 1993), and as a university operating with an international, global outreach (Daniel, 1996a,b, 1997). Its current Vice Chancellor, Sir John Daniel, strongly believes that the British Open University's global strategy makes it an attractive and viable model of a *future university*: "A university that teaches through technology to students world-wide has to re-create itself continually. The Open University is a good place to imagine the kind of university that the 21st century will need" (Daniel, 1997, 12).

In the 1980s the British Open University started moving from being a domestic to becoming an international organisation (Tait, 1994b). Its North Regional Office began servicing students in Brussels, mostly British civil servants and their families who moved there to work for the European Commission. From 1980 to 1991 it expanded into Luxembourg and the Netherlands. Thus, the Benelux Scheme was born. Students were admitted as associate students, not as undergraduates, and paid their fees in pounds. By 1991 there were 740 such students (*ibid.*, 84). By the late 1990s, the British Open University made its courses available throughout the European Community. This policy was driven by a highly competitive market in the UK, mainly in the field of Business and Management studies. Europe was marked out as a potential market for expansion. The new Vice Chancellor, John Daniel, "put his weight behind a move into Europe as a strategic goal of the University as a whole, not just for the Open Business School" (*ibid.*, 85).

The collapse of regimes in central and eastern Europe inspired the funding of a Planning Executive for the so-called Budapest Platform, a pan European distance education network which set itself the goal of creating a formal structure to bring together distance educators and all those involved in such developments in the media and in industry, both from eastern and western European countries. This goal was reached by setting up the European Distance Education Network. A special Eurodesk was established at the Cambridge Regional Centre in East Anglia. Coordinators were appointed in France, Germany, Spain, and Switzerland. Later, coordinators were also appointed in Greece, Italy, Portugal, and Austria. By early 1994, 3,650 students were enrolled from continental western Europe (*ibid.*). Currently, the British Open Business School operates in Hungary, Slovakia, Bulgaria, Russia, Romania, and the Czech Republic.

The British Open University also reaches out beyond Europe. Three of its operations are based in Ethiopia and Eritrea, Singapore and Hong Kong (Open University, 1997). In Ethiopia and Eritrea managers and senior government officers enrolled in the MBA programme, with study centres established there and seminars conducted by British Open University's staff. The programme started in 1992 for Ethiopia, and in 1996 for Eritrea. The Open University Degree Programme (OUDP) has developed in Singapore. In 1997, over 4,000 students studied 29 British Open University courses in language, literature, management, mathematics, and computer science at the Singapore Institute of Management. OUDP programmes are the only foreign degrees recognised by Singapore's Public Service Commission and Ministry of Education to qualify graduates eligible to be civil servants and graduate teachers. Students are registered with the British Open University and are subject to the same quality assurance as other British Open University's students. On the programmes, the pass rate in Singapore is very high (97%).

The Open Learning Institute (OLI) of Hong Kong was established in 1989. Some 7,000 to 8,000 students follow courses each year in arts, social science, mathematics, computing, science, technology, management and education, using the British Open University's materials and methods. The OLI was so successful that the Hong Kong Council of Academic Accreditation granted it self-accrediting status. In 1995, the Open Learning Institute launched an MBA based on the British Open University's materials.

Although Athabasca University is a provincial university, and was founded to serve mainly students in Alberta, it has in the last decade reached into a broader market, both in Canada and internationally. In recent publications, it claims that: "Athabasca University's student body spans the globe" (ICDL, 1997). The three other distance teaching universities, the Spanish UNED, the Open University of Israel and the German FernUniversität, have gone beyond their national territory, as we said earlier in Chapter 6. The potential which globalisation holds for the role of distance teaching universities is explored further in the concluding chapter.

8

Lessons from the Past and Trends of the Future

In a world of complexity, boundaries are constructed only to be torn away. Invisible barriers arise and disappear as do formal barriers.

Rothblatt and Wittrock (1993a, 9)

As universities themselves, under increasing financial pressure, begin to question some of the certainties of the last three decades in a rather more flexible way, there is now a chance for the open universities of the future to develop in a more challenging and less cautious fashion. It is important, however, that, if we are to develop sensible alternatives, they should be based on a truer interpretation of our universities' past, and on a fuller understanding of the line of well-tried open university traditions.

Bell and Tight (1993, 158)

The only thing we can be sure of in forecasting the future is that whatever happens will not be what is forecast—which, of course, leaves one saying, "But why bother?" The answer is that by attempting to visualise the shape we would like the future to have we can influence the shape it actually takes.

Tifflin and Rajasingham (1995, 186)

Introduction

Distance teaching universities were born less than three decades ago. They are relative newcomers in the higher education arena. While still subjected to occasional scepticism, both within and outside higher education circles, they have demonstrated in their short period of existence a remarkable resilience and genuine creativity in facing problems and dealing with sustained challenges. Distance teaching universities have proved beyond the practices of the preceding generation of correspondence institutions. They have won for distance higher education prestige and legitimacy. Many distance teaching universities were designed as large-scale universities catering for huge numbers of students and operating over a wide national, where not international, scale and scope. Distance teaching universities, particularly the more innovative and bold, assumed tasks that their traditional counterparts were either reluctant to undertake or unable to deal with. They were presented with the challenge to experiment with new teaching modes appropriate for reaching out to diverse, large and heterogeneous clienteles; to probe the relative strengths and weaknesses of delivery and communication technologies in distance education settings; to cut the costs of university education while providing high-level study experiences; and to develop new academic curricula and study programmes responsive to the demands of the labour market and to the needs of both students as individuals and society as a collective learning community.

Since their foundation in the early 1970s, many distance teaching universities were looked upon by their conventional counterparts as unique establishments entrusted with special missions outside the realm of mainstream higher education. However, as Archer pointed out: "Once a given form of education exists, it exerts influence on future educational change" (Archer, 1979, 30). The very presence of distance teaching universities sparked off debate as to what universities were and should be. It generated changes and revisions within classical universities and other institutions of higher education. The workings and experience of distance teaching universities over nearly thirty years carry interesting lessons and important implications for government officials, academics, administrators and policy makers of universities and in society at large, and most particularly for new universities and other higher education institutions, born in the past decade and which have to handle many tasks similar to those which initially fell to the distance teaching universities. For those of recent foundation and for universities faced with the challenge of change, the distance teaching universities' experience can be of special interest. Distance teaching universities may be seen in many lights as pioneers in dealing with delicate, if not burning social and academic issues which today confront higher education systems across the planet (Guri-Rosenblit, 1997b).

On the road towards education for tomorrow, distance teaching universities have, in several domains, provided a pioneering leadership (Morrison,

1992; Daniel, 1996a,b, 1997). Success has been achieved in part by maintaining a delicate balance between tradition and change. In some areas, they operated at the cutting edge of educational developments which today feature on the agendas of higher education systems worldwide. Clearly, a challenge exists today for nations and inter-governmental organisations to design and plan the agendas for universities in the near future. The challenges facing higher education nowadays are immense. Some argue that what is currently needed is a wholesale transformation of the higher education system in its totality (Coffield & Williamson, 1997a). Options and models of higher education for the twenty-first century have to relate to the missions and essence of universities both in the past and present (Scott, 1995; Coffield & Williamson, 1997b; Johnstone, 1997; Rothblatt, 1997). Distance teaching universities encapsulate a highly interesting model since from the outset they were designed for the *many*, as opposed to most traditional universities which expanded their boundaries, absorbed large numbers of students, but continued to function on the basis of the historic, elitist model designed for the select *few*. Most universities expanded without great change in the meritocratic model of higher education and without altering significantly the underlying premises in their social mission. Many campuses became more impersonal as student numbers expanded (Daniel, 1996a). Coffield and Williamson (1997b) have suggested that the dominant, though profoundly contested, model of what higher education is or should be, a model which shapes the thinking about higher education in both government and academia, still harks back to the institutions of the past. Against this, the accumulated experience of distance teaching universities—some of which have literally open doors, but are no less insistent on promoting opportunities to study at a high level—bring some illuminating insights to bear on the crucial dilemma: how to strike a delicate balance between quantity and quality in higher education.

Without question, massification and universalisation of access to higher education pose serious challenges to the enduring ethos of academic tradition (Trow, 1974, 1993; Scott, 1995). Across the planet, many universities have found themselves in the last few decades floundering within the framework of a dialectical and well-nigh unsolvable contradiction. On one hand, some have been dedicated to social equality both in theory and in practice, by creating and disseminating ideas vehemently defending social opportunity and by extending and enlarging their access base. On the other hand, they have continued to reproduce social elites, and thus reinforce social and occupational stratification (Gellert, 1997).

In this final chapter, we will examine the main lessons one might derive from the past experiences of the distance teaching universities as they might apply to the future planning of both conventional, mass-oriented universities and the providers of distance higher education. In addition, we shall outline some possible scenarios in the development of single-mode distance teaching universities. Given the rapid pace of change that has taken place in higher education systems in the last decades, distance teaching universities have had to rethink their missions carefully and redefine their goals accordingly. Self evidently, boundaries between distance teaching universities and campus universities are in a continued process of blurring and convergence. It is a situation which reflects one of the most noteworthy phenomena in our changing society, as Rothblatt and Wittrock have noted: "In a world of complexity, boundaries are constructed only to be torn away. Invisible barriers arise and disappear as do formal barriers" (Rothblatt & Wittrock, 1993a, 9). It is a most intriguing exercise to foretell where the new boundaries and new horizons of universities in the future, both distance and campus-based will emerge. Based on the lessons of the past and on the foreseeable trends of the future, some leading guidelines for those considering setting up a new distance teaching university in any part of the world are laid out in the Annexes.

Lessons from the Past

In their initial stages, many distance teaching universities fulfilled what Morrison (1992) calls an *emancipatory ethos*, a kind of barrier-removal element in their mission and goal statements. Space, time, prior level of education, social class, work and family obligations were defined as barriers to be overturned through the emancipatory actions of distance teaching universities. By their very existence, they spotlighted the boundaries of traditional higher education systems and pushed for a reconfiguration of thinking of prevailing academic models. Thus, in several areas, distance teaching universities had emphasised their *moving away* from rather than moving *towards* established practice. It was *freedom from* rather than *freedom to*. In addition to their *emancipatory ethos*, distance teaching universities also pioneered several important innovative mechanisms and structures, which have implications for the way traditional universities work as well.

In some national settings, distance teaching universities provided a controlled outlet for opening up and widening access to higher education, while enabling traditional universities to preserve their elitist *modus operandi*. In others, they played a leading role by ushering their national higher education systems into a new era (Guri-Rosenblit, 1997b). By their very nature, distance teaching universities probed higher education environments to learn everything possible. They experimented with elements to see what succeeds and what fails. Morrison noted that: "This trial and error approach often generates high levels of excitement. The basic motivation, in this start-up phase, is invention and the drive to find a repeatable pattern of success" (Morrison, 1992, 39). Brand new universities have naturally more degrees of freedom to try innovative ways and novel models of operation without having to invest energy and time to alter long-standing practices and routines. Some distance teaching universities, like the British Open University, the Open

University of Israel and Canadian Athabasca University, were highly innovative in their national settings, challenging many existing and cherished truisms rooted in classical universities, whereas others, such as the Spanish UNED and the German FernUniversität tried to keep in step with their conventional counterparts as much as possible.

One of the most important lessons to be retained from a comparative examination of the distance teaching universities' past must surely be that it is impossible to treat them as a generic group. Vast and profound differences exist between them. It is most vital to pay attention to such differences, both to understand the peculiar innovative cluster of each distance teaching university in its own national environment, and to draw up basic guidelines for those considering the establishment of a new university based on distance teaching methods. Distance teaching universities clearly provide more than one grand model of an innovative university. In reality they offer several models, differentiated by various characteristics: some are national universities, others are regional. Some encompass a wide international scale and scope. Others are more locally-oriented. Some are mega-universities teaching hundreds of thousands of students, compared to relatively small-scale distance teaching universities. Few distance teaching universities exercise an open admission policy, while most of the others adhere to conventional admission procedures. Some distance teaching universities offer a broad academic curriculum, while others focus on more restricted professional and vocational-oriented programmes. Some distance teaching universities are comprehensive, offering the full range of degrees at the undergraduate and graduate levels, whereas others offer mainly first level degrees. Some distance teaching universities have designed elaborate and efficient support mechanisms, while others provide sparse and weak support. Some distance teaching universities are based solely on the concept of self-study, while others provide ample opportunities of student–student and student–faculty interaction. A handful of distance teaching universities move steadily and systematically towards the application of advanced communication and delivery technologies. Yet, most still rely heavily on the written word. Some possess a large academic faculty, while others have minimal academic staff and rely on cooperation with academics from conventional universities. Some distance teaching universities control and monitor tightly the network of their study centres, while others work through a system of highly decentralised study centres.

Though it is impossible to refer to all distance teaching universities as a generic group, since they differ from each other in so many respects, nevertheless some interesting general lessons may be had from their diverse and rich experience that are relevant to many higher education systems. An examination of the lessons flowing from the relatively short past of the distance teaching universities will focus on: equality, quantity and quality in higher education; lifelong learning and flexible curricula; interface with labour markets; support systems in mass higher education; putting the accent on teaching and learning in higher education; technologies in the service of higher education; merits of inter-institutional and international collaboration.

Equality, Quantity and Quality in Higher Education

Distance teaching universities constitute a most illuminating example of how it is possible to combine equality in access with the ability to absorb huge numbers of students whilst insisting on high quality teaching and high-level exit requirements. Distance teaching universities provide a powerful solution to the two dilemmas of access and cost in higher education. Daniel asserted that distance teaching universities were established "with the express purpose of breaking the perceived link between quality of education and exclusivity of access" (Daniel, 1997, 10). Distance teaching universities demonstrate that wider access and lower costs can go together.

The continuous and massive increase in the numbers of students entering universities is the most noteworthy development in many higher education systems since the 1960s (Scott, 1995; Daniel, 1996a). The move from elite premises to equal opportunity and equity in access ideologies characterises higher education in all developed countries and some of their developing counterparts, in the last three decades. Yet, the two major concerns that have burdened both politicians and academics with regard to the massification of higher education, bear down on the deterioration of academic standards and high costs to the public purse. Annan (1990) believed that the expansion of universities brought about the diversification of higher education and the inevitable distinction between elite-type institutions and mass-oriented estab-lishments: "It had been right to expand higher education. What had been wrong was to imagine that all students could be given a Rolls-Royce higher education. No country could afford it... No country could afford centres of excellence (the equivalent of Harvard and Berkeley, the Grandes Ecoles and Max Planck Institutes) and declare that all other universities were to be given equal status" (Annan, 1990, 515–16). In short, Annan argued that it is imposs-ible to provide elite-style higher education in a mass or universal access framework.

Not only is it impossible to provide elite-type education on a mass basis due to financial constraints. It is also inappropriate to offer a restricted and limited model of higher education to heterogeneous clienteles characterised by diverse demands, abilities and needs. The Oxbridge model, for instance, based to a great extent on the principle of self-regulation that requires students to construct and pursue their own curriculum, would hardly fit the study require-ments of most undergraduate students populating universities at present. Burton Clark has pointed out that the: "So-called *mass* higher education is not simply elite higher education written ten times larger. More students mean more different types of students that need a greater variety of programmes" (Clark, 1997, 92). Mandell and Herman (1996) emphasised that student preferences and inclinations at present differ significantly from those in the past. Students no longer have to adapt so entirely to the university. They can expect, and do expect, the university to adapt to them. Faculty has to accommodate students whose attention and time are not primarily focused on school.

Obviously, elite sectors will continue to preserve their specific social and political functions in many higher education systems (Gellert, 1997). But, the crucial question arises as to how to reconcile *equality* and *quality* in mass-oriented universities (Guri, 1986; Scott, 1995; Coffield & Williamson, 1997a; Guri-Rosenblit, 1997a; Middlehurst, 1997; Roberston, 1997). This question reflects one of the most troubling dilemmas of contemporary higher education.

The notion that universities should be accessible to most or even to the entire population, is without doubt a revolutionary concept. Distance teaching universities have been in the forefront of opening up and democratising university education to large segments of the population which were either denied, or unable to pursue, academic studies. Distance teaching allows universities to reach out to great numbers of potential students within and beyond local and national boundaries. To broaden access, distance teaching universities designed flexible access systems, ranging from open entry to special preparatory courses for targeted populations. Those distance teaching universities that have adopted open admissions have made higher education equally accessible to all, and most particularly to hitherto less privileged and *second chance* constituencies (Guri-Rosenblit, 1996b, 1997b). The British Open University and the Open University of Israel were born into highly selective higher education systems; their open access policy was profoundly innovative in their national contexts. Even in less selective systems, distance teaching universities opened their doors to sectors of the population which otherwise would have never pursued academic studies, most specifically to adults in employment, studying part time.

One of the most important lessons to be drawn from the distance teaching universities is that open access or flexible admission policies do not necessarily imply the lowering of academic standards. The accumulated experience acquired by distance teaching universities suggests that their large size allowed them to invest in producing high quality materials and to assist independent learners by comprehensive and cohesive support networks. From their very start, distance teaching universities have been designed for the *many* and not for the *few*. In their continuous search for effective teaching methods that provide an intimate study environment within the setting of a mass-oriented system, they have initiated new models of student–faculty, student–student and student–content encounters and a wide range of caring and guidance mechanisms. Paradoxically, teaching large numbers of students at a distance provided the distance teaching universities with a sound economic base from which to create a close interaction between individual students, various faculty ranks, support personnel, and a means for cutting the per student cost of university education. Many conventional campus universities absorbed *many* and continued teaching them in frameworks suitable for the *few*, often resulting in the alienation of undergraduates from academic faculty, at least in their first years of study, and in the deterioration of academic standards.

The flexible approach of most distance teaching universities in admitting adult students part time, and catering for the needs of diverse student clienteles is reflected at present in access policies of many conventional, campus universities reaching out to wider student populations. Many conventional universities operate currently as large-scale undertakings and are developing quality assurance measures to ensure high standard education in the face of massification (van Vught & Westerheijden, 1993; Trow, 1994, 1996b; van Vught, 1994; Scott, 1995; Tait, 1997). Furthermore, over recent years, many established universities have adopted distance education technologies. Paul and Brindley (1996) observed that superficially distance education provides a ready response to the two pressures of absorbing many students and coping with mounting deficits in the overall university budgets. But if applied inappropriately, distance education can lead to considerable disillusionment. Paul and Brindley also urged politicians and academics, when considering the adoption of distance education strategies, to pay attention to the *softer* rather than the *technological* lessons from the operation of distance teaching universities, lessons which relate directly to the process of learning and to the support systems which are essential in running distance education systems.

Mass-oriented universities or consortia-type ventures might draw some lessons from the distance teaching universities' practice especially how to deliver high-level academic instruction to hundreds of thousands of students, as well as to the interesting relationships between *equality*, *quantity* and *quality* in higher education. It is no easy matter to manage efficient distance teaching systems on a small scale. Thus, to improve cost effectiveness of university education in a distance teaching mode and to insist on high quality learning, it is essential to enrol large numbers. Small ventures of distance teaching, operating on the margins of the traditional universities' activity, may find it difficult and nearly impossible to provide both high level education and economies of scale at the same time.

Lifelong Learning and Flexible Curricula

Today, lifelong learning has become the leitmotif and dominant slogan for most higher education institutions worldwide. This was not the case in the late 1960s and early 1970s when the distance teaching universities were born. *Lifelong learning* forms the cornerstone of the idea of a *learning society*, which encourages its citizens to study on an on-going basis and which should result, among other things, in the enrichment of the social fabric and in collective well-being. Grosso modo, *lifelong learning* is based on part-time education proceedings throughout the whole life cycle. Part-time higher education is an essential element in lifelong, recurrent education. Part-time students are typically adults in full or partial employment and/or having family and social commitments.

In several national contexts distance teaching universities were pioneers in introducing part-time higher education. In the 1970s the provision of part-time university education was fully exercised by the British Open University and partly by the polytechnics. Universities were totally given over to enrolling and teaching high-school graduates. Higher education in Spain, Germany, Israel and Canada offered some opportunities for part-time study within campus universities, but the majority of their students were young adults. Distance teaching universities are based almost entirely on part-timers. Part-time provision and lifelong learning schemes grew rapidly in many higher education systems since the 1980s, particularly in postgraduate programmes and short-cycle courses. In some systems of higher education part-timers currently outnumber full-time students.

An important lesson that flows from the distance teaching universities' experience is that if lifelong learning is to be promoted and supported, it is not enough to enrol part-time students in a full-time curriculum, and just have them learn for a longer time. For genuine lifelong study opportunities it is essential to design flexible curricula, which permit students to drop in and out of the study process and to define *academic currency* as transferable across national and even international institutions; to offer modular, non-linear degree and diploma programmes, side by side with short professional update and refresher courses; and make learning in a variety of fields available at any time required (Duke, 1997). The British Open University, for example, was the first English university to offer a modular degree which allowed students to accumulate credits. In the 1970s, most English campus-based universities offered students entry to a fixed programme in a named subject area with increasing specialisation towards a honours degree. Only the Scottish universities exercised a modular credit system. Since 1992 most English universities employ a modular credit system based on a unified frame of reference (Scott, 1995; Parry, 1997). A modularised curriculum is central to a lifelong learning scheme.

Students at many distance teaching universities may choose between a specialised or a multi-disciplinary programme—an option that was non-existent in most conventional universities during the 1970s. The choice presented to students to construct their own curriculum and to decide which kind of programme they would like to pursue is one of the pillars of lifelong learning. Interestingly, over the years, most distance teaching universities moved towards offering specialised degrees in their undergraduate programmes as a response to student demand. The experience of many distance teaching universities clearly points out to the fact that many students studying a full programme towards a degree prefer to focus on a defined disciplinary area.

Such a programme eases their admission to graduate studies, which by and large are based on restricted disciplinary foci. This characteristic underlines the immense impact of what Burton Clark calls the "dominant rule of disciplinary higher education" (Clark, 1993, 1997). The force of disciplinarity in higher education is so great that it transcends both institutional and national boundaries. Though distance teaching universities were expected to promote multi- and inter-disciplinary courses and degrees, disciplinary hegemony proved stronger. Since the 1990s, the trend is towards inter- and trans-disciplinary research (Gibbons et al., 1994; Gibbons, 1997), which has yet to prove its transferability to teaching practice at universities.

The modular and more general degrees of some distance teaching universities have led to the introduction of comparable programmes at several conventional universities. While distance teaching universities moved steadily towards more specialised degrees, often as an alternative study path, many conventional universities offer nowadays a wider range of academic curricula, from general liberal arts degrees to distinctly defined single-subject honours programmes, from full degrees to short cycle courses and specialised professional diplomas. On a more general level, it is evident that many students seeking to earn an academic degree, and with the intention of pursuing postgraduate studies, prefer to focus on specialised disciplinary programmes. By contrast, students who aim at broadening their education or upgrading their professional status are inclined more towards a general or wide education curriculum or short continuing education packages.

The distance teaching universities' experience has also highlighted the need to redefine and rethink the hidden meanings attached to *drop-out* and *attrition* in higher education. One should distinguish between students who fail in their studies and, as a result of their failure, drop out from students who successfully complete one or several courses, and decide to quit for personal and professional reasons. In many national systems, the funding of universities is based on the numbers of students graduating. However, the growth of part-time students within distance teaching universities, other distance education providers and conventional universities demands serious debate just as it requires revision of current funding schemes, the better to take account of changing patterns of study in the setting of lifelong education.

Closer Interface with Labour Markets

Distance teaching universities have become especially conscious of society's needs and hence more inclined to respond to market developments than classical universities. From the outset many of them appealed to professional groups—teachers, nurses, technicians, engineers, lawyers, and public employees—and have designed a variety of programmes geared towards professional upgrading. The British Open University and the Open University of Israel, for instance, from the start, invested considerable efforts in upgrading the professional status of teachers in the UK and in Israel to bring them up to an academic level. The Spanish UNED, German FernUniversität and Athabasca University designed a wide range of continuing education programmes for vocational and professional training. The ability to study part-time wherever and whenever one wishes greatly helps the provision of update and professional refresher courses. Distance higher education by its nature encourages adults in employment to pursue academic study and professional diplomas concurrently with their work.

One of the most noteworthy lessons to be gained from the history of distance teaching universities underscores the importance of and the real gains associated with, responding swiftly to changing needs of the surrounding environment. Several distance teaching universities have modified their priorities to meet changes in labour markets and in societal demands. From defining *second chance* students as their main constituency in the 1970s, many distance teaching universities moved progressively towards providing continuing education and professional upgrading for professional workers, many of whom already possess academic qualifications. The profiles, interests and study habits of these two distinct groups of adult students have brought about the introduction of new programmes and innovative study paths. The British Open University's Business School is nowadays the biggest Business School in Europe, yet it was established only in the second decade of the British Open University's existence. The majority of students at the German FernUniversität take courses in economics, computer science and engineering. A large proportion of students at Athabasca University and at the Open University of Israel take management and business administration courses leading on to academic degrees or professional diplomas. Many students in distance teaching universities prefer to study subjects that have a direct payoff in the job market.

In many respects, distance teaching universities are in the forefront of the academic world in launching collaborative ventures and creating links with business and industry in the areas of teaching and training. They offer degree and continuing education programmes, tailored to the special needs of particular professions, and to the unique requirements of special firms. Spain's UNED and the German FernUniversität run their study centres in collaboration with local authorities and business and industry firms. Such collaboration is beneficial for all parties. Business and industry ensure the provision of continuing education for their workers on a structured basis, in keeping with real and emerging needs. The universities demonstrate for their part social accountability and functional relevance, and improve their balance sheet.

Collaboration with the work place also permits more sophisticated technological devices to be inserted in the study process, amongst which computer-mediated communication, computer-based programmes, or video disc technologies. These do not lend themselves to extensive use, since such technologies are not easily accessible.

Cooperation between universities and consumer and job markets is highly important for both universities and society. It is likely to develop and expand in the future. Universities exist within an increasingly entrepreneurial and competitive market. In a recent international conference on *What Kind of University?* which dealt with future scenarios for universities, Michael Gibbons in his address on research and generation of knowledge within higher education systems, drew a crucial lesson for universities in the future: The rubric of survival in academic research, he suggested, has changed from *publish* or *perish* to *partnership* or *perish*, i.e. *collaborate* or *evaporate*! (Gibbons, 1997). Universities can no longer allow themselves to conduct research in isolation. Knowledge generation today has to be flexible to respond to labour market developments. Professional demands must go forward in a context of application. And this requires cooperation between academics within universities and researchers and policy makers on the outside. Gibbon's lesson, applied mainly to research and knowledge generation, also extends to the spheres of lifelong education and professional training. Distance teaching universities have an excellent potential for cooperating with industry and business not only in research, but also, and even primarily, in on-the-job training and professional upgrading.

Frequent career changes and the need for retraining make higher and continuing education attractive to many more. The more responsive and attentive a university is to the changing trends of the society surrounding it and to labour market developments, the more it may revitalise its academic mission, raising its student numbers, improving its cash flow and strengthening its accountability to society.

Support Systems in Mass Higher Education

The expansion of higher education should imply the inclusion of less privileged students within its circles. For those who are less well prepared, less motivated and less socially advantaged, the success rate depends to a great extent on support and assistance provided when learning. Most distance teaching universities have recognised the need for general support services and devoted resources to them. The distance teaching universities show, without the slightest doubt, that to deal effectively with large numbers of students from widely differing backgrounds, it is indispensable to reinforce teaching and learning by efficient delivery and support (Mills, 1996; Tait, 1996). Many distance teaching universities have developed first-rate tutorial and counselling services, personal tutors, tutors, tutor-counsellors, intensive tutorials, seminar meetings, summer and residential schools, and campus-like provisions. All these are extremely important for the effective management of distance higher education. Student support systems should be flexible and attentive to change in face of new technologies and their impact on the conditions of learning and teaching.

Not a few conventional universities are engaged in teaching large numbers of students, and plan to widen access and broaden their student intake. Provision for comprehensive student support is needed in conventional mass-oriented universities, as well, especially as, quite frequently, hundreds of students gather in huge lecture rooms or auditoria to listen to a lecturer and take notes. The trend is today—and will continue to be tomorrow—towards even less homogeneity of students and a similar diversity in relationship with the campus (Scott, 1995; Mandell & Herman, 1996; Silver & Silver, 1996; Barnett, 1997). It is highly likely that the new students that the universities hope to attract will need more individual guidance to help them acquire appropriate study habits, overcome social and work constraints, and to manage their time efficiently. This challenge faces traditional and non-traditional higher education. In the coming decade, it will bring to the forefront of academia, the issue of having to rethink learning and teaching in higher education, and thus to redefine both the roles of faculty and students (Mandell & Herman, 1996).

An additional lesson that may be had from the experience of running distance teaching universities underlines the importance of social learning. Contrary to some initial theories which assumed that adult students choosing to study via distance methods prefer to learn on their own and to interact only from time to time with academic staff, experience of distance teaching universities shows clearly that many prefer frequent contact, both with academic faculty and fellow students. Evidence suggests that the separation of learning from social relationships creates problems, ranging from feelings of deep isolation and loneliness, through to lack of immediate feedback to questions and queries posed in the study process and even to dangers of indoctrination. A growing literature has developed, mainly since the 1990s, which criticises the one-way, linear, industrial model, which accompanied course production and teaching at most distance teaching universities, a model which exposes all students to the same instructional design, irrespective of individual differences and preferences (Hamilton, 1990; Rumble, 1992, 1995a,b, 1996; Raggatt, 1993; Evans & Nation, 1993; Paul & Brindley, 1996). One of the major pitfalls of the linear model of teaching must surely be indoctrination—political, social or intellectual.

In future the development of distance and open learning will face an important task, namely, to find an optimal balance between autonomous self-guided study and social interaction with fellow students, with faculty and with student support personnel, a balance which meets the needs of individual students and which is feasible in each contextual setting. Otto Peters, the father of the *industrialised theory* of the 1960s, predicted that distance education in post-industrial society will feature "combinations of intensified and sustained group work" and "increased telecommunication between the participants" (Peters, 1994f, 239). Peters was also alert to the possible social dangers of intellectual training based solely on self-study. Distance education, he warned, "could also be interpreted as an astounding expression of the exaggerated and often excessive industrialisation of our world. It produces students who fit perfectly into a competitive achievement-oriented society... Could it be that distance education reinforces processes which are not wholesome as they help to disintegrate society by isolating people, reducing the form of shared knowledge, keeping learners away from personal interactions and critical intercourse?... This development does not comply with the educational goal of developing full and balanced persons with a sense of social obligation and responsibility" (Peters, 1997, 77–78). The subsequent experience of distance teaching universities convinced Peters that social interaction was markedly absent from the idea of a *distance teaching university*, and that this lacuna is likely to acquire further weight in the future.

In some instances where distance does not present a real physical obstacle, as in Israel for example, many distant learners urged the university to provide more intensive and frequent meetings with their tutors. In other countries, initiatives have been taken to increase the number of active study centres where such exchange and social interaction may take place (Mills, 1996). In South Africa, for example, there is a national effort since the mid 1990s to create a network of *community learning centres* to support distance learners (Glennie, 1996). In most distance teaching universities, where students are scattered over vast geographical areas, new information and communication technologies have made frequent interpersonal dialogues and discussions possible. Daniel stressed that the potential success of innovative and advanced electronic technologies depends to a great extent on the ability to provide individual learners with adequate backup throughout their studies: "We believe that good distance education means first-rate tutorial support for each student... We will not operate... anywhere else unless we can provide this tutorial support, either through a partnership or by electronic means. Can we, through electronic mail, computer conferencing, and the World Wide Web, provide the level of individual student support that we think necessary? We are experimenting with that, but despite all the arm waving, I think the jury is still out. If the jury comes back and declares us guilty of being able to provide effective, personal tutorial support to students on a large scale, then all sorts of things become possible" (Daniel, 1996b, 38).

As more conventional universities offer distance education to students in remote areas, it becomes a priority for them to devote resources and efforts to design effective support systems and to improve communication on a person to person basis between students and teachers and among students themselves. Student support services are costly. To some extent they go counter to the drive for cost effectiveness in distance teaching. But they are a necessary condition to manage effectively the teaching of, and learning by, large numbers. Both politicians and academics should understand that teaching via distance education technologies demands a variety of support as an integral part in running the organisation. Distance education on a wide scale is more complex by far

than managing small-scale correspondence institutions and extension departments (Daniel, 1996a). In the future, one of the intriguing challenges for
universities will be to provide means for close and sensitive caring to individual
students, with ample opportunities for social interaction with students and
specialists within mass-oriented institutions of higher education.

Reviving the Focus on Teaching and Learning in Higher Education

Distance teaching universities have assigned top priority to *teaching* and
student *learning* in their mission goals and practical operation. By paying
particular attention to these two activities, they have gone beyond the practices
of most correspondence institutions, which paid little attention to the quality of
studying, and also beyond most campus universities, heavily dominated by
research. By emphasising their role as *teaching universities*, they have revived
the long-established tradition of the ancient universities. Daniel declared that:
"Indeed, most modern universities, such as the Open University, resemble in
their essence the early University of Oxford more than other academic models
that have come and gone between" (Daniel, 1997, 4). For over 800 years, until
the birth of the ideal of the *Humboldtian* university (Rothblatt, 1989, 1997),
teaching was the most important task of academics. Throughout the twentieth
century universities added the generation of new knowledge to their previous
responsibilities of preserving knowledge and transmitting it. They turned
research into a supreme core value which guided their overall raison d'être
(Altbach, 1996; Gibbons, 1997).

Distance teaching universities have refocused attention on *teaching* and
learning within academia. In mass or universal access universities, most
students do not aim at an academic career. Thus, research is less relevant to
their careers or to their educational goals. In the future, universities will be
obliged to pay greater attention to teaching while accommodating divergent
student profiles (Annan, 1990; Guri-Rosenblit, 1990b; Scott, 1995; Mandell &
Herman, 1996; McNair, 1997).

To find appropriate ways of accommodating different styles of learning and
different needs of students from many different backgrounds, with different
achievements on entry and study behaviours, it was essential to experiment
with a variety of teaching techniques. Distance teaching universities have
developed quality assurance procedures to monitor teaching, and to provide
students with learning at a high level. Since the early 1970s they have tried out
various types of teaching methods and scattered their efforts over several
domains. The 1970 stood out by the emphasis on producing *high quality
self-study materials*, user-friendly and self-guiding. Ten years later, priorities
shifted towards supplementing study materials by more elaborate and *intensive
support*, with greater weight on social learning and social interaction. The
1990s have been marked by hectic experimentation with *advanced interactive
media*. The production of high-level study texts, the design of sophisticated

support procedures and the incorporation of new delivery and communication media have the purpose of improving the quality of teaching, of providing individual students with an attentive and protective learning environment. Added to this, distance teaching universities have moved over the years from a *teaching-centred* ethos to a *learner-centred* approach, offering more flexible study paths, and responding to diverse individual needs and requests.

An important lesson from the distance teaching universities' experimentation with a variety of teaching techniques, approaches and delivery mechanisms bears upon the changing roles of academics in teaching. Being entrusted with writing self-study materials has drastically altered the roles of the distance teaching universities professors as teachers when this is compared with the requirements teachers in conventional universities are called upon to fulfil. In some cases, working with a team may restrict their *academic freedom*. The involvement of new types of academic and support staff in the development of learning texts, if not in the actual process of study, has redistributed responsibility for teaching between several actors and redefined the place of the lecturer. The introduction of new interactive technology posed new challenges to academics and with it the need to assume new roles. In future, the role of academic faculty as teachers in many universities will change profoundly; it will require on-the-job retraining. Continuous changes in the learning environment also change the traditional student–faculty relations. They create new expectations and new definitions in the role of lecturers. Mandell and Herman (1996) claimed that the changing profile of students would also lead to a drastic shift in the roles of faculty. Faculty are expected nowadays not merely to teach, but to act as counsellors and mentors. They have to deal with issues for which their scholarly and disciplinary expertise never prepared them. In addition, new ranks of academic and support staff will become members of the universities' professional personnel, and assume distinct roles in teaching and learning.

Over the last decade, interest of national governments and international organisations in defining and assessing quality in higher education institutions for both research and teaching performance has grown (Tait, 1993, 1997; van Vught & Westerheijden, 1993; van Vught, 1994). Quality assurance schemes are currently employed in the UK, other European Community countries, and elsewhere. They will continue to feature on the agendas of universities for a long time. In the future both distance teaching universities and campus universities will pay greater attention to learning and teaching and will have to invest further effort in trying out more innovative approaches and techniques to improve their everyday practices.

Technologies in the Service of Higher Education

Distance teaching universities have an unparalleled experience of employing a very wide range of media and technologies. Some have proven disappointing. Others have been most promising. The use of a multi-media approach and the harnessing of different technologies to the production and delivery of study materials and to improve exchange in learning lie at the heart of all distance teaching universities. Other universities might skip over some of the early stages of adapting multi-media systems by contemplating the lessons and recommendations amassed by distance teaching universities.

The experience of distance teaching universities suggests that it takes a very considerable time for a new technology to work its way into the study system on a large scale. Audio cassettes, for example, were successfully adopted for instructional purposes in the British Open University after nearly twenty years of small scale trials. For wholesale application, the relevant medium or technology has to be easily accessed, easily operated, preferably low-cost to produce and cheap enough to purchase (Bates, 1989b, 1995).

Furthermore, the greater the control a student has over any given medium greatly influences its instructional efficacy. The ability to stop and re-start a medium during study was astoundingly important for students. Audio cassettes and video cassettes, for example, were preferred by many students over radio and television broadcasts. Thus, many of the tasks assigned to radio and television were gradually transferred to audio and video cassettes. Learning from ephemeral media—radio, television and satellite transmissions—appears to be more difficult for distance students than learning from permanent materials—books, audio and video cassettes, discs and computer-based programmes.

Some technologies, mainly educational television and radio, have not met the initial expectations placed on them in the planning phase of the distance teaching universities during the early 1970s. They became peripheral to the distance teaching universities world. In fact, careful experimentation is needed before large-scale implementation of a new technology. In addition, different technologies lend themselves to different teaching approaches. Thus, instructional television and satellite conferencing are more appropriate for information transmission, and are not dissimilar to the function of a lecture. Computer-mediated communication, however, allows a greater range of collaborative learning methods and dialogues (Bates, 1995, 1997). Choosing a balanced mix of media appropriate for each instructional context is of prime importance.

Distance education targeted at specific professional groups, managers or teachers, either at work or attending local centres, is less restrictive as to the media that may be used. Satellite transmission and computer-based learning become realistic propositions for individuals at their place of work, or gathered together in virtual class settings. Even video discs become a viable option for local centres. They can be shared by several users.

New delivery and interactive technologies have a huge potential to improve learning experiences in distant learning environments, and for raising social learning. However, their initial implementation requires high investments. So, increased use of technology does not lead automatically to increased cost effectiveness. One cannot expect immediate cost reductions when setting up the infrastructure for elaborate and complex technologies. Some will always be expensive. Their use will be justified only by improved efficiency of the study process, or by adding an important dimension—interactivity—to distance learning environments. Finally, for new interactive technologies to be implemented effectively, demands that major, structural and organisational changes accompany them (Bates, 1995, 1997; Miller, 1996; Paul & Brindley, 1996). Paul and Brindley (1996) claimed that: "Changing the way we teach or expect students to learn may change our universities in ways that may not be anticipated" (*ibid.*, 48). Thus, before adapting a new technology, its suitability and integration into overall learning and teaching has to be taken into consideration.

New technologies challenge the organisation of academic life both within distance teaching universities and classical universities. Interactive technologies will affect the relations between students and faculty, change the nature and essence of academic curricula and alter the ways in which knowledge is both acquired and generated. The time is not yet ripe to predict the full impact new information and interactive technologies might have on the organisation of higher education institutions. What is obvious, however, is that technologies should be treated as means to an end, as vehicles to achieve educational goals, and not as ends in themselves.

Inter-institutional and International Cooperation

The relations between distance teaching universities and their conventional counterparts showed up the enormous advantages to be gained from a fruitful inter-university collaboration. To some extent, most distance teaching universities rely on the academic staff of neighbouring universities to design and develop study materials, in teaching, and in monitoring final exams. On the other hand, high quality textbooks from distance teaching universities, their special television production and their other study packages, are used extensively by students and faculty of mainstream universities. They contribute continuously to the improvement of the quality of learning and teaching within higher education institutions at large (Guri-Rosenblit, 1990b, 1996b). Both students and faculty could benefit greatly from increasing cooperation between distance and campus universities, utilising and exploiting the strengths of each.

The late 1980s and the 1990s witnessed substantial working together between campus universities and distance teaching universities, in utilising advanced technology, in developing mutual academic and continuing education programmes, and that side by side with sharper competition over potential clienteles. This was discussed in Chapter 7. Successful inter-institutional collaboration could well expand educational opportunities, broaden the scope of the curriculum and contribute to cost-efficiency (Coffey, 1989; Guri-Rosenblit, 1991, 1997b; Daniel, 1996a,b). Some distance teaching universities have attempted to develop high-cost multi-media programmes jointly with other higher education institutions. They have proven that such endeavours were mutually beneficial (Bates, 1995, 1997). The tendency of universities to rely only on their own staff to design and develop study programmes in the face of shrinking resources and growing student numbers may perhaps be seen as unwise and costly. Inter-university collaboration, national and international might reduce production costs of study materials and of academic programmes, and free up money to sustain more effective teaching techniques and student support services.

Internationalisation and globalisation today are high on the agendas of intergovernmental organisations and universities. The major contribution of universities to globalisation lies in knowledge generation and knowledge transmission. Skilbeck argued that: "The importance of knowledge and innovation in the so-called post-industrialised age underlines the role of university in the global environment, since it is a major source of innovative and applicable knowledge and... has the best structures and organisations for knowledge dissemination" (Skilbeck, 1997, 106). Distance teaching universities are well able to transcend national borders, and to reach out to students across the globe. Their infrastructure allows them with relative ease to develop international collaboration between different types of distance education providers, between distance and campus universities, and between universities and the corporate world of business. Most of those studied here work successfully beyond their national borders. The British Open University's operation embraces literally all continents and girdles the Earth.

Well-established distance teaching universities have the capacity to help new distance education institutions, particularly in developing countries, in their start up phase as well as helping them gradually build credibility in their own countries. Newly born institutions in developing regions often lack the initial capital investment to set up the infrastructure to be self-standing. The experience, advice, materials and programmes of senior and successful distance teaching universities gives the new institutions that boost which enables them to gain academic status on their home ground. Several institutions were able to assume full autonomy as degree granting establishments. In a few cases, new distance teaching institutions have even forced out "some of the shoddier providers of higher education" (Daniel, 1996b, 38) from their local markets. By their ability to reach out to less privileged and under-developed regions of the world, as well as offering attractive programmes in developed countries, distance teaching universities have shown themselves as potentially a most powerful tool for upgrading and providing continuing, professional and higher education in any part of the world. Distance education, in general, clearly stands as a first-rate vehicle for raising the educational level in the most remote areas. The sheer size of many distance teaching universities provides them with a positive advantage in accommodating a wide variety of needs from very different student constituencies of diverse nationalities. Obviously, language adaptation and additional adoption mechanisms are needed to fit programmes to local markets.

Main Lessons: A Brief Summary

Here, we draw together the main lessons which may be said to follow from the experience of distance teaching universities and which are summarised below.

1. Massification and flexible access policies do not necessarily imply the lowering of academic standards. Even in mass-oriented universities it is possible to provide high-level learning opportunities and insist on high exit requirements.

2. There is an interesting correlation between equality, quantity and quality in higher education, and most specifically in distance higher education. Operating on a large scale and enrolling large numbers of students provides universities with a sound financial base from which they may design small-scale and convivial conditions for student and faculty to meet. Sound finances permit large investments to provide high quality materials and study at a high level. It is difficult, if not well-nigh impossible, to run small-scale distance education programmes, and at the same time to provide high-level education and to achieve favourable economies of scale.

3. Flexible and modular curricula are essential for promoting and consoli-dating lifelong learning, enabling students to choose the programmes they would like to pursue, which may range from full degree programmes, short-cycle diplomas to professional in-service courses.

4. Many undergraduates who opt for an academic degree with the intention of pursuing postgraduate studies, prefer a specialised disciplinary curriculum over broad programmes even within distance teaching universities. This highlights the overarching power of the disciplines in higher education.

5. Lifelong learning calls for a redefinition of *drop-out* and *attrition* within higher education institutions. Many adult students successfully complete different paths of study and exit the university for a variety of professional and personal reasons without obtaining an official degree. Their study behaviour does not, by any standard, reflect *failure*. The number of older students already possessing academic qualifications and aiming at pro-fessional upgrading and continuing education are likely to grow in the future. Funding formulas of higher education systems should respond to the variation in lifelong study patterns, and should fund part-time students on a basis comparable to full-timers.

6.   Universities should be attentive and alert to changes in their immediate environments and should respond to changing job and consumer markets rapidly. Successful collaboration between business, industry and universities is of mutual benefit. It helps universities to revitalise their academic mission, to broaden their student constituencies, to improve their financial base and to strengthen their social accountability.

7.   Student support systems are of key importance for running and maintaining large-scale universities. Creating a friendly and sympathetic environment for individual students is equally a key factor in managing mass-oriented universities successfully.

8.   The accumulated experience of distance teaching universities highlights the importance of social learning and social interaction within distance learning environments. Many distant students prefer contacts with both faculty and fellow students to be more frequent. New and advanced technologies make it possible to increase the intensity of exchange among students and between students and academic staff. Distance higher education in the future will provide even greater opportunities for interpersonal dialogues and group work.

9.   Developing high-level study material requires heavy investment in human capital, time and money, but generates great benefits for student learning. The development of such materials is justified particularly in fields studied by large numbers of students and/or shared by students across many institutions.

10.   The advent of widely different student clienteles compels universities to place greater weight on teaching and learning, and to search for effective ways to improve both—a task which has been hitherto largely neglected.

11.   Changes in learning environments affect the teaching roles of academic staff, as too the ethos of academic freedom. In all probability, the teaching tasks of lecturers and professors in the future will undergo radical change, and require on-the-job training.

12.   Adjunct academic faculty and student support personnel are likely to become an integral part of the teaching force in many universities. Consequently, traditional teaching responsibilities will be divided between several different parties—tutors, counsellors, Internet specialists, computer interface designers, instructional technologists, data resource personnel, etc.

13.   A new technology takes considerable time to work its way into the study system. For it to be implemented on a large-scale it is advisable that the new technology be easily accessed and operated, and that it be preferably low-cost to develop and relatively cheap to buy.

14. The degree of control a student has over any medium greatly influences that medium's efficacy. The ability to stop and re-start a medium in the study process has proven to be highly important for distance students.

15. Different technologies lend themselves to different teaching and learning approaches. Thus, the choice of an appropriate mix of media for each instructional context is an important prior consideration.

16. Distance education targeted at specific professional groups, managers or teachers, either in the work place or in local centres, is less restricted in the media it may bring to bear, from courses based on open or universal access.

17. New delivery and interactive technologies have a huge potential for improving learning in distant learning environments, and for enhancing social learning. However, their setting up requires high investments. It is not realistic to expect cost effectiveness when installing an infrastructure for elaborate and complex technological systems. The high costs of certain advanced technologies might be justified given either their proven educational efficiency or by their capacity to add a new dimension, interactivity for example to distance education.

18. For the potential of new technologies to be fully realised, it is of paramount importance that their implementation go hand in hand with far-reaching structural and organisational changes in the overall management and provision of learning/teaching.

19. Both students and faculty might benefit from closer collaboration between distance and campus universities, by each having use of the advantages of the other. Successful inter-institutional collaboration has the potential to broaden educational opportunities, to enrich the range of the curriculum and by being cost-efficient.

20. Distance education by its very nature easily transcends national borders, and may reach out to diverse student constituencies around the world. The infrastructure of distance teaching universities enables them to extend international collaboration between different distance education providers, between distance and campus universities, and between universities and the world of business and enterprises.

Future Trends

Over the past decade, the pace of change in higher education has been so outstandingly rapid that the visible and palpable barriers between distance and conventional higher education are clear no longer. The environments in which higher education evolves will change dramatically as they respond to new demands, new markets and shifting consumer needs. We are already well into this process. We see distance and conventional higher education blending together in many countries. In all likelihood, the next decade will see a further blurring of the boundaries between campus and distance universities. Developments that were vaguely emerging only as possibilities when I started writing this book in 1992, have become realities by the time of its completion. In June 1997, an international conference on *What Kind of University?* took place in London. Many of the scenarios that were presented, predicted and analysed there had equal application to both distance and campus universities. Providing lifelong education on a part-time basis across a variety and wide spectrum of fields through new knowledge technologies and other distance teaching means seem to feature prominently on the future agendas of most higher education systems and that across the planet!

The blurring frontiers between distance and campus universities is particularly evident in the move by conventional universities into providing distance education programmes. Some universities have converted in the course of the last decade to dual-mode institutions, offering education and training to both on- and off-campus students. The creation of national or regional ventures based on the consortium format which offer distance education programmes is another flourishing example, most particularly in Europe, Canada and the USA. In both cases, conventional universities are expanding their student base by using distance teaching methods either single-handedly (the dual-mode) or in partnerships with other universities (the consortium-type model).

Faced with these developments, distance teaching universities clearly have to readjust and articulate their vision for the future. They have to define their specific and special missions, strategic and logistic planning, if not the whole range of their operational activities. To carry out these demanding and challenging tasks, distance teaching universities will have to consider alternative operational scenarios and provide tentative answers to some crucial questions: Who are likely to be their potential target clienteles? Which kind of special functional roles, if any, will the distance teaching universities undertake? (Will they for instance compete with other higher education providers for the same student constituencies whilst offering comparable programmes? Or will they launch new and focused initiatives?) What roles will their academic faculty be required to perform? Which form of academic curricula are they going to offer? How will such planned and visible changes affect their basic organisational infrastructure? What relationship will they develop with their surrounding communities and with other higher education institutions? How far will their operation be grounded and divided between local, national and international markets?

Defining a clear vision for the future is a key to shaping each institution's development. Coffield and Williamson took the view that universities, in general, must take the initiative in defining radically different arrangements for their future if only for their own good: "Universities must themselves change, as otherwise their future will be defined by political and business elites" (Coffield & Williamson, 1997b, 5). Universities have to envision their future in a most creative way in order to escape the trap of offering more of what already exists: "The task facing people in higher education is to think beyond the constrains of conventional wisdom. If universities are to respond to the challenges and uncertainties of the new century, they must find fresh ways to do so. The old frameworks of planning and managing them are no longer fit for repositioning them for the new century" (Williamson & Coffield, 1997, 117).

Morrison argued that as distance teaching universities chart their futures, they must recognise the distinction between growth and development: "To grow means to increase in size by the assimilation or accretion of demand. To develop means to expand or realise the potentialities of; to bring to a fuller, greater and better state... When something grows, it gets quantitatively bigger. When it develops it gets qualitatively better or at least different. Quantitative growth and qualitative improvement follow different laws and require different visions and strategies...The critical issue facing open universities is not increasing growth, but selecting the pathways to development. Although there are limits to growth within a given model, there are no limits to development" (Morrison, 1992, 41). Morrison concluded by pressing distance teaching universities not merely *to do things differently*, but *to do also different things*. Distance teaching universities should open up and permit what was never allowed to become part of their systems.

The discussion of trends likely to mark the development of distance teaching universities in their search to realise their potential, touches upon six domains: Potential student constituencies; the roles of academic faculty; knowledge generation, delivery and dissemination; organisational infrastructure; university–society dialogue; global outreach.

Potential Student Constituencies

Initially, most distance teaching universities were designed mainly for older part-time students. Throughout the last two decades more diverse student clienteles joined them, and it is likely that the future student cohorts will be even more heterogeneous. In discussing potential student constituencies, four categories are considered: (a) *older* versus *younger* students; (b) *second chance* versus *first chance* clienteles; (c) *degree* versus *continuing education* populations; (d) *national* versus *international* learners.

Older versus younger students: More younger students joined distance teaching universities since the 1980s. This trend is likely to grow. Increasing mobility amongst professionals and the willingness of many high-school graduates to pursue specific fields of study, which are either hard to get admitted to at a conventional university, or require full residency, have drawn, and will continue to draw, young adults to highly acclaimed and reputable distance teaching universities, and to other distance education providers. The fact is that the average age of distance students is currently younger than it used to be in the 1970s and the 1980s, whilst the average age of traditional students in campus universities is older. There is an evident convergence in the demographic characteristics of distance education students and on-campus populations. Young students are similar in many respects to conventional age cohorts in traditional universities. Social interaction and campus-like provisions, either real or virtual, through electronic communication media, are highly significant for their progress and success in studying.

Among the older students at least three distinct groups can be identified: Second-chance students; professional workers; and adults seeking to broaden their education and to become better acquainted with new fields of knowledge. Adults at distance teaching universities, in the 1970s and in the 1980s, were regarded mainly as *second chancers* who had missed out earlier by premature school leaving or by insufficient entry qualifications, for a wide range of personal, social and political (such as war time) reasons and circumstances. Since the 1980s, a sizeable and noteworthy group entered both distance teaching universities and classical universities, as well as non-university institutions—professionals seeking career upgrading either through graduate degrees or through short specialised courses and diplomas. Many already held academic qualifications. Their numbers will increase significantly in the coming decade at many distance teaching universities. A third group comprises adults seeking to upgrade their general education or to pursue fields of study different from their professional or academic careers, for recreational purposes. These three groups of older students display highly distinctive preferences and study habits. Each requires a very different treatment and a broad range of courses and study opportunities. Many distance teaching universities have already started to adjust their curricular planning to fit the diverse range of their varying student constituencies, and will continue to be attentive to potential new clienteles.

Second chance versus first chance students: We noted earlier, *second chance* students were the main target population of most distance teaching universities. With the rising tide of equity of access to universities and the expansion of higher education, distance teaching universities will absorb students from even less privileged backgrounds, less well prepared for academic studies by comparison with current students. The new contractual ties of distance teaching universities with the locality which are discussed further on, will open up their gates to more second chancers, with whom conventional universities are likely to be both unwilling and unequipped to deal. Distance teaching universities with an open admission will see such groups as an important target population to be accommodated, thus fulfilling both an important mission and extending their student base. Strong and comprehensive student support will be needed for those who hail from highly underprivileged segments of the society.

Even so, the ratio between *second chance* and *first chance* students will tip in favour of the latter. If at the start distance teaching universities were designed by and large to meet the needs of *second chancers*, currently several teach many *first chance* students and this trend will intensify. By *first chance* student clienteles we mean both young and older adults who chose, and will choose, to study at a distance teaching university after comparing the merits of several higher education options available to them. Since many conventional universities are already offering distance education programmes, the choice to study at a distance teaching university will be based both on the feasibility of studying by distance teaching methods, and to a greater extent on the standing of each distance teaching university. Such *first chance* students will usually be well prepared for academic studies, and many will pursue graduate and continuing education studies, rather than undergraduate programmes.

Degree versus continuing education students: Currently, many distance teaching universities focus on undergraduate students. The Open University of Israel and Athabasca University have for over two decades, offered only undergraduate level courses. Only in the 1990s did they start to offer a limited range of Master's degrees. Both also provide several continuing education programmes. Most of Athabasca University students pursue professional and continuing education study rather than opt for an academic degree. The British Open University teaches all types of degrees up to the PhD. Most of its students, however, are undergraduates. At Spain's UNED and at the German FernUniversität the story is different. Their degrees resemble those at conventional universities, and usually lead to diplomas comparable to master level qualifications. Many distance teaching universities already provide further non-credit, certificate and diploma programmes, as well as more specialised graduate level studies to meet the needs of new student groups, joining their students. Here too it is likely indeed this trend will become more pronounced. Students opting for non-credit and diploma studies will come from the business and industry sectors, enrolling either as individuals or more likely as members of organised groups, on the basis of contracts signed between distance teaching universities and firms and enterprises.

National versus international students: International students too will be a growing component of the student body of large-scale distance teaching universities. This development will require distance teaching universities to pay more attention to ways of taking up and adapting to diverse local markets, by translating study materials, finding suitable tutors, counsellors and additional personnel to run study centres and support services and giving them various levels of responsibility to monitor exams in other languages, etc. Undoubtedly, they will figure among the leading universities that promote globalisation in higher education, and among the pioneers of international networks and collaborative projects.

Roles of Academic Staff

Distance teaching universities were forerunners in redefining and reshaping the roles of their academic staff to match their new and very different learning/teaching environments. By doing so they highlighted the future role of academic staff elsewhere. Distance teaching universities may lead the way in working out new training models and appropriate reward structures to bring about changes in academic teaching. Bates believed that: "University teaching is probably the last craft- or guild-based profession. However, the changing nature and variety of learners, the growing complexity and volume of knowledge, and the impact of technology on teaching now really require that university teachers should have formal training and qualifications in instructional methods. This should eventually become a condition for tenure" (Bates, 1997, 21). To improve teaching within academia is a long-range goal to be pursued by all universities and other higher education providers. As relatively new institutions, distance teaching universities are better situated to take the initiative in reshaping the roles of their faculty. Many academics joining them are aware of their innovative nature, and arguably are likely to be less conservative in their overall views on change and reform. Distance teaching universities can take the lead in retraining both their *veteran* academics and *newly recruited* staff with a clear vision of what the required competencies are and what are likely to be teaching responsibilities of a faculty member in a future university setting.

First, academics will have to become reconciled to collaborating with other professionals, junior or adjunct staff, in designing and teaching. Academics at most distance teaching universities had to accommodate to working in teams without any former preparation or training. Teamwork requires lecturers to give up some degree of the most valued *academic freedom* on the one hand, and on the other to exercise social interaction and communication skills. Teaching responsibility is distributed between several actors. Increasing employment of advanced interactive technologies will most assuredly require academic staff to work with other experts to develop course materials of high quality delivered by a broad spectrum of media.

Second, academic staff will become more facilitators and mediators between knowledge bases and students, rather than the main vehicle and transmitter of bodies of knowledge. Interestingly, such a trend has grown widely in the last decade in lower levels of education, namely nursery to high school education, but is practised to a most restricted degree within universities. Distance teaching universities lead and will continue to lead the transformation of academic faculty teaching roles from the archetypal *sage on the stage* to the ideal of *guide on the site*.

Third, the new teaching and learning environment will require academics to assume new responsibilities and to develop a range of new skills and talents. Until now, most staff in distance teaching universities have been writing and developing self-study materials. The emergence of new delivery technologies and new interactive communication media will divert their activities to additional fields. New technologies challenge profoundly the organisation of academic life. Faculty members will be expected to lead teleconferencing sessions via computer or video or audio channels, become more expert in desktop publishing, design computer software, put their lessons on the World Wide Web, or lecture through satellite or instructional television. In the foreseeable future, many of these skills will be required of faculty at campus universities as well. Some of the new technologies will restore the individual professor to the centre of teaching and learning (Rumble, 1997), as is the case with video-based lecturing. The new study environment will extend the variety of teaching techniques and demand greater instructional expertise from faculty. At the same time, teachers will have greater flexibility to choose the teaching styles best suited to their personal strengths and individual preferences.

Fourth, more of the staff in distance teaching universities will undertake research, which focuses on adult teaching and learning and on effective application models of new technologies to various disciplinary and inter-disciplinary fields of inquiry. Already, new research institutes, studying knowledge acquisition, virtual learning environments, and technology application, have been established in the last few years in both campus and distance education universities.

Changes such as those just mentioned will require setting up special human, technical and organisational infrastructures for on-the-job training of faculty, and defining appropriate rewards and incentives. The current reward system based mainly, and even solely, on research products will have to adjust its priorities in the near future to include excellence in teaching and mentoring.

Generation of Knowledge, its Delivery and Dissemination

Different forms of knowledge generation are currently being debated and developed in academic circles. As discussed earlier in Chapter 4, Gibbons introduced an interesting distinction between two modes of research which he labelled *Mode 1* and *Mode 2* (Gibbons et al., 1984; Gibbons, 1997). According to this interpretation, the teaching infrastructure of universities is based mainly on the transmission of knowledge generated in *Mode 1* within the confines of disciplinary departments. One of the problems with which Gibbons and other scholars are preoccupied is how the new knowledge forms—*Mode 2*—will be translated into an academic curriculum, within knowledge structures existing in most universities.

Most distance teaching universities focus mainly on teaching. They were not established as research institutes. Arguably, they are better equipped than classical universities to translate *Mode 2* research into a teaching programme. The development of their study materials resembles the teamwork essential in the knowledge generation typical to *Mode 2*. Distance teaching universities have deliberately decided not to offer academic programmes that are too different from those of their conventional counterparts, in part to secure academic standing for their degrees, and in part to enable their students to move freely from and to other higher education institutes. They have the potential infrastructure both to develop and to deliver inter- and multi-disciplinary courses with relative ease. In the future distance teaching universities may well play an important role in linking new types of knowledge generation and their transmission to students. In addition, many distance teaching universities could find themselves in a favourable position to participate in inter-institutional research ventures, coordinating the work of specialists from a wide range of institutions and monitoring the translation of research into instructional texts. In nearly thirty years of operation distance teaching universities have gained ample experience in managing and operating teams of scholars. The lessons they have acquired may prove beneficial to traditional universities should they attempt to coordinate *Mode 2* research and teaching practices.

Evidently, the new delivery and communication technologies will substantially change course development and delivery practices at distance teaching universities. Learning units and textbooks will develop through sophisticated electronic publishing. Less time will be taken to produce them, and they will be far more easily and immediately updated. As more students own or have access to computers with modems, materials can be directly delivered from the lecturer's computer to students' homes.

Providing a wider variety of programmes, tailored to the special needs of various student clienteles, will be an additional potential change in the domains of knowledge delivery and dissemination within distance teaching universities. The new technologies will allow core materials easily to be modified to suit different markets and individual students, as opposed to highly standardised products of self-study texts in a one-way industrial model. The global market will require distance teaching universities to set up appropriate translation and adaptation facilities. A growing tendency will be the development of modular materials, serving many uses and potential target populations, ranging from full degree programmes, through certificates and diplomas, to stand-alone textbooks, units, study kits and media products, to be purchased both by individuals and organisations.

Growing inter-institutional and international collaboration in producing academic curricula is another important area. Courses covering international topics, on *European Culture and Civilisation* for example, or multi-disciplinary and inter-disciplinary topics will be designed and co-produced by several partners. Such ventures may make for a better quality of end-products, and further economies of scale, by widening the potential student clientele. Distance teaching universities will assume a leading role in initiating and monitoring such projects with other distance education providers, conventional campus-based universities, and non-university institutions both nationally and internationally. Quality of materials and courses will be central in a telelearning market, where there are no physical limits to the number of courses that can be offered by any single institution. Unquestionably, an international trade in academic and professional education will take shape, when individual learners may access courses and teachers anywhere in the world in whatever subject they wish, provided someone, somewhere, wants to teach it. The more qualitative the programmes, the more likely they are to be accessed by wide numbers of students, and the greater their advantage in a competitive higher education market.

Organisational Infrastructure

An infrastructure based on printed materials, warehouses and delivery via mail does not fit future learning and teaching in which distance teaching universities will work in the next millennium. Distance teaching universities will be obliged to alter their organisational infrastructure and overhaul the management of both headquarters, local and regional centres. In Bates' estimation, the issue before all distance education providers in setting an infrastructure to accommodate present and future developments "is to develop a system that encourages teaching units to be flexible, innovative and able to respond quickly to changes in subject matter, student needs and technology, while at the same time avoiding duplication, redundancy and conflicting standards and policies" (Bates, 1997, 23–24).

The present reliance of most distance teaching universities on the physical production of study materials will shift in the coming decade to very different ways of operating. Large warehouses storing tens of thousands of study units and millions of course elements will be abolished, when course production moves on towards electronic publishing. Communication between students and teaching staff will rely less on postal mail, and more on e-mail and other teleconferencing technologies.

Large-scale distance teaching universities may decentralise their plant. More autonomy and power may accrue to local and regional centres which will have the responsibility to monitor student learning from the initial registration to final examination. Such a development reflects a trend elsewhere in complex and large institutions, in general. Skilbeck argued that: "The larger and more complex the institution and the more diverse or ambitious its mission, the greater the need to break it down into self-governing, but well-coordinated units" (Skilbeck, 1997, 109). Local study centres will take on more responsibility for teaching, tutoring and counselling, both within national boundaries, and even more so beyond them.

Large-scale distance teaching universities will also establish more centres abroad. Here, it will be even more important to work out the detailed and respective responsibilities of each cooperating local partner, and the margin of freedom it may have to innovate and meet whatever special needs its enrolled students might pose.

Enhancing University–Society Dialogue

Coffield and Williamson (1997a) in their recent book on *Repositioning Higher Education*, which focuses mainly on British higher education asserted vehemently that all debates about the future of higher education are inseparable from debates about society. The limits on what universities can achieve are set by the societies in which they function. The central argument succinctly stated that: "The universities, despite all the changes they have made, have not responded and are not responding, with sufficient speed or at an appropriate level, to the technological, economic, social and demographic changes of the past twenty years" (Coffield & Williamson, 1997b, 2). From this we may go on to state that: "It is not sufficient for higher education institutions, universities in particular, to reform themselves. They must seek to engage in a wide-ranging and critical dialogue within society to secure the conditions of the future growth and sustainable development of both" (*ibid.*, 5).

If dialogue with society is essential to securing the proper functioning of all universities in the future, it is assuredly an imperative for distance teaching universities, whose core mission is to be attentive to societal needs, many of which were left aside by other higher education institutes. Distance teaching universities possess in high degree what Lindblom (1990) terms a capacity for *mutual adjustment*. This quality permits individuals and institution leaders acting without a central decision-maker to "mutually control and adapt to each other to reach an outcome" (*ibid.*, 239). As we saw earlier in Chapter 6, the organs of decision making in some distance teaching universities were set to respond fast to external initiatives and to continuously take account of emerging needs and to tackle them as efficiently as possible.

Distance teaching universities have both the drive and the potential to extend university–society dialogue at local community and on broader national levels. The British Open University and the Spanish UNED, for example, are the only universities in their system to be defined as *national universities*. After the British higher education system was restructured in 1992, the British Open University is now the only university to participate in all four funding councils (of England, Wales, Scotland and Northern Ireland). As *national universities*, distance teaching universities fulfil nationwide missions. One aspect of their remit could be directed towards stimulating regional mobility, breaking ethnic boundaries, and bringing various groups together. The Open University of Israel, for instance, might act as an important vehicle for promoting higher and continuing education within the Arab population in Israel and in neighbouring countries. It already runs study centres in several Arab communities, and is looking for creative avenues of cooperation with more Arab communities, in fields such as in-service teacher training, professional training in medicine and agriculture, and the teaching of English as a second language.

At a more local level, distance teaching universities should enhance collaboration with local leaders through their existing network of study centres. Distance teaching universities should seek to become more involved in the life of the communities where they are located, and respond attentively to emerging needs on an ongoing basis. Investing their local/regional centres with greater responsibility and allowing them greater freedom to initiate special initiatives, to deal with problems at the local level, could conceivably strengthen their social dimension.

Global Outreach

The global economy is only now beginning to bear upon the international role of higher education. Universities are at present frantically engaged in enrolling international students, becoming partners in inter-institutional schemes, and pushing forward in the drive towards globalisation (Skilbeck, 1997). Students, academic staff and curricula are transferred and exchanged between institutions; accreditation agencies ensure promptness in accrediting previous experiential learning and previous academic studies; governments append their signatures to cooperative projects in higher education. A European-based programme such as *Erasmus*, which promotes the exchange and mobility of students, faculty and academic programmes, has expanded markedly over the last decade. Within ten years students participating in *Erasmus* activities grew from 3,000 to more than 200,000 (European Commission, 1996; Teichler & Maiworm, 1994, 1997).

Distance teaching universities by definition exert global outreach. Their operation is not bound by territory. They can easily reach out to students beyond national frontiers. Not surprisingly therefore many national distance teaching universities have ramifications elsewhere. As Chapter 7 noted, since the 1980s, several distance education international associations and networks have been established; the ICDE (International Council of Distance Education), EDEN (European Distance Education Network), EADTU (European Distance Teaching Universities), COL (Commonwealth of Open Learning), AAOU (Association of Asian Open Universities). The 1990s have seen a drive towards consortium-type programmes and ventures, and extensive collaboration between distance education providers. The plan for a European Open University, led by the British Open University and other distance education in Europe, exemplifies this development.

The outreach of distance teaching universities at a global level could be activated at different levels, ranging from individual students, through collaboration with other institutions (universities, colleges, industry and businesses) to cooperative undertakings with governments, international corporations and intergovernmental organisations.

It may well be that in future many distance education students will not be nationally based. The European Community networks and organisations, for example, anticipate the emergence of the mobile professional, for whom distance education would be the most feasible option for lifelong learning and professional upgrade. In the international market individual students are, and will be even more so, able to approach any university, whose access policy encourages and extends to international students. Strengthening agreements between academic institutions within particular country and across national borders will be central to the mobility of adult students.

Rumble (1997) predicted that in the future, many students, perhaps the majority, would study while they work. Being highly mobile, they will expect to continue studying as they move within, or between, jurisdictions, and will expect to carry their credits with them. In Rumble's view: "Whether an institution's credits are recognised or not by a validating body may become a significant factor in access to the global education market" (*ibid.*, 6). For distance teaching universities to gain recognition from as many national and international validating bodies as possible is clearly no small matter of importance.

Experience shared among distance teaching universities, assistance and guidance of veteran distance teaching universities to new arrivals is an important aspect in the distance teaching universities' global outreach, both at institutional and national levels. Many distance teaching universities set up after the early 1980s acknowledged their debt to more experienced distance teaching universities elsewhere, on the experience of which they shaped their own institution (Mugridge, 1997a). The British Open University is by far the most noticeable and conspicuous distance teaching university in assisting distance teaching institutions all around the world. The Spanish UNED has a leading role in Latin America and the hispanophone. The FernUniversität plays an important role in East and West Germany, and operates in several Eastern European countries, such as Hungary and the Czech Republic. Israel has in the last decade greatly extended its ties in countries of the former Soviet Union, and with other Jewish communities.

Gottfried Leibbrandt, the founding president of the Dutch Open Universiteit between 1981 and 1987, remarked in his memoirs that the planners of the new university were much helped by *older sister* institutions on what could and what could not be done. For example: "It was recommended by the British Open University not to put too much emphasis on television and video as it turned out to be very expensive with comparatively low contribution to learning results" (Leibbrandt, 1997, 103). From the German Fern-Universität the Dutch learned: "that from the beginning one campus should be built instead of renting buildings spread all over the city" (*ibid.*). And the Israeli experience of the Open University of Israel showed that: "It is possible to run an open university with much smaller academic staff than, for example, the German and British institutions" (*ibid.*, 103–104). Advice such as this is just one example of the close relations between experienced and wealthy distance teaching universities and newly established distance teaching institutions.

Some believe that the widespread use of distance and open education methods can serve far-reaching human goals, such as social cohesion within and between nations, breaking national and ethnic barriers as well as promoting understanding and peace (Hommadi, 1989). Morrison (1992) suggested that in the turbulent days of the present, distance teaching universities may play a transformative role through providing models of innovative and generative learning—learning which leads to change and renewal and which allows a society to learn on a sustained basis. We live in a world of global scope, in which traditional boundaries between the local and the global are seemingly fast disappearing: "Open universities have a unique opportunity to take the lead in the globalisation of learning... Open universities can serve, through the development of collaborative, and pan-national programmes, as conduits through which the diversity and variety of human experience can flower on a global level. If globalisation calls for one thing, it is for the new ways and means to understand and build upon the diversity of human experience on this planet. Open universities, functioning within regional and global learning networks, can provide a unique opportunity to legitimate this *diversification of experience*" (*ibid.*, 32–33).

Many large, established and prestigious distance teaching universities will play a very important role in advancing international cooperation and globalisation. They will act on different levels and through their international organs and specific outreach infrastructure, intensify collaboration: among distance education institutions within continental and global frameworks; between distance and classical universities; between universities and non-university institutions; between universities and industry and business corporations; and between universities and society at large. Distance teaching universities will undoubtedly mobilise their proven features of creativity, flexibility of thought and action, persistence and a special pioneering *esprit de corps*, to respond originally and resourcefully to the multiple challenges facing them over the coming decades.

Annex I

Basic Guidelines for Initiating and Establishing a New Distance Teaching University

In the literature of current distance education there is a sustained discussion over the future prospects and "life expectancy" of distance teaching universities. One of the critical issues revolves around whether new large-scale distance teaching universities, which operate on a national and international basis, are in fact truly needed. Some claim that the day of the large distance teaching universities has passed. Their sheer size and industrial way of working made them vulnerable to increasing competition in the markets of higher education. Both factors might well hinder them from responding to meet rapid developments of a post-industrial age (Hamilton, 1990; Rumble, 1992; Evans & Nation, 1992, 1993; Raggatt, 1993; Bates, 1995). Others strongly defend the superiority of the large distance teaching university compared with other forms of distance education (Daniel, 1996a; Ginzburg, 1997). When asked about the viability of the distance teaching university model, Ginzburg—who served for 12 years as the Open University of Israel's president—said that: "In my opinion, every country, large or small, with many or with few universities, should have at least one open university, if not for everybody, if not for *every man*, then at least for those for whom this is the only way to get an academic education" (Ginzburg, 1997, 86).

Obviously, distance teaching universities cannot be treated as homogeneous. Apart from their great variety, an important distinction exists between the veterans, the well-to-do and the newcomers. The future of the well-established seems secure. One cannot doubt that *old* distance teaching universities, some of which we have examined here, will continue and will flourish in a variety of fields which have been analysed and discussed earlier. The prospects of large national distance teaching universities, the British Open University and Spain's UNED, are especially promising. The more interesting question is, of course, the viability and applicability of the distance teaching university model to further expansion in the future.

The establishment of distance teaching universities has slowed down since the mid-1980s (Mugridge, 1997a). First, in most national systems, there is no need for more than one large distance teaching university. Unlike the campus university which has served, and will continue to serve, as an inspiration for continuous multiplication and imitation, one distance teaching university can absorb hundreds of thousands of students. In short, in any given national or provincial setting, there is no room for many distance teaching universities. Since distance teaching universities operate currently in nearly forty countries (Holmberg, 1995; Moore & Kearsley, 1996), naturally the emergence of new distance teaching universities, which was particularly rapid in the 1970s and early 1980s, has slowed.

Second, most higher education systems today differ in many central dimensions from the situation in the 1960s and 1970s. Universities have changed profoundly over the last two decades. Consequently, many of the issues that distance teaching universities tackled as pioneers in the 1970s are common practice today. They lie at the heart of the consensus in higher education systems at large: accommodating part-time working adults, employing flexible access policies, providing lifelong education, offering a broad range of academic and professional curricula, reaching out to remote students, the utilisation of information technology and multi-media, etc. (Guri-Rosenblit, 1997b). Most advanced higher education systems have either entered, or stand at the threshold of entering, the phase of universal access, in which, according to Martin Trow (1974), over 30% of the relevant age cohort participates in various forms of higher education. Many of the background issues that led to the creation of the distance teaching universities examined here are almost absent today and most particularly so in developed states.

It is, I think, not unreasonable to predict that very few, if any, new distance teaching universities will emerge in the near future in the developed countries. It is more likely that dual-mode or consortia-type universities, providing distance education, will expand considerably in the near future. Even so, the idea and practice of a distance teaching university remains, in my opinion, a most attractive model for those developing countries which suffer from scarce resources, both human and material, and which seek to raise the education level of their population. Developing countries can benefit enormously from establishing a distance teaching university.

Add to this the fact that countries which today are considering the establishment of a new distance teaching university are in an advantageous position, when compared with distance teaching universities born in the 1970s. They may compare in retrospect several working models of distance teaching universities, analyse their strengths, evaluate their weaknesses, and avoid mistakes. New distance teaching universities can lean on the support and assistance of well-established distance teaching universities, on international distance education networks and associations. They have the option partially to adapt ready-made materials, obtain the help of counsellors and experts in guidance, in planning their student support services at the initial stages of development, and for determining the mix of media, to fit their particular objectives. Some basic parameters to be considered when comparing distance education providers and for setting up a new distance teaching university are specified below. The analysis of each distance teaching university in the light of the parameters suggested has the purpose of identifying the specific and salient characteristics of each institution and thus (Guri-Rosenblit, 1993b) to provide constructive guidelines for those who are considering establishing a new distance education university anywhere in the world.

Political Support

The saga of the five distance teaching universities in this study showed very clearly the decisive role played by leading politicians in establishing them. The enthusiasm of determined and forceful personalities for the idea of a distance teaching university, irrespective of country, was paramount. For the fathers of a new distance teaching university, it is indispensable to list their supporters and potential opponents, in order to ascertain the feasibility of bringing the venture into the world. The following variables warrant particular attention:

* *Political Support*—Is there a strong political commitment, expressed by prominent individuals for the establishment of a distance teaching university?
* *Potential Alliances*—Which political, social, educational and academic parties might be potential allies of the distance teaching university? How is it best to approach them, in order to strengthen their support?
* *Potential Opponents*—Which political, social, educational and academic parties might be potential opponents of the distance teaching university? In what ways may their views and influence be countered?
* *International Involvement*—Are there international networks or institutions involved actively in the establishment of the new distance teaching university? In which activities or which part of the campaign might they assist?

Target Population

Defining the target population of an institution is central to defining its overall purpose, its educational tasks and its function in its surrounding milieu. Developing countries might obtain relevant information about how to implement a distance education model in their particular circumstances from institutions that teach equivalent or similar populations, rather than those dealing with totally different student populations. In defining the characteristics of an institution's population, whether that institution is already running or is planned, the following elements should be attended to:

- *Level of Education*—Does the distance teaching university intend to teach undergraduate, graduate, professional or continuing education programmes?
- *Age*—Is the target population composed mainly of young or students older than 25 years of age? What is the age breakdown of the student body?
- *Sex*—Is the university set up to cater for both female and male students? Do study programmes reflect any preference towards one gender? (In several developing countries, where women and men are separated in all educational institutions, the students' gender may be an important factor in designing a new distance teaching university).
- *Full- or Part-time Students*—Is the distance teaching university to offer only part-time study, or allow also full-time study? How will the organisation of the distance teaching university accommodate both part-time students and full-timers?
- *Size*—How many students is the distance teaching university planned to serve?
- *Geographical Distribution*—How widely are the students distributed geographically? How is it planned to reach small numbers of dispersed students?

Innovative Cluster

Defining the innovative dimension of each distance teaching university in its particular setting, is of major importance in laying down its specific roles, and in identifying potential tensions or even clashes with mainstream institutions. The following variables are worth considering:

- *University Education by Distance*—Is distance higher education a novel or an old and practised phenomenon in the particular country?
- *Access–Exit Requirements*—Does the distance teaching university employ open admissions? In what ways, if at all, do entry and exit requirements of the distance teaching university differ from those of conventional institutions?
- *Ethos of Academic Freedom*—What is the prevailing form of academic freedom in mainstream institutions? How might it affect the working of the distance teaching university?
- *Size of Faculty*—Is the distance teaching university based, or planned to be based, on a small or large number of academic staff?

- *Flexibility of the Academic Curricula*—Does the distance teaching university offer more flexible or different programmes compared to classical universities?
- *Use of Media*—Which kind of media does the distance teaching university employ, or plan to employ?
- *Place of Study*—Are studies conducted at home, study centres, work places, summer schools, or in virtual environments, etc.?
- *Pace of Study*—How far can students pace the length of their studies in each course, and in the overall programme?

Teaching/Tutoring System

The nature of the teaching/tutoring system in any distance teaching university depends largely on its initial goals, conceptual framework and available resources. The roles of academic and adjunct faculty should be clearly defined on the basis of such critical variables:

- *Functions of Senior Academic Faculty*—What are the main roles expected of the faculty, e.g., to write self-study materials, to adapt or translate materials written elsewhere, to teach or tutor students, to monitor the overall teaching of any given course under their academic responsibility?
- *Functions of Junior Academic Faculty*—What are the functions of junior or adjunct faculty in developing and teaching courses?
- *Ratio between Internal and External Staff*—To what extent is the distance teaching university based on internal staff? How many external members participate in the production and teaching of the courses?
- *Interrelations between Faculty–Junior Staff–Students*—Which kind of relationship exists between these parties in learning and teaching? Who is most in contact with students and who is responsible for monitoring learning?

Study Programmes

The range, flexibility and novelty, of the university's study programmes are important variables for consideration in the initial planning of a distance teaching university:

- *Range*—Which study tracks is the distance teaching university offering? Is the curriculum to be broad or focused? Is the emphasis on full degree programmes or professional and vocational courses? Does the curriculum offer courses for recreational purposes?
- *Development of the Study Materials*—Is the distance teaching university responsible for developing the whole range of study materials it uses, or does it adapt part of them from other institutions? Which kind of learning packages are to be designed? How are study materials to be developed and by whom?

- *Quality Assurance*—What quality assurance procedures are to be utilised in designing, developing and implementing study materials?
- *Scope of Distribution*—Are the materials intended for local or international audiences? How large are the potential audiences?
- *Estimated Costs*—How much does it cost to produce a given course, a full length degree or a short-cycle diploma?

Choice of Media

The choice of media is also important in defining the profile of each distance teaching university. New distance teaching universities may skip over some technologies, experimented with by veterans, and embark on the new generation of advanced media. For a new distance teaching university it might even be easier to adapt new technologies, by contrast with the well-established one who would be obliged to change their basic infrastructure if they were to replace their old media. In choosing appropriate media, the main issues are:

- *Accessibility*—How feasible and accessible are relevant technologies to target populations?
- *Delivery Media*—What are the most appropriate delivery media given the specific setting in which they are to be installed?
- *Communication Media*—What are the most appropriate communication media in these specific circumstances?
- *Costs*—What are the costs for using various media? Who is responsible for bearing them?

Student Support Services

Student support services have proved to be most significant in explaining the success rate of students at distance teaching universities. Support systems are essential for all students, but most particularly for students from under-privileged backgrounds. Since it is probable that developing countries cater for large numbers of students from such backgrounds, the weight given to the design of student support services in a new distance teaching university must be very high. It should be an integral part of the overall design of a new university. The main variables to be considered here are:

- *Functions of Support Services*—What are the main roles of different support services (e.g., helping students with study materials, providing psychological counselling and support, assisting disabled students, providing money, study grants, etc.)?
- *Headquarters and Study Centres*—What links exist between headquarters and local study centres? Who bears financial responsibility for study

centres? Who is responsible for academic affairs at the study centres? What activities are offered there?

- *Additional Support Mechanisms*—Aside from study centres, are there additional forms of support available to students?
- *Access to Support Systems*—How accessible are the support services and are they available to students in different locations?

Cooperation with Other Universities

Mapping areas for potential cooperation with conventional higher education institutes is an important step in both consolidating the academic standing of a new distance teaching university, and in reducing its operating costs. Successful collaboration between distance teaching universities and mainstream universities has proven to be beneficial to both. The mapping of areas for collaboration calls for the following questions to be addressed:

- *Faculty Employment*—How far are external faculty to be engaged to work at the distance teaching university?
- *Academic Programmes*—Are the study materials designed from the outset to be used by students from conventional universities as well?
- *Media Utilisation*—How far may joint ventures for media utilisation be envisaged and planned, for example teleconferencing via satellite, interactive computer telelearning, setting up shared data bases and Internet sites?
- *Credit Transfer Schemes*—Do credit transfer schemes exist which enable students to move freely between different higher education institutes?
- *Collaborative Degree and Diploma Programmes*—Is it feasible to plan such collaborative programmes?

Collaboration with International Distance Education Institutes and Networks

As we have seen, new distance teaching universities have been—and may in future be—greatly assisted by international networks, for instance, the Commonwealth of Learning, the International Association of Distance Education, the European Distance Education Network, the Association of Asian Open Universities, etc. The assistance of such international bodies requires delineating potential and actual areas of collaboration on the basis of the following considerations:

- *Participating Partners*—What kind of institutions are ready to offer their help and are willing to collaborate?
- *Dimensions of Collaboration*—Which elements are best suited to laying down the basis of collaboration (study materials production, material adaptation, setting up teaching/learning mechanisms, designing student support services, installing and developing new technology)?

- *Financial Commitments*—What are the exact financial commitments of each participating partner?
- *Review Procedures*—What form of agreed review procedures are to monitor the collaboration?

Collaboration with the World of Work and Business

Collaboration with work places and the world of business and industry bears an immense potential both for intensifying the social accountability of a distance teaching university and for improving its financial base. The relevant aspects to be taken into account are:

- *Participating Parties*—Which work places and corporations may be approached for future collaboration?
- *Dimensions of Collaboration*—On which fields and levels of activity is collaboration to be built (vocational upgrading, utilisation of advanced technology, full degree programmes, running of local study centres)?
- *Financial Commitments*—What are the exact financial commitments of each participating partner?
- *Review Procedures*—What form of agreed review procedures should monitor the collaboration?

Annex II

Summarised Check List

For the sake of convenience, the guidelines suggested in Annex I for starting up and developing a new distance teaching university, or for examining a veteran one, are summarised in a brief check list:

1. Political Support
   - Political commitment
   - Potential alliances
   - Potential opponents
   - International involvement

2. Target Population
   - Level of education
   - Age
   - Full- or part-time students
   - Size
   - Geographical distribution

3. Innovative Cluster
   - University education by distance
   - Access–exit requirements
   - Ethos of academic freedom
   - Size of faculty
   - Flexibility of academic curricula
   - Use of media
   - Place of study
   - Pace of study

4. Teaching/Tutoring System
    – Functions of senior academic faculty
    – Functions of junior academic faculty
    – Ratio between internal and external staff
    – Interrelations between students and senior/junior staff

5. Study Programmes
    – Range
    – Development of study materials
    – Quality assurance
    – Scope of distribution
    – Estimated costs

6. Choice of Media
    – Accessibility
    – Delivery media
    – Communication media
    – Costs

7. Support systems
    – Functions of support systems
    – Headquarters and study centres
    – Additional support mechanisms
    – Access to support systems

8. Cooperation with other Universities
    – Employment of faculty
    – Academic programmes
    – Media utilisation
    – Credit transfer schemes
    – Collaborative degree and diploma programmes

9. Collaboration with International Distance Education Networks and
    Institutes
    – Participating parties
    – Dimensions of collaboration
    – Financial obligations
    – Review procedures

10. Collaboration with the Work and Corporate Worlds
    – Participating parties
    – Dimensions of collaboration
    – Financial obligations
    – Review procedures

References

AAUC (1996) *Trends: The Canadian University in Profile,* Association of Universities and Colleges in Canada.

Adelman, C. & Alexander, R. (1982) *The Self-Evaluating Institution*, London: Methuen.

Allon, Y. (1973) *A Letter to Dorothy de Rothschild*, 11 November 1973.

Altbach, P. G. (ed.) (1996) *The International Academic Profession: Portraits of Fourteen Countries*, Princeton, NJ: The Carnegie Foundation for the Advancement of Teaching.

Anderson, C. (1960) *Grants to Students,* London, HMSO, Cmnd. 1051.

Andrews, M. B., Holdaway, E. A. & Mowat, G. L. (1997) Postsecondary education in Alberta since 1945. In: G. A. Jones (ed.) *Higher Education in Canada: Different Systems, Different Perspectives.* New York: Garland Publishing, 59–92.

Annan, N. (1990) Our Age: *The Generation that Made Post-War Britain.* London: Fontana.

Archer, E. A. (ed.) (1992) *Commonwealth Universities Yearbook*, London: The Association of Commonwealth Universities, 67th edition.

Archer, M. (1979) *Social Origins of Educational Systems*, London: Sage Publications.

Athabasca University (1992a) *Athabasca University 1992-3 Calendar—Canada's Open University,* Athabasca University.

Athabasca University (1992b) *Demographic Profile of AU Students*, Athabasca University.

Athabasca University (1992c) *Role Description: Academic Faculty of Arts and Faculty of Science*, Athabasca University.

Athabasca University (1992d) *Registrations by Discipline*, Athabasca University.

Athabasca University (1991) *Role Description: Course Coordinator, Telephone Tutor and Seminar Tutor*, Athabasca University.

Baath J. A. (1984) Essentials of distance education, *Teaching at a Distance*, 25, 120–122.

Baath, J. A. (1979) *Correspondence Education in the Light of a Number of Contemporary Teaching Methods*, Malmo: Liber Hermods.

Bacsich, P. (1990) Electronic publishing in distance teaching universities. In: A. W. Bates (ed.), *Media and Technology in European Distance Education*, European Association of Distance Teaching Universities, Milton Keynes: The Open University Press, 49–56.

Barnett, R. (1997) Beyond competences. In: F. Coffield & B. Williamson (eds.), *Repositioning Higher Education*, Buckingham: The Society for Research into Higher Education and the Open University Press, 27–44.

Barnett, R. (1992) *The Idea of Higher Education.* Buckingham: The Society of Research into Higher Education and the Open University Press.

Bartels, J. & Peters, O. (1986) The German FernUniversität: Its main features and functions. In: G. van Enckevort, K. Harry. & H. G. Schutze (eds.), *Distance Education and the Adult Learner*, Herleen: Dutch Open University, 97–110.

Bartels, J., von Prümmer, C. & Rossie, U. (1988) *Subjektive Studienziele*. Hagen: FernUniversität, ZFE.

Bates, A. W. (1997) Restructuring the University for Technological Change, *A keynote address at the 'What Kind of University?' International Conference*, June 1997, London.

Bates, A. W. (1995) *Technology, Open Learning and Distance Education*, London: Routledge.

Bates, A. W. (ed.) (1990a) *Media and Technology in European Distance Education*, European Association of Distance Teaching Universities, Milton Keynes: The Open University Press.

Bates, A. W. (1990b) The challenge of technology for European distance education. In: A. W. Bates (ed.), *Media and Technology in European Distance Education*, European Association of Distance Teaching Universities, Milton Keynes: The Open University Press, 17–26.

Bates, A. W. (1990c) Audio cassettes in the British Open University. In: A. W. Bates (ed.), *Media and Technology in European Distance Education*, European Association of Distance Teaching Universities, Milton Keynes: The Open University Press, 101–104.

Bates, A. W. (1990d) The future. In: A. W. Bates (ed.), *Media and Technology in European Distance Education*, European Association of Distance Teaching Universities, Milton Keynes: The Open University Press, 285–287.

Bates, A. W. (1989a) Delivery and new technology. In: N. Paine (ed.), *Open Learning in Transaction: An Agenda for Action*, London: Kogan Page, 290–304.

Bates, A. W. (1989b) Towards a European Electronic University: Technology and Course Design for European-wide Distance Education Courses, *Working Group on Media and Technology*, Herleen: European Association of Distance Teaching Universities.

Bates, A. W. (ed.) (1984) *The Role of Technology in Distance Education*, London: Croom Helm.

Bayliss, H. (1995) Postgraduate distance learning in British dual mode universities, *Open Learning*, 10 (1), 46–51.

Beaudoin, M. F. (1995) Introduction. In: M. F. Beaudoin (ed.), Distance Education Symposium 3: Instruction, *Selected Papers Presented at the Third Distance Education Research Symposium*, The Pennsylvania State University, May 1995, 1–4.

Belanger, R., Lynd, D. & Mouelhi, M. (1982) *Part-time Degree Students: Tomorrow's Majority?* Ottawa: Statistics, Canada.

Bell, R. & Tight, M. (1995) Open universities in the nineteenth century Britain, *Open Learning*, 10 (2), 3–11.

Bell, R. & Tight, M. (1993) *Open Universities: A British Tradition?* Buckingham: The Society of Research into Higher Education and the Open University Press.

Ben-David, J. (1986) Universities: Dilemmas of Growth, diversification and administration, *Studies in Higher Education*, 11, 105–130.

Birnbaum, R. (1989) The cybernetic institution: Toward an integration of governance theories, *Higher Education*, 18, 239–253.

Birnbaum, R. (1988) *How Colleges Work: The Cybernetics of Academic Organisation and Leadership*, San Francisco: Jossey Bass.

Blackburn, R. M. & Jarman, J. (1993) Changing inequalities in access to British universities, *Oxford Review of Education*, 19 (2), 197–215.

Boucher, M. (1973) *Spes in Arduis: A History of the University of South Africa*, Pretoria: UNISA Press.

Brindley, J. E. (1987) *Attrition and Completion in Distance Education: The Student's Perspective*, A Master Thesis, University of British Columbia.

Brindley, J. E. & Paul, R. (1993) The way of the future? Transfer credit and credit banking. In: L. Moran & I. Mugridge (eds.), *Collaboration in Distance Education: International Case Studies*, London: Routledge, 83–96.

Bull, G. M. (1994) United Kingdom. In: G. M. Bull, C. Dallinga-Hunter, Y. Epelboin, E. Frackmann & D. Jennings (eds.), *Information Technology: Issues for Higher Education*, London: Jessica Kingsley Publishers & OECD, 169–199.

Burpee, P. & Wilson, B. (1995). Professional development: What teachers want and universities provide—a Canadian perspective. In: D. Sewart (ed.), *One World Many Voices: Quality in Distance Learning,* Volume 1, ICDE and the Open University, 236–239.

Byrne, T. C. (1989) *Athabasca University: The Evolution of Distance Education, Calgary:* The University of Calgary Press.

Campion, M. & Renner, W. (1992) The supposed demise of Fordism: Implications for distance education and higher education, *Distance Education,* 13 (1), 7–28.

Carr, R. (1990) Open Learning: An imprecise term, *ICDE Bulletin,* 22, 47–50.

Carter, C. (1992) Counseling Distance Learners: Preferred Support Strategies for Social and Personal Difficulties, Sydney: TAFE Commission, *Open Training and Education Network Occasional Papers* 4.

Central Bureau of Statistics (1997) Candidates for First Degree Studies in Universities: 1996/7, *Current Briefings in Statistics–Findings from Recent Surveys, No. 32,* Jerusalem : The State of Israel.

Cerych, L. & Sabatier, P. (1986) *Great Expectations and Mixed Performance: The Implementation of Higher Education Reforms in Europe,* Paris, European Institute of Educational and Social Policy, Stoke-on-Trent: Trentham Books.

Christoffel, P. (1986) The impact on higher education of new information and telecommunication technologies. In: G. van Enckevort, K. Harry. & H. G. Schutze (eds.), *Distance Education and the Adult Learner,* Herleen: Dutch Open University, 174–184.

Chu, G. C. & Schramm, W. (1967) *Learning from the Television: What the Research Says,* Washington, D.C.: National Association of Educational Broadcasters.

Clark, B. R. (1997) Higher education as a self-guiding society, *Tertiary Education and Management,* 3 (2), 91–99.

Clark, B. R. (1993) The problem of complexity in modern higher education. In: S. Rothblatt & B. Wittrock (eds.), *The European and American University since* 1800, Cambridge University Press, 263–279.

Clark, B. R. (ed.) (1987) *The Academic Profession: National, Disciplinary and Institutional Settings,* Berkeley: University of California Press.

Clark, B. R. (1986) Implementation in the US: A comparison with European higher education. In: L. Cerych & P. Sabatier (eds*.), Great Expectations and Mixed Performances: The Implementation of Higher Education Reforms in Europe,* European Institute of Educational and Social Policy, Stoke-on-Trent,: Trentham Books.

Clark, B. R. (1983) *The Higher Education System: Academic Organisation in Cross-National Perspective,* Berkeley: The University of California Press.

Clark, B. R. & Neave, G. (1992) Preface. In: B. Clark & G. Neave (eds.), *The Encyclopedia of Higher Education,* Vol 1, Oxford: Pergamon Press, xxiii–xxviii.

Coffey, J. (1989) The basis for effective collaboration: 1 + 1=3. In: N. Paine (ed.), *Open Learning in Transition: An Agenda for Action,* London: Kogan Page, 277–289.

Coffield, F. & Williamson, B. (eds.) (1997a) *Repositioning Higher Education,* Buckingham: The Society for Research into Higher Education and the Open University Press.

Coffield, F. & Williamson, B. (1997b) The challenges facing higher education. In: F. Coffield & B. Williamson (eds.), *Repositioning Higher Education,* Buckingham: The Society for Research into Higher Education and the Open University Press, 1–26.

Cohen, M. D. & March, J. G. (1986) *Leadership and Ambiguity: The American College,* New York: McGraw Hill, Second Edition.

Council for Higher Education (1995) *The Higher Education System In Israel—Statistical Data,* Jerusalem.

Cowan, J. (1994) How can you assure quality in my support, as a distance learner? *Open Learning,* 9 (1), 59–63.

Crawford, G. & Spronk B. (1995) Graduate degrees at a distance: Issues in planning and delivery. In: D. Sewart (ed.), *One World Many Voices: Quality in Open and Distance Learning,* Volume 1, ICDE & The Open University, 61–63.

Crooks, B. & Kirkwood, A. (1990) Videocassettes by design in Open University courses. In: A. W. Bates (ed.), *Media and Technology in European Distance Education,* European Association of Distance Teaching Universities, Milton Keynes: The Open University Press, 135–143.

Cross, K. P. (1981) *Adults as Learners.* San Francisco: Jossey Bass.

Curran, C. (1990) Factors affecting the costs of media in distance education. In: A. W. Bates (ed.), *Media and Technology in European Distance Education*, European Association of Distance Teaching Universities, Milton Keynes: The Open University Press, 27–39.

Curran, C. & Wickham, A. (1994) *Directory of Media, Methods and Technology in Memebr Institutions*. Herleen: European Association of Distance Teaching Universities.

Daniel, J. S. (1997) Reflections of a Scholar Gypsy, *A keynote address at the 'What Kind of University?' International Conference*, June 1997, London.

Daniel, J. S. (1996a) *The Mega-Universities and the Knowledge Media*. London: Kogan Page.

Daniel, J. S. (1996b) Global Reach: A Vice Chancellor's Perspective on Distance Learning, *International Educator*, Fall 1996, 37–38.

Daniel, J. S. (1995a) *The Mega-Universities and the Knowledge Media: Implications of the New Technologies for Large Distance Teaching Universities*, A Master Thesis, Department of Education, Concordia University, Montreal, Canada.

Daniel, J. S. (1995b) What has the Open University achieved in 25 years? In: D. Sewart (ed.), *One World Many Voices: Quality in Open and Distance Learning*, Volume 1, ICDE and the Open University, 400–403.

Daniel, J. S. (1993) The challenge of mass higher education, *Studies in Higher Education*, 18 (2), 197–203.

Daniel, J. S. (1990) Distance education and developing countries. In: M. Croft, I. Mugridge, J. S. Daniel & A. Hershfield (eds.), *Distance Education: Development and Access*, Caracas: ICDE Proceedings, 101–110.

Daniel, J. S. (1989) The worlds of learning. In: N. Paine (ed.), *Open Learning in Transition: An Agenda for Action*, London: Kogan Page, 48–59.

Daniel, J. S., Peters, G. & Watkison, M. (1994) The funding of the UKOU. In: I. Mugridge (ed.) *The Funding of Open Universities: Perspectives on Distance Education*, Vancouver: The Commonwealth of Learning, 13–20.

Daniel, J. S. & Marquis, C. (1979) Interaction and independence: Getting the mixture right, *Teaching at a Distance*, 14, 29–44.

Davies, P. (ed.) (1995) *Adults in Higher Education: International Perspectives in Access and Participation*, London: Jessica Kingsley.

Davies, P. & Reisinger, E. (1995) Germany. In: P. Davies (ed.) *Adults in Higher Education: International Perspectives in Access and Participation,* London: Jessica Kingsley, 159–180.

Department for Education (1993) *The Charter for Higher Education: Higher Quality and Choice*, London: DfE.

Doerfer, F. & Schuemer, R. (1988) *Preliminary Descriptors of Some Distance Education Institutions*, Hagen: FernUniversität, ZIFF.

Duke, C. (1997) Towards a lifelong curriculum. In: F. Coffield & B. Williamson (eds.), *Repositioning Higher Education*, Buckingham: The Society for Research into Higher Education and the Open University Press, 57–73.

Duke, C. (1967) *The London External Degree and the English Part-Time Student*, Leeds: Leeds University Press.

EADTU (1994a) *Universities Membership 1994*, Herleen: European Association of Distance Teaching Universities.

EADTU (1994b) *EuroStudy Centers*, Herleen: European Association of Distance Teaching Universities.

EADTU (1993a) *Directory of Study Centers in Europe*, Herleen: European Association of Distance Teaching Universities.

EADTU (1993b) *Mini-Directory*, Herleen: European Association of Distance Teaching Universities.

European Commission (1996) *Teaching and Learning: Towards the Learning Society, White Paper on Education and Training*, Luxembourg: Office for official Publications of the European Union.

Eustace, R. (1992) United Kingdom. In: Clark, B. R. & Neave, G. (eds.), *The Encyclopedia of Higher Education*, Vol 1, Oxford: Pergamon, 760–776.

Evans, T. D. & Nation, D. (eds.) (1993) *Reforming Open and Distance Education*, London: Kogan

Page.

Evans, T. D. & Nation, D. (1992) Theorising open and distance education, *Open Learning*, 7 (2), 3–13.

Everyman's University (1982) *Statutes and General Regulations*, Everyman's University Press.

Fage, J. (1995) Studying with the UK Open University—a CD-Rom presentation. In: D. Sewart (ed.), *One World Many Voices: Quality in Open and Distance Learning*, Volume 1, ICDE and the Open University, 20–23.

FernUniversität (1993) *Personal und Kursverzeichnis: Hinweise für Studierende*, Hagen: Fern-Universität.

FernUniversität (1992) *Das Studium an der FernUniversität: Informationen zum Studium*, Hagen: FernUniversität.

Fox, J. (1987) Towards open learning. In: P. Smith & M. Kelly (eds.), *Distance Education and the Mainstream*, London: Croom Helm, 74–92.

Frackmann, E. (1994) Germany. In: G. M. Bull, C. Dallinga-Hunter, Y. Epelboin, E. Frackmann & D. Jennings (eds.), Information *Technology: Issues for Higher Education*, London: Jessica Kingsley Publishers & OECD, 89–127.

Frackmann, E. & De Weert, E. (1994) Higher education policy in Germany. In: L. Goedgebuure, F. Kaiser, P. Maassen, L. Meek, F. A. van Vught & E. de Weert (eds.), *Higher Education Policy: An International Comparative Perspective*, Oxford: Pergamon Press, 132–161.

Fritsch, H. (1988) *Drop-out is a Matter of Definition*, Hagen: FernUniversität, ZEF.

García-Aretio, L. (1995) Advantages and drawbacks to a macroinstitution: Spain's UNED. In: D. Sewart (ed.), *One World Many Voices: Quality in Open and Distance Learning*, Volume 1, ICDE and the Open University, 92–95.

García-Garrido, J. L. (1994) *Personal Communication*.

García-Garrido, J. L. (1993) *Personal Communication*.

García-Garrido, J. L. (1988) The Spanish UNED : One way to a new future. In: G. R. Reddy (ed.), *Open Universities: The Ivory Towers Thrown Open*, New Delhi: Sterling Publishers Ltd, 200–214.

García-Garrido, M. J. (1976) *La Universidad Nacional de Educación a Distancia: Su Implantación y Desarrollo Inicial*, Barcelona: Ediciones CEAC.

Garrison, D. R. (1987) Researching drop-out in distance education, *Distance Education*, 8 (1), 95–101.

Garrison, D. R. (1993) Quality access in distance education: Theoretical considerations. In: D. Keegan (ed.), *Theoretical Principles of Distance Education*, London: Routledge, 9–21.

Garrison, D. R. (1987) Researching drop-out in distance education, *Distance Education*, 8 (1), 95–101.

Garrison, D. R. (1985) Three generations of technological innovation in distance education, *Distance Education*, 6 (2), 235–241.

Garrison, D. R. & Shale, D. G. (1989) Mapping boundaries of distance education. In: M. G. Moore & G. C. Clark (eds.), *Readings in Principles of Distance Education*, University Park, PA: American Center for Study of Distance Education, 1–8.

Gellert, C. (1997) Access to Mass Higher Education: The End of Elite Reproduction? *A paper presented at 'What Kind of University?' International Conference*, June 1997, London.

Gibbons, M. (1997) Choices Concerning Knowledge and Curricula, *A keynote address at the 'What Kind of University?' International Conference*, June 1997, London.

Gibbons, M., Limoges, C., Nowtry, H., Schwartzman, S., Scott, P., Trow, M. (1994) *The New Production of Knowledge: The Dynamics of Science and Research in Contemporary Societies*, London: Sage.

Ginzburg, A. (1997) Everyman's University. In: Mugridge, I. (ed.), *Founding the Open Universities*, New Delhi: Sterling Publishers Private Ltd, 80–86.

Ginzburg, A. (1995) *Personal Communication*.

Glatter, R. & Wedell, E. G. (1971) *Study by Correspondence: An Inquiry into Correspondence Study for Examinations for Degrees and Other Advanced Qualifications*, London: Longman.

Glennie, J. (1996) Towards learner-centered distance education in the changing South African context. In: Mills, R. & Tait, A. (eds.), *Supporting the Learner in Open and Distance Learning*, London: Pitman Publishing, 19–33.

Globerson, A. (1978) *Higher Education and Employment: A Case Study of Israel*, New-York: Praeger.

Gottlieb, E. E. & Chen, M. (1995) The visible and invisible crises in Israeli higher education, *Higher Education*, 30 (2), 153–173.

Granger, D. (1990) Open universities: Closing the distances to learning, *Change*, 22 (4), 45–50.

Groof, J. de, Neave, G. & Svec, J. (1998) *Governance and Democracy in Higher Education*. Dordrecht: Kluwer Legal Publications for the Council of Europe Legislative Reform Program Studies, Vol. 2.

Groten, H. (1992) The role of study centers at the FernUniversität, *Open Learning*, 7 (1), 50–56.

Gunawardena, G. N. & Zittle, R. (1995) An examination of teaching and learning processes in distance education, and implications for designing instruction. In: M. F. Beaudoin (ed.), *Distance Education: Symposium 3 on Instruction,* Number 12, Pennsylvania State University, 51–63.

Guri, S. (1987) Quality control in distance learning, *Open Learning* ,2 (2), 16–21.

Guri, S. (1986) Equality and excellence in higher education: Is it possible? *Higher Education,* 15, 59–71.

Guri-Rosenblit, S. (1997a) Quality assurance procedures at the Open University of Israel . In: A. Tait (ed.), *Quality Assurance in Higher Education: Selected Case Studies,* Vancouver: The Commonwealth of Learning, 29–41.

Guri-Rosenblit, S. (1997b) The Agendas of Distance Teaching Universities: Moving from the Margins to the Center Stage of Higher Education, *A paper presented at 'What Kind of University?' International Conference*, June 1997, London.

Guri-Rosenblit, S. (1996a) Trends in access to Israeli higher education 1981–1996: From a privilege to a right, *European Journal of Education*, 31 (30), 321–340.

Guri-Rosenblit, S. (1996b) Campus-Based and Distance Teaching Universities: Differential Functions and Mutual Impacts, *Tertiary Education and Management*, 2 (2), 110–118.

Guri-Rosenblit, S. (1996c) Improving University teaching at a Distance through Interactive Studies via Satellite, *A paper presented at the 21st Improving University Teaching,* July 1996, Nottingham.

Guri-Rosenblit, S. (1994a) Collaborative teacher education programs between teacher training colleges and the Open University of Israel, *Teaching Education Journal*, 7 (2), 59–69.

Guri-Rosenblit, S. (1994b). Reforms and curricular changes in Israeli teacher education, *Curriculum & Teaching*, 8 (2), 3–13.

Guri-Rosenblit, S. (1993a) Trends of diversification and expansion in the Israeli Higher Education System, *Higher Education*, 25 (4), 457–472.

Guri-Rosenblit, S. (1993b) Differentiation between distance/open education systems: Parameters for comparison, *International Review of Education*, 39 (4), 287–306.

Guri-Rosenblit, S. (1993c) Quality assurance procedures in developing academic courses: A comparative study of five distance teaching universities. In: A. Tait (ed.), *Quality Assurance in Open and Distance Learning: European and International Perspectives*, Cambridge: The Open University, 99–113.

Guri-Rosenblit, S. (1991) Distance/open learning: Trends and developments as reflected in recent literature, *Studies in Higher Education*, 16 (1), 83–90.

Guri-Rosenblit, S. (1990a) Selectivity and openness in the Israeli higher education system, *Higher Education Review*, 22 (2), 24–38.

Guri-Rosenblit, S. (1990b) The potential contribution of distance teaching universities to improving the learning/teaching practices in conventional universities, *Higher Education,* 19, 73–80.

Guri-Rosenblit, S. (1990c) Assessing perseverance in studies at the Open University of Israel, *Assessment and Evaluation in Higher Education*, 15 (2), 105–114.

Guri-Rosenblit, S. (1989) Providing higher education to socially disadvantaged populations, *Studies in Higher Education*, 14 (3), 321–329.

Halperin, S. (1984) *Any Home a Campus: Everyman's University of Israel*, Washington: The Institute of Educational Leadership.

Halsey, A. H. (1993) Trends in access and equity in higher education: Britain in international perspective, *Oxford Review of Education*, 19 (2), 129–140.

Hamilton, D. (1990) *Learning about Education: The Unfinished Curriculum,* Buckingham: Open University Press.

Harry, K. (1986) The Open University of the United Kingdom. In: G. van Enckevort, K. Harry. & H. G. Schutze (eds.), *Distance Education and the Adult Learner,* Herleen: Dutch Open University, 90–97.

Harry, K. (1982) The Open University —United Kingdom. In: G. Rumble & K. Harry (eds.), *The Distance Teaching Universities,* London: Croom Helm, 167–186.

Harry K., Magnus, J. & Keegan, D. (eds.) (1993) *Distance Education: New Perspectives,* London: Routledge.

Hayduk, A. W. (1994) Distance education and niche markets in conventional education, *Open Learning,* 9 (1), 44–48.

Herskovic, S. (1995) *The Israeli Higher Education System: Trends and Developments,* Jerusalem: Council for Higher Education and Planning and Budgeting Committee (in Hebrew).

Holmberg, B. (1995) *Theory and Practice of Distance Education,* London: Routledge, second edition.

Holmberg, B. (1990) The role of media in distance education as a key academic issue. In: A. W. Bates (ed.), *Media and Technology in European Distance Education,* European Association of Distance Teaching Universities, Milton Keynes: The Open University Press, 41–46.

Holmberg, B. (1989) *Theory and Practice of Distance Education,* London: Routledge.

Holmberg, B. (1986). *Growth and Structure of Distance Education,* Beckenhem: Croom Helm.

Hommadi, A. H. (1989) *Open University: Retrospect and Prospect,* Delhi: Indian Bibliographies Bureau.

Houle, D. (1974) *The External Degree,* San Francisco: Jossey-Bass.

Hughes, L. J. (1980) *The First Athabasca University,* Athabasca University Press.

ICDL (1997) *International Centre for Distance Learning—Data Base,* Milton Keynes: The Open University.

International Association of Universities (1993) *International Handbook of Universities,* New York: Stockton Press and the IAU Press, Thirteenth Edition.

Iram, Y. (1991) Israel. In: P. G. Altbach (ed.), *International Higher Education: An Encyclopedia,* Volume 2, New York: Garland Publishing, 1027–1041.

Israel Central Bureau of Statistics (1995) *Statistical Abstracts of Israel, Jerusalem: Governmental Press* (in Hebrew).

Jablonska-Skinder, H. & Teichler, U. (1992) *Handbook of Higher Education Diplomas,* UNESCO, European Centre for Higher Education (CEPES), München: K. G. Saur.

James, A. (1982) The Universidad Nacional de Educación a Distancia. In: G. Rumble, & K. Harry (eds.), *The Distance Teaching Universities,* London: Croom Helm, 147–166.

Jenkins, A. & Walker, L. (eds.) (1995) *Developing Student Capability Through Modular Courses,* London: Kogan Page.

Jennings, P. L. & Ottewill, R. (1996) Integrating open learning with face-to-face tuition: A strategy for competitive advantage, *Open learning* 11 (2), 13–19.

Johnstone, B. (1997) The Future of the University: Reasonable Predictions, Hoped-For Reforms, or Technological Possibilities, A keynote address at the 'What Kind of University?' *International Conference,* June 1997, London.

Jones, G. A. (ed.) (1997) *Higher Education in Canada: Different Systems, Different Perspectives.* New York: Garland Publishing.

Kaye, T. (1990) Building the foundation for the electronic campus. In: A. W. Bates (ed.), *Media and Technology in European Distance Education, European Association of Distance Teaching Universities,* Milton Keynes: The Open University Press, 227–234.

Keegan, D. (1993a) A typology of distance teaching systems. In: K. Harry, J. Magnus & D. Keegan (eds.), *Distance Education: New Perspectives,* London: Routledge, 62–76.

Keegan, D. (ed.) (1993b) *Theoretical Principles of Distance Education,* London: Routledge.

Keegan, D. (ed.) (1994a) *Otto Peters on Distance Education,* London: Routledge.

Keegan, D. (1994b) *Distance Training in the European Union,* Hagen: FernUniversität, ZIFF Papiere 96.

Keegan, D. (1986) *The Foundations of Distance Education,* Beckenham: Croom Helm.

Keegan, D. (1982) The FernUniversität—Federal Republic of Germany. In: G. Rumble & K. Harry (eds.), *The Distance Teaching Universities*, London: Croom Helm, 88–106.

Keegan, D. (1980a) On defining distance education, *Distance Education*, 1 (1), 13–36.

Keegan, D. (1980b) Drop-outs at the Open University, *The Australian Journal of Education*, 24 (1), 44–55.

Keegan, D. & Rumble, G. (1982) Distance teaching at university level. In: G. Rumble & K. Harry (eds.), *The Distance Teaching Universities*, London: Croom Helm, 15–31.

Kerr, K. (1963) *The Uses of University*, Cambridge, MA: Harvard University Press.

Kirkup, G. (1996) The importance of gender. In: Mills, R. & Tait, A. (eds.), *Supporting the Learner in Open and Distance Learning*, London: Pitman Publishing, 146–164.

Kirkup, G. & van Prümmer, C. (1992) Value of Study Centers and Support Services for Women and Men in a Comparative Perspective, *Selective Results from a Research Project at the FernUniversität and the Open University*, Hagen.

Kirkup, G. & van Prummer, C. (1990) Support and connectedness: The needs of women distance education students, *Journal of Distance Education*, 5 (2), 9–31.

Kurland, N. D. (1986) Computer communication: A new tool for distance education. In: G. van Enckevort, K. Harry. & H. G. Schutze (eds.), *Distance Education and the Adult Learner*, Herleen: Dutch Open University, 209–220.

Kwong, J. (1993) Canadian universities in an age of austerity: Moving towards the business model, *Oxford Review of Education*, 19 (1), 65–77.

Laaser, W. (1990) Teaching economics by video and television. In: A. W. Bates (ed.), *Media and Technology in European Distance Education*, European Association of Distance Teaching Universities, Milton Keynes: The Open University Press, 121–125.

Lacasa, P. & Padro de Leon, P. (1990) Using radio to learn psychology. In: A. W. Bates (ed.), *Media and Technology in European Distance Education, European Association of Distance Teaching Universities*, Milton Keynes: The Open University Press, 85–93.

Leibbrandt, G. (1997) The Open Universiteit of the Netherlands. In: Mugridge, I. (ed.), *Founding the Open Universities*, New Delhi: Sterling Publishers Private Ltd, 101–108.

Levtzion, N. (1992) *The Open University: 1988–1992*, Tel-Aviv: The Open University Press.

Lewis, R. (1997) Open learning in higher education, *Open Learning*, 12 (3), 3–13.

Lewis, R. (1989) The open school. In: N. Paine (ed.), Open *Learning in Transition: An Agenda for Action*, London: Kogan Page, 170–187.

Lindblom, C. E. (1990) *Inquiry and Change: The Troubled Attempt to Understand and Shape Society.* New Haven: Yale University Press.

Mandell, A. & Herman, L. (1996) From teachers to mentors: Acknowledging openings in the faculty role. In: R. Mills & A. Tait (eds.), *Supporting the Learner in Open and Distance Learning*, London: Pitman Publishing, 3–18.

Mason, R. (1990) Computer conferencing in distance education. In: A. W. Bates (ed.), *Media and Technology in European Distance Education,* European Association of Distance Teaching Universities, Milton Keynes: The Open University Press, 221–226.

Mason, R. & Kaye, A. (eds.) (1989) *Mindweave: Communication, Computer and Distance Education,* Oxford: Pergamon Press.

McIntosh, N., Calder, J. & Swift, B. (1976) *A Degree of Difference. A Study of the First Year's Intake to the Open University of the United Kingdom*, Guilford: Society of Research into Higher Education.

McIntosh, N., Woodley, A. & Morrison, V. (1980) Student demand and progress at the Open University—the first eight years, *Distance Education*, 1 (1), 37–60.

McNair, S. (1997) Changing frameworks and qualifications. In: F. Coffield & B. Williamson (eds.), *Repositioning Higher Education*, Buckingham: The Society for Research into Higher Education and the Open University Press, 100–115.

Menand, L. (1993) The future of academic freedom, *Academe,* May–June 1993, 11–17.

Merriam, S. & Caffaerlla, R. (1991) *Learning in Adulthood*, San Francisco: Jossey Bass.

Messer-Davidow, E., Shumway, D. & Sylvan, D. (eds.) (1993) Historical *and Critical Studies in Disciplinarity*, Charlottesville: University Press of Virginia.

Middlehurst, R. (1997) Enhancing quality. In: F. Coffield & B. Williamson (eds.), *Repositioning*

Higher Education, Buckingham: The Society for Research into Higher Education and the Open University Press, 45–56.

Middlehurst, R. & Elton, L. (1992) Leadership and management in higher education, *Studies in Higher Education*, 17 (3), 251–264.

Miller, G. (1996) Technology, the curriculum and the learner: Opportunities for open and distance education. In: R. Mills & A. Tait (eds.), *Supporting the Learner in Open and Distance Learning*, London: Pitman Publishing, 34–42.

Mills, R. (1996) The role of study centers in open and distance education: A glimpse of the future. In: R. Mills & A. Tait (eds.), *Supporting the Learner in Open and Distance Learning*, London: Pitman Publishing, 73–87.

Mills, R. & Tait, A. (eds.) (1996) *Supporting the Learner in Open and Distance Learning,* London: Pitman Publishing.

Mood, T. A. (1995) *Distance Education: An Annotated Bibliography*, Englewood: Libraries Unlimited.

Moore, M. G. (1989) Three types of interaction, *American Journal of Distance Education*, 3 (2), 1–6.

Moore, M. G. (1987) University distance education of adults, *Tech Trends*, 32 (4), 13–18.

Moore, M. G. (1986) Self directed learning and distance education, *Journal of Distance Education*, 1 (1), 7–24.

Moore, M. G. & Kearsley, G. (1996) *Distance Education: A Systems View*, Belmont: Wadsworth Publishing Company.

Moran L. & Mugridge, I. (eds.) (1993a) *Collaboration in Distance Education: International Case Studies*, London: Routledge.

Moran L. & Mugridge, I. (1993b) Collaboration in distance education: An introduction. In: L. Moran & I. Mugridge (eds.), *Collaboration in Distance Education: International Case Studies*, London: Routledge, 1–11.

Moran L. & Mugridge, I. (1993c) Policies and Trends in inter-institutional collaboration. In: L. Moran & I. Mugridge (eds.), *Collaboration in Distance Education: International Case Studies*, London: Routledge, 151–164.

Morgan, C. & Morris, G. (1994) The student view of tutorial support: Report of a survey of Open University Education Studies, *Open learning*, 9 (1), 22–33.

Morrison, T. R. & Saraswati, D. (1988) Athabasca University: Responding and adapting to change. In G. R. Reddy (ed.), *Open Universities: The Ivory Towers Thrown Open*, New Delhi: Sterling Publishers Ltd., 19–43.

Morrison, T. R. (1992) Learning, Change and Synergism: The Potential of Open Universities, *A paper presented at the Annual Asian Association of Open Universities,* Seoul, Korea, September, 1992, Proceedings, 19–54.

Mugridge, I. (ed.) (1997a) *Founding the Open Universities*, New Delhi: Sterling Publishers Private, Ltd.

Mugridge, I. (1997b) Conclusion. In: I. Mugridge (ed.), *Founding the Open Universities*, New Delhi: Sterling Publishers Private, Ltd, 166–171.

Mugridge, I. (ed.) (1994a) *The Funding of Open Universities: Perspectives on Distance Education*, Vancouver: The Commonwealth of Learning.

Mugridge, I. (1994b) Conclusions. In: I. Mugridge (ed.), *The Funding of Open Universities: Perspectives on Distance Education*, Vancouver: The Commonwealth of Learning, 17–22.

Mugridge, I. & Kaufman, D. (eds.) (1986) *Distance Education in Canada*, London: Croom Helm.

National Committee of Inquiry into Higher Education (1997) *Higher Education in the Learning Society.* Report of the Dearing Committee.

Neave, G. (1997) *Personal Communication.*

Neave, G. (1995) *The Core Functions of Government: Six European Perspectives on a Shifting Educational Landscape*, Leiden: The National Advisory Council for Education.

Neave, G. & van Vught, F. A. (eds.) (1991) *Prometheus Bound: The Changing Relationship between Government and Higher Education in Western Europe*, Oxford: Pergamon Press.

Newport, K. (1990) Radio in the British Open University. In: A. W. Bates (ed.), *Media and Technology in European Distance Education*, European Association of Distance Teaching

Universities, Milton Keynes: The Open University Press, 95–100.

Nicoll, K. & Edwards, R. (1997) Open learning and the demise of discipline? *Open Learning*, 12 (3), 14–24.

Nipper, S. (1989) Third generation distance learning and computer conferencing. In: R. Mason & A. Kaye (eds.), *Mindweave: Communication, Computers and Distance Education,* Oxford: Pergamon Press, 63–73.

Open University (1997) *Supported Open Learning Throughout the World*, Milton Keynes: The Open University Press.

Open University (1995) *Pocket Guide to OU Figures*, Milton Keynes: The Open University Press.

Open University (1993a) *Pocket Guide to OU Figures*, Milton Keynes: The Open University Press.

Open University (1993b) *Undergraduate Courses—1993*, Milton Keynes: The Open University Press.

Open University (1992) An Introduction to the Open University, *Fact Sheet, Number 1*, Milton Keynes: The Open University Press.

Open University Planning Committee (1969) *The Open University: Report of the Planning Committee to the Secretary of State for Education and Science*, London: HMSO.

Open University of Israel (1997) *New Enrollments for the 1998 Year*, The Open University of Israel.

Open University of Israel (1995) *Accelerated Growth: The Dilemmas Facing the Open University, An internal document.*

Open University of Israel (1993) *Handbook of Courses,* The Open University of Israel.

Open University of Israel (1986) *Statutes and General Regulations*, The Open University of Israel.

O'Rourke, J., Roberts, J., Spronk, B. & Wong, A. (1995) Distance Education in Canada, 1995. In: D. Sewart (ed.), *One World Many Voices: Quality in Open and Distance Learning,* Volume 1, ICDE and the Open University, 28–32.

Ortner, G. E. , Graff, K. & Wilmersdoerfer, H. (eds.) (1992*) Distance Education as Two-Way Communication, Essays in Honour of Borje Holmberg,* Frankfurt: Peter Lang.

Osborne, M. (1995) Spain. In: P. Davies (ed.), *Adults in Higher Education: International Perspectives in Access and Participation*, London: Croom Helm, 252–277.

Paine, N. (ed.) (1989) *Open Learning in Transition: An Agenda for Action*, London: Kogan Page.

Parer, M. S. (ed.) (1989a) *Development, Design and Distance Education,* Victoria: Centre for Distance Leaning, Gippsland Institute.

Parer, M. S (1989b) Clarifying development and design in distance education. In: M. S. Parer (ed.), *Development, Design and Distance Education*, Victoria: Centre for Distance Leaning, Gippsland Institute, 11–30.

Parry, G. (1997) Patterns of participation in higher education in England: A statistical summary and commentary, *Higher Education Quarterly*, 51 (1), 6–28.

Parry, G. (1995) England, Wales and Northern Ireland. In: P. Davies (ed.), *Adults in Higher Education: International Perspectives in Access and Participation*, London: Croom Helm, 102–133.

Patten, P. (1997) *Personal Communication.*

Paul, R. H. (1990) *Open Learning and Open Management: Leadership and Integrity in Distance Education,* London: Kogan Page.

Paul, R. H. (1987) Staff development for universities: Mainstream and distance education. In: A. Smith & M. Kelly (eds.), *Distance Education and the Mainstream,* London: Croom Helm, 139–155.

Paul, R. & Brindley, G. (1996) Lessons from distance education for the university of the future. In: Mills, R. & Tait, A. (eds.), *Supporting the Learner in Open and Distance Learning*, London: Pitman Publishing, 43–55.

Pazy, A. (1994*) Higher Education in Israel.* Jerusalem: Planning and Budgeting Committee, the Council for Higher Education.

Pedro, F. (1988) Higher education in Spain : Setting the condition for an evaluative state, *European Journal of Education*, 23 (1–2), 125–139.

Peisert, H. & Framhein, G. (1990) *Higher Education in the Federal Republic of Germany,* Bucharest: CEPES, UNESCO.

Peraya, D. & Haessig, C. (1995) Course development process: Design and production of teaching material at the FernUniversität and the Open Universiteit: A comparison between two European universities, *Journal of Distance Education*, 10 (1), 25–52.

Perkin, H. (1987) The academic profession in the United Kingdom. In: B. R. Clark (ed.), *The Academic Profession: National, Disciplinary and Institutional Settings*, Berkeley: University of California Press, 13–59.

Perraton, H. (1993) The costs. In: H. Perraton (ed.), *Distance Education for Teacher Education*, London: Routledge, 381–390.

Perraton, H. (1988) A theory for distance education. In: D. Sewart, D. Keegan & B. Holmberg (eds.), *Distance Education: International Perspectives*, New York: Routledge, 34–45.,

Perraton, H. (1981) A theory for distance education, *Prospects*, XI (1), 13–24.

Perry, W. (1997) The Open University. In: I. Mugridge (ed.), *Founding the Open Universities,* New Delhi: Sterling Publishers Private Ltd, 5–20.

Perry, W. (1996) Distance systems in Europe. In: A. Burgen (ed.), *Goals and Purposes of Higher Education in the 21st Century*, London: Jessica Kingsley Publications, 62–68.

Perry, W. (1992) The birth of the Open University: The unwanted infant and its children. In: G. E. Ortner, K. Graff & H. Wilmersdoerfer (eds.), *Distance Education as Two-Way Communication,* Frankfurt: Peter Lang, 226–228.

Perry, W. (1991) *Education in the XXIst Century, Distinguished Guests Series* 2, Institute for Advanced Study, Indiana University.

Perry, W. (1986) Distance education, trends worldwide. In: G. van Enckevort, K. Harry. & H. G. Schutze (eds.), *Distance Education and the Adult Learner*, Herleen: Dutch Open University, 15–21.

Perry, W. (1984) *The State of Distance-Learning Worldwide*, Milton Keynes: The Open University, International Centre for Distance Learning.

Perry, W. (1977) *The Open University*, San Francisco: Jossey Bass.

Perry, W. (1976) *Open University: A Personal Account of the First Vice-Chancellor*, Milton Keynes: The Open University Press.

Peters, O. (1997) FernUniversität. In: I. Mugridge (ed.), *Founding the Open Universities*, New Delhi: Sterling Publishers Private Ltd, 53–79.

Peters, O. (1994a) Didactic analysis. In: D. Keegan (ed.), *Otto Peters on Distance Education,* London: Routledge, 57–106.

Peters, O. (1994b) The FernUniversität after ten years. In: D. Keegen (ed.), *Otto Peters on Distance Education*, London: Routledge, 179–191.

Peters, O. (1994c) The concept of the FernUniversität. In: D. Keegan (ed.), *Otto Peters on Distance Education,* London: Routledge, 173–178.

Peters, O. (1994d) Distance education and industrial production: A comparative interpretation in outline. In: D. Keegan (ed.), *Otto Peters on Distance Education*, London: Routledge, 107–127.

Peters, O. (1994f) Distance education in a post-industrial society. In: D. Keegan (ed.), *Otto Peters on Distance Education,* London: Routledge, 220–240.

Peters, O. (1994e) Introduction. In: G. Keegan (ed.), *Otto Peters on Distance Education,* London: Routledge, 1–23.

Peters, O. (1992a) Distance education: A revolutionary concept. In: Ortner, G.E., Graff, K. & Wilmersdoerfer, H. (eds.), *Distance Education as Two-Way Communication*, Frankfurt: Peter Lang, 28–34.

Peters, O. (1992b) Some observations of dropping out in distance education, *Distance Education*, 13 (2), 234–269.

Peters, O. (1988) Tradition and innovation—the FernUniversität in Hagen. In: G.R. Reddy (ed.), *Open Universities; The Ivory Towers Thrown Open*, New Delhi: Sterling Publishers Ltd., 82–93.

Peters, O. (1983) Distance teaching and industrial production: A comparative interpretation in outline. In: D. Sewart, D. Keegan & B. Holmberg (eds.), *Distance Education: International Perspectives*, London: Croom Helm, 95–113.

Peters, O. (1981) *Die FernUniversität im Fünften Jahr: Bildungspolitische und Fernstudiendidaktische Aspekte*, Köln: Verlagsgesellschaft Schulfernsehen.

Peters, O. (1965) *Der Fernunterricht*, Weinheim: Julius Beltz.

Platt, E. (1997) *Personal Communication*.

276   Sarah Guri-Rosenblit

Popa-Lisseanu, D. (1986) The Universidad Nacional de Educacíon a Distancia, Spain. In: G. van
    Enckevort, K. Harry. & H. G. Schutze (eds.), *Distance Education and the Adult Learner*,
    Herleen: Dutch Open University, 115–122.
Potashnik, M. (1996) Distance Education: Lessons from Experience , Challenges for the Future, *A
    paper presented at the UNICEF Regional Seminar on 'Multi Channel Learning'*, 28 October–1
    November, 1996, Cairo, Egypt.
Powell, R. (1991) *Success and Persistence at Two Open Universities*, Centre for Distance Education,
    Athabasca University.
Powell, R. & McGuire, S. (1995) Filling the cracks: How distance education can complement
    conventional education? In: D. Sewart (ed.), *One World Many Voices: Quality in Open and
    Distance Learning*, Volume 1, ICDE and the Open University, 455–458.
Powell, R. & Woodley, A. (1995) Re-thinking drop-out in distance education. In: D. Sewart (ed.),
    One World Many Voices: Quality in Open and Distance Learning, Volume 1, ICDE and the
    Open University, 283–287.
President's Report (1997) *The Open University of Israel—1996/97*, Tel Aviv: The Open University
    of Israel Press.
President's Report (1995) *The Open University of Israel—1994/95*, Tel Aviv: The Open University
    of Israel Press.
President's Report (1993) *The Open University of Israel—1992/93*, Tel Aviv: The Open University
    of Israel Press.
Prime Minister's Committee on Higher Education (1963) *Higher Education, Appendix 1—The
    Demand for Places in Higher Education*, Robbins Report, London: HMSO, Cmnd. 2154.
Pritchard, R. M. O. (1994) Government power in British higher education, *Studies in Higher
    Education*, 19 (3), 253–265.
Radcliffe, J. (1990) Television and distance education in Europe: Current roles and future
    challenges. In: A. W. Bates (ed.), *Media and Technology in European Distance Education*,
    European Association of Distance Teaching Universities, Milton Keynes: The Open
    University Press, 113–120.
Raggatt, P. (1993) Post-Fordism and distance education—a flexible strategy for change, *Open
    Learning*, 8 (1), 21–31.
Rawlence, D. (1994) *Personal Communication*.
Reddy, G. R. (ed.) (1988a) *Open Universities: The Ivory Towers Thrown Open*, New Delhi: Sterling
    Publishers Ltd.
Reddy, G. R. (1988b) Open universities: The new temples of learning. In: G. R. Reddy (ed.) *Open
    Universities: The Ivory Towers Thrown Open*, New Delhi: Sterling Publishers Ltd, 1–18.
Reddy, G. R. (1988c) The FernUniversität. In: G. R. Reddy (ed.) *Open Universities: The Ivory
    Towers Thrown Open*, New Delhi: Sterling Publishers Ltd, 75–81.
Rickwood, P. (1995) Others like us?—A study of part-time degree provision outside the Open
    University, *Open Learning*, 10 (3), 16–24.
Ritter, I. (1986) Part-time students: Rule or exception? *Proceedings of the Twelfth International
    Conference of Improving University Teaching*, Heidelberg, 114–122.
Roberston, D. (1997) Social justice in a learning market. In: F. Coffield & B. Williamson (eds.),
    Repositioning Higher Education, Buckingham: The Society for Research into Higher
    Education and the Open University Press, 74–99.
Robinson, B. (1990) Telephone teaching and audio-conferencing at the British Open University.
    In: A. W. Bates (ed.), *Media and Technology in European Distance Education*, European
    Association of Distance Teaching Universities, Milton Keynes: The Open University Press,
    105–110.
Robinson, J. (1982) *Learning over the Air: 60 Years of Partnership in Adult Education*, London:
    British Broadcasting Corporation.
Roll, R. (1995) Foreword. In: J. Tifflin & L. Rajasingham (eds.), *In Search of the Virtual Class:
    Education in an Information Society*, London: Routledge, xi–xvi.
Ross, M. G. (1976) *The University—The Anatomy of Academe*, New-York: McGraw Hill.
Rossetti, A. (1989) Open learning and the youth training scheme. In: N. Paine (ed.), *Open Learning
    in Transition: An Agenda for Action*, London: Kogan Page, 232–244.

Rossman, P. (1992) *The Emerging Worldwide Electronic University: Information Age Global Higher Education*, Westport: Greenwood Press.

Rothblatt, S. (1997) *The Modern University and its Discontents: The Fate of Newman's Legacies in Britain and America*, Cambridge University Press.

Rothblatt, S. (1993) The limbs of Osiris: Liberal education in the English-speaking world. In: S. Rothblatt & B. Wittrock (eds.), *The European and American University Since 1800*, Cambridge University Press, 19–73.

Rothblatt, S. (1991) The American modular system. In: R. O. Berdahl, G. C. Moddie & I. S. Spitzberg, Jr. (eds.), *Quality and Access in Higher Education,* Buckingham: The Society of Research into Higher Education and The Open University Press, 129–141.

Rothblatt, S. (1989) The idea of the idea of a University and its antithesis, *Conversazione,* La Trobe University, Bundoora, Australia.

Rothblatt, S. (1987) Historical and comparative remarks on the federal principle in higher education, *History of Education*, 16 (3), 151–180.

Rothblatt, S. & Wittrock, B. (1993a) Introduction: Universities and 'Higher Education'. In: S. Rothblatt & B Wittrock (eds.), *The European and American University Since 1800*, Cambridge University Press, 1–15.

Rothblatt, S. & Wittrock, B. (eds.) (1993b) *The European and American University Since 1800*, Cambridge University Press.

Rowntree, D. (1993) *Preparing Materials for Open, Distance and Flexible Learning: An Action Guide for Teachers and Trainers*, New York: Nichols Publishing.

Rowntree, D. (1992) *Exploring Open and Distance Learning*, London: Kogan Page.

Rowntree, D. (1990) *Teaching Through Self-Instruction: How to Develop Open Learning Materials,* New York: Nichols Publishing.

Rowntree, D. (1981) *Developing Courses for Students*, New York: McGraw-Hill.

Rumble, G. (1997) University's Labour Markets for the 21st Century, *A paper presented at the 'What Kind of University?' International Conference*, June 1997, London.

Rumble, G. (1996) Labour market theories and distance education: A response, *Open Learning,* 11 (2), 47–51.

Rumble, G. (1995a) Labour market theories and distance education II: How Fordist is distance education? *Open Learning,* 10 (2), 12–28.

Rumble, G. (1995b) Labour market theories and distance education III: Post-Fordism—the way forward? *Open Learning*, 10 (3), 25–42.

Rumble, G. (1994) The competitive vulnerability of distance teaching universities: A reply, *Open Learning,* 9 (3), 47–49.

Rumble, G. (1993) The economics of mass distance education. In: K. Harry, J. Magnus & D. Keegan (eds.), *Distance Education: New Perspectives*, London: Routledge, 94–107.

Rumble, G. (1992a) *The Management of Distance Learning Systems*, Paris: UNESCO, International Institute for Educational Planning.

Rumble, G. (1992b) The competitive vulnerability of distance teaching universities, *Open Learning*, 7 (2), 31–45.

Rumble, G. (1989a) On defining distance education, *American Journal of Distance Education*, 3 (2), 8–21.

Rumble, G. (1989b) 'Open learning', 'distance learning' and the misuse of language, *Open Learning* 4 (20), 26–28.

Rumble, G.& Harry, K. (eds.) (1982) *The Distance Teaching Universities*, London: Croom Helm.

Rumble, G. & Keegan, D. (1982) General characteristics of distance teaching universities. In: G. Rumble & K. Harry (eds.), *The Distance Teaching Universities,* London: Croom Helm, 204–224.

Schlosser, C. A. & Anderson, M. L. (1994) *Distance Education: Review of the Literature*, Ames, Iowa: Research Institute for Studies in Education.

Schmidtchen, V. (1993) FernUniversität Gesamthochschule Hagen, *EADTU News*, 12, Special Institutional Insert, 1–12.

Schramm, W. (1977) *Big Media, Little Media*. Beverley Hills: Sage Publications.

Schramm, W., Coombs, P., Kahnert, F. & Lyle, J. (1967) *The New Media: Memo to Educational*

278   Sarah Guri-Rosenblit

Planners, Paris: UNESCO.

Schramm, W., Hawkridge, D. & Howe, H. (1972) *An Everyman's University for Israel,* Jerusalem: Hanadiv.

Schuemer, R. (1997) *Personal Communication.*

Schuemer, R. (1993) *Personal Communication.*

Schutze, H. G. (1986) Adults in higher education: Lowering the barriers by teaching and learning at a distance. In: G. van Enckevort, K. Harry. & H. G. Schutze (eds.), *Distance Education and the Adult Learner,* Herleen: Dutch Open University, 21–39.

Scott, P. (1995) *The Meanings of Mass Higher Education,* Buckingham: The Society for Research into Higher Education and the Open University Press.

Seligman, D. (1982) Everyman's University—Ha Universita Ha'Petucha. In : G. Rumble & K. Harry (eds.), *The Distance Teaching Universities,* London: Croom Helm, 107–121.

Sewart, D. (1993) Students support systems in distance education, *Open Learning,* 8 (3), 3–12.

Sewart, D. (1992) Mass higher education: Where are we going? In: Ortner, G. E. , Graff, K. & Wilmersdoerfer, H. (eds.) (1992) *Distance Education as Two-Way Communication, Essays in Honour of Borje Holmberg,* Frankfurt: Peter Lang, 229–239.

Sewart, D., Keegan, D. & Holmberg, B. (eds.) (1983*) Distance Education: International Perspectives,* London: Croom Helm.

Shale, D. (1982) Athabasca University, Canada. In: G. Rumble & K. Harry (eds.), The *Distance Teaching Universities* , London: Croom Helm, 32–53.

Shaw, B. & Taylor, J.C. (1984) Instructional design: Distance education and academic tradition, *Distance Education,* 5 (2), 277–285.

Silberberg, R. (1987) *Undergraduate Studies in Israeli Higher Education,* Jerusalem: Council for Higher Education and Planning and Budgeting Committee (in Hebrew).

Silver, H. (1996*) Personal Communication.*

Silver, H. & Silver, P. (1996) *Students: Changing Roles, Changing Lives,* London: Society of Research into Higher Education and the Open University Press.

Silver, H. , Stennett, A. & Williams, R. (1995) *The External Examiner System: Possible Futures, Report of a Project Commissioned by the Higher Education Quality Center,* London: Quality Support Center.

Skilbeck, M. (1997) Higher education in a changing environment: Regional, national and trans-national issues, *Tertiary Education and Management,* 3 (2), 101–111.

Smart, R. (1968) Literate ladies: A fifty year experiment, *St. Andrews University Alumnus Chronicle,* 59, 21–31.

Smith, A. (1992) *The Open University: The Key to Wider Opportunities,* London: The Labour Party, Spokesperson of Higher and Continuing Education.

Smith, K. C. (1980) Course development procedures, *Distance Education,* 1(1), 61–67.

Smith, R. C. (1988) Developing distance learning systems—The UKOU experiment: Some lessons. In: G. R. Reddy (ed.) *Open Universities: The Ivory Towers Thrown Open,* New Delhi: Sterling Publishers Ltd, 235–249.

Smith, A. & Kelly, M. (eds.) (1987) *Distance Education and the Mainstream,* London: Croom Helm.

Smith, K. & Small, I. (1982) Student support: How much is enough? In: J. S. Daniel, M. A. Strand & J. R. Thomson (eds.) *Learning at a Distance: A World Perspective,* Edmonton: Athabasca University, 27–39.

Snowden, B. L. & Daniel, J. S. (1980) The economics and management of small post-secondary distance education systems, *Distance Education* 1 (1), 68–91.

Sparkes, J. (1984) Selection of technology and course design. In: Bates, A. W. (ed.), *The Role of Technology in Distance Education,* London: Croom Helm.

Spear, G. E. (1989) Beyond the organizing circumstance. In: H. Blong (ed.) *Self-Directed Learning: Application and Theory,* University of Georgia, 44–67.

Stevenson, K., Sander, P. & Naylor, P. (1996) Student perception of the tutor's role in distance learning, *Open Learning,* 11 (1), 22–30.

Tait, A. (ed.) (1997) *Quality Assurance in Higher Education: Selected Case Studies,* Vancouver: The Commonwealth of Learning.

Tait, A. (1996) Conversation and community: Student Support in open and distance learning. In: Mills, R. & Tait, A. (eds.), *Supporting the Learner in Open and Distance Learning*, London: Pitman Publishing, 59–72.

Tait, A. (1994a) The end of innocence: Critical approaches to open and distance open learning, *Open Learning*, 9 (3), 27–36.

Tait, A. (1994b) From domestic to an international organisation: The Open University, the United Kingdom, and Europe, *Higher Education in Europe*, XIX (2), 82–93.

Tait, A. (1994c) *Conference Report: Seminar on a Student Charter for Distance Education,* May 25, 1993, Laurentian University, Sudbury, Ontario, Canada, Open Learning, 9 (1), 64–65.

Tait, A. (1993) Approaches to quality assurance for student support in Europe, *Open Learning*, 8 (3), 50–53.

Teichler, U. (1994a) Professional and Social Competence: Higher Education and New Socio-Economic Challenges, *A paper presented at the OECD and PHARE Seminar,* Warsaw, European Commission.

Teichler, U. (1994b) The Changing Nature of Higher education in Western Europe, *A paper presented at the conference on 'Future Role of Universities in South African Tertiary Education',* July 1994.

Teichler, U. (1993a) Structures of higher education systems in Europe. In: C. Gellert (ed.), *Higher Education in Europe*, London: Jessica Kingsley, 23–36.

Teichler, U. (1993b) Curricula and Graduate Employment in Comparative Perspective, *Keynote Speech at the Annual Conference of the Society of Research into Higher Education*, Brighton, December 1993.

Teichler, U. (1986) *Higher Education in the Federal Republic of Germany*, New York/Kassel: Wissenschftliches Zentrum fur Berüfs und Hochschulforschung der Gesamthochschule Kassel Universität.

Teichler, U. & Maiworm, F. (1997) *The ERASMUS Experience: Major Findings of the ERASMUS Evaluation Research Project*, Brussels: European Commission, Education, Training and Youth.

Teichler, U. & Maiworm, F. (1994) *Transition to Work: The Experiences of Former ERASMUS Students*, London: Jessica Kingsley.

Thach, L. & Murphy, K. (1994) Collaboration in distance education: From local to international perspectives, *The American Journal of Distance Education*, 8 (3), 5–17.

Thorpe, M. (1995) The expansion of open and distance learning—A reflection on market forces, *Open Learning,* 10 (1), 21–30.

Tifflin, , J. & Rajasingham, L. (1995*) In Search of the Virtual Class: Education in an Information Society*, London: Routledge.

Tight, M. (1994) Models of part-time higher education : Canada and the United Kingdom, *Comparative Education*, 30 (3), 183–192.

Tight, M. (1991) *Higher Education: A Part-time Perspective*, The Society of Research into Higher Education and the Open University Press.

Tight, M. (1987) Mixing distance and face-to-face higher education, *Open Learning*, 2 (1), 14–18.

Timmons, J. A & Williams, I. A. (1990) *Handbook on the Organization and Management of Distance Education Study Centers*, Bangkok: UNESCO Principal Regional office for Asia and the Pacific.

Trow, M. (1996a) Continuities and change in American higher education. In : A. Burgen (ed.), *Goals and Purposes of Higher Education,* London: Jessica Kingsley Publ., 24–36.

Trow, M. (1996b) Trust, Markets and Accountability in Higher Education, *A Paper presented at a seminar organized by the Society of Research into Higher Education*, Oxford, June 12, 1996.

Trow, M. (1994) Managerialsim and the academic profession: The case of England, *Higher Education Policy*, 7 (2), 11–18.

Trow, M. (1993) Comparative perspectives on British and American higher education. In: S. Rothblatt & B. Wittrock, (eds.), *The European and American University since 1800,* Cambridge University Press, 280–299.

Trow, M. (1988) Comparative perspectives on higher education policy in the UK and US, *Oxford Review of Education*, 14, 81–96.

Trow, M. (1974) Problems of transition from elite to mass higher education, *Policies for Higher Education*, Paris: OECD.

Tunshall, J. (ed.) (1980) *The Open University Opens*, London: Routledge and Keegan Paul.

Turner, P. V. (1984) *Campus—An American Planning Tradition,* Cambridge, Massachusetts: The MIT Press.

UNED (1996) *Información General,* Madrid: Universidad Nacional de Educación a Distancia.

UNED (1995) *Memorio Curso Academico,* Madrid: Universidad Nacional de Educación a Distancia.

UNED (1993) *Información General,* Madrid: Universidad Nacional de Educación a Distancia.

UNED (1992a) *Memorio Curso Academico,* Madrid: Universidad Nacional de Educación a Distancia.

UNED (1992b) *Past and Present,* Madrid: Universidad Nacional de Educación a Distancia.

Usher, R. (1993) Re-examining the place of disciplines in adult education, *Studies in Continuing Education,* 15 (1), 15–25.

van Enckevort, G. & Woodely, A. (1995) *Quality and Performance at UNISA: Some Indicators, Comments and Proposals,* Unpublished Report.

van Enckevort, G., Harry, K. & Schutze, H. G. (eds.) (1986) *Distance Higher Education and the Adult Learner,* Herleen: Dutch Open University.

van Prümmer, C. (1994) Women-friendly perspective in distance education, *Open Learning,* 9 (1), 3–12.

van Seventer, C. W. (1990) Towards 1992: The European Association of Distance Teaching Universities and media and technology in European distance teaching. In: A. W. Bates (ed.), *Media and Technology in European Distance Education*, Milton Keynes: The Open University, 11–14.

van Vught, F. A. (1994) Intrinsic and extrinsic aspects of quality assessment in higher education. In: D. F. Westerheijden, J. Brennan & P. A. M. Maassen (eds.), *Changing Contexts of Quality Assessment: Recent Trends in West European Higher Education,* Utrecht: Uitgeverij Lemma B. V., 31–50.

van Vught, F. A. & Westerheijden, D. F. (1993) *Quality Management and Quality Assurance in European Higher Education,* Luxemburg: Office of Official Publications, EC.

Verduin, J. R. & Clark, T. A. (1991) *Distance Education: The Foundation of Effective Practice*, San Francisco: Jossey Bass.

Wagner, L. (1984) What are the main innovative features of new (reform) universities and other new institutions of higher education and what is their impact, if any, on traditional institutions? The Changing Functions of Higher Education: Implications for Innovation, *Reports from the 1984 OECD/Japan Seminar on Higher Education,* Research Institute for Higher Education: Hiroshima University, pp. 104–113.

Wagner, L. (1980) The economic implications. In: J. Tunshall (ed.), *The Open University Opens,* London: Routledge and Kegan Paul, 21–27.

Wagner, L. (1977) The economics of the Open University revisited, *Higher Education*, 6, 359–381.

Wallace, L. (1996) Changes in the demographics and motivations of distance education students, *Journal of Distance Education,* 11 (1), 1–31.

Watkin, B. L. & Wright, S. J. (1991) *The Foundations of American Distance Education: A Century of Correspondence Collegiate Correspondence Study*, Dubuque, Iowa: Kendall/Hunt.

Watson, K. (1989) The changing pattern of higher education in England and Wales—the end of an era? *International Review of Education*, 35 (3), 283–304.

Watts, S. (1995) Quality assurance in regional centers. In: D. Sewart (ed.), *One World Many Voices: Quality in Open and Distance Learning,* Volume I1, ICDE and the Open University, 59–63.

Wedemeyer, C. A. (1983) Back door learning in the learning society. In: D. Sewart, D. Keegan & B. Holmberg (eds.) *Distance Education: International Perspectives,* London: Croom Helm, 128–140.

Wedemeyer, C. A. (1981) *Learning at the Back Door*, Madison: University of Wisconsin Press.

Wedemeyer, C. A. & Childs, G. B. (1961) *New Perspectives in University Correspondence Study,* Chicago: Center for the Study of Liberal Education for Adults.

Weston, C., McAlpine, L. & Wiseman, C. (1996) How Outstanding Professors View Teaching and

Learning, *A paper presented at the annual AERA conference*, San Francisco, April 1996.

Williamson, B. & Coffield, F. (1997) Repositioning higher education. In: F. Coffield & B. Williamson (eds.), *Repositioning Higher Education*, Buckingham: The Society for Research into Higher Education and the Open University Press, 116–132.

Wilson, B. (1992) Studies in the conceptualization of a University, *Studies in Higher Education,* 17 (3), 295–303.

Wittrock, B. (1993) The modern university: The three transformations. In: S. Rothblatt & B. Wittrock (eds.), *The European and American University since 1800*, Cambridge University Press, 303–362.

Woodley, A. & McIntosh, N. (1980) *The Door Stood Open: An Evaluation of the OU Younger Students Pilot Scheme*, Brighton: Palmer Press.

Woodley, A. & Parlett, M. (1983) Student drop-out, *Teaching at a Distance*, 25, 2–23.

Yaari, M. (1995) *Cost of Studies at the Open University,* An internal document.

Young, M. (1995) The prospects of open learning, *Open Learning,* 10 (1), 3–9.

Zajkowski, M. E. (1997) Price and persistence in distance education, *Open Learning,* 12 (1), 12–23.

Index